the produce bible

Leanne Kitchen

the produce bible

essential ingredient information
and more than 200 recipes
for fruits, vegetables, herbs & nuts

Foreword by Deborah Madison

Stewart, Tabori & Chang   New York.

contents

foreword by Deborah Madison

I'm thinking of fruit loops. Not the cereal, but of how fruits and vegetables loop through the framework of time, and how they express the wealth of biodiversity associated with plant foods. At times the cultural mode of expression has been to ignore diversity altogether, offering only the barest bones of possibilities. The fifties and much of the sixties were decades that saw just this kind of minimalism. Those of us who grew up then knew, for example, only iceberg, butter (or Boston) lettuce, and the occasional head of romaine. We knew Red Delicious apples, a smattering of Newtown Pippins, and a rare Rome Beauty, and when it came to potatoes, there were bakers and boilers, that is, russets and reds. With variety held at bay, choosing was easy when you shopped—there simply wasn't much to choose from.

"Who knew?" asked our parents much later. Who knew, indeed, that those three lettuces existed against a background of hundreds of varieties? Who knew that there were still more than 800 kinds of apples extant in America during those decades? Certainly no one knew about Peruvian blues, Yukon Golds, Russian red bananas, Yellow Finns, Dutch Creamers, and all the other potatoes we know today. Those who did know, and there were some, were eccentrics, people who remembered what had been before and who were somehow in love with plants—farmers, gardeners, good eaters with an awareness of what they ate—rarities in themselves.

Food at this time was confined to a narrow world of tastes and possibilities. Fortunately, it's not in our nature to enjoy vacuums, and we don't tolerate the boredom that comes with a paucity of choice. Once diversity was taken away from us, we started to look towards it with a yearning that was ultimately fierce enough to ignite an era of good growing and selling through farmer's markets, places where produce—in all its speckled and spotted glory—was offered to eager buyers hungry for difference, thirsty for variety.

Because farmer's markets are local markets, the kind of diversity displayed there is vertical, meaning that within one kind of food, say lettuce, there may be twenty kinds offered, or fifty kinds of apples, a dozen new squashes. Supermarkets explore a more horizontal kind of diversity. They express, for better or worse, the season of the world since they abound with examples of fruits and vegetables from all over the planet—one or two of this tuber from the Caribbean, some star fruit, pineapples, and passion fruit from the tropics, four or five kinds of apples from America. No one kind of food is given a deeply varietal expression—it's more like a sampler. But even among single groups of foods, there are certainly more offerings than there were a generation ago, as well as foods that we didn't know about twenty years ago, but now take for granted, like arugula and radicchio.

There's been change, much change, and here we are today, a nation of people that knows it needs to partake of the bounty that fills the enormous produce sections of our markets, but is frequently at a loss as to how to go about it. Yes, there are three kinds of beets, but what do we do with them? Do they taste the same, or are they different? What is the difference between a boysenberry and a gooseberry? Are they interchangeable? And what's what with all those different mandarins?

Many of us need a guide, and *The Produce Bible* provides just that. It's an appropriately limited kind of guide, too. Leanne Kitchen does not explore all the possibilities that exist, just those that are helpful. Quince are quince and not Smynra, Pineapple, Emek, or other varieties. For most home cooks, it's quite enough to know about quince in general, and useful, too, because there's a buzz in the air about this ancient fruit. But when it comes to potatoes, we learn about all the different kinds because everyone eats potatoes, likes potatoes, and is sooner or later going to be faced with having to choose from a large array of them. This makes *The Produce Bible*, at heart, a practical guide—one that leads the reader, via avenues of great ideas and enticing recipes, to those foods most likely to be encountered. And for those of us who dwell in the world of deep varietal differences, this book offers the hope that such a guide will provoke curiosity in its users to explore the fascinating world of plant biodiversity.

introduction

In developed countries, the weekly expedition to the supermarket to stock up on necessary supplies has become routine. Everything you need to run a household can be procured there; from detergents to deli items, greeting cards to green vegetables, and frozen sweet treats to fresh fruits, meats, and fish. Convenient and one-stop, those wide aisles, piercing fluorescent lights, and commodious shopping carts make food shopping a no-brainer—in fact, we've almost forgotten that there was once an entirely different way to hunt and gather. Almost, that is, but not quite.

Over the past decade, there has been a quiet, significant shift in food shopping options with the rise in popularity of farmer's markets. Ironically, this represents a return to more traditional food retail, and a time when every town had its own market—farmers would typically bring their produce, freshly dug, picked, or gathered and sell direct to buyers. There were no middlemen, no transportation issues, no drawn-out storage, no gas-induced ripening, and no specially developed varieties bred to withstand the rigors of long-distance distribution and supply. In fact, nothing fancy at all—just good, simple, honest food, delivered at its seasonal peak.

While it is a sad fact that many of our seasonal foods have been reduced to mere commodity items (think of tomatoes, apples, or strawberries, for example), thankfully not everyone is prepared to settle for the attendant loss of both flavor and varietal quirks that go with it. While it is handy to have salad vegetables in the dead of winter, or out-of-season produce shipped in from far-flung hemispheres, there is no doubt that a rising number of cooks, rather than embracing bland convenience, are instead returning to such underthreat values as "flavor," "seasonal usage," "heirloom varieties," and "boutique-scale production."

To an extent, this interest is driven by a modern breed of restaurant chef, who increasingly favors "top quality seasonal produce cooked simply." Another contributing factor is fatigue with our complex, rat-race lifestyle and a nostalgic yearning for the values of a slower time when one ate what the earth offered up when it saw fit, and each season's bounty was a refreshing change from the previous one. International travel and exposure to true food cultures, where seasonal availability dictates what is put on the table, and where taste and quality of even the humblest of ingredients are extolled above all else, has done much to alert us to the emptiness of a wholly supermarket-dependent existence.

The fact is, we've become increasingly separated from the source of our food—farmer's markets, and the spirit that motivates them, are bridging this gap. Urbanites can't hope to turn back clocks and exist in rural idylls, but they can, through patronage of a local market, move closer to that place and that person that is the source of their food—and be enriched in the process.

Shopping at farmer's markets requires thought, planning, and effort but the results are not just superior-flavored food. Ambling, basket-in-arm, through stalls bursting with fragrantly ripe fruits, just-dug potatoes splotched with rich, damp earth, and bright, perky leaves, shoots, and herbs, is as much nourishment for the soul as it is for the body. Stallholders offer tastings, insights, advice, and information that often can't be found elsewhere. Buying in-season represents better monetary value too, and gluts provide opportunities to make jams, preserves, or to freeze in bulk such fleeting delights as cherries, apricots, or figs, for out-of-season use. There's no wasteful packaging or exposure to blinding display lights (which can diminish nutrient content and shorten produce life) at the market, not to mention the refreshing absence of congested checkouts and harried shoppers.

Not everyone though has access to a farmer's market, and in such instances, sleuthing to find a reputable greengrocer becomes necessary. Find a purveyor who is passionate about their suppliers and produce, who can give you information about fruit and vegetable varieties and details about how, when, and where they were grown. Settle for nothing less than perfectly in-season, full-flavored produce, cook them beautifully and reconnect with the seasonal rhythms that give such a meaningful pace to each and every year.

fruit

grapefruit

fruit ■ **citrus**
season ■ **peak season winter–early spring**

A relatively modern fruit, the grapefruit is the result of cross-pollination between the pomelo and sweet orange; it was discovered in Barbados around 300 years ago. The fruit is named for the way it grows—in heavy bunches on an attractive tree with thick, glossy leaves.

The original grapefruit were white-fleshed, had many seeds, and were smaller than the fruit we know today. Modern grapefruit varieties have been bred for appearance and size, and their flavor is less intense than that of older varieties —if you happen to find smaller, not-so-perfect looking fruits, which will most likely be full of seeds, do buy them and savor their sharp-sweet, juicy difference.

culinary uses

A halved grapefruit, hot and bubbling with melted sugar and garnished with a maraschino cherry, is a breakfast cliché, but delicious nonetheless. Often relegated to the marmalade pot, the grapefruit can be a most elegant fruit—its slightly bitter edge is a wonderful complement to seafood, salad greens, avocado, and even Campari.

Pink grapefruit tossed through a Thai-style shrimp or crab salad, or a mixture of yellow and pink grapefruit doused in a cinnamon and mint-infused syrup, are memorable combinations. Grapefruit makes a refreshing granita, while sweetened, frozen juice (perhaps fortified with quantities of vodka) is a tasty, popsicle-style treat.

selection and storage

Grapefruit are classified as white, pink, or ruby; these describe the flesh, not the skin color. Choose fruit that feels heavy for its size, with tight skin and no soft spots. Grapefruit has optimum flavor when not chilled so, if refrigerated, bring to room temperature before eating.

Grapefruit will keep for 3–4 weeks, stored in the crisper section of the refrigerator— or for about 1 week at room temperature. The membranes and pith are rather bitter and are best removed—to do this, use a small, sharp knife to slice off all the peel and pith and then cut between membranes to remove each segment.

ginger and grapefruit pudding with mascarpone cream

Preheat the oven to 325°F. Grease six ⅔-cup ramekins or pudding molds.

Finely grate 2 teaspoons of zest from the ruby grapefruit and set aside. Cut the grapefruit widthwise, about one third of the way down, to give two uneven-size pieces. Peel the larger piece of grapefruit, removing any white pith, and cut the flesh into six ½-inch slices. Squeeze 3 teaspoons of juice from the remaining grapefruit. Finely chop the stem ginger.

Combine the grapefruit juice, ginger syrup, and corn syrup in a small bowl. Divide the mixture among the ramekins and top with a slice of grapefruit, trimming to fit.

Put the butter and sugar in a bowl and beat with electric beaters until pale and smooth. Beat in the eggs, one at a time. Sift in the flour and ground ginger, add the grapefruit zest, chopped ginger, and milk and mix well. Divide the mixture among the ramekins.

Cover each ramekin with foil and put them in a deep roasting pan. Pour in enough boiling water to come halfway up the sides of the ramekins. Cover the pan with foil, sealing the edges well. Bake the puddings for 30–35 minutes or until set.

To make the mascarpone cream, mix the mascarpone cheese, cream, and confectioners' sugar in a small bowl until smooth. Gently invert the puddings onto serving plates and serve with the mascarpone cream.

1 large ruby grapefruit
⅓ cup drained stem ginger in syrup, plus 3 teaspoons syrup
1½ tablespoons dark corn syrup
½ cup unsalted butter, softened
½ cup superfine sugar
2 eggs, at room temperature
1½ cups self-rising flour
1 teaspoon ground ginger
⅓ cup milk

mascarpone cream
½ cup mascarpone cheese
½ cup whipping cream
1 tablespoon confectioners' sugar, sifted

citrus ■ grapefruit

kumquat

selection and storage

Choose kumquats that have firm, shiny, unblemished skin—check carefully for any signs of mold, or fruit that has been squashed, and avoid these. Store kumquats in the refrigerator for up to 2 weeks, or at cool room temperature for several days.

The kumquat, despite its resemblance to a dwarfed orange and its bittersweet tangy, citric taste, is technically not a citrus fruit at all; it has a genus, *Fortunella*, all its own. To qualify as citrus, fruit needs to have 8–15 segments, where kumquats have just 3–6. Generally though, it is classified with citrus fruits because in many respects it truly is a citruslike fruit.

With its small oblong to round fruit, the kumquat has attractive golden-red, sweetish skin that does not need to be peeled before eating, and somewhat biting flesh. Although it can be eaten raw, most find the kumquat too tart and intensely flavored for this purpose. Kumquats are most commonly pickled to make a delicious accompaniment to smoked or gamey meats, made into a particularly delicious marmalade (either on its own or in combination with oranges or grapefruit), preserved in a brandied syrup, or candied whole for use as a flavoring in ice creams, fruit compotes, and other desserts.

varieties

The nagami *(Fortunella margarita)* is the most commonly grown kumquat and has slightly ovoid fruits with tart flesh and quite pungent, sweet skin. Marumi *(F. japonica)* is rounder in shape and is generally sweeter than the nagami. There is also the meiwa *(F. crassifolia)*, which, with its pale-colored, thick skin, and often seedless flesh, is the best type for eating raw.

caramelized kumquats
with honey parfait

Put the honey in a small saucepan and bring to a boil. Whisk the egg yolks in a bowl until thick and pale, then add the hot honey in a slow stream, whisking constantly. Allow to cool, then gently fold in the whipped cream and liqueur. Pour the mixture into six ½-cup ramekins or pudding molds. Freeze for 4 hours or until firm.

Wash the kumquats and prick the skins with a skewer. Put the kumquats in a large saucepan, cover with boiling water and simmer for 20 minutes. Strain the kumquats and reserve 2 cups of the liquid. Return the liquid to the saucepan, add the sugar and stir over medium heat until the sugar has dissolved. Increase the heat and boil for 10 minutes. Add the kumquats and simmer for 20 minutes, until the kumquats are soft and the skins are smooth and shiny. Remove from the heat and set aside to cool. Lift the kumquats out of the syrup, reserving the syrup.

To serve, dip the molds in hot water for 5–10 seconds before inverting the parfaits onto serving plates. Serve with the caramelized kumquats alongside and the syrup spooned over the top.

note Kumquats in syrup also make a delicious topping for ice cream, sponge cakes, and puddings.

¼ cup honey
4 egg yolks, at room temperature
1¼ cups whipping cream, whipped
1 tablespoon orange liqueur, such as Grand Marnier
1 pound (about 3½ cups) kumquats
1½ cups superfine sugar

citrus ■ kumquat

A Cantonese native, the kumquat is associated in China (and other Asian nations, such as Vietnam) with prosperity; its name in Chinese, jingua, *means "gold melon."*

For other kumquat recipes see:
lime (or kumquat) marmalade..........26

lemon

fruit ▪ citrus
season ▪ **peak season winter–spring**

selection and storage

Choose lemons that have firm, unblemished, glossy yellow skin. Avoid buying lemons that are wrinkled, have cuts or soft spots, or are still green—the flavor of the latter will not be fully developed. Avoid too, any fruits that are damp, as this causes mold to quickly grow and spread among other lemons that sit nearby.

Lemons will store for up to 2 weeks in the refrigerator or up to 1 week at cool room temperature.

The lemon is surely one of the kitchen's most useful and versatile fruits, lending its unmistakable, sharp-sweet fragrance to myriad dishes; in fact, we take the lemon quite for granted. Its juice and finely grated zest spike dressings and drinks, sauces both sweet and savory, and a plethora of desserts, cakes, fillings, and preserves. Its juice can be used for everything from preventing discoloration in other fruits and vegetables given to oxidation (apples, pears, bananas, quince, artichokes), to "cooking" fresh raw seafood, as in the famous raw fish dishes of Central and South America.

Lemons are believed to have originated in northern India; from there it was a short step to adoption into Arabic cuisines, from which language it got its name—*limun*. Arabs planted the fruit in Andalusia and Sicily, regions still famed for the quality and profusion of their lemons. Christian crusaders also helped spread the lemon far and wide; today about a quarter of the world's lemons are grown in California.

Lemons are stunningly nutritious—aside from their high vitamin C content, they are high in flavonoids, an antioxidant thought to help fight off cancer and heart disease. The membranes between lemon segments are a rich source of pectin, a fiber that can be helpful in controlling blood cholesterol.

citrus ■ lemon

varieties

The two most common lemon varieties are the lisbon and the eureka, both almost identical in size and shape. Oblong, with vivid yellow skin and acidic, juicy flesh, these are the workhorses of the lemon world; they can be used in any recipe where lemons, their juice, or zest are called for.

The meyer lemon is a "sweet" variety, with thin, yellow-orange skin and oceans of deeply lemony, slightly sweet juice. Its flesh is a rich yellow-orange color. Meyer lemons are worth seeking out for their fabulously full flavor and particularly high yield of juice. These lemons, thought to be a lemon-orange hybrid, are good in drinks, such as homemade lemonade, and Middle Eastern-style raw lemon salads, relishes, and desserts.

preparation

Check with your supplier whether lemons have been waxed or not, and scrub very lightly before use if they have. If you have a surplus of lemons, the juice can be frozen for several months; heat the fruit in a bowl of hot water before juicing as this will greatly boost the yield.

To use the zest of a lemon, grate it using the finest holes of a grater, applying light pressure and turning the fruit as you go so that you don't grate any of the bitter white pith.

Use a small, sharp knife to remove the peel in slices, working from the top to the bottom of the lemon, having first cut off the ends of the fruit to give it a stable base as you work. Lay the strips, pith side up, on a work surface and use the knife, held at a deep angle, to remove all remaining pith from them, then cut the peel into super-thin shreds. It is a good idea to briefly blanch fine strips of zest in boiling water before using (especially in desserts), as this will remove some of the more volatile, harsher flavors.

culinary uses

The culinary world is dotted with lemon classics: French tarte au citron, English lemon curd, North African preserved lemons, Greek avgolemono soup (and sauce), and the Italian liqueur limoncello, for example.

There are also many food partnerships that rely for success on the jolt of lemon: think of simply cooked fish eaten with a good dousing of lemon juice; tender veal slices napped in a creamy lemon sauce; billowy, meringue-topped pie saved from sickly sweetness by its bracing, lemony layer; and a cup of perfectly brewed black tea with its finishing float of sliced fresh lemon.

preserved lemons

Wash and scrub the lemons in warm water to remove any wax coating. Cut each lemon in half lengthwise, stopping just before the base and keeping the base intact, then make another cut to form four attached quarters. Open each lemon, remove any visible seeds, and pack 1 tablespoon of the salt against the cut edges of each lemon. Push the lemons back into shape and pack into an 8-cup sterilized airtight jar. Depending on their size, you may not need all 12 lemons—they should be firmly packed and the jar should be full.

Add 1 cup of the lemon juice, the remaining rock salt, the peppercorns, and bay leaf to the jar. Fill the jar to the top with the remaining lemon juice. Seal and shake to combine all the ingredients. Leave in a cool, dark place for 6 weeks, inverting the jar each week. The liquid will be cloudy initially, but will clear by the fourth week.

To test if the lemons are ready, cut through the center of one of the quarters. If the pith is still white, the lemons are not ready. Seal and test again in another week.

Once the lemons are preserved, cover the brine with a layer of olive oil. Preserved lemons can be stored for up to 6 months in a cool, dark place.

note To prepare preserved lemons for cooking, remove the required number from the jar with a fork, separate into quarters, and rinse under cold running water. Remove and discard the pulp (you can add it to dishes, if desired, but use it sparingly as it has a bitter taste). Rinse the rind, pat dry with paper towels, and finely slice. Replace the oil each time you remove some of the lemon. Refrigerate the jar once it has been opened.

8–12 thin-skinned lemons
1 cup rock salt
2 cups lemon juice
1/2 teaspoon black peppercorns
1 bay leaf
1 tablespoon olive oil

citrus ■ lemon

warm olives with lemon and herbs

serves 6

2 cups black kalamata olives
1/3 cup olive oil
1 teaspoon fennel seeds
2 garlic cloves, finely chopped
1 pinch cayenne pepper
finely grated zest of 1 lemon
juice of 1 lemon
1 tablespoon finely chopped
  Italian parsley
1 tablespoon finely chopped
  cilantro leaves

Rinse the olives, drain, and place in a saucepan with enough water to cover. Bring to a boil and cook for 5 minutes, then drain in a sieve.

Add the olive oil and fennel seeds to the saucepan and heat until fragrant. Add the drained olives, garlic, cayenne pepper, lemon zest, and juice. Toss for 2 minutes or until the olives are heated through.

Transfer to a bowl and toss with the parsley and cilantro. Serve hot as part of an antipasti selection, or with crusty bread to soak up the juices.

lemon cake with sugar crust

serves 6–8

1 cup unsalted butter, softened
scant 1 cup superfine sugar
2 teaspoons finely grated lemon
  zest
4 eggs, lightly beaten
2 cups self-rising flour
1 teaspoon baking powder
2 tablespoons lemon juice

sugar crust
1/2 cup sugar
1/4 cup lemon juice

Preheat the oven to 325°F. Lightly grease and line an 8 1/2-inch square cake pan with baking paper.

Cream the butter and sugar in a small bowl until pale and fluffy. Beat in the lemon zest, then gradually add the egg in stages, beating well after each addition. Transfer to a large bowl. Using a metal spoon, fold in the combined sifted flour, baking powder, and 1/4 teaspoon salt. Stir in the lemon juice, mixing until smooth.

Spoon the mixture into the cake pan and smooth the surface. Bake for 1 hour 20 minutes or until a skewer inserted into the center of the cake comes out clean. Remove from the pan and turn out onto a wire rack.

To make the sugar crust, mix together the sugar and lemon juice and quickly brush over the top of the warm cake. Cool before serving (the crust forms as the cake cools).

lemon delicious

Preheat the oven to 350°F. Lightly grease a 5-cup ovenproof ceramic dish.

Using an electric beater, beat the butter, sugar, and lemon zest together in a bowl until the mixture is pale and fluffy. Gradually add the egg yolks one at a time, beating well after each addition. Fold in the flour and milk alternately to make a smooth, thin batter. Stir in the lemon juice; don't worry if the batter looks separated.

Whisk the egg whites in a clean, dry bowl until firm peaks form, then, with a large metal spoon, fold a third of the egg whites into the batter to loosen. Gently fold in the remaining egg whites, being careful not to overmix.

Pour the batter into the prepared dish and place in a deep roasting pan. Pour enough hot water into the pan to come one third of the way up the side of the dish. Bake for 55 minutes or until the top is golden, risen, and firm to touch. Leave for 5 minutes before serving. Dust with confectioners' sugar and serve with cream.

1/4 cup unsalted butter, at room temperature
3/4 cup sugar
2 teaspoons finely grated lemon zest
3 eggs, separated
1/4 cup self-rising flour
3/4 cup milk
1/3 cup lemon juice
confectioners' sugar, to dust
heavy cream, to serve

citrus ■ lemon

For other lemon recipes see:

lime

fruit ▪ **citrus**
season ▪ **peaking late summer–fall**

Kaffir lime

Could there be a brighter, purer, more alluring smell than that of a just-cut lime? And where would the culinary world be without them—their penetrating flavor spikes everything from drinks (margaritas, mojitos, daiquiris, limeade) to Latin staples such as guacamole, ceviche, salsa, and the legendary Floridian key lime pie. Their juice perks up low-acid tropical fruits (papaya, mango, custard apple) like nothing else and imagine, if you will, the tequila-salt-lime ritual without this crucial citric element.

The origins of the lime, a close lemon relative, are quite obscure, but it is generally believed they are native to modern-day Malaysia or Indonesia. The "original" lime is the key lime—smaller, sourer, and more difficult to pick than today's common Tahitian lime hybrid, but with a far more rewarding and complex flavor. Limes have long been an important feature of Middle Eastern and Persian cookery—there is even a reference from the stories of the famed Arabian Nights to "Egyptian limes" which dates back to 1450 A.D.

Limes can be used interchangeably with lemons, but remember that their flavor is much more assertive than lemon so less is generally required. Hence, lime marmalade, lime curd, lime meringue pie, lime syrup cakes, and lime dressings and sauces are all as delicious as their lemony prototypes.

selection and storage

Limes are picked and sold while still under-ripe as this is when their flavor is best—when fully ripe their skin turns yellow and they lose that hallmark fragrant acidity. Look for fruits that are bright darkish green, glossy-skinned, feel firm, and are heavy for their size. There should be no spots or brown, soft patches.

Store limes for up to 2 weeks in the refrigerator or for 1 week at cool room temperature. Lime juice and the finely grated zest can be frozen for up to 3 months.

varieties

key lime Lime etymology is a little confusing. It's thought the "original" lime is the key lime, which is really the Mexican lime (also known as West Indian lime). Native to the East Indies, this lime is golf-ball small with highly acidic, intensely flavored, juicy flesh. It is difficult to source outside of the Florida Keys area in the United States, from where it derived its common name.

tahitian The Tahitian or Persian lime is the fruit you are most likely to encounter at the fruit stand. It is thought to be a hybrid of the original East Indian lime and was developed early in the twentieth century. Seedless and thin-skinned, the pale, juicy flesh is not as forceful or aromatic as that of its Mexican cousin.

kaffir Also known as makrut, these are dispersed throughout Southeast Asia, have thick, knobby skin, highly aromatic leaves, and very little juice. They are not strictly a lime at all but rather a citrus subspecies—the word *kaffir* is Arabic for "unbeliever" or "infidel" and has racist connotations in South Africa, so increasingly the fruit goes by the Thai name, makrut.

preparation

Lime juice brings out many flavors and can be used as a part-substitute for salt in cooking. To make the juice easier to extract, first submerge the limes in very hot water for 1 minute. Drain well and allow to cool slightly, then roll them on a hard surface, using the palm of your hand and applying firm pressure. Halve the limes and squeeze the juice, which should flow quite readily.

Lime juice is very useful in meat marinades as it has a natural tenderizing effect and will "cook" the diced flesh of fresh fish and other tender seafoods when it is used in quantity. As a useful guide, 1 lime will yield about 2 tablespoons of juice and 1½ teaspoons of finely grated zest.

Don't cook limes in aluminum or iron cookware as the acids will react with the metal, causing changes in the color and taste of your food.

lime pie (in the style of key lime)

Sift the flour and 1/4 teaspoon salt into a large bowl. Add the butter and rub it into the flour using your fingertips until the mixture resembles fine bread crumbs. Fold in the sugar.

Make a well in the center, add nearly all the water and mix with a flat-bladed knife, using a cutting rather than a stirring action. The mixture will come together in small beads of dough. If necessary, add more water, a teaspoon at a time, until the dough comes together. Test the dough by pinching a little piece between your fingers—if it doesn't hold together, it needs more water. Gather the dough together and lift out onto a lightly floured surface. Press the dough into a ball and then flatten it slightly. Cover in plastic wrap and refrigerate for 20–30 minutes.

Preheat the oven to 350°F. Lightly grease a 9-inch round loose-bottomed tart pan. Roll the dough out between two sheets of baking paper until it is large enough to fit into the pan. Remove the top sheet of paper and invert the pastry into the pan. Use a small ball of pastry to help press the pastry into the pan, allowing any excess to hang over the side. Use a small, sharp knife to trim away excess pastry.

Line the pastry shell with baking paper and pour in some baking beads or rice. Bake for 10 minutes, remove the paper and beads, and return the pastry to the oven for 5 minutes or until the base is dry to touch. Leave to cool.

Using electric beaters, beat the egg yolks, condensed milk, lime juice, and zest in a large bowl for 2 minutes or until well combined. Pour into the pastry shell and smooth the surface. Bake for 20–25 minutes or until set. Allow the pie to cool, then refrigerate for 2 hours or until well chilled. Garnish with lime slices, dust with sifted confectioners' sugar, and serve with whipped cream.

sweet shortcrust pastry
2 cups all-purpose flour
1/2 cup chilled butter, cut into cubes
2 tablespoons superfine sugar
2–3 tablespoons iced water

filling
4 egg yolks
1 (14-ounce) can sweetened condensed milk
1/2 cup lime juice
2 teaspoons grated lime zest
lime slices, to garnish
confectioners' sugar, to dust
whipped cream, to serve

citrus ▪ lime

lime (or kumquat) marmalade

2 pounds (about 12) limes
8 cups water
10¼ cups sugar, warmed (see
    note)
4-inch square of cheesecloth

Scrub the limes (or kumquats) under running water to remove any wax. Cut the fruit in half lengthwise, reserving any seeds, then slice thinly. Place in a large nonmetallic bowl with the water. Tie any seeds securely in the cheesecloth and add to the bowl. Cover and leave overnight.

Put two small plates in the freezer. Put the fruit, water, and cheesecloth bag in a large saucepan. (If making kumquat marmalade, add the lemon juice to the pan.) Bring slowly to a boil, then reduce the heat and simmer, covered, for 30–45 minutes or until the fruit is tender.

2 pounds (7 cups) kumquats
5 cups water
¼ cup lemon juice
5⅔ cups sugar, warmed (see
    note)
4-inch square of cheesecloth

Add the warmed sugar and stir over low heat, without boiling, for 5 minutes or until dissolved. Return to a boil and boil rapidly, stirring often, for 20 minutes. Remove any scum during cooking with a slotted spoon. When the syrup falls from a wooden spoon in thick sheets, test for setting point.

To do this, remove from the heat, put a little marmalade onto one of the cold plates and place in the freezer for 30 seconds. A skin should form on the surface and the marmalade should wrinkle when pushed with your finger. If not, return to the heat, then retest a few minutes later with the other plate. Discard the cheesecloth bag.

Carefully ladle into hot sterilized jars and seal. Allow to cool, then label and date each jar. Store in a cool, dark place for 6–12 months. Refrigerate after opening for up to 6 weeks.

note To warm the sugar, preheat the oven to 300°F. Spread the sugar evenly in a baking dish and put in the oven for 10–15 minutes or until warmed through. To save time you can warm the sugar while you are cooking the jam. Do not add the sugar until the fruit has softened. If sugar is added before the fruit has fully softened, the fruit will remain firm.

mandarin and tangerine

fruit ▪ citrus
season ▪ early fall–late spring

With their characteristic baggy, easy-peel skin, segments that fall neatly and messlessly apart, thin pith and (mostly) sweet, sweet flesh, there's much to like about the mandarin. It's another native of China where for centuries it was reserved exclusively for the privileged classes, or Mandarins, which is, some speculate, how it acquired its name.

Visitors to China, where it was cultivated as early as 300 B.C., would take seeds of the fruit back home with them, hence its early spread to Japan and the Philippines. It wasn't until the nineteenth century that the mandarin found its way to Europe, North and South America, Australia, and North Africa.

The first mandarins imported into Europe came in through the Moroccan port city of Tangiers, giving rise to the name "tangerine." This nomenclature causes confusion today—all tangerines are varieties, sub-varieties, or hybrids of the mandarin, but not all mandarins are tangerines, even though the names are often used interchangeably. Indeed "differences" between tangerine types of mandarins are subtle, at best. David Arthur and Daemmon Reeve (*Perfumer and Flavorist* magazine) state differences in juice flavor and essential oil characters, which took careful scientific analysis to detect. In general though, tangerines have a darker, red-orange skin than non-tangerine types of mandarin.

selection and storage

Mandarins are often, but not always, sold by variety. As with all citrus, select fruits that are heavy for their size and, if possible, try before you buy.

Avoid mandarins with overly puffy skin as this indicates over-ripeness; also avoid fruits with any soft or weepy areas.

Mandarins don't keep as well as other citrus fruits. Store them in the refrigerator for up to 10 days or up to 1 week at cool room temperature.

varieties

clementine A cross between a mandarin and a bitter, seedless orange, the clementine was discovered by Father Clement Rodier in Algeria in 1902. Generally, but not always, the clementine has seedless flesh and loose, smooth, bright reddish-orange skin. The flesh is juicy and deep-flavored.

honey mandarin A cross between a mandarin and sweet orange hybrids, these are classified as a tangerine. They are thin-skinned and have a smooth and shiny peel that hugs the flesh and is particularly sweet, juicy, and meaty. In some countries they are called murcotts. Tangerine types are classified by their large size and have deep orange-red skin.

satsuma The satsuma originated in Japan centuries ago. There are over seventy varieties of satsumas, most of which are seedless, with loose, easily removed peel. Their flavor should be slightly tart, perfumed, and sweet.

tangelo A cross between a mandarin and a grapefruit, tangelos are orange-sized with a thin, tapering stem end. Their bright orange skin is easily peeled and their flesh is at once acid, sweet, and fragrant.

tangor Another hybrid, this time between a mandarin and a sweet orange, the tangor is a largish fruit with close-fitting skin and sweet, perfumed, juicy flesh.

culinary uses

Mandarin juice is a flavorsome alternative to orange juice and the segments are worthy additions to fruit salads and compotes. Mandarins make fabulous marmalade, either on their own or in tandem with other citrus fruits, and can also be put to excellent use in homemade ice creams, sorbets, and other ices. Use their grated zest and juice in baking recipes (cakes, puddings, and pies) that usually call for orange and enjoy the fragrant difference.

tangerine gelato

Whisk the egg yolks and half the sugar together until pale and creamy. Put the milk, tangerine zest, and remaining sugar in a saucepan and bring to a boil. Pour over the egg mixture and whisk to combine. Pour the custard back into the saucepan and cook over low heat, stirring continuously, until the mixture is thick enough to coat the back of a wooden spoon—do not allow the custard to boil.

Strain the custard into a bowl, add the tangerine juice and cream and then cool over ice. Churn in an ice-cream maker following the manufacturer's instructions. Alternatively, pour into a plastic freezer box, cover and freeze. Stir every 30 minutes with a whisk during freezing to break up the ice crystals and give a better texture. Keep in the freezer until ready to serve.

5 egg yolks
1/2 cup sugar
2 cups milk
2 tablespoons grated tangerine zest
3/4 cup tangerine juice
3 tablespoons heavy cream

citrus ■ mandarin and tangerine

mandarin soda

makes 2 1/4 cups syrup

Put the sugar and water in a large saucepan. Dissolve the sugar over low heat, stirring occasionally. Bring to a boil and cook, uncovered, for 5 minutes.

Add the mandarin juice and boil for 5 minutes. Allow to cool, then pour the syrup into a hot sterilized airtight jar and refrigerate for 1 hour. Dilute about 2–3 tablespoons of syrup per glass and top up with soda or sparkling mineral water and ice cubes.

heaping 1 cup sugar
2 1/2 cups water
1 1/2 cups mandarin juice
soda water or sparkling mineral water, to serve
ice cubes, to serve

orange

fruit ■ citrus
season ■ peaking in winter

selection and storage

Oranges should feel heavy with juice for their size, firm to the touch, and give when gentle pressure is applied. They should not be shriveled, bruised, or moldy, and should have no soft spongy spots.

A winter fruit, oranges can be stored at room temperature for 3 days or will keep for up to 2 weeks in a loosely sealed plastic bag in the crisper section of the refrigerator.

A wake-up glass of freshly squeezed orange juice, with its bracing acid-sweetness and healthy wallop of vitamin C, is a morning ritual the world over. But, while orange juice may hold the fruit's flavor, the zest encapsulates its heady essence.

A most prosaic fresh fruit, thanks to year-round availability and the competition from so many more "interesting" fruits, the orange is hardly associated with high gastronomy. But this wasn't always the case. The French, for example, who were introduced to the sweet orange around the fifteenth century, have contributed some of the most enduring, sophisticated orange dishes to the culinary lexicon. Think of duck à l'orange, that apotheosis of rich-flesh-meets-tangy-citrus, or the iconic crêpes suzette, where flaming pancakes are infused with the orange's bright aromas and flavor. In England, oranges star in traditional festive dishes, the juice in Cumberland sauce for ham and the grated zest stirred into dense fruitcake batter.

Widely known for its rich vitamin C content, a single orange contains more than 100 percent of the recommended daily intake. Oranges also contain vitamin A, dietary fiber, thiamine, folate, potassium, antioxidants and, surprisingly, a little protein. They aid the body in healing, in absorbing iron, and in boosting immunity.

bitter and sweet

Oranges can roughly be divided into two groups: bitter and sweet. Bitter oranges, such as Sevilles and bergamots, are too tart to eat out of hand and are most often used for marmalades, general cooking, and to add zing to mixed drinks. They are also prized for their peel, which is often candied, and their essential oils, which are used in making the liqueur Curaçao. In the Middle East, the blossoms of bitter oranges are distilled, then transformed into the fragrantly floral orange-flower water.

Sweet oranges are those that are eaten as a table fruit, added raw to salads and used for juice. Generally large, they have skins that are relatively difficult to peel and include navels, valencias, and the exceptionally sweet and richly flavored blood oranges. Sweet oranges can have seeds or be seed-free.

blood oranges

varieties

blood orange The red pigmentation varies depending on growing conditions—those blood oranges from cooler climates seem to be redder than those from warmer areas. With their complex, spicy, almost berried flavors and ruby good looks, blood oranges are a favorite choice for use in salads, fresh drinks, and the classic pinkish French sauce, maltaise (a derivative of hollandaise sauce).

hamlin This orange has sweet, pale, and juicy flesh and, while not the world's most interesting orange, is tasty and useful nonetheless. It is widely grown in Florida.

navel So-named for the distinctive, navel-shaped dimple on its base, the popular navel orange is actually a secondary fruit, produced at the blossom end of the primary fruit—in Portugal and Spain they were once called pregnant oranges. They are also characterized by their rich-colored skin (particularly Washington navels), juicy, sweet, and almost always seedless flesh, and ability to peel easily.

pineapple With hints of pineapple flavor in its flesh, the pineapple orange is a deeply flavored, brightly colored, heavily juicy orange, perfect for eating, juicing, or using in cooking—its only shortcoming is the large number of seeds, which require straining out.

seville A cooking orange, on account of its very bitter flavor, the Seville is thick-skinned and contains many seeds. It is the best orange for most savory recipes requiring orange juice, and for marmalade.

valencia The classic juicing orange and a late-ripening variety, the Valencia is a large fruit with more seeds than a navel and often green-tinged skin. This greening in no way affects their flavor—oranges need a cool temperature to retain their orange skin color and valencias harvested in summer may lose some color as a result.

preparation

To segment an orange, cut off the base and top to create flat ends. Put the orange, flat side down, on a work surface. Using a small, sharp knife and working from the top of the orange to the base, remove the peel in strips, taking care to remove all the bitter white pith. Holding the orange over a bowl to catch juices, cut between the white membranes to remove sections of flesh—the leftover membranes can be squeezed to extract more juice, then discarded.

Orange zest can first be removed with a small, sharp knife or using the fine holes of a grater; either way it is important to remove as little of the bitter white pith as possible. This is a tricky job and involves placing strips, skin side down, on a work surface and cutting away the pith on an angle. When preparing oranges for candying the zest or making orange confit (cooking unpeeled slices for a very long time in dense sugar syrup until translucent and semicandied), it is best to first blanch the fruit in several changes of boiling water, as this both softens the fruit and eliminates excess bitterness.

culinary uses

Like their lemon cousins, oranges lift the flavor of ingredients they are cooked with and go particularly well with chocolate, almonds, walnuts, duck liver, cumin, ginger, Madeira, Marsala, pork, winter squash, spinach, Belgian endive, and beets.

As with all premium ingredients, the simplest treatments are often the best—a bowl of cinnamon-infused caramelized oranges is an ode to this maxim. Or to take it up a notch, slice some peeled blood oranges and serve them with a sublime chocolate mousse or in an airy, blood orange rind-flecked soufflé. Oranges are also greatly used in confectionery and desserts in glacé or crystallized form, and they have contributed their inimitable flavor to some of the world's most famed liqueurs—Grand Marnier, Cointreau, and Triple Sec.

Moving away from desserts to more savory offerings, an orange, avocado, and watercress salad is an excellent combination. Chilies are a surprisingly good partner for oranges, used to great effect in Mexico, where their juice is excellent in shrimp ceviche. Regularly baste a turkey with a mixture of orange juice and zest, sherry, oregano, and garlic, or drizzle orange and Dijon mustard vinaigrette over a baby beet, spinach, and feta salad, or any beet-based salad or soup for that matter, as the two have a special affinity.

orange hollandaise sauce

makes 1¼ cups

¾ cup butter
4 egg yolks
2 tablespoons orange juice

Melt the butter in a small saucepan. Skim any froth from the top and discard; cool the melted butter. Combine 2 tablespoons water and the egg yolks in a separate pan. Whisk for about 30 seconds or until the mixture is pale and creamy.

Put the pan over very low heat and continue whisking for 3 minutes or until thick and foamy, then remove from the heat. (Make sure the saucepan does not get too hot or you will end up with scrambled eggs.)

Add the cooled butter slowly, a little at a time at first, whisking well after each addition. Keep adding the butter in a thin stream, whisking continuously, until all of the butter has been used. Try to avoid using the milky white whey in the bottom of the pan, but don't worry if a little gets in. Stir in the orange juice and season with sea salt and white pepper.

variation To make a basic hollandaise sauce, replace the 2 tablespoons of orange juice with 1 tablespoon of lemon juice. (Strain through a fine sieve to remove any pulp before measuring.)

In Scotland, chunky bittersweet seville marmalade was invented by accident in 1700, when a Spanish ship took refuge in Dundee harbor and its entire load of oranges was purchased by an enterprising local— he discovered them to be too bitter to eat so his wife turned them into a sweetened preserve.

orange, hazelnut, and goat cheese salad

Preheat the oven to 350°F. Put the hazelnuts on a baking sheet and roast in the oven for 5–6 minutes or until the skins turn dark brown. Wrap the hazelnuts in a clean dishtowel and rub them together to remove the skins.

To make the dressing, combine the nuts, orange juice, lemon juice, and a pinch of salt in a food processor. With the motor running, gradually add the olive oil a few drops at a time. When about half the oil has been added, pour in the remainder in a steady stream.

Remove the stems from the watercress and place the leaves in a bowl with the spinach, orange segments, and 2 tablespoons of the dressing. Toss to combine, then season with sea salt and freshly ground black pepper. Arrange the salad on four plates.

Heat a small nonstick frying pan over medium-high heat and brush lightly with olive oil. When hot, carefully press each slice of goat cheese firmly into the pan and cook for 1–2 minutes or until a crust has formed on the cheese. Carefully remove the cheese from the pan and arrange over the salads, crust side up. Drizzle over the remaining dressing, to serve.

¼ cup hazelnuts
1 tablespoon orange juice
1 tablespoon lemon juice
½ cup olive oil
1 bunch (9 ounces) watercress, rinsed and dried
1 cup baby English spinach leaves, rinsed and dried
24 orange segments (about 2 oranges)
10 ounces firm goat cheese, sliced into four equal portions

citrus ▪ orange

A source of nutrition for Christopher Columbus and his sailors, the orange undoubtedly contributed to their seafaring success. Columbus took the seeds of oranges, lemons and citrons with him to Haiti and the Caribbean, where they took root to become an integral ingredient of the local cuisine. As long as oranges have been eaten, they have been associated with fertility—perhaps because they come from an evergreen tree that can simultaneously produce foliage, flowers, and fruit.

orange and almond cake

Lightly grease an 8½-inch springform pan and line the base with baking paper.

Scrub the oranges under warm running water to remove any wax coating from the skins. Put the whole oranges in a saucepan, cover with water and boil for 1 hour. Remove from the water and set aside to cool.

Preheat the oven to 350°F. Using a plate to catch any juice, cut the cooled oranges into quarters and remove any seeds. Blend the orange quarters, including the skin, in a food processor or blender until they turn to a pulp.

Beat the eggs in a large bowl with electric beaters until light and fluffy. Add the orange pulp and any reserved juice to the bowl with the almonds, sugar, and baking powder. Mix thoroughly to combine.

Pour the cake batter into the pan. Bake for 1 hour or until the cake is firm to touch and lightly golden. Cook the cake a little longer if it is still wet. Cool in the pan before turning out onto a wire rack to cool completely. Dust with sifted confectioners' sugar before serving.

2 large oranges
5 eggs
2½ cups ground almonds
1 cup sugar
1 teaspoon baking powder
confectioners' sugar, sifted,
   to dust

citrus ■ orange

Contrary to popular belief, the word "orange" actually refers to the fruit's aroma, not its color, as it comes from the Sanskrit word naranga, *meaning "fragrant." The fruit itself is thought to have come from China and perhaps India, as the name would suggest. From there it traveled west to the Mediterranean, and Arab, Dutch, Portuguese, and Spanish sailors planted oranges along the shores of their trade routes to guard against scurvy.*

blackberries

fruit ▪ **soft**
season ▪ **late summer–fall**

selection and storage

Blackberries remain sour long after they turn black and are not truly ripe and ready to eat until they are soft. Consume them quickly, as they lose their flavor fast. Blackberries should be plump and their stems removed—attached stems are a sign that they were picked too early and may be under-ripe and tasteless.

Like all berries, blackberries can be frozen. To freeze berries so they "free-flow" (as opposed to being frozen in a lump), spread them in a single layer on baking sheets lined with baking paper, then freeze solid. Transfer to an airtight container or freezer bag, pressing all the air out of the bag, then seal and use within 6 months.

Once considered a noxious weed, blackberries have gained in popularity over the years and their price has risen accordingly. Growing on bushes and made up of a congregation of smaller fruits called drupelets, blackberries are botanically not classified as berries at all, but are part of the rose (Rosaceae) family.

Wild blackberries grow freely throughout the English, European, and United States late-summer countryside. Smaller than their cultivated cousins, they are more intensely flavored, but do lose their flavor quickly. The cultivation of the blackberry has resulted in the complete elimination of the thorny branches, which once made the wild crop difficult to harvest. Blackberries are a good source of calcium, iron, potassium, and vitamin C.

culinary uses

Containing high levels of pectin, slightly under-ripe blackberries are ideal for making jams, jellies, and preserves—a few drops of geranium water is an excellent addition. If you are lucky enough to have a surplus of blackberries, then purple-stained blackberry butter takes minutes to make and is divine over crumpets, pancakes, and scones—simply combine the blackberries, a little confectioners' sugar and some softened, unsalted butter in a food processor until smooth. Blackberries can be macerated in sweetened Prosecco (a sparkling wine) and served with a dollop of mascarpone cheese, or, with the addition of some softened gelatin they can be poured into champagne glasses to set, becoming elegantly jellied.

soft fruit ■ blackberries

serves 4

venison with blackberry sauce

1/4 cup clarified butter
12 baby onions, peeled with root left intact
1 cup blackberries or black currants
3 tablespoons red currant jelly
16 (2-ounce) venison medallions
1/4 cup red wine
1²/₃ cups beef stock
1/2 tablespoon butter, softened
2 teaspoons all-purpose flour

Heat half the clarified butter in a saucepan. Add the onions, cover, then cook for 20–25 minutes, stirring occasionally, until the onions are browned and softened. Set aside. Put the berries in a separate saucepan with the red currant jelly and 3 tablespoons water. Boil for 5 minutes or until the fruit is softened and the liquid reduced and syrupy. Set aside.

Season the venison with sea salt and freshly ground black pepper. Heat the remaining clarified butter in a frying pan and cook the medallions in batches over high heat for 1–2 minutes, turning once. Transfer the venison to a plate, cover loosely with foil and keep warm in a 235°F oven.

Add the wine to the reserved juices in the frying pan and boil for 30 seconds. Add the stock and boil until reduced by half. Mix together the butter and flour separately to make a smooth paste and then whisk into the stock. Boil, stirring constantly to avoid lumps forming, for 2 minutes or until slightly thickened.

Drain the syrup from the fruit into the stock to make a sauce. Stir well, season, and serve with the venison and onions, using the drained fruit as a garnish.

Called brambles in the United Kingdom, local folklore has it that blackberries should not be picked after September 29 (Michaelmas or the feast of St Michael), when it is said that the devil claims them for his own evil uses.

blackberry and apple jam

Peel, core, and chop the apples. Put the apple pieces in a large saucepan with the berries and 1/2 cup water. Cook, covered, over medium heat, stirring often, for 30 minutes or until the fruit has softened.

Add the warmed sugar to the fruit and stir, without boiling, for 5 minutes or until all the sugar has dissolved.

Put two small plates in the freezer. Bring the jam to a boil and boil for 20 minutes, stirring often. Stir across the bottom of the pan to check that the jam is not sticking or burning. When the jam falls from a wooden spoon in thick sheets without dripping, start testing for setting point. To do this, remove from the heat, put a little jam onto one of the cold plates and place in the freezer for 30 seconds. A skin should form on the surface and the jam should wrinkle when pushed with your finger. If not, continue to reduce the syrup over heat, then use the second testing plate to test for setting point.

Carefully ladle into hot sterilized jars and seal. Allow to cool, then label and date each jar. Store in a cool, dark place for 6–12 months. Refrigerate after opening for up to 6 weeks.

note To warm sugar, preheat the oven to 300°F. Spread the sugar evenly in a baking dish and put in the oven for about 10–15 minutes or until warmed through. Do not overheat the sugar or it will start to lump together. To save time you can warm the sugar while cooking the jam. Do not add the sugar until the fruit has softened. If sugar is added before the fruit has fully softened, the fruit will remain firm.

1 pound 10 ounces (about 5) green apples
8 cups fresh blackberries, boysenberries, or raspberries
7 cups sugar, warmed (see note)

soft fruit ■ blackberries

For other blackberry recipes see:
boysenberry pie 51
summer pudding 45

black currants

selection and storage

Choose currants that are plump, firm, and show no signs of crushing. Currants are best kept refrigerated, covered tightly, for up to 4 days, then washed just prior to using. They can also be frozen for up to 3 months.

Black currants are the jewels of the summer fruit bowl, their shiny, tiny, purple-black looks adding a glamorous touch to any dish they grace. They have a unique, astringent, somewhat musky sourness, and are one of the few fruits that require cooking to render them palatable. With their tartness tempered by sugar, black currants make garnet-hued jellies, preserves, sauces, and syrups. Of all the black currant-based alcohols, the French liqueur crème de cassis, the essential ingredient in the champagne cocktail kir royale, is the most famed. Offering manganese, vitamin C, dietary fiber, folate, and bioflavonoids that reduce blood pressure, black currants are extremely nutritious too.

culinary uses

Explore the culinary potential of black currants by adding handfuls to a mixed berry clafoutis (see page 83), stirring some through a citrus-scented pound cake mixture, or sprinkling them over a black currant-tea-infused crème brûlée.

On a savory note, gently heat black currants in warmed butter until they just burst, add a spoonful of black currant jelly, a splash of balsamic vinegar and brown sugar, then spoon over slices of roast pork, pan-fried duck breasts, or pot-roasted guinea fowl. The flavor of black currants is complemented by flavors found in Northern European cuisines, such as juniper berries, cinnamon, cloves, nutmeg, dark chocolate, vanilla beans, and venison.

summer pudding

Put all the berries, except the strawberries, in a large saucepan with 1/2 cup water and heat gently until the berries begin to collapse. Add the strawberries and turn off the heat. Add sugar to taste (the amount you need will depend on how ripe the fruit is). Set aside to cool.

Line a 4-cup pudding basin or mold with the bread, cutting a large circle out of one slice for the base and slicing the rest into "fingers" to line the sides. Drain a little juice off the fruit mixture. Dip one side of each piece of bread in the juice before fitting it, juice side down, into the basin, leaving no gaps. Do not squeeze or flatten the bread or it will not absorb the juices well.

Fill the center of the basin with the fruit, reserving any leftovers, and add a little juice. Cover the top with a layer of dipped bread, juice side up, and cover with plastic wrap. Put a plate that fits tightly inside the basin onto the plastic wrap to weigh the pudding down. Refrigerate overnight. Carefully turn out the pudding onto a serving plate and serve with any reserved berry mixture and cream.

1¼ cups black currants
1¼ cups red currants
1¼ cups raspberries
1¼ cups blackberries
1⅓ cups strawberries, hulled and halved
superfine sugar, to taste
6–8 slices good-quality day-old sliced white bread, crusts removed
whipping cream, to serve

soft fruit ■ black currants

Currants are relatives of the gooseberry family—red currants were domesticated in the sixteenth century in Scandinavia, with whose cuisines they are largely associated (although they are the key component in the singularly British cumberland sauce). Red currants and their many hybrids, of which the pretty, translucent white currant is one, have thinner skins and sweeter flesh than black currents and can be eaten raw. They are often used in Northern European-style soups, plus jellies, drinks, and summer desserts.

For other black currant recipes see:
venison with blackberry (or black currant) sauce 42

blueberries

fruit ▪ **soft**
season ▪ **late spring–summer**

selection and storage

Look for plump, firm, uniform-sized blueberries that are coated with a dusty, silver-white bloom—as well as indicating freshness, this is their natural protection against the sun.

Blueberries are generally sold in punnets, so check there are no squashed or moldy berries lurking at the bottom of the storage container.

If not using immediately, transfer any unwashed blueberries to a dish lined with paper towels, cover with plastic wrap and refrigerate for up to 2 days. Blueberries can be frozen for up to 6 months—do not wash before freezing, as this tends to toughen their skin.

Blueberries are one of the few fruits native to North America. It is hardly surprising then that the very best blueberry recipes—blueberry-studded muffins, velvety blueberry cheesecakes, and homely pies spilling sticky juices—come from there too.

Their deep indigo blue exterior covers sweet, greenish flesh, containing tiny, almost invisible seeds. For baking or making jams, pancakes, and salads, blueberries work well with the flavors of lemon (which can turn them red), cinnamon, cloves, pecans, almonds, peaches, and yogurt.

Containing cholesterol-lowering compounds, antioxidants, vitamin C, potassium, folate, and dietary fiber, blueberries are now regarded as one of the so-called super foods. It is even thought that their consumption can have anti-aging effects.

preparation

Blueberries are one of the easiest fruits to eat, requiring absolutely no preparation—no peeling, seeding, topping, or tailing. Just wash them immediately before eating, then drain on paper towels. If adding blueberries to cake and muffin batters, do this at the very last moment to prevent their vibrant juices from streaking the mixture. When including them in pancakes, sprinkle over half-cooked batter in the pan before turning, to minimize the risk of overcooking them and to seal in their luscious juices. Lightly heated with sugar and a splash of brandy, blueberries make a wonderful topping for waffles with vanilla ice cream.

soft fruit ■ blueberries

blueberry muffins

3 cups all-purpose flour
1 tablespoon baking powder
¾ cup firmly packed soft brown
  sugar
½ cup unsalted butter, melted
2 eggs, lightly beaten
1 cup milk
1¼ cups blueberries

Preheat the oven to 415°F. Grease two trays of six ½-cup muffin holes.

Sift the flour and baking powder into a large bowl. Stir in the sugar and make a well in the center. Working quickly, pour the combined melted butter, eggs, and milk into the well and stir until just combined. Do not overmix; the batter should look quite lumpy.

Gently fold in the blueberries. Spoon the batter into the prepared muffin pans. Bake for 20 minutes or until golden brown. Cool on a wire rack or serve warm.

hot blueberry sauce

3¼ cups blueberries
¼ cup sugar
1 tablespoon balsamic vinegar
vanilla ice cream or warm
  chocolate cake, to serve

In a nonmetallic bowl, combine the blueberries, sugar, and balsamic vinegar. Allow to marinate for 30 minutes.

Place the berry mixture in a saucepan with 2 tablespoons water and stir over low heat for 4–5 minutes or until sugar dissolves. Bring to a boil and simmer for 5 minutes. Serve warm with vanilla ice cream or warm chocolate cake.

blueberry cheesecake

Grease an 8-inch springform pan and line the base with baking paper. Melt the butter in a saucepan, add the oats and crushed graham crackers and mix well. Stir in the brown sugar. Press half the mixture into the base of the pan in an even layer, and gradually press the remainder around the side, but not quite all the way up to the rim, using a glass to firm it into place. Refrigerate for 10–15 minutes.

Preheat the oven to 350°F. To make the filling, beat the cream cheese, ricotta cheese, sugar, and sour cream with electric beaters until smooth. Beat in the eggs, orange zest, and flour. Put the pan on a baking sheet to catch any drips. Pour the filling into the crust and bake for 40–45 minutes or until the filling is just set. Remove from the oven and leave in the pan to cool to room temperature.

To make the topping, sprinkle the blueberries over the cheesecake. Push the jam through a sieve into a small saucepan with the cherry brandy. Stir over medium heat until smooth, then simmer for 2–3 minutes. Carefully brush the hot mixture over the blueberries. Refrigerate for several hours or overnight, until well chilled.

variation Other berries, such as blackberries, raspberries, or strawberries can be used instead of blueberries for the topping—just substitute the same weight in berries. If using strawberries, they need to be quartered or sliced first.

Blueberries were a key source of nutrition to the Native American population, who added them to soups, stews, and meat dishes and dried them for nourishment during the harsh winter months. Colonizing pilgrims did likewise, contributing to their survival in their new home, and since then blueberries have become an ingrained part of the American diet.

½ cup unsalted butter
1 cup rolled oats
¾ cup finely crushed graham crackers
2 tablespoons soft brown sugar

filling
1½ cups light cream cheese, at room temperature
⅓ cup ricotta cheese
⅓ cup superfine sugar
½ cup sour cream
2 eggs
1 tablespoon finely grated orange zest
1 tablespoon all-purpose flour

topping
1⅔ cups blueberries
¾ cup blackberry jam
¼ cup cherry brandy

soft fruit ■ blueberries

boysenberries

fruit ■ **soft**
season ■ **summer**

Shaped like an elongated blackberry but lacking its gritty seeds, with the deep purple color and acid note of loganberries and hints of the aromatic flavor of raspberries, boysenberries feature the best characteristics of these three delectable berries. Named after American horticulturalist Rudolph Boysen, who hybridized them in 1923, boysenberries can be used interchangeably or in combination with any of their progenitors.

Boysenberries taste delicious when pureed with superfine sugar, a little grated orange zest, and Grand Marnier for a quickly prepared crepe filling, or paired with pistachio and vanilla gelato for a grown-up sundae. Sprinkled over the base of a small baking dish, splashed with crème de cassis, slathered with crème fraîche and topped with brown sugar, they can be placed under a hot broiler to create a bubbling boysenberry gratin. Or, for an extremely easy dessert, stir boysenberries through whipped cream with some ground almonds, brown sugar, lemon juice, and natural vanilla extract, spoon into glasses and serve.

Rich in fiber, vitamin C, and potassium, their luscious sweet-sour flavor marries especially well with vanilla or other berry ice creams, citrus flavors, chocolate, apples, mangoes, pastry, and meringue.

selection and storage

Boysenberries should be firm and uniform in size, with no signs of mold or shriveling. Highly perishable, they should be gently wiped with a damp cloth before eating, preferably on the day of purchase. Alternatively, put them, unwashed and in a single layer, on paper towels in an airtight container and refrigerate for up to 2 days. If faced with a surplus, you can freeze boysenberries for up to 3 months; they'll only be good for cooking; use them for greatest effect in preserves, sauces, sorbets, or granitas.

boysenberry (or blackberry) pie

Sift the flour and 1/4 teaspoon salt into a large bowl. Add the butter and rub it into the flour using your fingertips until the mixture resembles fine bread crumbs. Fold in the sugar.

Make a well in the center, add nearly all the water and mix with a flat-bladed knife, using a cutting rather than a stirring action. The mixture will come together in small beads of dough. If necessary, add more water, a teaspoon at a time, until the dough comes together. Test the dough by pinching a little piece between your fingers—if it doesn't hold together, it needs more water. Gather the dough together and lift out onto a lightly floured surface. Press the dough into a ball and then flatten it slightly. Cover in plastic wrap and refrigerate for 20–30 minutes.

Preheat the oven to 350°F. Grease a 10 inch (top) x 8 inch (bottom) pie dish. Roll half the dough out between two sheets of baking paper, until it is large enough to fit into the dish. Remove the top sheet of paper and invert the pastry into the dish. Use a small ball of pastry to help press it down, allowing it to hang over the side. Use a small sharp knife to trim away excess pastry.

To make the filling, toss the boysenberries, sugar, and cornstarch together in a bowl until well combined, then transfer to the pie dish. Roll out the remaining pastry between two sheets of baking paper until large enough to cover the pie. Moisten the rim of the pie base with milk and press the pastry lid firmly into place. Trim and crimp the edge. Brush with egg and sprinkle with the extra sugar. Pierce the top of the pie with a knife.

Bake on the bottom shelf of the oven for 10 minutes, then move the pie to the center shelf and bake for an additional 30 minutes or until golden on top. Cool before cutting into wedges and serving with cream or ice cream.

sweet shortcrust pastry
3 1/4 cups all-purpose flour
3/4 cup chilled unsalted butter, cut into cubes
2 tablespoons superfine sugar
3–4 tablespoons iced water

filling
4 cups boysenberries or blackberries
2/3 cup superfine sugar
2 tablespoons cornstarch
milk, to brush
1 egg, lightly beaten
superfine sugar, extra, to sprinkle
whipping cream or vanilla ice cream, to serve

soft fruit ■ boysenberries

For other boysenberry recipes see:
blackberry and apple jam...................43

fig

One of the most sensual of all fruits, with their velvety skins, succulent rose-tinted, seedy flesh, and delicate, distinctly musky flavor, it's no wonder figs have long been associated with temptation. They achieved mythological status in ancient Rome and Greece, where they were not only a chief source of sustenance for the original Olympians, but so important to the Greek diet that it became illegal to export them. The ancient Greeks were certainly on to something, as modern research indicates that figs have one of the highest combined mineral counts of any popular cultivated fruit. Rich in calcium, potassium, phosphorus, and iron, they are also packed with dietary fiber.

While fig trees are extremely hardy and flourish in tough conditions, the fruit is extremely delicate and must be handled with care. Figs must be picked when completely ripe, for once they are picked they will not ripen further, and can't be kept very long in cold storage before spoiling. The difficulty of getting them to market in prime condition makes it hardly surprising that fig aficionados eagerly anticipate their appearance each fall, and will search to find a supplier of quality, ripe fruit.

selection and storage

There are hundreds of varieties of figs; all are highly perishable, ranging in skin color from purple, brown, and green to white, with flesh color from crimson and pinkish brown to amber.

Choose figs that feel yielding but not squashy, and that have no splits, bruises, black spots, leaking, or wrinkling on their skin. Ripe figs are sometimes coated with a natural, light whitish bloom; this is desirable.

Store figs on an uncovered tray or plate in the refrigerator for 2–3 days, but be sure to allow them to come to room temperature before eating, as chilling tends to dull their glorious flavor.

soft fruit ■ fig

varieties

black genoa A large purple-skinned fruit with sweet, pulpy, deep pink flesh.

brown turkey Another large fig with copper-brown skin, brown-pink flesh and a mild flavor.

mission Also known as Franciscan figs, these are the mainstay of Californian fig-growing with deep purple-black skin and pink flesh which has a coarse texture but sweet, lush flavor.

white adriatic Characterized by a vivid green skin and a flame-red interior, these figs have a brightly pronounced flavor.

preparation

Figs do not need to be washed before eating, just lightly wiped with a damp cloth. Some figs have thicker skins than others and it may be necessary to peel these—use a peeler for this or just pull the skin off gently using a paring knife to assist, working from the stem end down. Always trim off the stem as this contains an oozy white substance which is unpleasant to eat.

culinary uses

Flavor lightly poached figs with orange-flower water and they'll need little more than some honeyed yogurt and a sprinkling of crushed walnuts. A most luscious dessert consists of nothing more than halved, ripe figs doused in sweetened whipped cream into which has been folded plenty of pureed raspberries.

Dried figs are perfect on a cheese platter, add texture and character to a sticky golden syrup pudding, make a glorious sweet compote (cook them in a red wine and fresh thyme-flavored syrup), and are the vital ingredient in the eponymous American cookie, the Fig Newton. Figs can be roasted or baked, or halved, brushed with olive oil and carefully broiled.

Other worthy companions for this luscious fruit include honey, walnuts, pistachios, yogurt, citrus, rose water, raspberries, and cheeses, especially those of the blue and soft goat varieties.

chicken stuffed
with figs and fennel

To make the stuffing, heat 4 tablespoons of olive oil in a saucepan. Add the pancetta and onion and cook over medium-high heat, stirring often, for 5 minutes or until golden. Add the fennel and potato and cook for 2 minutes. Add the garlic and rosemary and season with sea salt and freshly ground black pepper. Stir in the wine, reduce the heat, then cover the pan. Cook for about 15 minutes or until the potato is tender and has absorbed the wine. Remove the saucepan from the heat and add the orange zest and figs. Set aside to cool if not using immediately. Stuffing can be made several hours in advance.

Preheat the oven to 500°F. Season the cavity of the chicken, then fill with the stuffing. If there is any stuffing left over, add it to the roasting pan 15 minutes before removing the chicken from the oven.

Put the chicken, breast side up, in a roasting pan, drizzle over the remaining oil and cook for 15 minutes. Remove the chicken from the oven and turn it over, then cook for an additional 15 minutes. After this time, remove from the oven again and turn the chicken onto its back, then reduce the heat to 350°F and cook for 30 minutes.

Check that the chicken is cooked by piercing the thickest part of the thigh with a skewer—the juices should run clear. Check that the stuffing is cooked through by pushing a skewer into the cavity for 3 seconds—the skewer should feel very hot when you pull it out. If it isn't, cover the chicken with foil and cook for an additional 10–15 minutes or until stuffing is heated through. Remove from the oven and rest for 10 minutes before serving. Serve with any extra stuffing and pour over any juices.

⅔ cup olive oil
1 cup diced smoked pancetta
1 onion, chopped
1 fennel bulb, chopped
1 large potato, cut into ¾-inch
   cubes
2 garlic cloves, chopped
1 tablespoon chopped rosemary
½ cup white wine
zest of 1 large orange
4 figs, chopped
4 pounds 8 ounces whole
   chicken

soft fruit ▪ fig

For other fig recipes see:

makes 12

figs wrapped in prosciutto

1½ tablespoons unsalted butter
1 tablespoon orange juice
12 small ripe figs
12 sage leaves
6 slices prosciutto, trimmed and
  halved lengthwise

Put the butter in a small heavy-bottomed saucepan. Melt the butter over low heat, then cook for 8–10 minutes or until the froth subsides and the milk solids appear as brown specks on the bottom of the saucepan. Strain the butter through a sieve lined with paper towels into a clean bowl, then stir in the orange juice.

Wash the figs gently and pat them dry with paper towels. Cut each fig into quarters, starting from the stem end and cutting almost to the base, then gently open out—figs will open like a flower. Put a sage leaf in the opening of each fig, then wrap a piece of prosciutto around each one, tucking the ends under the base of the fig. Arrange the figs, cut side up, in a baking dish and brush with the butter mixture.

Put the figs under a hot broiler and broil for 1–2 minutes or until the prosciutto is slightly crisp. Serve the figs warm or at room temperature.

serves 6

figs with rose water, almonds, and honey

12 purple-skinned figs
⅓ cup blanched almonds, lightly
  toasted
3–4 teaspoons rose water
1–2 tablespoons honey

Wash the figs gently and pat them dry with paper towels. Cut each fig into quarters, starting from the stem end and cutting almost to the base, then gently open out—figs will open like a flower. Put on a serving dish, cover with plastic wrap and chill in the refrigerator for 1 hour or until required.

Coarsely chop the toasted almonds and set aside. Carefully drizzle about ¼ teaspoon of rosewater into the center of each fig, then sprinkle over 1 teaspoon of the chopped almonds. Drizzle a little honey over the nuts, to serve.

gooseberries

fruit ▪ **soft**
season ▪ **summer**

Gooseberries have opaque, finely veined skins, which can be either furry or smooth. They are highly popular in Britain and Northern Europe, where their pleasing acidity and unique taste are utilized in tarts, pies, sauces, desserts, and preserves. Gooseberries are an old-fashioned fruit, with recipes for their use included in cookbooks dating back to the 1700s.

Depending on their cultivar and state of ripeness, gooseberries can be red, yellow, or green. Boasting high levels of vitamin C, potassium, and citric acid, they always require some sweetening ingredient, even when used in savory dishes. In England, they are traditionally associated with Whitsuntide, a time when they are made into gooseberry pies or the elderflower-scented Wiltshire Whitsun cake.

selection and storage

Gooseberries do continue ripening after picking, unlike other berries. Look for shiny, firm berries that show no signs of crushing or bruising, then handle them as little as possible. They must be topped and tailed before using.

Gooseberries will keep for 1–2 days at room temperature or for about 1 week in the refrigerator. Gooseberries can be frozen for later use—remove stems, put in a flat layer in an airtight freezer bag and seal; use within 6 months.

culinary uses

Gooseberries are one of the few fruits that are not eaten raw and the only berry at its finest when unripe. This quality makes them perfect for cutting the richness of oily fish, as the numerous recipes for smoked or pan-fried mackerel with gooseberry sauce attest. High in pectin, gooseberries make delightful jams and conserves, and spiced gooseberry chutney is great with roast goose and game. Gently sauté sliced gooseberries with a splash of sherry vinegar, thyme, and brown sugar, then serve with pan-fried duck breasts, pork chops, or use to top a sweet crème fraîche or crème pâtissière-filled tart.

gooseberry cream shortcake

To make the pastry, combine the flour and sugar in a large bowl and stir to mix well. Add the butter and rub it in until the mixture resembles coarse bread crumbs. Add the egg and, using a fork, mix until a soft dough forms. Form the dough into a flat disc, wrap in plastic wrap, then refrigerate while you prepare the filling.

To make the filling, combine the gooseberries and 1 cup of the sugar in a saucepan. Bring slowly to a boil over medium heat and cook, uncovered, for 10–15 minutes or until berries are cooked and liquid is thick and syrupy. Remove from the heat and cool.

Using an electric mixer or food processor, mix the cream cheese, sour cream, and remaining sugar together until the mixture is smooth. Stir in the flour and egg yolk until well combined.

Preheat the oven to 350°F. On a lightly floured surface, roll out two thirds of the pastry to cover the base and side of a lightly greased 10-inch round loose-bottomed tart pan. Press the pastry into the tart pan using a small ball of dough, then trim the excess pastry.

Spoon the gooseberry mixture into the pan, then spoon the cream cheese mixture over the berries. Roll the remaining pastry out on a floured surface to about 1/4-inch thick and cut into 5/8-inch strips. Arrange strips on a slight diagonal over the top to form a lattice pattern, trimming and joining pieces of pastry as needed.

Mix the egg yolk with 2 teaspoons water, then brush lattice strips with the mixture. Bake the shortcake for 35–40 minutes or until pastry is firm and golden. Cool, then serve warm or at room temperature with whipped cream.

pastry
2 1/2 cups self-rising flour
1/3 cup superfine sugar
1/2 cup chilled unsalted butter, cut into cubes
1 egg, lightly beaten

3 cups gooseberries, topped and tailed
1 1/4 cups superfine sugar
2/3 cup cream cheese
1/4 cup sour cream
1 tablespoon all-purpose flour
1 egg yolk
whipped cream, to serve

soft fruit ■ gooseberries

grapes

Whether classified as white or black, red or green, all grapes have smooth skins surrounding translucent, juicy flesh, some with seeds and others without. Grapes are actually true berries, unlike many fruits bearing that moniker, such as strawberries.

There are over 8,000 grape varieties in existence, although the vast majority of cultivated grapes are used for making wine rather than eating out of hand, and this has long been the case.

Archeological evidence suggests that not long after grapes were first found growing in the Fertile Crescent (an historical region in the Middle East and the world's original "fruit bowl," from where many other fruits originated), people quickly realized their juice could be fermented into wine. This fortuitous discovery has been appreciated by civilizations ever since, and utilizes grape varieties that are generally too tart for eating.

Used to make vinegar, verjuice, jam, jelly, grapeseed oil, and even the leavening agent cream of tartar, the versatility of grapes makes them an extremely valuable crop, second only to olives as the most widely cultivated temperate-climate fruit.

Containing vitamins B and C, dietary fiber, some potassium, protein, and a cancer-inhibiting compound called resveratrol, grapes are also rich in tannins, as any fan of red wine will appreciate.

selection and storage

Developing sugar as they ripen, grapes do not sweeten further after picking—bunches of table grapes are hand harvested to preserve their fruit-laden clusters.

Choose grapes that are well-colored for their variety, plump, and still firmly attached to their stems—a gentle shake will show whether the bunch is too old, as grapes will tellingly fall from their stems. Green grapes should have a slightly pale, yellowish hue rather than be grassy green, whereas red varieties are at their best when deeply colored.

Store unwashed grapes in a plastic bag in the refrigerator for 5–7 days. Wash grapes and gently pat dry just before eating.

varieties

There are many table grapes produced and these are differentiated by skin thickness and color, shape, juiciness, intensity of flavor, and sweetness, and whether the variety is seeded or seedless. Seedless types are increasingly preferred by consumers, although most experts agree that seeded grapes have a better flavor.

flame seedless A dark red, seedless grape with a juicy, somewhat "crisp" flesh with a tart edge.

muscat An ancient grape that is used for making wine, raisins, and as a table fruit. There are many varieties: the Muscat of Alexandria has yellowish skin, is large and seeded, with a very sweet and juicy flesh; Muscat Hamburg is a blue-black grape with oval, medium-large fruit. The flesh is pleasantly winey in flavor, is sweet and seeded.

red globe An extremely large, round red grape with subtle flavor, mealy flesh and a large seed.

thompson seedless Popular for processing into raisins, the medium-size Thompson seedless have yellowish green skin and a pronounced sweet flavor.

preparation

Although eating peeled grapes is associated with indolent Roman aristocracy, for some uses (in sauces to go with meats, for example), particularly if the skins are tough and tannic, peeling is necessary. To do this, cut a small incision at the stem end, then simply pull the skin off carefully. For particularly thick-skinned grapes, put them in a bowl, add boiling water to cover, then refresh in iced water and peel.

Similarly, if seeds are large and chewy, remove these by simply cutting grapes in half and picking them out.

culinary uses

Generally, there's no beating the classics—the Italians got it right with schiacciata, a flat bread studded with red or black grapes, as did the Spanish with ajo blanco (see page 160), the almond-based gazpacho topped with a few refreshing green grapes.

A handful of grapes tossed into a poached chicken, tarragon, and watercress salad makes memorable summer fare, as does an idea from Umbrian vintners—slow-roasting pork sausages with muscatel grapes until they become a delicious, crimson mass. Serve this as a satisfying lunch to combat fall's chill.

Perfect, sweet grapes served with freshly cracked walnuts and a delicious chunk of soft cheese (something decadent like a triple cream or an oozing Brie) is an unbeatable way to end a meal.

grape fritters
with cinnamon sugar

To make the cinnamon sugar, combine the sugar and cinnamon in a bowl. Set aside.

Whisk the egg yolks with the vanilla extract and sugar until pale and creamy. Slice each grape into four and stir into the egg yolk mixture. Sift the flour into the mixture and stir to combine. Beat the egg whites in a separate bowl until soft peaks form. Gently fold half of the egg whites into the grape mixture with a metal spoon until just combined, then fold in the remaining egg whites.

Melt 2 teaspoons of butter in a frying pan over low heat. Drop 6 heaping teaspoons of the batter separately into the pan, and cook over low-medium heat for 2–3 minutes, turning carefully when the base becomes firm and bubbles appear around the edges. Cook for an additional 2 minutes or until golden. Remove to a plate and keep warm, covered, in a 235°F oven. Repeat to make 24 fritters. Dust the fritters with cinnamon sugar and serve immediately.

cinnamon sugar
2 tablespoons superfine sugar
1 teaspoon ground cinnamon

fritters
2 eggs, separated
1/2 teaspoon natural vanilla extract
1/4 cup superfine sugar
3/4 cup large seedless red or black grapes
1/3 cup self-rising flour
2 tablespoons unsalted butter

soft fruit ■ grapes

The ancient Greeks and Romans were the first to dry grapes, the precursors of dried currants, golden raisins, and raisins; their very reduced juices were widely used as a sweetening agent before the advent of sugar. Italians also distil grape skins, seeds, and stems (the "waste" product of winemaking) to make a type of clear brandy called grappa.

schiacciata con uva
(sweet grape flat bread)

serves 6

¾ cup raisins
5 tablespoons sweet Marsala
⅔ cup milk
½ cup superfine sugar
1 (¼-ounce) package active
   dried yeast
2½ cups all-purpose flour
olive oil
2¾ cups black seedless grapes

Combine the raisins and Marsala in a bowl. Warm the milk and put in a small bowl. Stir in 1 teaspoon of the sugar, then sprinkle over the yeast, and set aside in a draft-free place for 7 minutes or until the mixture becomes foamy.

Put the flour, ⅓ cup of the sugar, and a pinch of salt in a bowl and mix together. Add the yeast mixture and mix until a dough forms. Transfer to a lightly floured surface and knead for 6–8 minutes or until smooth and elastic. Add a little more flour or a few drops of warm water if necessary to give a soft, but not sticky, dough.

Lightly oil the inside of a large bowl with olive oil, put the dough in the bowl and roll to coat in oil. Cut a cross on the top of the ball of dough with a sharp knife. Leave the dough in the bowl and cover with plastic wrap. Set aside in a draft-free place for 1 hour or until doubled in size.

Preheat the oven to 350°F. Drain the raisins and squeeze them dry. Lightly dust a baking sheet with flour. Punch down the dough and divide in two. Shape each half into a flattened round about 8 inches in diameter, and place one round on the baking sheet. Sprinkle half the grapes and half the raisins over the dough, then cover with the second round of dough. Sprinkle the remaining grapes and raisins over the top. Cover loosely with a dishtowel and leave in a draft-free place for 1 hour or until doubled in size.

Sprinkle the dough with the remaining sugar. Bake for 40–50 minutes or until golden. Serve warm or at room temperature, cut into thick slices.

raspberries

fruit ▪ **soft**
season ▪ **late summer**

Squiggles of raspberry coulis became an overused 1980's menu staple, adorning everything from chocolate mud cake and brownies to duck liver pâté. These days, cooks are rediscovering the simpler delights of raspberries, as the resurgence in popularity of dishes such as peach Melba, with its essential raspberry sauce, and squidgy summer pudding, can attest.

The red raspberry and its rarer golden relative both hail from the Caucasus, while the lesser known black version is indigenous to North America. If you are fortunate enough to spy yellow raspberries at the market, try them, as they have a particularly concentrated flavor. Like all berries, raspberries are rich in vitamins A and C, potassium, and iron.

culinary uses

Although raspberries are undoubtedly one of the finest flavored of the berries and do not need too many competing flavors, they are luxurious when paired with dark or white chocolate, almonds, hazelnuts, vanilla, lavender, rose water, coconut, sparkling wine, rosé, or crème de framboise.

Showcase their glorious color and flavor by using them in simple, classic desserts, such as Eton mess, a sherry-sodden trifle, a Sauternes syllabub, or a humble berry crumble. For a very lush dessert, top raspberries with fresh clotted cream. Raspberries, in the form of raspberry vinegar, can add a special note to savory food, such as a dressing for spinach or beet-based salads, or splashed into a sauce destined for pairing with a roasted duck.

selection and storage

Labor intensive to harvest due to their extreme fragility, raspberries should be eaten within 2 days of purchase and stored in the refrigerator.

Choose deeply-colored raspberries, as these are the most strongly flavored, and do try to buy those that have escaped spraying as they won't need washing (raspberries don't respond well to drenching in water).

When purchasing, look to see that the hulls have been removed when picked, leaving the characteristic hollow center; if they are still there, it's an indication that the berries were picked when under-ripe and will be sour. Raspberries can be frozen for up to 3 months.

soft fruit ▪ raspberries

duck breast with raspberries and cassis

serves 4

4 (7-ounce) duck breasts
2 teaspoons ground cinnamon
1 tablespoon raw sugar
1 cup red wine
2/3 cup crème de cassis
1 tablespoon cornstarch or
   arrowroot
2 cups raspberries

Using a sharp knife, score the duck breasts through the skin and fat, taking care not to cut into the meat. In a frying pan, cook the duck breasts over medium-high heat for 4–5 minutes, skin side down, until the skin browns and the fat runs out. Remove the meat from the pan and drain excess fat, reserving the pan.

Combine the cinnamon, sugar, and 2 teaspoons sea salt in a small bowl. Sprinkle over the skin of the duck breasts, then press in with your hands. Season with black pepper. Reheat the frying pan and cook the duck breasts, skin side up, for 10 minutes or until the duck is cooked through but still a little pink in the middle. Remove from pan and leave to rest on a carving board, reserving the pan and 2 tablespoons of cooking juices. Preheat the broiler.

Meanwhile, combine the red wine and cassis in a measuring cup. Pour 1/2 cup of the liquid into a small bowl and mix in the cornstarch. Pour this back into the cup.

Return the pan with the cooking juices to the heat and pour in the red wine mixture. Simmer for 2–3 minutes, stirring constantly, until the sauce has thickened. Add the raspberries and simmer for an additional minute to warm the fruit through. Season to taste.

Broil the duck breasts, skin side up, for 1 minute or until the sugar mixture starts to caramelize. Remove from heat and slice the duck breasts thinly. Pour a little of the hot sauce over the top and serve the rest of the sauce separately.

white chocolate and raspberry mousse

Melt the white chocolate in a heatproof bowl over a saucepan of simmering water, making sure that the water does not touch the bowl. Cool slightly, then stir in the cream. Stir in the yolks and mix well.

Whisk the egg whites until stiff peaks form. Fold a third of the egg whites into the chocolate mixture to loosen them. Fold in the remaining egg white until just combined. Fold in the raspberries, then divide among four serving bowls. Refrigerate for at least 4 hours. Decorate with extra fresh raspberries, to serve.

1 cup chopped good-quality white chocolate
2/3 cup whipping cream
4 eggs, separated
2 cups raspberries, crushed
raspberries, extra, to serve

soft fruit ■ raspberries

fig and raspberry cake

serves 6–8

Preheat the oven to 350°F. Grease a 9-inch springform pan.

Cream the butter and sugar in a bowl until light and pale. Add the egg and egg yolk and beat again. Sift the flour and baking powder into the bowl and add a pinch of salt. Stir to combine. Chill for 15 minutes or until firm enough to roll out.

Divide the dough in two equal halves, and roll out one half large enough to fit the base of the pan. Cover with the figs, orange zest, and raspberries. Roll out the remaining dough and place it over the filling. Lightly brush the top with water and sprinkle with extra sugar. Bake for 30 minutes or until a skewer inserted into the center of the cake comes out clean. Cut into slices and serve with cream or mascarpone cheese.

3/4 cup unsalted butter, at room temperature
3/4 cup superfine sugar
1 egg
1 egg yolk
2 2/3 cups all-purpose flour
1 teaspoon baking powder
4 figs, quartered
grated zest of 1 orange
1 2/3 cups raspberries
2 tablespoons superfine sugar, extra
whipping cream or mascarpone cheese, to serve

strawberries

fruit ■ **soft**
season ■ **summer**

Arguably the most beloved of all the soft fruits, strawberries belong to the rose family, so it's no surprise that adding a few judicious drops of rose water enhances their floral flavor. Strawberries are the only fruit whose seeds grow around the exterior rather than interior. While their botanic name, *Fragaria*, means "fragrance," describing perfectly their perfumed essence, strawberries had romantic associations long before chocolate-dipped fruits and strawberries floating in champagne became Valentine's Day staples. Once regarded as an aphrodisiac in provincial France, they are also the symbol of Venus, goddess of love, due to their ruby color and unique heart shape.

Cultivated strawberry varieties abound, ranging in color from scarlet to yellow and even white. The smaller, sweeter wild strawberries, known in France as *frais de bois*, meaning "strawberries of the woods," are the most highly prized, on account of their exquisite, concentrated flavor.

Strawberries contain more vitamin C than oranges. A good source of potassium and folic acid, they also contain ellagic acid, a compound that guards against cancer. Be warned though: strawberries can cause a severe allergic reaction in babies, so it is best to wait until they are over one year old before introducing them to the fruit.

preparation

Don't wash or hull strawberries before storing, or soak them in water before using, as they readily absorb moisture, which dilutes their flavor. Wash just before eating, then remove leaves and stems with a small, sharp knife or strawberry huller.

culinary uses

Who can resist a luscious bowl of sun-ripened strawberries? Imagine the ritual of afternoon tea without scones adorned with strawberry jam and cream, or Neapolitan ice cream minus the obligatory strip of strawberry. The marriage of strawberries and cream may have evolved into more refined expressions, but the original combination remains one of summer's purest pleasures.

Take a cue from the Italians and sprinkle perfect strawberries with superfine sugar, then drizzle with a little aged balsamic vinegar; finish with a light grinding of black pepper and mascarpone cheese. Crush strawberries with sugar and a dash of orange-flower water or rose water, then fold through whipped cream and serve as a fool, or use as a filling for sponge cake or a pavlova topping (see page 109). Along with sliced cucumber, lemon, lime, and mint, strawberries are a vital ingredient in an authentic Pimm's No. 1 Cup. Strawberries' sweetness offsets rhubarb's tartness; together the pair make excellent pies, crumbles, jams, and preserves.

selection and storage

As delicate as the hearts they resemble, strawberries should be handled with care. They do not ripen further after picking but just soften.

Choose strawberries that are plump, fragrant, and firm, with no signs of bruising, leaking, or mold festering in the bottom of the container and no greenish white "shoulders" at the stem end. Carefully store and handle them—ideally eat them on the day of purchase.

An excess of strawberries will be best used by making jam or freezing for up to 6 months for later use—hull them first and freeze them in a single layer on trays before transferring to freezer bags or containers.

For other strawberry recipes see:

summer pudding 45

serves 6

balsamic strawberries

3⅓ cups strawberries, hulled
  and halved
¼ cup balsamic vinegar
2 tablespoons superfine sugar
2 teaspoons lemon juice
small handful mint leaves
vanilla ice cream, to serve

Put the strawberries in a glass bowl. Combine the balsamic vinegar, sugar, and lemon juice in a small saucepan and stir over medium heat for 5 minutes or until the sugar dissolves. Remove from the heat and cool.

Pour the balsamic mixture over the strawberries, add the mint leaves and toss together. Cover with plastic wrap and refrigerate for 1 hour to allow the flavors to develop. Serve with vanilla ice cream.

makes 2 cups

strawberry curd

1⅔ cups strawberries, hulled
  and roughly chopped
¾ cup superfine sugar
½ cup unsalted butter, softened
1 teaspoon grated lemon zest
1 tablespoon lemon juice
4 egg yolks

Put the strawberries in a saucepan with the sugar, butter, lemon zest, and lemon juice. Stir over low heat until the butter has melted and the sugar dissolved. Simmer gently for 5 minutes, then remove from the heat.

Lightly beat the egg yolks in a large bowl, then, stirring constantly, slowly add the strawberry mixture in a thin stream. The mixture will thicken as you add it.

Return to low heat and cook for 2 minutes, stirring constantly. Do not allow the mixture to boil or the curd will separate. Pour into hot sterilized jars and seal while hot. Curd will keep in the refrigerator for up to 2 months. Once opened, the curd will keep, refrigerated, for 5 days.

apricot

fruit ▪ **stone**
season ▪ **summer**

If you have only ever eaten supermarket-supplied apricots, on the whole sadly tasteless specimens, you could be forgiven for wondering what the fuss over apricots is about. All too often, this eagerly anticipated summer fruit, which should brim with sweet, fragrant juices and have satisfyingly lush flesh, has all the mouth-appeal of the boxes it arrives in and is rather similar in taste. The fact is, the highly perishable apricot doesn't travel well when ripe and doesn't much ripen once picked, although a few days at room temperature will improve flavor a little. The best way to obtain full-flavored fruit is to buy it sun-ripened and just picked from a caring supplier. Only then will the "fuss" become apparent as there can be few lovelier experiences than eating a juicy apricot, warm with the flavors of high summer.

The apricot hails from China where it has been cultivated for over 4,000 years. Marco Polo is credited with the westward spread of the fruit, via the legendary Silk Road. This was a highly successful migration; assorted Turkish, Spanish, Arab, and other Mediterranean cooks have, over time, embraced the fruit with great enthusiasm, producing some of the most memorable apricot recipes, including savory preparations where the fruit is cooked with lamb, chicken, or rice and a plethora of exotic sweet spices, such as cardamom, ginger, and cinnamon.

preparation

There is no need to peel apricots; this would be tediously difficult anyway. They split in half easily and neatly along their natural crease. Do beware, the flesh will oxidize (turn brown) on contact with the air, so work quickly and if serving raw, prepare just before you plan to serve them.

culinary uses

Fresh apricots make sublime jam and if you are blessed with an excess, they are perfectly suited to being bottled in syrup. They are fabulous in tarts, pies, cakes (upside-down cake springs to mind), and crumbles; they can be poached, pureed, and even stuffed and roasted—there, the classic Italian filling for stuffed roast peaches, comprising chopped almonds, chocolate, and amaretti biscuits, translates perfectly to apricots.

Their flavor also goes particularly well with those of vanilla beans, almonds, hazelnuts and pistachios, fresh rosemary, honey, saffron, some cheeses (Camembert, Brie and mascarpone, for example), dessert wines, and orange-flower and rose waters. Simple desserts can be made by lightly poaching apricots in syrup spiked with one (or some) of these flavors—saffron-poached apricots served with yogurt and pistachios are delicious, as are honey and rosemary poached apricots served chilled with dollops of mascarpone cheese.

selection and storage

Buy directly from a grower, then you'll know what apricot variety you are purchasing; otherwise it's something of a lottery. If possible, seek out older varieties like blenheim or the peerless moorpark, a large apricot with particularly fine flavor.

Buy fruits that are firm but not hard, and ones with clear, unblemished skin. They should feel slightly soft when pressed and have a faintly sweet fragrance; they should be a deep, clear orange and some may blush with red.

Once purchased, apricots should be consumed within 1–2 days and stored carefully at cool room temperature (chilling masks their flavor); cradled in a single layer on several layers of paper towel is the best way.

serves 4

chicken with apricots and honey

2 tablespoons butter
1 teaspoon ground cinnamon
1 teaspoon ground ginger
⅛ teaspoon cayenne pepper
4 (6-ounce) chicken breasts, trimmed
1 onion, sliced
1 cup chicken stock
6 cilantro sprigs, tied in a bunch
10 apricots, halved and pits removed
2 tablespoons honey
2 tablespoons slivered almonds, toasted, to serve
couscous, to serve

Melt the butter in a large frying pan. Add the spices, season with freshly ground black pepper, and stir over low heat for about 1 minute or until fragrant. Increase the heat to medium and add the chicken breasts. Cook for 1 minute on each side, taking care not to let the spices burn.

Add the onion and cook for 5 minutes, stirring the onion and turning the chicken occasionally. Add the stock and cilantro sprigs and season, to taste. Reduce the heat to low, cover, and simmer for 5 minutes, turning the chicken once.

Transfer the chicken to a serving dish, cover, then rest for 2–3 minutes. Put the apricots, cut side down, into the frying pan with the juices and drizzle with the honey. Cover the pan, then simmer for 7–8 minutes, turning the apricots after 5 minutes. Remove the cilantro and discard.

Spoon the apricots and sauce over the chicken, sprinkle with almonds and serve with couscous.

Apricot kernels, found inside the hard pit, look somewhat like an almond and, when blanched and used sparingly, impart a delicious bitter almond flavor—this is particularly lovely in apricot jam, or stewed or poached apricots. Beware, however, as apricot kernels can be toxic eaten in any quantity—always use just a few (four kernels in a large batch of jam or three in a brew of poached fruit to serve 6–8), and retrieve them before serving.

makes 3 cups **apricot jam**

2 pounds (about 20) apricots,
  halved and pits removed
4½ cups sugar, warmed (see
  note)

Put the apricots in a large saucepan with 1½ cups water.
Bring to a boil, stirring, for 20 minutes or until the fruit
has softened.

Put two plates in the freezer. Add the sugar to the pan and
stir, without boiling, for 5 minutes or until all the sugar has
dissolved. Return to the boil and boil for 20 minutes, stirring
often. Remove any scum during cooking with a slotted
spoon. When the jam falls from the back of a tilted wooden
spoon in thick sheets without dripping, start testing for
setting point. To do this, remove from heat, put a little jam
onto one of the cold plates and place in the freezer for
30 seconds. A skin will form on the surface and the jam will
wrinkle when pushed with your finger. If not, return to the
heat for a few minutes, then retest with the other plate.

Carefully ladle into hot sterilized jars and seal. Allow to cool,
then label and date each jar. Store in a cool, dark place for
6–12 months. Refrigerate after opening for up to 6 weeks.

note To warm the sugar, preheat the oven to 300°F. Spread
the sugar evenly in a baking dish and put in the oven for
10–15 minutes or until warmed through. To save time you
can warm the sugar while you are cooking the jam. Do not
add the sugar until the fruit has softened. If sugar is added
before the fruit has fully softened, the fruit will remain firm.

apricot meringue torte

Combine 1 1/2 cups water, 1/2 cup of the sugar, cinnamon stick, and 1 teaspoon of the vanilla extract in a large saucepan. Stir over low heat until the sugar has dissolved, then increase the heat and simmer for 15 minutes. Add the quartered apricots and simmer over low heat for 20 minutes or until the apricots are very soft. Set aside to cool.

Preheat the oven to 300°F. Draw an 8 1/2-inch circle on two sheets of baking paper. Put the sheets, pencil side down, on two baking sheets.

Using electric beaters, whisk the egg whites in a bowl until stiff peaks form. Add the remaining sugar, a little at a time, and continue beating until the mixture is stiff and glossy. Beat in the vinegar and remaining vanilla extract. Gently fold in the ground hazelnuts.

Divide the meringue mixture between the two circles on the prepared baking sheets and smooth the surface. Bake for 35–40 minutes or until the meringues are firm and dry. Turn off the oven and leave the meringues in the oven to cool completely.

Peel off the baking paper and put one meringue on a serving plate. Whip the cream until stiff peaks form. Discard the cinnamon stick from the syrup and drain the apricots. Gently stir the apricots through the whipped cream and then spread over the meringue. Put the second meringue on top of the apricot cream and dust with confectioners' sugar to serve.

1 2/3 cups superfine sugar
1 cinnamon stick
2 teaspoons natural vanilla extract
1 pound (about 10) apricots, quartered and pits removed
6 egg whites, at room temperature
1 1/2 teaspoons white vinegar
1/3 cup ground hazelnuts
1 1/4 cups heavy whipping cream
confectioners' sugar, to dust

stone fruit ■ apricot

cherries

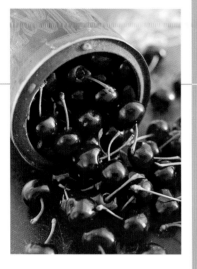

fruit ■ **stone**
season ■ **summer**

No fruit epitomizes lazy, hazy summer days like cherries, those cheerful, shiny, and ruby-red (or pink or yellowish) globes that seem to come and then go all too quickly. Even in these days of year-round produce supply, cherries remain stubbornly seasonal, making them a highly anticipated treat. Divinely juicy and addictively sweet, cherries are at their best eaten out of hand, although they can also lend their subtle but unmistakable flavor to any number of sweet and savory preparations.

It seems too, that cherries are not just delicious —they burst with good things for the body. Particularly rich in cancer-fighting antioxidants, cherries also contain anti-inflammatory compounds plus abundant quantities of melatonin, which helps regulate the body's circadian rhythms. Cherry consumption is being credited with everything from helping arthritis and gout sufferers, to preventing diabetes and heart disease.

A venerable fruit, the first recorded mention of the cherry was in Theophrastus' (372–287 B.C.) *History of Plants*, where he suggests the Greeks had been cultivating the fruit, a native of Asia Minor, for centuries. The Romans spread the cherry throughout Europe, leaving it in the wake of their conquests, and it is thought to have been an important part of the Legionnaires' diet.

varieties

Cherries can be divided into two basic categories—sweet and sour. Some of the most popular and well-known sweet cherry varieties are the Bing (large and very dark red-black fruit), Napoleon, Florence, and Ranier—these latter three types have yellowish skins that blush pink when ripe.

Perhaps the two most popular sour varieties are the maraschino (used to produce the classic preserved cherry used in desserts) and the Morello. Sour cherries, with their complex flavor and slightly tart edge, are perfectly suited for cooking (in fact they're too tart to eat raw) and are the cherry behind some of the world's most beloved cherry preparations—think black forest cake, Hungarian-style chilled cherry soup, the liqueur kirsch, and sour cherry strudel. Sweet cherries also work well when cooked; witness the timeless cherry clafoutis from France, that fabulous batter-based pudding which is utterly delicious and particularly easy to prepare.

preparation

Cherry pits contain kernels that can contribute a complementary, slightly bitter-almond flavor to cherry dishes. If you want this flavor, leave them in when freezing or, if dealing with fresh fruit, crack a few kernels, tie them in a piece of cheesecloth and add them to the cooking liquid or poaching syrup when making jam, compotes, or puddings.

culinary uses

Cherries are such a special treat that it is unlikely you will have to deal with extras. However, if fortunate enough to be in possession of more fruit than you can possibly use, they can be made into gorgeous jams or pickled in a lightly spiced, vinegared syrup to serve with smoked meats, such as ham, pâtés, and terrines.

selection and storage

Buy cherries with the stalk still on—they'll keep better. Make sure the fruits have been kept cool as their flavor and texture degrade if they have been exposed to warmth. Ripe sweet cherries will last for 2–3 days in a plastic bag in the refrigerator. Sour cherries keep for up to 2 weeks, refrigerated.

Both sweet and sour types can be frozen successfully and if doing this, consider investing in a cherry pitter to remove pits before freezing so they'll be easier to deal with once thawed.

Always take the time to choose your own cherries from the piles typically heaped high at markets. Pick out fruit that is unblemished, shiny, large (cherries gain 30 percent of their flavor and volume in the last week before picking), heavy and with no soft, wrinkled, spotted, or burst patches. Generally, the deeper the skin color (according to variety), the riper the fruit.

serves 8

cherry and cream cheese strudel

1 cup cream cheese, at room
temperature
1/2 cup whipping cream
1/4 cup superfine sugar
1 tablespoon brandy or cherry
brandy
1 teaspoon natural vanilla extract
10 sheets phyllo pastry
1/3 cup unsalted butter, melted
1/3 cup dry bread crumbs
1/3 cup ground almonds
2 tablespoons superfine sugar,
extra
1 1/4 cups cherries, pitted
confectioners' sugar, to dust

Preheat the oven to 400°F. Lightly grease a large baking
sheet. Put the cream cheese, cream, sugar, brandy, and vanilla
extract in a bowl and beat with electric beaters until smooth.

Take one sheet of phyllo pastry. Keep the rest covered with
a damp dishtowel to prevent them drying out. Brush with
some of the melted butter and sprinkle with some of the
combined crumbs, almonds, and extra sugar. Put another
sheet of pastry on top. Repeat brushing and sprinkling until
all the sheets are used.

Spread the cream cheese mixture evenly over the pastry,
leaving a 1 1/2-inch border all around. Brush butter over the
border. Arrange the cherries over the cream cheese.

Roll the pastry from one long side and fold in the ends
as you roll. Form into a firm roll and place, seam side
down, on the greased baking sheet. Brush all over with the
remaining butter. Bake for 10 minutes, then reduce the oven
to 350°F and continue to bake for 30 minutes or until crisp
and golden. Cool on a wire rack. To serve, dust the strudel
liberally with confectioners' sugar and cut into slices using
a sharp serrated knife.

cherry clafoutis

Preheat the oven to 350°F. Put the cream in a small saucepan. Scrape out the seeds of the vanilla bean and add the seeds and scraped bean to the cream. Heat gently for 2–5 minutes, then remove from the heat, add the milk, then cool. Strain to remove the vanilla bean and seeds.

Whisk the eggs with the sugar and flour, then stir into the cream. Add the kirsch and cherries and stir well. Pour into a 9-inch round baking dish and bake for 30–35 minutes or until golden on top. Dust with confectioners' sugar and serve.

note It is traditional to leave the pits in the cherries when you make a clafoutis (they add a bitter, almost-almond flavor during the cooking), but you should point this out when you're serving the pudding.

¾ cup heavy cream
1 vanilla bean, halved lengthwise
½ cup milk
3 eggs
¼ cup superfine sugar
⅔ cup all-purpose flour
1 tablespoon cherry brandy, such as kirsch
2¼ cups sweet black cherries
confectioners' sugar

stone fruit ■ cherries

Today, much of the world's sweet cherry crop is produced in Turkey, Iran, the United States, Italy, and Spain, while Russia and Poland grow huge quantities of sour cherry varieties.

date

fruit ■ **stone**
season ■ **fall–winter**

selection and storage

Select dates that haven't been prepackaged (typically on small trays, wrapped tightly in plastic wrap) as it is difficult to tell their condition. Choose dates that are plump, with unbroken, slightly wrinkled skins. Avoid any with sugary surfaces as this indicates their sugars are crystallizing (due to inappropriate storing or age).

Store dates in a sealed container in the refrigerator. Fresh dates will keep for 12 months—they can also be frozen for several years.

With a sugar content of around 60 percent, it's little wonder that dates taste so good! They are one of the world's oldest food crops; some believe they were cultivated as early as 8,000 B.C. Known as "the tree of life" in the Arab countries where they flourish, date palms are also one of the world's most useful crops. Legendarily the palm has 800 uses—the sap is drunk, the fiber woven, the seeds are ground and used for camel fodder, the palm-hearts are eaten and the bark is used as building material, to name a few.

Aside from the usual sweet uses for dates (in scones, cakes, and muffins, for example), dates also star in salads, tagines, sauces, rice and grain dishes; even in an intriguing rice-based stuffing for fish.

varieties

There are countless varieties of dates; they are rarely sold by name but the two sorts most likely to be encountered are the famous medjool (crinkly skinned, mellow, sticky, and sweet) and the noble deglet noor, "date of light," which has a translucent, smooth skin, chewy texture, and delicate flavor.

Usually we buy dates by type—namely, "soft," "semidry," or "dry." Soft dates, which are very fresh, have soft flesh, with a high moisture content and relatively low sugar levels. "Semidry" (often erroneously labelled "fresh dates") have firmer but still softish flesh, lower moisture, and higher sugar content; these are "soft" dates that have been partially dried to develop the sugars and extend shelf-life. "Dry" or "bread" dates are quite hard and contain little moisture and loads of sugar. Dry dates are usually packaged and used extensively in Western countries for baking.

stone fruit ▪ date

trout stuffed with dates

serves 4

4 medium-size trout
1 cup chopped fresh dates
¼ cup cooked rice
1 onion, finely chopped
4 tablespoons chopped cilantro
  leaves
¼ teaspoon ground ginger
¼ teaspoon ground cinnamon
⅓ cup roughly chopped
  blanched almonds
2 tablespoons butter, softened
ground cinnamon, to dust

Preheat the oven to 350°F. Rinse the trout under cold running water and pat dry with paper towels. Season with sea salt and freshly ground black pepper.

Combine the dates, rice, half the onion, the cilantro, ground ginger, cinnamon, almonds, and half the butter in a bowl. Season well.

Spoon the stuffing into the fish cavities and put each fish on a well-greased double sheet of foil. Brush the fish with the remaining butter and divide the remaining onion among the four packages. Wrap the fish neatly and seal the edges of the foil. Put the packages on a large baking sheet and bake for 15–20 minutes or until cooked to your liking. Serve dusted with cinnamon.

dates poached in earl grey syrup

serves 2–4

2 Earl Grey tea bags
1 cup sugar
12 fresh dates
heavy cream or mascarpone
  cheese, to serve

Infuse the tea bags in 1 cup boiling water for 30 minutes.

Discard the tea bags and place the liquid in a small saucepan with the sugar. Stir over medium heat until the sugar has dissolved. Bring to a boil, then reduce the heat and simmer for 10 minutes, without stirring.

Add the dates to the pan and cook for 2–3 minutes, turning once, until the dates are tender. Serve with heavy cream or mascarpone cheese.

sticky date pudding with caramel sauce

Preheat the oven to 350°F. Grease a deep 9-inch springform pan and line the base with baking paper. Chop the dates and put them in a saucepan with 1¾ cups water. Bring to a boil, then remove from the heat, add the baking soda and ginger and leave to stand for 5 minutes.

Cream together the butter, sugar, and 1 egg. Beat in the remaining eggs one at a time, mixing well after each addition. Fold in the sifted flour and pumpkin pie spice, add the date mixture and stir until well combined. Pour into the pan and bake for 55–60 minutes or until a skewer inserted into the center of the pudding comes out clean. Cover with foil if overbrowning during cooking. Leave to stand for 5 minutes before turning out onto a serving plate.

To make the caramel sauce, stir all the ingredients in a saucepan over low heat until the sugar has dissolved. Simmer, uncovered, for about 3 minutes or until thickened slightly. Brush some sauce over the top and side of the pudding until well glazed. Serve the pudding immediately with extra sauce and a dollop of crème fraîche.

2 cups fresh dates
1½ teaspoons baking soda
1 teaspoon grated ginger
⅓ cup unsalted butter, at room
   temperature
heaping 1 cup superfine sugar
3 eggs
1½ cups self-rising flour
½ teaspoon pumpkin pie spice
crème fraîche, to serve

caramel sauce
⅔ cup unsalted butter, cut into
   cubes
1¼ cups soft brown sugar
⅓ cup maple syrup
¾ cup whipping cream

stone fruit ■ date

The date palm takes 30 years to mature, grows up to 100 feet and can live for up to 150 years—if it doesn't topple over first, which is commonly the way date palms die.

peach and nectarine

fruit ▪ **stone**
season ▪ **summer**

Raw fruit perfection doesn't come any more complete than a ripe, fragrant peach or nectarine, served in simple slices or eaten, complete with the inevitable drips and mess, out of sticky hands. Like apricots, these fragile stone fruits taste best when purchased as near to where they grow as possible, as they bruise easily when transported and are most scrumptious when ripened on the tree.

Nectarines are no more than a subspecies of the peach and not, as is often supposed, a cross between a peach and a plum; essentially, the nectarine is a fuzz-free peach. Nectarine and peach trees are virtually indistinguishable from each other, producing the same leaves, buds, and flowers. In fact, no more than a single recessive gene (the one for "fuzzlessness") separates the two fruit. Nectarines and peaches come with either white or yellow flesh—purists claim that white fruits have a finer flavor.

varieties

In general, mid-to-late summer peach and nectarine varieties taste better than those first fruits of summer. There are dozens of types cultivated commercially and yet all too often they are not sold by variety. Many of these stone fruits have very, very brief seasons, so as one disappears from the stands, another will take its place— you will need to purchase what's around and go back for more if you particularly love a variety you've discovered.

freestone Peaches and nectarines are classified as either freestone or clingstone. Freestone varieties, as the name implies, separate easily from their stone or pit—all that is needed is to cut through to the pit, all the way around the fruit, then gently twist the cut halves in opposite directions and pull them off the pit. Freestone fruits are perfect when you want to poach whole halves or if you want to roast, stuff, or bake intact halves. If you plan to bottle quantities of fruits or make preserves, such as jams, chutneys, or relishes, freestone fruits make preparation a breeze.

clingstone Clingstones will not yield their pits at all and the flesh must be cut away to separate it. Clingstones are fine when you want to serve whole, poached peaches, require a puree, or want to cook something else that doesn't require neat halves.

preparation

Nectarines don't need to be peeled, but fuzzy peaches do, especially if served poached or in pies, jams, or ice creams. To peel clingstones, score a tiny cross at the base of each peach and plunge, a few at a time, into boiling water for 15–20 seconds. Using a slotted spoon, transfer each one carefully to a bowl of iced water to cool, then peel away the skin.

To peel freestones, score the peach through the skin all the way around and right through to the pit, then plunge into boiling water and iced water as above—the skin will easily peel off.

culinary uses

If they are to be cooked (and with the exception of a few chutney, salsa, and savory salad recipes), peaches and nectarines are best suited to sweet recipes. They are complemented well by the flavors of almonds, champagne, vanilla, raspberries, wine (poached in either white or red wine, these fruits are transcendental), dashes of cinnamon or cardamom, yogurt, and cream.

selection and storage

Choose unblemished specimens that give slightly to gentle pressure but don't feel too soft. Peaches in particular should smell sweetly fragrant when ripe so follow your nose when selecting them.

Both peaches and nectarines will soften at room temperature but not ripen once they are picked. Refrigerate ripe fruits for a day or so only and bring them to room temperature before serving, as their flavor is diminished by chilling.

stone fruit ▪ peach and nectarine

makes 8

nectarine feuilletées

2 sheets butter puff pastry
3 tablespoons unsalted butter,
    softened
1/2 cup ground almonds
1/2 teaspoon natural vanilla
    extract
5 large nectarines
1/4 cup superfine sugar
1/3 cup apricot or peach jam,
    warmed and sieved

Preheat the oven to 400°F. Line two large baking sheets with baking paper.

Cut the pastry sheets into eight 41/2-inch rounds and put on the prepared baking sheets. Combine the butter, ground almonds, and vanilla extract, then stir to form a paste. Divide the paste among the pastry rounds and spread evenly, leaving a 5/8-inch border around the edge of each.

Halve the nectarines, remove the pits, and cut into 1/4-inch slices. Arrange the nectarine slices over the pastry rounds, overlapping the slices and leaving a thin border. Sprinkle the sugar over the nectarines.

Bake for 15 minutes or until the pastry is puffed and golden. Brush the nectarines and pastry with the warm jam while still hot. Serve hot or at room temperature.

serves 6

cointreau-glazed peaches

6 peaches
1–2 tablespoons soft brown
    sugar
1/3 cup Cointreau
1 cup mascarpone cheese
ground nutmeg, to dust

Line a broiler tray with foil and lightly grease the foil. Preheat the broiler to medium. Cut the peaches in half, remove the pits, then place the peaches, cut side up, on the tray.

Sprinkle peaches with the sugar and Cointreau and broil for 6 minutes, until the peaches are soft and the tops are glazed.

Serve immediately with dollops of mascarpone cheese, dusted lightly with ground nutmeg.

bottled peaches

Using a small, sharp knife, score a small cross in the base of each peach. Put the peaches in a heatproof bowl and cover with boiling water. Leave for 30 seconds, then transfer to a bowl of cold water. Peel the peaches, cut in half and remove the pits. Cut each peach into ⁵⁄₈-inch-thick slices. Arrange the fruit in six 2-cup hot sterilized airtight bottles.

To make a sugar syrup, put the sugar and 5 cups water into a saucepan over low heat. Stir for 8–10 minutes or until the sugar has dissolved. Bring to a boil and boil for 3 minutes. Cover the fruit with the hot syrup. Tap the bottles while filling to remove any air bubbles and carefully close the lids.

Put a folded dishtowel in the base of a stockpot. Fill the pot with enough warm water to cover the bottles. Gradually bring the water to simmering point (about 30–35 minutes), then simmer steadily for 15 minutes. Do not allow the water to boil. Check the water level regularly and top up with boiling water, if required.

Remove the stockpot from the heat. Wear rubber gloves or use kitchen tongs to remove the bottles. Do not put any pressure on the lids. Allow to cool overnight, then label and date each bottle.

5 pounds 8 ounces (about 10) freestone peaches
1¾ cups sugar

stone fruit ■ peach and nectarine

It is quite easy to breathe sweet life into slightly under-ripe peaches or nectarines or those lacking in flavor. Cut unpeeled pitted fruit into wedges, then pour boiling sugar syrup over them in a bowl—they will cook as they cool. Make the syrup interesting by making it half red wine and half water, and add a sprig of rosemary and a cinnamon stick, or a few whole cloves and a couple of star anise.

poached vanilla peaches with raspberry puree and passion fruit sauce

serves 4

1½ cups superfine sugar
1 vanilla bean, halved lengthwise
4 freestone peaches
1 cup raspberries
4 scoops vanilla ice cream

passion fruit sauce
¼ cup passion fruit pulp (from about 4 passion fruit)
2 tablespoons superfine sugar

Put the sugar, vanilla bean, and 2½ cups water in a large saucepan. Stir over low heat for 8–10 minutes or until the sugar has dissolved. Bring to a slow boil, then add the peaches and simmer for 5 minutes or until the peaches are just tender and softened. Cool the peaches in the syrup, then remove with a slotted spoon. Peel and halve the peaches, removing the pits.

Put the raspberries in a food processor and process until pureed. Push the puree through a sieve, discarding the pulp.

To make the passion fruit sauce, combine the passion fruit pulp and the sugar in a small bowl and stir until the sugar has dissolved.

To serve, divide the raspberry puree between four glasses. Arrange a scoop of ice cream and two peach halves on top. Spoon over the passion fruit sauce and serve immediately.

The word peach is a corruption of the Latin persica, *meaning "Persian," whereas nectarine comes from the Greek* nektar, *meaning "sweet." Both fruits are thought to have originated in China, where even today, mythology and symbology shroud the delicious peach. It is a potent symbol there for long life, and the word peach in Chinese was once slang for "young bride."*

plum

stone fruit ■ plum

In China, where they are believed to have first been cultivated, plums symbolize good fortune—the tree is favorably associated with age and wisdom.

Plums are a varied bunch. The skins of some are green, some yellow; others are pink, red, or blue-black. The flesh varies widely in color, texture, sweetness, and juiciness; and depending upon variety, the fruit size and shape do too. Hence there are elongated and ovular, or rotund and plump plums.

From damsons to mirabelles, gages to satsumas, the plum world is populated with a startling selection of fruits. They star in all manner of sweet and savory dishes around the globe, from the ubiquitous pork in plum sauce found on many a Chinese restaurant menu, to Germany's repertoire of plum cakes. In the Balkans, plums are distilled to make the local high-octane beverage of choice, *slivovitz* (a brandy or schnapps made from bluish plums); the French use mirabelles to make an *eau de vie* (a clear brandy distillate made from fermented fruit juice, translating from the French as "water of life") of the same name.

Nutritionally, plums are a good source of calcium, magnesium, vitamin A, iron, potassium, and dietary fiber.

selection and storage

If lucky enough to find plums still covered with a silver, powdery bloom, snap them up as this indicates extreme freshness. Wash them just before using. When ripe, a plum should feel firm but not hard and be blemish-free.

Store ripe plums in the refrigerator and eat within a few days; unripe plums can be softened at room temperature, although they won't develop any more sweetness or flavor.

Choose larger, sweeter plum varieties for eating fresh or for use in desserts and baking—smaller, tart varieties are best used for savory recipes or for preserving in sugar syrup.

The skins of all varieties can be sour, but will easily slip off, like those of tomatoes. To skin a plum, make a small cross-shaped incision at the base with a sharp knife, then plunge briefly into boiling water. Transfer to ice water immediately and gently pull back the skin.

Although plums freeze for up to 3–4 months, the pits can impart a strong bitter almond aftertaste, so are best removed before freezing.

prunes

In dried form, plums are known as prunes. Unfortunately, prunes have come to be associated with bowel regulation (for which they were notoriously used by previous generations) and suffer a terrible image problem as a result. They are, however, utterly delicious and very versatile, and can be utilized in everything from a Persian-inspired savory rice pilaf, stuffing for the Christmas turkey, a lightly spiced fruit compote, or paired with almonds or hazelnuts in a fancy tart. Try plumping prunes in brandy, drain, then pat them dry and dip them in chocolate —you'll quite forget they're so good for you.

varieties

There are hundreds of cultivated plum varieties, which broadly fall into two main camps: European plums, which are said to come from the Caucasus and are mostly used for preserving and drying (making prunes, that is); and Japanese plums, which are actually the ones from China. The latter can be either eaten fresh or used in cooking. Japanese plums are generally round or heart-shaped and include all the blood plum varieties.

preparation

Plums can be peeled by first making a small cross-shaped incision in their base, then plunging them briefly (in batches if dealing with quantities) in boiling water. Drain the plums, cool in a bowl of iced water and the skins will easily slip off. Depending on the size of the plums and their intended use, it may not be necessary to bother—when making puree or jam, for example, the skins can simply be sieved out. To remove the pits, most varieties require the flesh to be cut away, although some types have pits which, once the fruits are halved, are quite easily lifted out.

culinary uses

While juicy, sun-ripened plums require little embellishment, they also pair well with sweet spices, especially cardamom, cloves, ginger, and star anise. More unusually, but just as successfully, plums team well with herbs such as mint, thyme, and rosemary.

Plums also make wonderful pies, tarts, and crumbles and can be baked into certain butter cakes. Pickled plums are excellent with pâtés and terrines, and their sweet, puckery flavor also complements the richness of pork, rabbit, and duck. Plums make excellent jam but they don't contain much pectin, which helps jam set. When using them for jam, crack a few pits and remove their kernels, tie these in a cheesecloth bag and add to the cooking jam to assist in setting.

plum sauce

Peel, core, and chop the apple and place in a large saucepan with 1/2 cup water. Cover and simmer for 10 minutes or until the apple is soft. Cut the chilies in half lengthwise. Remove the seeds, then chop the chilies finely. Add the plums, sugar, vinegar, onion, soy sauce, ginger, garlic, and chili to the pan.

Bring the mixture to a boil and cook, uncovered, over low heat for 45 minutes, stirring often. Remove the sauce from the pan and, using a wooden spoon, push it through a coarse sieve over a large bowl. Discard the solids. Rinse the pan, then return the sauce to the pan and bring to a boil.

Simmer the sauce over medium-high heat for 20 minutes or until it has thickened slightly. The sauce will thicken even further on cooling. Pour immediately into hot sterilized jars and seal. Label and date each jar. Leave for 1 month for the flavors to develop. Store in a cool, dark place for up to 12 months. Once opened, sauce will keep in the refrigerator for up to 6 weeks. Plum sauce is delicious with beef or pork spareribs, or Chinese barbecued pork and duck.

1 large green apple
2 red chilies
2 pounds 12 ounces (about 18 medium) plums, halved and pitted
2 1/2 cups soft brown sugar
1 1/2 cups white wine vinegar
1 onion, grated
1/4 cup soy sauce
2 tablespoons finely chopped ginger
2 garlic cloves, crushed

stone fruit ▪ plum

makes 1

plum and rosemary flat bread

¼ cup warm milk
1 (¼-ounce) package active
   dried yeast
½ cup superfine sugar
2 eggs, lightly beaten
grated zest of 1 lemon
2 teaspoons finely chopped
   rosemary
1¼ cups white bread flour
⅔ cup unsalted butter, cut into
   cubes, softened
10 plums, halved and pitted
whipped cream or mascarpone
   cheese, to serve

Grease a 10-inch springform pan or loose-bottomed tart pan with butter. Combine the milk and yeast in the bowl of an electric mixer. Stir in ¼ cup of the sugar, the eggs, lemon zest, and 1 teaspoon of the rosemary, then add the flour. Using the beater attachment, mix for 1 minute or until a soft dough forms. Add the butter, then continue mixing for a further minute or until the dough is smooth and shiny. Alternatively, mix the dough by hand using a wooden spoon.

Spoon into the prepared pan and cover with plastic wrap. Leave in a draft-free place for 1½–2 hours or until the dough has doubled in size.

Knock back the dough by punching it gently. Dampen the palms of your hands with water and press the dough into the edge of the pan. Arrange the plums, cut side up, over the top, pressing them gently into the dough. Leave for 30 minutes. Meanwhile, preheat the oven to 400°F.

Sprinkle the plums with the remaining sugar. Sprinkle the remaining rosemary over the top. Bake for 10 minutes, then reduce the oven to 350°F and bake for an additional 20 minutes or until light golden and slightly spongy when pressed in the center. Serve warm, cut into wedges, with cream or mascarpone cheese.

plum cobbler

Preheat the oven to 350°F. Lightly grease an 8-cup baking dish. Cut the plums into quarters, discarding the pits.

Put the plums in a saucepan with ¼ cup of the sugar and 1 tablespoon water. Stir over low heat for 5 minutes or until the sugar dissolves and the fruit softens slightly. Spread the plum mixture into the prepared dish.

Sift the flours into a bowl, add the remaining sugar and stir to combine. Rub in the butter, using your fingertips, until the mixture is fine and crumbly. In a separate bowl, combine the egg and milk and whisk until smooth. Stir into the flour mixture until a soft dough forms.

Drop heaping spoonfuls of the mixture on top of the plums, until the plums are covered or all the mixture has been used. Bake for 30–40 minutes or until the top is golden and cooked through. Dust with confectioners' sugar before serving.

1 pound 10 ounces plums
  (about 10)
½ cup superfine sugar
1 cup self-rising flour
½ cup all-purpose flour
½ cup unsalted butter, chopped
1 egg
½ cup milk
confectioners' sugar, to dust

stone fruit ■ plum

For other plum recipes see:

banana

fruit ▪ tropical
season ▪ available year-round

selection and storage

Bananas are harvested when they register about 20 percent starch content and one percent sugar content and continue to ripen until their starches have all converted to fructose, sucrose, and glucose. So you can buy quite green fruit and it will quickly turn to sunny yellow at ambient room temperature. Bananas are at their most flavorsome when the skin is lightly flecked with black spots. Fruit that has become over-ripe (very brown or verging on black) is perfect for baking in cakes, breads, or muffins.

Bananas can be refrigerated although this does turn the skin an unappealing black color—very ripe fruit can also be pureed then frozen and used, thawed, in baking.

If possible, store bananas away from other ripe fruits, as they produce ethylene, which will cause fruit or vegetables sitting near them to ripen prematurely.

How exotic the banana must have appeared to those Europeans who first encountered them and who so enthusiastically helped their global infiltration. Bananas are believed to be native to Malaysia, from where they traveled to India. It is here that Alexander the Great is reputed to have tasted them around 327 B.C. and subsequently introduced them to the Western world. The Portuguese, slave dealers, and Arabic traders (the word *banan* is Arabic for "finger")—everyone, it seems, had a hand in their spread.

Technically, the banana tree is a herb, the world's largest in fact, and is related to plants like grasses, palms, and orchids.

varieties

The vast majority of bananas available are the Cavendish variety. This is a longish, thin-skinned, pale-fleshed, and sweet banana that is favored by growers because it is particularly disease-resistant, although it does bruise easily. Other varieties include red bananas, with the reddish-brown skin and red-tinged, firm flesh, and the particularly sweet, flavorsome, and fragrant lady's finger.

The vast majority of commercially produced bananas are plantains, the hard, green-skinned cooking banana. In many cultures they are treated as a vital starch food crop, in a similar fashion to the way the potato is in other cuisines. Plantains have tough flesh that turns from green to black as they ripen, although they can be cooked whether ripe or unripe—they just can't be eaten raw.

banana and plum crumble

serves 4

¼ cup all-purpose flour
½ cup rolled oats
½ cup shredded coconut
¼ cup soft brown sugar
finely grated zest of 1 lime
⅓ cup chilled unsalted butter,
    cut into cubes
2 bananas, peeled and halved
    lengthwise
4 plums, halved and pits
    removed
¼ cup lime juice
whipped cream or vanilla ice
    cream, to serve

Preheat the oven to 350°F. Combine the flour, rolled oats, coconut, sugar, and zest in a small bowl. Add the butter and, using your fingertips, rub the butter into the flour mixture until crumbly.

Put the bananas and plums in a 5-cup baking dish, pour over the lime juice and then toss to coat. Sprinkle the crumble mixture evenly over the fruit. Bake for 25–30 minutes or until the crumble is golden. Serve hot with whipped cream or vanilla ice cream.

bananas foster

serves 4

2 bananas, thickly sliced
1 tablespoon unsalted butter
1 tablespoon soft brown sugar
1 tablespoon rum
vanilla ice cream, to serve

Melt the butter in a large frying pan, add the bananas, then cook over medium-high heat, turning bananas to coat. Add the sugar and fry until the bananas are caramelized. Drizzle with the rum. Divide the bananas between bowls and serve with vanilla ice cream.

banana bread

Preheat the oven to 350°F. Grease and line the base and sides of a 9 x 5 x 2½-inch loaf pan. Sift the flour, baking powder, pumpkin pie spice, and ¼ teaspoon salt into a bowl.

In a separate bowl, cream the butter and sugar using electric beaters until pale and fluffy. Add the eggs gradually, mixing well after each addition, and beat until smooth. Mix in the banana. Add the dry ingredients in several batches and stir the mixture until smooth.

Pour into the prepared loaf pan and bake on the middle shelf of the oven for 35–45 minutes or until a skewer inserted into the center of the bread comes out clean. Cool in the pan for 10 minutes before turning out onto a wire rack. Serve warm or at room temperature. Bread will keep for up to 3 days covered in plastic wrap in an airtight container.

2 cups all-purpose flour
2 teaspoons baking powder
1 teaspoon pumpkin pie spice
⅔ cup unsalted butter, softened
1 cup soft brown sugar
2 eggs, lightly beaten
1 cup mashed very ripe banana

tropical fruit ■ banana

Americans first sampled the banana in 1876, in Pennsylvania, as part of the celebrations for the 100th anniversary of the signing of the Declaration of Independence. The Domestic Cyclopaedia of Practical Information, published in the 1870s, advised that bananas should be "eaten raw … with sugar and cream or wine and orange juice. They are also roasted, fried, or boiled and are made into fritters, preserves, and marmalades."

coconut

fruit ■ **tropical**
season ■ **available year-round**

The coconut is a culinary marauder. It started life in India then, thanks to ocean currents and its ability to bob over vast stretches of water, made its way around the world, insinuating itself into every tropical region one could care to name. The Portuguese introduced the coconut to Brazil and the Spanish took it to the Caribbean, thereby completing the worldwide coconut invasion. Today, there are about 25 million acres of the nut planted around the world.

preparation

Punch through two of the "eyes" (place a screwdriver in each hole and deal it a heavy blow with a hammer), then drain it of the liquid, which can be used for drinking or in cooking. To facilitate the easy removal of the flesh, bake the coconut in a 350°F oven for 20 minutes, then cool. Crack the coconut open using a hammer. Peel away the brown skin from the meat using a potato peeler or small, sharp knife—partially frozen pieces are particularly easy to peel using this method.

culinary uses

Coconuts can be eaten when young (about six months old) when their meat is soft and has a fruity, nutty flavor. In this form, coconuts are commonly used in drinks and desserts, or just scraped out and eaten with a spoon. Mature coconut flesh, intrinsic to many Asian cuisines, is used (mainly grated) in soups, salads, fresh chutneys, curries, and coconut milk. Freshly grated it is wonderful in cakes, cookies, and desserts, being much sweeter and mellower in flavor than its dried counterpart.

selection and storage

Choose a coconut that feels heavy and sloshes with liquid when you shake it. Coconuts take about 12 months to mature on a plam tree, after which time they weigh about 5–6 pounds, although half of this weight is shell and husk. The three "eyes" on top of the nut should be uniformly dark and there should be no mold on the husk.

The meat can be used immediately or stored, frozen in plastic bags, for up to 1 month.

A coconut of average size will yield about 10 ounces of grated fresh coconut.

coconut chutney

serves 4

1 teaspoon gram lentils
 (chana dhal)
1 teaspoon black lentils
 (black urad dhal)
1/2 coconut, flesh grated
2 green chilies, seeded and
 chopped
1 tablespoon oil
1 teaspoon black mustard seeds
5 curry leaves
1 teaspoon tamarind puree

Soak the lentils in cold water for 2 hours, then drain well.

Put the grated coconut, chili, and 1/2 teaspoon salt in a food processor, or in a mortar with a pestle, and process or pound to a smooth paste.

Heat the oil in a small saucepan and add the black mustard seeds and lentils, then cover and shake the pan until the seeds pop. Add the curry leaves and fry for 1 minute or until the lentils brown. Combine with the coconut mixture and add the tamarind puree, stirring to mix well. Serve on the side with spicy meat dishes.

mango and coconut salad

serves 4

1 coconut, flesh grated (to give
 about 10 ounces or 2 1/4 cups)
2 dried chilies, seeded and
 chopped
1 tablespoon grated jaggery or
 soft brown sugar
2 ripe mangoes, flesh cut into
 cubes (1 3/4 cups cubed mango)
1 tablespoon oil
1/2 teaspoon coriander seeds
1/2 teaspoon black mustard
 seeds
6 curry leaves

Put the coconut, chili, and jaggery in a blender and process with just enough water to make a thick, coarse paste. If you don't have a blender, crush everything together in a mortar using a pestle, adding a little water as necessary. Transfer the paste to a bowl, add the mango and toss to combine. Season to taste, cover with plastic wrap, then refrigerate.

Heat the oil in a small frying pan over low heat and add the coriander seeds, mustard seeds, and curry leaves. Cover and shake the pan until the seeds start to pop. Pour the oil and seeds over the mango mixture and stir to coat mango. Serve with southern Indian-style curries or as an accompaniment to fish or chicken.

coconut cream and milk

1 coconut, flesh grated (to give
    about 10 ounces or 2 1/4 cups)

Drain the coconut by punching a hole in two of the dark-colored eyes. Drain out the liquid and use it as a refreshing drink. Holding the coconut in one hand, tap around the circumference firmly with a hammer or pestle. This should cause the coconut to split open evenly. If the coconut doesn't crack easily, put it in a 300°F oven for 15 minutes. This may cause it to crack as it cools. If it doesn't it will crack easily with a hammer.

If you don't have a coconut grater, prise the flesh out of the shell, trim off the hard brown outer skin, and either grate by hand on a box grater or chop in a food processor. If you would like to use a coconut grater, the easiest ones to use are the ones that you sit on at one end, then scrape out the coconut from each half on the serrated edge, catching the grated coconut meat in a large bowl. Grated coconut can be frozen in small portions until it is needed.

Mix the grated coconut with 1/2 cup hot water and leave to steep for 5 minutes. Pour the mixture into a container through a sieve lined with cheesecloth, then gather the cheesecloth into a ball to squeeze out any remaining liquid. This will make a thick coconut milk, which is usually called coconut cream.

Repeat this process with another 1 cup hot water to make a thinner coconut milk.

tropical fruit ■ coconut

For other coconut recipes see:
banana and plum crumble..............102
mango, coconut, and almond tart ..113
apple and passion fruit crumble 132

kiwifruit

fruit ▪ **tropical**
season ▪ **summer–fall**

The kiwifruit is properly called the Chinese gooseberry and is native to China, but New Zealand growers and marketers who championed the fruit and produced the first serious commercial offerings of it are responsible for the name we all know today. Kiwifruit grows on vines and is typically harvested in fall when still hard—the fruit can be cool-stored for up to 6 months and travels well, continuing to ripen to full softness after picking.

There are two types of kiwifruit available—the furry-skinned sort with its startlingly green interior and the less common yellow-fleshed kiwifruit, which is a recently developed cultivar. This type has smooth, bronze-colored skin and a pointed cap at one end.

selection and storage

Buy kiwifruit quite firm and you'll be able to keep them in the refrigerator for 4–5 weeks—bring them out to ripen at room temperature when you want sweet, soft, lush fruit.

To speed ripening, put the kiwifruit in a paper bag at room temperature with a banana or an apple, as these fruits produce ethylene gas, which accelerates fruit ripening.

When ripe, kiwifruit should give slightly when pressed and can be eaten simply cut in half and the flesh scooped out with a teaspoon. Steer clear of overly soft fruit or any whose skins are wrinkled, as this indicates they are well and truly past their prime.

preparation

Use kiwifruit in breakfast drinks such as smoothies, in fruit salads, or sliced to decorate sponge cake, fruit tarts, or pavlova. An excess can be turned into jam or chutney but use ever-so-slightly under-ripe fruit for the best flavor. Kiwifruit contains an enzyme that dissolves protein—hence it is used commercially as a meat tenderizer. Never use it uncooked (cooking destroys the enzyme) in dairy-based recipes; it will attack milk proteins and turn them bitter.

pavlova with kiwifruit

Preheat the oven to 315°F. Line a 13 x 11¼-inch baking sheet with baking paper.

Put the egg whites and a pinch of salt in a large, clean, dry stainless steel or glass bowl—any hint of grease will prevent the egg whites foaming. Using electric beaters, whisk slowly until the whites start to become foamy, then increase the speed until the bubbles in the foam have become small and even-size. Continue whisking until stiff peaks form, then add the sugar gradually, whisking constantly after each addition, until the mixture is thick and glossy and all the sugar has dissolved. Don't overbeat or the mixture will become grainy.

Using a metal spoon, fold in the sifted cornstarch and the vinegar. Spoon the mixture into a mound on the prepared baking sheet. Lightly flatten the top of the pavlova and smooth the sides; the pavlova should have a cake shape and be about 1 inch high. Bake for 1 hour or until pale cream and crisp on the outside. Remove from the oven while warm, carefully turn upside down onto a plate and cool to room temperature.

Lightly whip the cream until soft peaks form and spread over the pavlova. Decorate with passion fruit pulp and sliced kiwifruit. Cut into wedges to serve.

note The addition of cornstarch and vinegar gives the meringue a marshmallow-soft center.

4 egg whites, at room
   temperature
1 cup superfine sugar
2 teaspoons cornstarch
1 teaspoon white vinegar
1 cup whipping cream
pulp from 3 passion fruit,
   to decorate
2 kiwifruit, skinned and sliced,
   to decorate

tropical fruit ■ kiwifruit

For other kiwifruit recipes see:
tropical sprout salad 275

mango

The mango is referred to as "the king of fruits" and rightly so. "For taste, the nectarine, peach, and apricot fall short," exclaimed Englishman Dr. John Fryer upon sampling a mango in seventeenth-century India, and fans of the fruit have been heaping on the accolades ever since.

There are hundreds of varieties of mango in existence and these vary in size from plum-small to the gigantic Keitt mango, whose fruit weigh in at around 4 pounds. Mango skin ranges in hue from yellow, orange, red, blush-pink, or green to a patchy mix of these colors. The majority of the world's mangoes are grown in India where they play a sacred role and are considered a potent symbol of love; on holy days, Hindus even brush their teeth with twigs from the mango tree.

Mangoes don't just taste glorious, they are terribly good for you too. Low in calories, extremely high in fiber, mangoes are also rich sources of betacarotene plus minerals like potassium, magnesium, and antioxidants, as well as vitamins A, B, and C. They contain an enzyme, similar to papain in papaya, that aids digestion and is reputed to add to that undeniable feeling of contentment that eating a mango brings.

selection and storage

The size of a mango depends upon type, not quality or ripeness, so check the varietal characteristics with your supplier.

When ripe, mangoes should yield slightly to pressure and their stem end should emit sweet, fragrant, tropical smells. According to type, the skin color will deepen and may develop pink or red patches. Black speckles on the skin can indicate damaged flesh underneath or over-ripeness; avoid fruits with loose or wrinkled skin as these are past their best.

Under-ripe fruit will continue to ripen at room temperature, and once ripe, should be stored in the refrigerator and used within 1–2 days.

tropical fruit ■ mango

green mangoes

In Southeast Asia green mangoes are used in refreshing salads, curries, chutneys, and other savory preparations. Green-skinned, with hard, pale flesh, they are prepared by peeling off the skin with a small, sharp knife, then either coarsely grating the flesh or cutting it off the seed in very thin slices and then into fine matchsticks.

Green mango has a pleasantly tart, fruity flavor which combines well with lime juice, jaggery, shrimp, chicken, peanuts, chili, and fresh Asian herbs such as cilantro and Thai basil. Amchoor (mango powder), a fragrant Indian seasoning made from ground, dried green mangoes, is also used widely as a meat tenderizer.

Green mangoes can be used in the same way as green papaya (see pages 116–117).

varieties

It is estimated there are about 350 varieties of mangoes cultivated commercially—these are sometimes, but not always, sold by variety so if not, ask your supplier to identify the type. The variables between varieties are their sweetness, amount of fiber in their flesh, the flesh-to-seed ratio, and their size. Some of the more popular varieties are listed below.

keitt An Indian strain of mango producing prodigiously large fruit with an oval shape and a slightly tapering protruberance above the tip. It has lush, firm flesh, minimal fiber, and thick skin that remains green even when it is fully ripe.

kensington pride Also known as bowen, this orange-skinned variety (blushing red when ripe) is popular in Australia. Fruits are large with particularly juicy flesh and have a slightly tangy flavor. The flesh has minimal fiber.

kent Fruits are large with plum cheeks and form a regular oval shape. When ripe the skin is yellow with red shoulders, while the flesh is very sweet, fiber-free, and butter-soft.

nam doc mai This mango is small-medium in size and has a fattish, slipper shape with a long, thin seed. Traditionally used green in salads, curries, and chutneys, this mango is also prized for its deep, slightly acid and sweet flavors when fully ripe.

R2E2 A recently developed Australian hybrid, initially exported to Asia, R2E2 is an enormous fruit with thin orange skin. It has a very sweet flavor with a high flesh-to-seed ratio.

tommy atkins One of the most common mango varieties, with oval, medium to large fruit that has thick skin, a mild flavor and more fibrous flesh than most others.

preparation

The mango has a large central seed that clings to the flesh—you need to cut the "cheeks" away from this. The most effective method is to hold the mango with a narrow side facing you. Using a large, sharp serrated knife, cut from the top down to the base of one side, feeling with your knife for the seed as you go and trying to cut as close to the seed as possible to remove the cheek. Repeat with the other side of the mango—the flesh left clinging to the seed is generally considered the "cook's treat."

Use a sharp knife to score deep parallel cuts in the flesh of each cheek, then score the flesh in the other direction to form square shapes—the mango cheek can then be pushed inside out and the little squares easily removed for further preparation or just eaten as is, with a teaspoon.

mango, coconut, and almond tart

To make the pastry, put the flour, sugar, ground almonds, and butter in a food processor. Process until the mixture resembles fine crumbs. Add the egg yolks and process until smooth. Add the water, 1/2 teaspoon at a time, until a firm dough forms. Flatten the dough to a rectangle shape, wrap in plastic wrap and refrigerate for 30 minutes.

Preheat the oven to 375°F. Grease a 71/2 x 103/4-inch loose-bottomed tart pan.

To make the filling, cream the butter and sugar with electric beaters for about 3 minutes. Add the eggs, one at a time, beating well after each addition. Fold in the ground almonds, flour, and shredded coconut. Gently stir in the coconut cream and coconut liqueur.

Roll out the pastry on a sheet of baking paper until large enough to line the base and side of the pan. Ease it into the pan, pressing gently to fit, and trim any excess. Line the pastry with baking paper and pour in some baking beads or uncooked rice. Bake for 10 minutes, remove the paper and beads, and bake for an additional 5 minutes. Reduce the oven temperature to 325°F.

Cut the cheeks from the mango. Using a large spoon, scoop the flesh from the skin and cut into 1/8-inch-thick slices. Spread the filling in the pastry case and arrange the mango slices in two rows down the length of the filling. Sprinkle the shaved coconut over the top and press it into the exposed filling with your fingertips, giving an uneven surface. Bake for 30 minutes or until the coconut begins to brown, then cover loosely with foil. Bake for 35 minutes or until the filling is set and the top is golden brown. Serve warm with cream or ice cream.

almond pastry
12/3 cups all-purpose flour
1/4 cup superfine sugar
1/4 cup ground almonds
2/3 cup chilled unsalted butter, cut into cubes
2 egg yolks, at room temperature
1–2 tablespoons iced water

filling
3/4 cup unsalted butter, softened
heaping 3/4 cup superfine sugar
2 eggs, at room temperature
2/3 cup ground almonds
1/2 cup all-purpose flour
1 cup dried shredded coconut
2 tablespoons coconut cream
1 tablespoon coconut liqueur
1 mango
1/2 cup shaved coconut
whipped cream or ice cream, to serve

tropical fruit ■ mango

serves 6

mango ice cream

flesh from 2½ mangoes
  (or 2¼ cups cubed flesh)
⅔ cup superfine sugar
3 tablespoons mango or apricot
  nectar
1 cup whipping cream
mango slices, extra, to serve

Put the mango in a food processor and process until smooth. Transfer the mango puree to a bowl and add the sugar and nectar. Stir until the sugar has dissolved.

Beat the cream in a small bowl until stiff peaks form, then gently fold into the mango mixture. Spoon into a shallow loaf pan, cover the pan, and freeze for 1½ hours or until the mixture is half frozen. Quickly spoon the mixture into a food processor and process for 30 seconds or until smooth. Return the mixture to the pan or a plastic container, then cover and freeze completely. Remove the ice cream from the freezer 15 minutes before serving to allow it to soften a little. Serve the ice cream in scoops with some extra fresh mango.

serves 4

mango lassi

2 large mangoes
2 cups plain yogurt
2 teaspoons lemon juice
3–4 tablespoons superfine sugar,
  to taste
ice cubes, optional, to serve
diced mango, extra, to serve

Prepare the mangoes by slicing off the cheeks with a sharp knife. Using a large spoon, scoop the flesh from the skin. Cut the flesh into chunks and put in a blender with the yogurt, lemon juice, and 3 tablespoons of sugar.

Add ¾ cup cold water and blend for 40–60 seconds or until the mixture is smooth. Taste for sweetness and add extra sugar, if desired.

Put some ice cubes, if using, in the bottom of four glasses. Pour the lassi over the top and serve immediately, topped with diced mango.

papaya

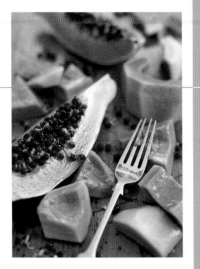

fruit ▪ **tropical**
season ▪ **peaking summer–fall**

The papaya plant (technically not a tree but a rather tall herb) is a prolific bearer of fruit. Hanging like pendulous melons under a canopy of leaves, from a slim, branchless trunk, the fruit varies in size and skin color—from green to pink, orange, or yellow.

Papayas grow prodigiously throughout tropical and semitropical regions of the world from where they are exported widely to cooler climates. They are a thin-skinned fruit and susceptible to damage, so are harvested unripe, for travel.

There are two main varieties you will likely encounter—the larger, pear-shaped yellow papaya, with its orange, slightly pungent-smelling flesh and the smaller, sweeter, rose-fleshed type.

selection and storage

Before buying papaya be aware that it is often marketed as "pawpaw"—the pawpaw is in fact a wild American fruit completely unrelated to the papaya—the confusion is likely to have sprung from the fact that throughout the Caribbean, papayas are called "pawpaws."

Papayas continue to ripen once picked (leave in a dark place at room temperature for several days to ripen) but their flavor suffers when not fully tree-ripened. When ripe, the skin, which will have lost all trace of green and may have a spotty appearance, will yield to gentle pressure (about the same amount as that of a ripe avocado).

Use ripe papaya within 2 days, storing it in the refrigerator and covering any cut portions in plastic wrap.

culinary uses

The taste of a ripe papaya is unforgettable—at once musky, sweet, the merest touch bitter, and distinctly floral. The crinkly black seeds, which tend to be discarded, are perfectly edible, and possess a black pepper flavor. The soft flesh is best enjoyed raw, tossed through fruit salads, whipped into orange-based drinks, or just spooned directly from its skin.

Papaya has a particular affinity for the flavors of lemon, lime, chili, and ginger. Like mango, hard, unripe green papaya is much-used throughout Southeast Asia as a vegetable; it mainly appears shredded in salads, dressed, like green mango, with the tart, spicy, sweet flavors of lime juice, fish sauce, jaggery, chili, and garlic. Once skinned and seeded it can be used in the same way as green mangoes (see page 112).

green papaya and peanut salad

Pound the dried shrimp in a mortar using a pestle, or chop finely.

Cook the beans in a saucepan of boiling water for 2 minutes. Drain and then plunge them into iced water; drain again. Shred the lettuce and arrange it on a serving plate. Top with the shrimp, beans, and papaya.

Combine the lime juice, fish sauce, sugar, and chopped chili in a small bowl and mix well. Pour over the salad. Sprinkle the peanuts and extra chili over the top.

note When grating papaya, lightly oil your hands or wear gloves as it can be very sticky and hard to wash off.

1/2 cup dried small shrimp
20 green beans, trimmed and cut into short pieces
1 head lettuce
1/2 green papaya or green mango, peeled and grated
1/4 cup lime juice
2 tablespoons fish sauce
2 teaspoons soft brown sugar
1–2 teaspoons chopped red chili
1/2 cup unsalted roasted peanuts, chopped
1 small red chili, extra, finely chopped

papaya lime fool

serves 4

Peel the papayas, remove the seeds, and mash the flesh until smooth. Do not do this in a food processor or the puree will be too thin. Add the lime juice and vanilla sugar, to taste—the amount will vary according to the sweetness of the fruit.

Whisk the cream until soft peaks form, then fold it into the mashed papaya. Spoon into serving glasses and chill until ready to serve.

variation 1 pound stewed rhubarb can be substituted for the papaya. If using rhubarb, replace the lime juice with the same amount of orange juice.

2 ripe papayas
1–2 tablespoons lime juice
3 tablespoons vanilla sugar
1 1/4 cups whipping cream

For other papaya recipes see:

passion fruit

fruit ■ tropical
season ■ late summer–early fall

The haunting flavor of the passion fruit defines for many the true taste of the tropics. This most unusual fruit, with its tough, protective exterior and seed-filled, pulpy, and intensely fragrant interior, is known to us via a couple of edible varieties—there are many more in South America but these either don't travel well or are poisonous (the *Passiflora* genus is associated with cyanide). There's the small purple sort, also called "purple granadilla," and the smoother skinned yellow variety, which is larger but has less flavor than the purple passion fruit.

preparation

Although the seeds are perfectly edible, for some recipes it is necessary to strain them out; this can be done by simply pushing the pulp through a sieve using a ladle or the back of a spoon, pressing firmly on the seeds to extract as much juice as possible.

As a guide, 10 ripe passion fruit will yield around 1 cup of pulp and about 1/2 cup of strained juice.

culinary uses

Passion fruit can be halved and eaten directly from the shell. Their concentrated, fruity flavors are a wonderful addition to drinks, icing for sponge or banana cake, to shortbread dough, and fruit salads. The pulp is also great dribbled over yogurt, ice cream, and other creamy desserts. A little passion fruit goes a long way—its powerful flavors quickly pervade whatever it is added to.

selection and storage

Passion fruit grow on a vine, from which they drop when the fruit are ready. Purple passion fruit should be avoided if the skin is smooth, as they will be too tart to enjoy—when ripe their skin thins a little and becomes wrinkled.

Ripe passion fruit will keep at cool room temperature for about 1 week and up to 3 weeks if refrigerated. Both passion fruit pulp and the strained juice can be frozen.

serves 4

hot passion fruit soufflé

superfine sugar, to coat ramekins
2 egg yolks
1/2 cup passion fruit pulp (from
    about 10 passion fruit)
2 tablespoons lemon juice
3/4 cup confectioners' sugar
6 egg whites
passion fruit sauce (see page
    92), to serve
confectioners' sugar, to dust,
    optional

Preheat the oven to 415°F. Place a collar of baking paper to come about 1¼ inches above the outside of four small ½-cup ramekins. Tie collars securely with string. Lightly grease the ramekins (including the paper) and pour in the superfine sugar. Turn the dishes to coat with the sugar and then shake out any excess.

Combine the egg yolks, passion fruit pulp, lemon juice, and half the confectioners' sugar in a large bowl. Whisk until well combined.

Using electric beaters, whisk the egg whites in a separate bowl until soft peaks form. Gradually add the remaining confectioners' sugar, beating well after each addition. Using a large metal spoon, fold the egg white mixture, in batches, into the passion fruit mixture. Divide the mixture among the four ramekins. Using a flat-bladed knife, cut through the mixture in a circular motion 3/4 inch from the edge.

Put the ramekins on a large baking sheet and bake for 20–25 minutes or until the soufflés are well-risen and cooked through. Remove the collars and serve the soufflés immediately, drizzled with passion fruit sauce and dusted with sifted confectioners' sugar, if desired.

Hailing from tropical South America, the passion fruit was named by Spanish missionaries who saw in its flower various references to Christ's passion—the five wounds in the anthers, the three nails in the stigmas, and the crown of thorns in the filaments.

pineapple

fruit ■ tropical
season ■ peaking spring–summer

Pineapple has become ubiquitous; think of the mountains of canned rings swimming in syrup that fill supermarket shelves, or those piles of the fresh fruit that often hover on the wrong side of ripeness and, when eaten, are disappointingly sour.

But what a revelation this curiously spiny, spiky South American native must have been to Christopher Columbus when he first saw it on the island of Guadeloupe in 1493—it is recorded that his men were "astonished and delighted" when they sampled it. And, if further reminders are needed of what we should expect from this incredible fruit, it's worth noting that the indigenous South American name, *ananas*, translates as "fragrant excellent fruit."

If you buy a pineapple that is neither fragrant nor excellent, you've been short-changed. The problem is that the pineapple doesn't continue to ripen after picking and, for convenience of transport and storage, is often harvested a little early.

Generally, pineapples aren't sold by variety. Rather, they fall into one of two categories—the "rough-leafed" or the "smooth-leafed." The former are typified by small, sweet, deep-golden-fleshed fruit, which are particularly aromatic, while the latter are large and very juicy when ripe, but are not as sweet as "roughies."

preparation

To trim and peel a pineapple, you need a sharp, sturdy knife. Cut off the leafy top, a little below the leaves, and cut off the base. Then, with the pineapple standing firmly on a cut end, run your knife down the fruit, cutting off the thick skin in strips. To remove the "eyes," use a small, sharp knife to cut v-shaped grooves that follow the pattern of the eyes around the fruit. Slice the pineapple in half lengthwise, and cut out the tough core. The pineapple is now ready to be sliced, diced, or chopped.

culinary uses

Luscious, juicy pineapple needs little to improve upon its raw perfection and is best enjoyed in sweet, dripping slices after a meal, or as an easy snack. However it is undeniably delicious when caramelized in a hot pan in the company of some butter and sugar and, perhaps, a dash of cardamom, then served as a warm dessert. It marries beautifully with other tropical fruits in a fruit salad and benefits too from a splash of kirsch or Grand Marnier.

If lucky enough to find yourself with an excess of pineapples, they do make terrific jam and, in combination with the bracing influence of lime or lemon, marmalade too. Pineapple is also sublime in certain curries and other Asian dishes as it has a special affinity for the flavors of those places, such as cilantro, coconut milk, chili, spices, and fish sauce.

Pineapple is rich in the enzyme bromelin, which attacks protein and turns it to mush. Therefore, never use raw pineapple in gelatin-based desserts as they won't set, nor combine it with cream or yogurt (unless stirred in just before serving) as it will cause them to separate. Heat destroys the enzyme so you can make jellies and uncooked cheesecakes with pineapple that has first been cooked.

selection and storage

In choosing a good pineapple, let your nose be your guide—ripe, rich, sweet aromas should waft from within. There should be no soft spots or dark patches whatsoever. The color of the skin doesn't necessarily indicate the ripeness of the fruit either—depending on the variety, the skin can be golden, reddish-yellow or even green-tinged.

Fully ripe pineapples are quite perishable—store at room temperature for no longer than 1–2 days, or in the refrigerator for up to 4 days, in a plastic bag and with the leaves still attached.

tropical fruit ■ pineapple

cilantro pork with fresh pineapple

serves 4

14 ounces pork loin or fillet, trimmed
¼ pineapple, peeled and trimmed
1 tablespoon oil
4 garlic cloves, chopped
4 scallions, chopped
1 tablespoon fish sauce
1 tablespoon lime juice
1 large handful cilantro leaves
1 large handful mint, chopped
steamed rice, to serve

Partially freeze the pork until it is just firm and then slice it thinly. Cut the pineapple flesh into bite-size pieces.

Heat the oil in a wok or heavy-bottomed frying pan. Add the garlic and scallions and cook over medium-high heat for 1 minute. Remove from the wok.

Heat the wok to very hot; add the pork in batches and stir-fry for 2–3 minutes or until just cooked. Return the garlic and scallions to the wok and then add the pineapple pieces, fish sauce, and lime juice. Toss to combine and cook for 1 minute or until the pineapple is heated through. Add cilantro and mint, toss to combine. Serve immediately with steamed rice.

sweet drunken pineapple

serves 6

1 large pineapple
oil, for brushing
¼ cup grated jaggery or soft brown sugar
2½ tablespoons rum
2 tablespoon lime juice
3 tablespoons small mint leaves
heavy cream, to serve

Preheat a barbecue grill plate or grill pan to medium. Trim the ends from the pineapple, remove the skin, then cut into quarters lengthwise. Brush the hot plate or pan with oil, add the pineapple quarters and cook for about 10 minutes, turning to brown all the cut sides.

Take the pineapple off the heat and cut each quarter into ⅝-inch-thick slices. Overlap the pineapple slices on a large serving plate.

Combine the jaggery, rum, and lime juice in a small bowl, mixing well to dissolve the sugar. Pour the mixture evenly over the warm pineapple slices, then cover with plastic wrap and refrigerate for several hours. Serve at room temperature, sprinkled with the mint leaves and a dollop of cream.

pineapple and mango jam

Remove the skin and tough eyes from the pineapple. Cut the pineapple into quarters lengthwise, remove the core, and chop the flesh into ½-inch pieces. Peel the mangoes and cut each cheek from the seeds. Using a large spoon, scoop out the flesh from the skin and cut into ½-inch pieces. Put the pineapple, mango, 1 teaspoon lemon zest, lemon juice, and warmed sugar in a large saucepan. Stir over medium heat for 5 minutes or until the sugar has dissolved.

Put two small plates in the freezer. Put the reserved lemon seeds and remaining zest on the cheesecloth and tie up securely with string. Add to the pan. Bring to a boil, then reduce the heat and simmer, stirring often, for 30–40 minutes. When the jam falls from a tilted wooden spoon in thick sheets without dripping, start testing for setting point. To do this, remove from the heat, put a little jam onto one of the cold plates and place in the freezer for 30 seconds. A skin should form on the surface and the jam should wrinkle when pushed with your finger. If not, return to the heat for a few minutes, then test again with the other plate.

Carefully ladle into hot sterilized jars and seal. Allow to cool, then label and date each jar. Store in a cool, dark place for 6–12 months. Refrigerate after opening for up to 6 weeks.

note To warm the sugar, preheat the oven to 300°F. Spread the sugar evenly in a baking dish and put in the oven for 10–15 minutes or until warmed through. Do not overheat the sugar or it will start to lump together.

1 pineapple
2 large mangoes
zest of 1 lemon
⅓ cup lemon juice, reserving the seeds
5⅔ cups sugar, warmed (see note)
4-inch square of cheesecloth

tropical fruit ■ pineapple

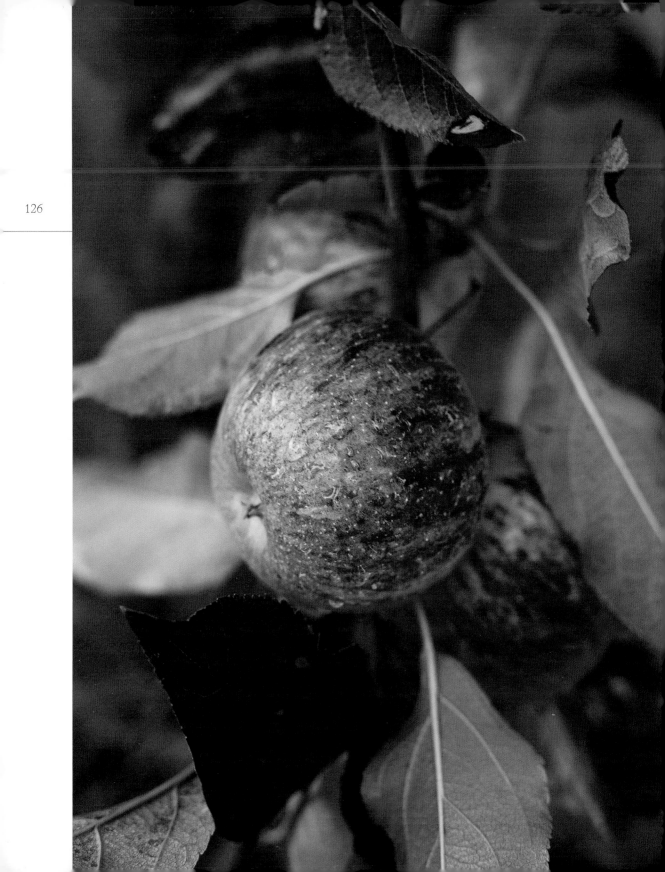

apple

Only a small proportion of the 8,000 named apple varieties are commercially cultivated. However, all modern day cultivars can trace their roots back to the earliest form of apple, the wild, sour crab apple that originated in the Caucasus, in what is now Kazakhstan. Along with pears and quinces, which also hail from this region, apples belong to the rose sub-family branch *Maloideae*.

Large-scale commercial growing and the advent of cold storage have driven demand for apple uniformity. Consistent size, color, and shape have become the predominant concern for farmers, as large retailers demand these qualities. They also favor those varieties that are disease-resistant and that travel and store well. In response to such standardization (and long storage), which has resulted in some quite "boring" and mealy fruit, there is a revival of interest in seasonally available heirloom apple varieties.

With so many varieties of apple, there are significant differences in nutritional value between them. However, the most commonly available varieties generally have decent amounts of vitamins A, B, and C, magnesium, iron, and manganese.

selection and storage

Apples kept in cold storage eventually lose flavor, juiciness and crispness, their most desirable qualities. It is best to either buy apple varieties as they come into season, or purchase fruit from farmers' or growers' markets and roadside stalls that dot the landscape of apple-orchard territory. Buying this way may also provide an opportunity to sample some lesser-known varieties.

Favor firm, smooth, and shiny-skinned apples that feel heavy for their size. Apples should still have their stalk intact and have dry, tight skin. Bruised apples deteriorate rapidly, so are best trimmed, then used immediately.

Apples slowly continue ripening after picking, so keep them in a ventilated plastic bag in the refrigerator crisper for up to 1 week. To store quantities of apples for out-of-season use, wrap firm fruit, individually, in tissue paper, then spread on slatted wooden boxes (or similar). They need to be stored in a cool, dry, well-ventilated place where they will keep for several months (check them occasionally for signs of deterioration).

varieties

While many apple varieties are multifunctional, there is a traditional division between cooking and eating apples, generally based on sugar and acid levels. Unpalatable as an eating fruit, the acidic, green-skinned British Bramley is perfectly suited to cooking—rich in pectin, it is excellent made into jellies and jams, and, as it collapses into a smooth puree, is ideal for sauces. Elsewhere, the tart, green Granny Smith is a cooking favorite. The French traditionally use the Pomme Reinette for tarte tatin, but also favor the Golden Delicious when the former is not available. Golden Delicious holds its shape without emitting too much moisture, making it the perfect pie or tart apple.

Like the Golden Delicious, others retain their shape, flavor and moisture when cooked (Gala, Jonagold, and Pink Lady, for example) so are suitable for stuffing and baking whole; they can also be poached or used in tarts, cakes, and pies. As a general rule, apples containing high sugar levels hold their shape better when cooked; however, these often need to be peeled before using, as their skins are prone to toughening when cooking with sugar.

In contrast, apple varieties best suited to eating raw are generally firm-textured, crisp, and juicy, with some acidity to counterbalance their sweetness. Red Delicious and Gala apples fall into this camp and are not suited to cooking at all.

braeburn The Braeburn apple was developed in New Zealand. It has firm, juicy flesh, is a medium-large apple, and has red-blushed skin with a delicate sweet-sour flavor. As such, Braeburns are an ideal eating apple, best reserved for table eating or adding raw to salads. They are at their crunchy best at the start of apple season, from fall to early winter.

cox's orange pippin Created by Englishman and retired brewer Richard Cox in 1825 by crossing a Ribston Pippin with a Blenheim orange, this heirloom mid-season English apple variety is generally small and round, with greenish-yellow skin flushed with some red russeting and creamy flesh. Its crisp, juicy, firm texture and sweet flavor is balanced by a little acidity. While this is an all-purpose apple, it is best when simply eaten out of hand. These apples are at their peak in fall.

fuji Originally from Japan and named after Mount Fuji, Fuji apples have juicy, crisp flesh and a high sugar content, which makes them one of the sweetest of all the cultivated apples. Their reddish-pink skins often have golden yellow highlights. With an appealing, highly perfumed aroma, they are the perfect eating apple. Holding their texture well, they are also suited to baking whole and adding to pies. Fujis are a late season variety.

golden delicious With yellowy green skin, golden freckles and tender sweet flesh, Golden Delicious apples maintain their shape during cooking, making them the perfect choice for tarts, caramelized apple desserts, and sautéing when cut into slices. Discovered in West Virginia in 1914, they are also a fine eating apple and, with a long season, are available in excellent condition throughout the winter months. Although it shares part of its name with the Red Delicious, the only relationship between the two is that the same people, the Stark brothers, marketed them.

granny smith Named after Australian Maria Ann Smith (aka "Granny" Smith), who found the seedlings growing in a spot in her suburban Sydney garden where she had thrown some apple cores. Mrs Smith recognized their cooking potential and began marketing these unusual new apples, said to be derived from French crab apples. Featuring thick, freckled, apple-green skin and hard, crisp, tart, white flesh, the medium-large Granny Smith is a great all-rounder, suiting both eating and cooking. As their flesh collapses upon cooking, they are the apple of choice for apple purees and sauces and their slightly sour flavor is the perfect foil for pork, goose, and duck. This quality makes them not so desirable for recipes requiring quarters or chunks.

pink lady Another Australian apple, the Pink Lady is one of the newest apple varieties. First grown in 1979 in the Margaret River region of Western Australia, it was the natural result of cross-pollination between the Golden Delicious and Lady Williams apples. Characterized by a distinct, pink-blushed skin surrounding crisp, juicy, sweet flesh, Pink Ladies are an excellent multipurpose fruit. Great for either eating or cooking, they are aromatic with a unique sugar-acid balance, so are ideal for baking whole and using in pies. Pink Ladies are a late season apple.

red delicious First appearing in a orchard in Iowa in 1880, this ubiquitous, elongated apple has thick, tough, deep red shiny skin and distinct ridged bumps at its base. With crisp, juicy, white flesh and a low level of acidity, Red Delicious is a good eating apple, due to its tender flesh, but does not suit cooking at all. An early season variety, Red Delicious tends toward flouriness when stored for too long, so buy it in winter months.

pome fruit ■ apple

As one of the oldest and most prolific cultivated fruits, apples have been the subject of legend, myth, and scientific discourse for centuries. The earliest records of apple cultivation go back to 8000 B.C.—dried apple slices dating to 2500 B.C. were found in the excavated tomb of an ancient Persian queen near Basra in modern-day Iraq. Apples are mentioned in Homer's Odyssey *and Pliny the Elder recorded twenty apple varieties in his definitive tome* Naturalis Historia. *In 1033, a falling apple inspired Sir Isaac Newton to discover the law of gravity, while the familiar edict of "an apple a day keeps the doctor away" has been repeated to children ever since first stated in a speech by J. T. Stinson in 1904.*

preparation

If coring quantities of apples, a purpose-made apple corer can be purchased for the job. Peeled, cored, and cut apples should either be placed in a bowl of acidulated water (water with lemon juice added) or lightly brushed with lemon juice to prevent them from browning.

culinary uses

A juicy ripe apple is the ultimate fast food—but served with a selection of cheese it becomes perfect picnic or after-dinner fare. Apples are a welcome addition to savory winter salads: a crisp salad of sliced apple, shaved cucumber, torn Belgian endive, and dill is a refreshing textural counterpoint to an extravagant whole poached salmon or cider-poached trout. A heart-warming plate of meat loaf and mashed potatoes makes the transformation from homely country staple to urbane sophisticate when reinvented as pork and fennel sausages with celeriac (or potato) and apple mash (see page 193).

Apple dessert possibilities are endless, from Austrian apple strudel and old-fashioned pastry-wrapped apple dumplings to the English cheddar-pastry-wrapped apple pie. Apples can also be used in muffins, cheesecakes, preserves (chutneys, jams, mincemeat), yeast-raised sweet breads, sweet omelettes, sorbets (particularly good here with mint), chilled mousses, hot soufflés, and the classic tarte tatin (see variation, page 139).

Flavors that complement apples in cooking include Calvados, cider, brandy, allspice, cinnamon, cloves, nutmeg, cheese, maple syrup, Barbados sugar, caramel, golden syrup, raisins, blackberries, pears, pastry, butter, lemon, pork, pickled herrings, horseradish, rhubarb, walnuts, almonds, vanilla beans, and cream. Or more adventurously, but equally compatibly, apples complement thyme, sage, quince, rabbit, pancetta, prosciutto, radicchio, endive, mayonnaise, mint, star anise, caraway, coriander seeds, polenta, parsnips, venison, hot-smoked trout, and beets.

layered potato and apple bake

Preheat the oven to 350°F. Grease a large, shallow baking dish. Peel the potatoes and cut into thin slices. Peel, halve, and core the apples, then cut into thin slices. Slice the peeled onion into very fine rings.

Layer the potatoes, apples, and onion in the prepared dish, finishing with a layer of potatoes. Sprinkle evenly with cheese, then pour over the cream.

Sprinkle with nutmeg and black pepper, to taste. Bake for 45 minutes, until golden brown. Remove from the oven and allow to stand for 5 minutes before serving.

note To prevent the potatoes and apples browning before assembling the dish, put them in a bowl of cold water with a squeeze of lemon juice. Drain and pat dry with paper towels before using.

2 large potatoes
3 green apples
1 onion
½ cup finely grated cheddar cheese
1 cup whipping cream
¼ teaspoon ground nutmeg

pome fruit ■ apple

traditional apple sauce

serves 6–8

Put the apple, sugar, cloves, cinnamon stick, and ½ cup water in a small saucepan. Cover and simmer over low heat for 10 minutes or until the apple is soft. Remove from the heat and discard the cloves and cinnamon stick.

Mash the apple, or press through a sieve for smooth-textured sauce. Stir in the lemon juice, to taste. Serve warm or cold with roast pork, pork chops, or pan-fried pork fillet. Will keep for 4 days stored, covered, in the refrigerator.

4 green apples, peeled, cored, and chopped
2 teaspoons superfine sugar
2 cloves
1 cinnamon stick
1–2 teaspoons lemon juice

serves 4–6

apple galette

1 sheet ready-made puff pastry
1/4 cup apricot jam
1 cooking apple, such as Granny
   Smith
2 teaspoons raw sugar

Preheat the oven to 415°F. Lightly grease a baking sheet. Trim the corners from the pastry to make a neat 9 1/2-inch circle (use a large plate as a guide).

Put the jam in a small saucepan and stir over low heat until melted. Strain the jam, discarding any solids, then brush over the puff pastry, leaving a 5/8-inch border.

Peel, quarter, and core the apple, and cut into 1/16-inch-thick slices. Arrange over the pastry in an overlapping circular pattern, leaving a 5/8-inch border around the edge. Sprinkle evenly with the sugar. Carefully place the galette on the prepared baking sheet and bake for 35 minutes or until the edge of the pastry is well browned and puffed.

serves 4–6

apple and passion fruit crumble

4 passion fruit
4 green apples
2/3 cup superfine sugar
1 cup shredded coconut
3/4 cup all-purpose flour
1/3 cup unsalted butter, softened

Preheat the oven to 350°F. Grease a 4-cup baking dish.

Sieve the passion fruit, discarding the pulp, and place the juice in a bowl. Peel, core, and thinly slice the apples and add to the passion fruit juice, along with 1/4 cup sugar. Mix well, then transfer to the prepared dish.

Combine the coconut, flour, remaining sugar, and butter in a bowl and rub together with your fingertips until the mixture resembles coarse crumbs. Pile evenly over the top of the apple mixture.

Bake the crumble for 25–30 minutes or until the topping is crisp and golden.

pear

fruit ▪ **pome**
season ▪ **peaking fall–end of winter**

"The pear is the grandfather of the apple, its poor relation, a fallen aristocrat ..." So said François Pierre de La Varenne (one of the greatest chefs and culinary writers of the seventeenth century), and perhaps that quite sums up how many of us feel about the pear. It isn't the satisfying daily staple that a crunchy apple is, nor does it have the treat value of, say, a mango or a bag of cherries. Once, however, the pear basked in star status.

The pear is thought to have originated in the Caucasus thousands of years ago but it wasn't taken seriously until European gardeners such as Louis XIV's own, Jean de la Quintinie (1626–1688)—the man responsible for the kitchen gardens of Versailles —showed some interest and gave us some of the buttery, creamy-fleshed varieties we have today. In fact, nobles at the French court could once find favor with the King by introducing delicious new varieties. By 1842, the English Horticultural Society had demonstrated the existence of over 700 types— today there are around 6,000 named varieties.

It could be we undervalue this fruit today because so often we experience them as under-ripe, bland, and hard, and it's true it can be tricky to know just when a pear is properly ripe. But when they are, they drip with juices and have sublimely sweet, aromatic flesh; a good pear is an irresistible thing.

nashi pear

varieties

Pears belong to the diverse Rosaceae family and are therefore related to apples and quinces. They fall into two basic groups —European pears and Asian pears.

European pears are classically "pear-shaped" (or pyriform) and have sweet, buttery, slightly gritty flesh that is balanced by an amount of acid. Asian pears, also called nashi (which simply means "pear" in Japanese), are round in shape and have extremely crisp, juicy, nonacidic sweet flesh that is very mild in flavor. More people worldwide eat nashi pears than the European varieties yet they are relatively little-known outside Asia.

beurre bosc An elegant pear with a long, tapering neck, the Beurre Bosc has greenish to brown skin and creamy, dense, full-flavored flesh. This pear will ripen at room temperature in 3–8 days but because it is a harder variety, will not become as burstingly soft as other types. This makes the Beurre Bosc an excellent choice for cooking—it keeps its shape beautifully when poached either whole or halved, sliced, and sautéed, or halved and roasted for use in sweet or savory dishes.

doyenne du comice This pear is regarded as one of the finest, with its excellent, smooth texture, rich aromas, and intense pear flavor. It bruises very easily so in some places, where more hardy, transportable varieties reign, it may be difficult to find. Fruits are large and squat, with pale green-yellow skin that blushes red when ripe. The Comice is best enjoyed raw and is perfect on the cheese board.

nashi The nashi is also known as the "pear apple" or "sand pear," the latter on account of the slight grittiness which often characterizes the texture of the flesh. Its consumption was once reserved for the Chinese ruling classes and to sink your teeth into its thirst-quenching flesh is to understand why— it is indeed a princely fruit. It comes from the Eastern regions of China, Korea, and Japan in which places it is wildly popular still—increasingly, it is becoming available in Western markets.

packham's triumph Also just called Packham, this variety was developed in Australia in 1896. It bears many similiarities to the Williams but has knobbly skin; it is reputedly the best-selling variety in the world. A large pear, the skin color changes from green to pale yellow when ripe and the flesh is white and juicy. Eat this pear ripe out of hand, or use for general cooking, but only when still on the firm side. Hard Packhams will ripen in 6–8 days at room temperature.

williams bon chrétien Also known as Bartlett or simply, Williams. Green when unripe but maturing to a light yellow with (sometimes) a reddish blush, this widely planted pear is

storage

As pears vary in color from green, yellow, brown, crimson to russet (and in shape and size), color is not necessarily an indicator of ripeness. Buy pears that are unblemished and firm, then ripen at room temperature—depending upon the variety, this could take anything from 3–10 days.

Unripe pears will keep in the refrigerator for several weeks but just make sure there is air circulating around them (don't seal them in plastic) or they may rot. Ideally, store pears in a single layer; if stacked, they will bruise. Asian pears store exceptionally well and will keep, refrigerated, for up to 2 weeks.

one of the world's most popular. They are medium-large in size with a thick neck and have sweet, buttery flesh that is quite juicy. These pears ripen quickly off the tree and will soften and sweeten at room temperature over 3 days. A red-skinned variety, which tastes the same, is variously called Red Bartlett, Red Williams, or Red Sensation. This all-purpose pear is a good eating pear but can also be poached, baked, and used in fruit or leafy salads.

winter nelis Originally from Belgium, Winter Nelis is not the prettiest of pears, with its squat shape and dull, rusted, yellow-green skin. Medium to small in size, the Nelis is however a useful pear, with sweet, slightly spicy flesh that lends itself to cooking and to eating raw, although it does have a tough skin.

culinary uses

European pears are versatile fruits. As noted above, they can be poached whole or halved (peel first), roasted in unpeeled halves, quarters or wedges, then used in sweet or savory dishes; they can also be sautéed, stewed, or simply sliced and used raw. Their flavor has an affinity with spices like ginger, nutmeg, cardamom, saffron, star anise, cloves, and cinnamon.

Pears are excellent poached in a red wine syrup, or in port or white dessert wine. Firm, poached, cooled pear halves work even better than raw pears in upside-down cakes and sweet tarts. Firmer pears, such as Beurre Bosc, make an admirable tarte Tatin in place of the usual apple.

Pears team beautifully with cheese, either in a salad or cheese course—partner them with Parmesan or blue cheese, a washed-rind or goat cheese. Nuts such as walnuts, hazelnuts, almonds, and pistachios also complement pears, as do salad leaves like radicchio, cress, spinach, and arugula. Like melon, pear also goes well with prosciutto, and firmer varieties are wonderful in braises with chicken, duck, or pork.

selection

Pears are picked when mature but still hard, then transferred to cool storage to cure for a period (the length of time here depends upon variety) and then, finally, bought to room temperature to complete ripening. During ripening, the starches are converted to sugars, and the pear, unusually, ripens from the inside out.

When allowed to fully tree-ripen, pears are fit to eat for a few days only, after which their flesh turns dry and mealy. Perhaps this is why, before the days of commercial cool storage, Ralph Waldo Emerson declared that, "There are only ten minutes in the life of a pear when it is perfect to eat."

To tell if a pear is ripe, it should give slightly when pressed (use your thumb) at the base of the "neck"; some varieties will also smell a little fragrant. Asian pears are the exception to the above rules as they are picked when ready to eat.

pear and walnut salad
with blue cheese dressing

serves 4

dressing
1/2 cup creamy blue cheese
1/4 cup olive oil
1 tablespoon walnut oil
1 tablespoon lemon juice
1 tablespoon whipping cream
2 teaspoons finely chopped sage

salad
1 cup walnut halves
4 small firm pears
2 tablespoons lemon juice
2 Belgian endives, trimmed and
   leaves separated
1 cup shaved Parmesan cheese

To make the dressing, process the blue cheese in a small processor until smooth, then add the olive oil, walnut oil, and lemon juice and blend until combined well. With the motor running, slowly add 2 teaspoons warm water. Stir in the cream and sage and season with sea salt and freshly ground black pepper.

Preheat the broiler to medium-hot. Place the walnuts in a bowl and cover with boiling water. Stand for 1 minute, then drain well. Spread the walnuts on the broiler tray and broil for 3 minutes or until lightly toasted. Chop coarsely.

Slice unpeeled pears widthwise to make thin rounds; discard the seeds. As each pear is sliced, brush slices with a little lemon juice to prevent browning.

Arrange three pear slices in a circle on a serving plate. Top with a sprinkling of walnuts, a few endive leaves, then a few more walnuts and some more Parmesan cheese. Repeat this layering, finishing with a layer of Parmesan cheese and some walnuts. Spoon some dressing over each stack. Serve as a first course or as an accompaniment to simple meat dishes.

pear tarte tatin

Preheat the oven to 425°F. Place an 8 1/2-inch heavy-bottomed frying pan with ovenproof handle over medium heat. Add the sugar and heat, shaking the pan constantly, until the sugar is a dark caramel color. Add the butter, ginger, and cinnamon and stir to combine. Arrange the pears on top, spoon over the syrup to coat, then reduce the heat to low and cook, covered, for 5 minutes or until the pears just begin to soften.

Remove the frying pan from the heat and arrange the pears over the base of the pan, overlapping them so they fit tightly and will look neat when turned out. Leave to cool slightly.

Roll out the pastry on a lightly floured work surface to a 9 1/2-inch round. Put the pastry over the pears in the frying pan, tucking the edges around the pears so they are enclosed in the pastry. Bake for 20–25 minutes or until the pastry is golden and puffed. Leave for 10 minutes, then run a knife around the edge of the pan to loosen the tart, and invert it onto a serving platter. Serve warm with cream. The tart is best served on the day it is made.

variation Make an apple tarte tatin by following the recipe instructions and substituting the pears for 2–3 green apples, such as Granny Smiths.

2/3 cup superfine sugar
1/4 cup butter, cut into cubes
1/2 teaspoon ground ginger
1/2 teaspoon ground cinnamon
3 Beurre Bosc pears, peeled, cored, and cut into wedges widthwise
1 pound block puff pastry
heavy cream, to serve

pome fruit ■ pear

For other pear recipes see:
pear and sprout salad with sesame
   dressing...275

serves 6

pears in red wine

1 tablespoon arrowroot
1 (750 ml) bottle red wine
1/2 cup sugar
1 cinnamon stick
6 cloves
zest of 1 small orange
zest of 1 small lemon
6 large firm pears
cream or crème fraîche, to serve

Combine the arrowroot with 2 tablespoons of the wine in a small bowl and stir to form a smooth paste. Heat the remaining wine in a saucepan with the sugar, cinnamon stick, cloves, and citrus zest. Simmer gently for 2–3 minutes or until the sugar has dissolved.

Peel the pears, leaving the stalks intact. Add pears to the saucepan, cover, and cook over medium heat for 25 minutes, turning pears occasionally. When the pears are very tender, lift out with a slotted spoon and put in a deep serving dish.

Strain the spiced wine, discarding solids, then return the wine to the pan. Stir the arrowroot and add to the hot wine. Simmer gently, stirring occasionally, until thickened. Pour over the pears and allow to cool. Serve with cream or crème fraîche.

serves 4

pear and raspberry crumble

3 pounds 5 ounces (about
    6 large) ripe but firm pears
2 tablespoons superfine sugar
3 star anise
1 cup raspberries
1 cup all-purpose flour
1/2 cup soft brown sugar
1/3 cup unsalted butter, cut into
    cubes
vanilla ice cream, to serve

Preheat the oven to 375°F. Peel, quarter, and core the pears, then cut each piece in half lengthwise. Put into a large saucepan and sprinkle the sugar over. Add 1 tablespoon water and the star anise. Cover and bring to a boil. Cook, covered, over medium-low heat for 10 minutes, stirring occasionally, until the fruit is tender but still holds its shape. Drain the pears and discard the star anise. Transfer to 6-cup baking dish. Sprinkle the raspberries over the pears.

Combine the flour, sugar, and butter in a bowl. Use your fingertips to rub the butter into the flour until the mixture resembles coarse crumbs. Sprinkle over the fruit, then bake for 20–25 minutes, until golden brown. Stand for 5 minutes, then serve with vanilla ice cream.

quince

fruit ▪ **pome**
season ▪ **late fall–winter**

The quince is an unpromising looking fruit, rock-hard (yet prone to bruising), thick-skinned, yellow, and covered with a strange fuzz. But the smell of quince (a complex, sweet perfume that invades your house with even a few of the fruit in a bowl), hints at the glorious flavors within, which require long, patient cooking to be fully unlocked.

An ancient fruit (one theory suggests that it was a quince or pomegranate that was Eve's downfall and not the apple), the quince originated around the Black and Caspian Seas and, after making its way westward, became a firm favorite throughout Mediterranean Europe, Northern Africa, and Portugal.

Quinces, like apples and pears, are a member of the Rosacaea, or rose family, and in times past was a popular tree in household orchards—in fact, it has been noted that seventeenth-century English cookbooks have more quince recipes than any other fruit. Over recent years the quince has been "rediscovered," becoming something of a winter favorite among professional chefs and enthusiastic home cooks alike. And little wonder—when cooked (quince can't be eaten raw as it is too astringent), the flesh takes on a glorious rosy color and a deep haunting flavor.

preparation

Wash quince well to get rid of any fuzz. If making jelly (and, with its particularly high pectin content, quince is ideal for this), don't bother to peel or core as the flavor will be better and the flotsam gets strained out anyway. Otherwise, peel and core your quinces—the flesh turns brown quickly on contact with air so if preparing a lot of the fruit put the pieces in acidulated water (water with lemon juice) as you go. Be sure to remove any brown patches—it's hard to tell if a quince is bruised until you come to peel it, so look out for soft, damaged spots at this stage.

culinary uses

Quinces are suited to poaching, baking, stewing, preserving in syrup, or being made into jam or dense, sweet quince paste—perfect to eat with cheese. They can also be pot-roasted, whole and unpeeled, in a very sweet, spiced syrup—this takes several hours and the fruit must be turned every now and then so it cooks evenly—the results of this treatment are especially luscious.

Quinces complement apples and pears and these other fruits can be used to extend your supply of quinces as, when cooked together, the quinces' flavor overpowers the more neutral flavors of the apples and pears. Although most often used in sweet preparations, Moroccan, Spanish, and Persian cooks also incorporate them into savory stews and tagines where they are an unexpected complement to the flavors of lamb, chicken, or fish.

selection and storage

There's little chance you'll get to buy quince by variety—generally you take what you can get—although pineapple quince (an early ripening variety with large, yellow fruit) and smyrna (a smaller quince with a very pronounced flavor and which doesn't break up even when cooked for a very long time) are two common varieties.

Choose fruit that has bright yellow or gold skin, with no signs of green or of discoloration. Riper fruit tends to have less fuzz on its skin although the amount of fuzz present can also be a feature of the variety.

Ripe quince will keep at cool room temperature for 10–14 days and for up to 3 weeks in the refrigerator. If choosing this option, seal the fruit in a large plastic bag to prevent their aroma permeating the entire contents of your refrigerator.

Called marmelos *by the Portugeuse and* membrillo *by the Spanish, the quince is the source of the English word "marmalade"—initially this jam was made using quinces.*

serves 4–6

lamb tagine with quince

3 pounds 5 ounces boned lamb shoulder
2 large handfuls cilantro leaves, chopped
2 large onions, diced
½ teaspoon ground ginger
½ teaspoon cayenne pepper
¼ teaspoon ground saffron threads
1 teasoon ground coriander
1 cinnamon stick
1 pound (about 4) quinces
2 tablespoons butter
¾ cup dried apricots
1 tablespoon superfine sugar
cilantro leaves, extra, to garnish
couscous or rice, to serve

Cut the lamb shoulder into 1¼-inch pieces. Put the lamb in a flameproof, heavy-bottomed casserole dish. Add the cilantro, half the onion, ginger, cayenne pepper, saffron threads, ground coriander, and cinnamon stick. Season with sea salt and freshly ground black pepper.

Cover with cold water and bring to a boil over medium heat. Lower the heat and simmer, partly covered, for 1½ hours or until the lamb is tender.

Meanwhile, core the quinces, then cut them into thick wedges. Melt the butter in a heavy-bottomed frying pan over medium heat and cook the quinces and remaining onion for 15 minutes or until lightly golden. When the lamb has been cooking for 1 hour, add the quince mixture, dried apricots, and sugar.

Taste the sauce and adjust the seasoning if necessary. Transfer to a warm serving dish and sprinkle with the extra cilantro. Serve immediately with couscous or rice.

"There is no fruit growing in this land that is of so many excellent uses as (the quince)." — John Parkinson (herbalist to King James I), 1629.

quince paste

Line an 11¼ x 7-inch rectangular cake pan or dish with plastic wrap. Wash the quinces, place in a saucepan and cover with water. Simmer for 30 minutes or until the quinces are tender, then drain. Peel and core the quinces, then push them through a sieve or potato ricer.

Put the pulp in a heavy-bottomed saucepan and add the sugar. Cook over low heat, stirring occasionally, for 3½–4½ hours or until very thick. Pour into the prepared pan. Allow to cool. Quince paste can be kept for several months in a tightly sealed container in the refrigerator. Serve before a meal with cheese and crackers as part of an antipasti selection, or with game such as pheasant.

note The amount of sugar will vary depending on the size of the quinces. The amount of sugar you use should equal the weight of quince pulp. You can measure this once strained.

3 large quinces
3⅔ cups sugar (see note)

pome fruit ▪ quince

slow-baked quinces in honey

serves 8

Preheat the oven to 300°F. Use half the butter to grease a shallow ovenproof dish, large enough to hold the halved quinces in one layer, overlapping slightly.

Peel and halve the quinces. Don't worry about them discoloring as they will turn very dark during cooking. Remove cores. Put them, cut side up, in the prepared dish.

Drizzle the honey and wine over the quinces and dot with the remaining butter. Cover with foil and bake for 2 hours, turn the quinces and bake for an additional 2 hours. The quinces should be a rich maroon red and the juices caramelized. Serve hot or warm with cream or softened vanilla ice cream.

¼ cup unsalted butter, softened
8 quinces
2 tablespoons honey
½ cup sweet white dessert wine, such as Sauternes
whipping cream or vanilla ice cream, to serve

melon

fruit ■ **other**
season ■ **cantaloupe, watermelon and netted melon peaking in summer; honeydew in fall**

A French poet is credited as saying, "there are three things which cannot support mediocrity—poetry, wine, and melons." Indeed, an unsatisfactory melon is quite horrible; there is no disguising any absence of the gentle flavors, voluptuous fragrance, or that sweet juiciness for which melons are so prized.

Melons are one of those fruits that are technically a vegetable, related as they are to other trailing, vine-borne crops such as gourds, cucumbers, and squash. They come from the cucurbit family, which includes many vegetables commonly used throughout Asia (bitter gourd, winter melon, and fuzzy melon, for example), where the words "gourd" and "melon" are virtually interchangeable.

Sweet melons fall into two broad groups—the genus *Cucumis melo* includes cantaloupe, netted melon (or muskmelon), and the honeydew; it is thought these originated in Persia, Afghanistan, or Armenia. The watermelon is from the *Citrullus lanatus* grouping; these are native to the Kalahari Desert of Africa.

Melons comprise around 90 percent water and it goes without saying they are very low in calories. Their nutritional profile varies according to type, but generally they provide generous quantities of vitamin C and betacarotene, with orange-fleshed varieties providing more than others.

cantaloupe

True cantaloupes are grown more widely in Europe (they take their name from a town near Rome called Cantalupo) and the Middle East than they are in North America or Australia—often what passes for cantaloupes in these latter countries are actually netted melons.

True cantaloupes are smaller and rounder than these and have tougher skin that is marked in clear sections—either smooth or slightly scaly, but never netted. The legendary Charentais and Ogen melons are regarded as the aristocrats of the cantaloupe. They possess fine, full-flavored and deep orange flesh. Charentais are smallish, with smooth, gray-green rind. The Ogen, which hails from Israel, has green flesh and an orange-green rind with dark green demarcations.

honeydew

The honeydew is distinguished by its smooth, creamy, thin skin and sweet green flesh. The Japanese adore honeydews—theirs is the fragrance supposedly encapsulated by Midori liqueur. The honeydew, which is unpleasantly bland when under-ripe, will continue to develop some flavor after picking, when stored at room temperature. It's a little tricky to tell when honeydews are ripe; some claim the skin turns yellow when ripe, while others insist it should be creamy or pale green; unlike other melons, honeydews will continue to ripen once harvested.

With many varieties of this melon now available (even orange-fleshed ones have been developed), the most reliable method of determining ripeness is to lightly press the stem end; it should be slightly soft when the fruit is mature. Store ripe honeydews in the refrigerator for up to 4 days, taking care to completely cover all cut surfaces, as the smell of melon permeates everything in its proximity. Bring honeydews back to room temperature before eating though, as chilling dulls their flavor.

netted melons

These melons are called "netted" because of the raised webbing on their skin, or sometimes are referred to as muskmelons on account of their glorious smell when ripe. The netted melon has deep, peachy-colored flesh which is rich in betacarotenes (vitamin A). Round or slightly ovoid in shape, these melons have a netted skin with lengthwise demarcations, called sutures.

Select melons with a deep, sweet aroma and pronounced netting on the skin—the background skin color should be beige to golden. A ripe melon should also have a paler, slightly flattened side where it rested on the ground before harvesting, and the stem end should be a little damp.

Netted melons are rather perishable; ripe ones (and these don't continue to ripen once picked, so select with care) should be eaten immediately. They will store for 1–2 days at cool room temperature or 2 days in the refrigerator. Avoid any melons that have soft, shrivelled, or sunken patches as this indicates spoilage.

watermelon

There are over 1,000 varieties of watermelon grown, ranging in skin color from pale green and faintly striped, to dark green with bold veining and stripes, to nearly black and unmarbled. Watermelons are rounded or oval in shape, although the Japanese, wishing to develop a melon that will fit cooperatively into a refrigerator, have even developed a square melon!

Under the skin of a watermelon lies a layer of thick, protective white rind which isn't edible raw, although certain culinary cultures either pickle or candy it. The many seeds contained in the flesh (large specimens can harbor over 1,000) can also be roasted for snacking, thereby making edible use of every part of the melon. In Russia, they even brew a beer from watermelon juice.

To tell if a watermelon is ripe, inspect the pale patch where it rested on the ground—it should be yellow, not white or light green. The skin should be matte and have a waxy rather than shiny appearance, and the fruit should be large for its type and feel heavy for its size. If you tap the fruit it should sound a little hollow. Many suppliers will let you taste from a cut specimen before you buy.

Don't store watermelon for too long (2–3 days maximum, covered in plastic wrap in the refrigerator). With age, the flesh takes on a deeper color, glassy appearance, and dry, almost gritty texture and, needless to say, is not so pleasant to eat.

Melons have extremely venerable origins; depictions of them have been found on Egyptian walls dating back to 5000 B.C. The Romans imported melons in great quantity from the Near Eastern reaches of their Empire, although these melons were tiny, orange-sized specimens, not the large ones we are familiar with today. In the fourteenth century, well after the Roman Empire had collapsed, the Italians finally began cultivating the fruit themselves and, as a result of their efforts, melons began to expand in size and weight. In seventeenth-century France, melons were called sucrins, *meaning "sweet," and little wonder, as gardeners hydrated them with honeyed water to make them even more so.*

culinary uses

A perfect melon demands little more than to be simply sliced, seeds removed, and served with a teaspoon for scooping— or in fleshy wedges to be eaten out of hand. There are, however, some utterly timeless dishes involving melon which deserve consideration. There's Italian prosciutto with melon— cantaloupe or netted melon are best used, as the perfumed sweetness is somehow the perfect foil for the salty, rich meat. From French cooking came the idea of melon (usually honeydew or cantaloupe, cut into balls with a special cutter, which can be purchased from specialist kitchen stores) doused with port. Greeks hit upon the combination of feta cheese and watermelon; sublime when tossed into a refreshing salad with sliced red onions, mint, and olives. Fragrant netted melon also goes well in cold dishes with smoked chicken, ham, and roast duck and with sweet crustaceans (shrimp, lobsters, crab), too.

In recent years it has become fashionable to fill a whole watermelon with vodka (using a funnel to poke through a small hole cut in the melon, the flesh absorbs great amounts of the alcohol), which is served in chilled, spirit-sodden wedges. Any melon will greatly enhance a fruit salad and they have an affinity for the flavor of ginger and rum.

Puree seeded melons and use in frappés and frozen ices— pureed netted melon, mixed with a little chicken stock, garlic, ground almonds, and sherry vinegar, makes an extremely pleasant gazpacho-style chilled soup.

other fruit ■ melon

makes 4 cups

melon and lemon conserve

6 lemons
4-inch square of cheesecloth
5 pounds 8 ounces honeydew
    melon, peeled, seeded, and
    cut into ½-inch cubes
1 tablespoon brandy
5⅔ cups sugar, warmed (see
    note)

Scrub the lemons under hot running water to remove any wax, then cut in half widthwise. Juice the lemons, strain the juice, and reserve the seeds. Put the juice in a large saucepan. Put the seeds on the cheesecloth and tie up securely with string. Roughly chop the lemon skins. Add the seeds to the pan, along with the chopped lemon skins, melon, brandy, and 3 cups water. Bring to a boil and boil for 40 minutes or until the fruit is soft.

Put two small plates in the freezer. Add the sugar to the pan and stir over low heat, without boiling, for 5 minutes or until the sugar has dissolved. Bring to a boil and boil, stirring often, for 30 minutes. As the mixture thickens and starts to darken, reduce the heat and simmer, stirring frequently, for 20–30 minutes. When the conserve falls from a tilted wooden spoon in thick sheets without dripping, start testing for setting point. To do this, remove from the heat, put a little conserve onto one of the cold plates and place in the freezer for 30 seconds. A skin should form on the surface and the conserve should wrinkle when pushed with your finger. If not, return the pan to the heat for a few minutes, then retest using the second plate. Discard the cheesecloth bag. Remove any scum from the surface.

Carefully ladle into hot sterilized jars and seal. Allow to cool, then label and date each jar. Store in a cool, dark place for 6–12 months. Refrigerate after opening for up to 6 weeks.

note To warm the sugar, preheat the oven to 300°F. Spread the sugar evenly in a baking dish and put in the oven for 10–15 minutes or until warmed through. To save time you can warm the sugar while cooking the conserve. Do not add the sugar until the fruit has softened. If sugar is added before the fruit has fully softened, the fruit will remain firm.

watermelon granita

Put the sugar in a saucepan with 1 cup water and stir over low heat, without boiling, until the sugar has dissolved. Increase the heat and bring to a boil, then reduce the heat and simmer, without stirring, for 5 minutes. Pour into a large bowl to cool.

Remove the rind from the watermelon, cut flesh into chunks and place in a food processor. Process melon until a puree forms, then strain, discarding seeds and fiber. Mix the watermelon puree with the sugar syrup and pour into a shallow metal pan. Freeze for 1 hour or until ice crystals start to form around the edges. Scrape frozen edges back into the mixture with a fork. Repeat this process at least twice more or until the mixture has large, even-size ice crystals. For refreshing extra flavor, add the chopped mint when freezing the last time.

Serve immediately, or beat well with a fork and refreeze until ready to serve. Scrape the granita into serving dishes with a fork, or serve in scoops in tall glasses.

heaping 1 cup superfine sugar
3 pounds 5 ounces watermelon
  (about ¼ average-size
  watermelon)
2 tablespoon chopped mint,
  optional

other fruit ■ melon

Watermelons are by far the largest of the sweet melons; the 1996 Guinness Book of Records *documents one that weighed 262 pounds, although generally, anywhere between 5–40 pounds is normal. Not surprisingly, watermelon flesh comprises a whopping 92 percent water— even today, in some parts of Africa, it is relied upon to satisfy thirst in times of water scarcity.*

pomegranate

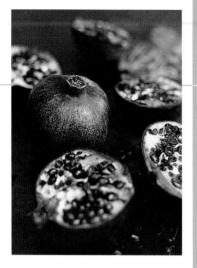

Pomegranates, also called Chinese apples, are an old, old fruit. The word "pomegranate" derives from the Latin meaning "apple with many seeds" and it is true that, under the tough, red, leathery skin of a pomegranate, lie hundreds of small seeds encased in cranberry-red sacs of juice. The fleshy seeds have a tart-sweetness and make a refreshing drink. So unique is the pomegranate that it is in a botanical family, *Punicaceae,* all its own; there are a few varieties but the differences are slight—skin may be darker, fruit may be larger, or seeds may be slightly sweeter.

selection and storage

As with many juicy fruits, it is important to choose pomegranates that feel heavy for their size—this indicates the presence of a lot of juice. Generally, larger pomegranates have sweeter flesh with well-developed flavor.

Store pomegranates at cool room temperature for up to 3 weeks or, if in good condition (with firm, unblemished skin), up to 8 weeks in the refrigerator; the skin becomes tougher and more leathery with time but is an effective protector of the fruits' interior. The seeds and juice can also be frozen for up to 6 months.

preparation

Whichever way you approach it, dealing with a pomegranate is going to require patience and a gentle hand. Avoid getting the juice on your clothes—it is such an effective stain that it is still used as a dye in the manufacture of Persian carpets.

The most effective way of extracting the seeds is to cut off the crown (top) of the pomegranate, then cut the fruit into quarters. Put in a bowl of cold water and carefully bend the skin back to open up the membranes, prising out the seeds—the bitter white membrane and skin will float to the top of the water, making for efficient disposal, while the seeds will sink (simply strain off water to retrieve the seeds).

To extract the juice, process the seeds briefly in a food processor, then strain off the juice. As a rough guide, a medium pomegranate should yield about 3/4 cup of seeds and about 1/2 cup juice.

pomegranate, green olive, and walnut salad

Soak the walnut halves in boiling water for 3–4 minutes or until the skins peel off readily. Drain, peel, and pat dry. Lightly toast, shaking often, under a broiler for 8 minutes or until golden. Cool, then roughly chop.

Combine the olive oil, pomegranate syrup, and chili flakes in a screwtop jar and shake well.

Put the olives, pomegranate seeds, onion, walnuts, and parsley in a bowl and toss. Just before serving, pour the dressing over. Season with sea salt and freshly ground black pepper and combine well.

note Pomegranate syrup is available from specialist Middle Eastern food stores and good delicatessens.

1 cup walnut halves
1/2 cup olive oil
1 1/2 tablespoons pomegranate syrup
1/2 teaspoon chili flakes
2 cups green olives, pitted and cut in halves
1/2 cup pomegranate seeds
1 large red onion, chopped
1 large handful Italian parsley

other fruit ■ pomegranate

Pomegranates have been found buried in ancient Egyptian tombs and are mentioned frequently throughout the Old Testament. They require serious heat in which to ripen to juicy sweetness, hence they grow best in the Middle East, to whose cuisines they are mainly connected, although they are native to Central Asia (Persia and Afghanistan).

For other pomegranate recipes see:
radicchio with figs and ginger
   vinaigrette 315

tamarillo

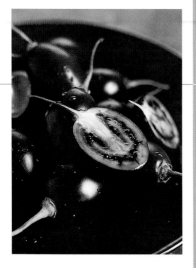

fruit ■ other
season ■ winter

The most common, commercially available varieties of tamarillo, which are elegant, tapered globes about 3 inches long, are rich red or yellow skinned, with apricot-colored flesh. The numerous seeds, contained in the center of the fruit in a large, pulpy, gel-like core, are perfectly edible but the bitter thin skin is not. Tamarillos can be enjoyed raw, although they need to be very ripe as their flesh can be somewhat tart—the yellow-skinned varieties being less acidic than the red. The fruit is highly nutritious, yielding good quantities of vitamins A, B6, C, and E, and is also rich in iron and potassium.

selection and storage

Tamarillos will ripen at room temperature—when fully ripe they should feel slightly soft and rather heavy for their size. Select fruit that has tight skin with no blemishes or wrinkles.

Once fully ripe, tamarillos should be stored in the refrigerator, where they will keep for about 10 days. When cutting a tamarillo, take care that the juice doesn't splash your clothing as it will stain.

preparation

Tamarillos are most effectively peeled by blanching in boiling water—prepared this way, they can then be poached whole. Using a small, sharp knife, make a tiny crisscross incision in the base of the fruit. Plunge the fruit (about six at a time; don't crowd the pan) into a saucepan of boiling water for 30 seconds, then transfer to a bowl of iced water to quickly cool. Drain them well; the skin should easily peel away.

culinary uses

Tamarillos make suburb jam, are wonderful stewed (perhaps with a few apples or chopped dates and bananas, to cut the acid) and then baked under a crisp crumble topping, or served sweetened and warmed with good vanilla ice cream or custard on the side. The whole, peeled fruit, still with their stems intact, make for a dramatic presentation when poached whole in a lightly spiced sugar syrup.

poached tamarillo with vanilla bean cream pots

Put six 1/2-cup ramekins in a deep roasting pan. Put the cream and vanilla bean in a saucepan, bring slowly to a boil, then reduce the heat and simmer for 5 minutes. Remove from the heat, split the vanilla bean, scrape out the seeds and return the bean and seeds to the cream. Cover and set aside for 30 minutes. Strain.

Preheat the oven to 315°F. Whisk the eggs, yolks, and sugar in a bowl. Whisk in the cream, then pour into the ramekins and cover each securely with foil. Pour enough hot water into the pan to come halfway up the sides of the ramekins. Bake for 30 minutes or until just set. Refrigerate, covered, for 4 hours or overnight.

To poach the tamarillos, score a cross in the base of the fruit, plunge them into boiling water for 10 seconds, then transfer to iced water and peel away the skins, leaving the stalks attached. Put the sugar in a saucepan with 3 cups water and the orange peel. Stir to dissolve the sugar. Bring to a boil and boil for 3 minutes. Reduce the heat to a simmer and add the tamarillos. Poach for 6–8 minutes, depending on their ripeness. Turn off the heat, add the liqueur and leave the fruit in the syrup to cool.

Remove the fruit from the pan, then bring the syrup to a boil. Boil for 5–10 minutes or until reduced and thickened. Pour into a bowl, cover and leave to cool. Cut each tamarillo in half, leaving the stalk end intact, and serve with the sauce and vanilla bean cream pots.

The tamarillo originates from the Peruvian and Bolivian Andes and is a relative of the potato, eggplant, and pepper. We have New Zealand to thank for its commercialization and renaming (originally it was known as the tree tomato). It became popular there during the lean, food-rationed years of World War II.

vanilla bean cream
2¾ cups whipping cream
1 vanilla bean
2 eggs
2 egg yolks
2 tablespoons superfine sugar

poached tamarillos
6 tamarillos with stalks
1⅔ cups superfine sugar
2-inch piece of orange peel
2–3 tablespoons kirsch or cherry
  liqueur, optional

other fruit ■ tamarillo

nuts

almonds

selection and storage

If purchased in their shells, almonds will keep for up to 1 year, stored in a cool dark place. Shelled nuts, as prone to rancidity as all other nut types, should be stored in an airtight container in the refrigerator for several months or in the freezer, for up to a year. Avoid any that show signs of mold, cracking, or holes in their shells—if purchasing shelled almonds, look for ones that are plump and unwrinkled.

Almonds are the most widely planted nut tree. They are part of the *Prunus* (plum, cherry, peach) genus, native to North Africa, West Asia, and the Mediterranean—it is thought the earliest almonds travelled along the Silk Road with explorers.

The word "almond" derives from the Greek word *"amygdalon"* which, via Latin, has become the botanical name for the species. The almond is a fruit, or drupe. It grows inside a hard oval shell, enclosed in a green-gray husk. The husks split open when the kernels, or nuts, are mature. In certain Mediterranean cultures the immature kernels, still moist, soft, pale, and cosseted in their furry green coat, are enjoyed with salty white cheese as an appetizer or snack.

varieties

There are two types of almonds—the common sweet almond and the bitter almond, a native to Asia although now virtually naturalized around the Mediterranean. The flavor of the bitter almond will be familiar thanks to the widespread use of natural almond extract (the making of which is one of bitter almond's main uses) in baking and confectionery. Bitter almond is also the defining flavor of Italian amaretti biscuits and, also from Italy, amaretto liqueur. Bitter almonds contain a poisonous compound (cyanide, essentially) that dissipates during processing, however they are very toxic when raw—about twenty kernels will kill an adult. Having said this, the taste of a raw bitter almond is so disagreeable that it is unlikely that anyone would eat enough of them to become seriously ill.

There are many varieties of the more familiar sweet almond, with over 100 different types grown in California alone. These are widely used in sweet and savory dishes the world over; whole, blanched, chopped, sliced, or ground. Their mild, milky flavor goes particularly well with vegetables, fish, and chicken—however they are used, a light roasting before use will accentuate their flavor. Almond milk, made by finely grinding whole almonds in water, then straining the mixture of solids, has long been appreciated as an alternative to cows' milk—one of the first European uses for this was during the Middle Ages, in making of the original blancmange.

preparation

shelling The best way to extract kernels from their shells is to use a nutcracker. The shells are not particlularly hard, so lots of force is not necessary.

roasting A light roasting significantly enhances the flavor of almonds and is easy to do. The most effective method is oven-roasting. Spread whole, shelled kernels (or blanched whole kernels) on a single layer in a roasting pan, then cook in a 350°F oven for 8–10 minutes or until light golden all the way through and fragrant.

blanching To blanch whole raw almonds, put almonds in a bowl, then cover them with boiling water. Stand for 1 minute and then drain well. Rinse under cold water and drain, then dry almonds using a clean dishtowel—the skins should just slip off.

almond milk To make almond milk, combine 1 cup chopped, blanched almonds and 1 cup water in a food processor and process until a smooth paste forms. Gradually add 2 cups water with the motor running. Strain mixture through a sieve lined with cheesecloth. Gather up the cloth and nut solids and wring tightly to extract all liquid, discarding the solids. Almond milk can be used in smoothies, blancmange, custards, and ice creams, or sweetened with honey to make a delicious milk jelly.

tamari roasted almonds with spicy green beans

serves 4–6

¾ cup almonds
tamari, for soaking
1 tablespoon oil
3 tablespoons sesame oil
2½ cups rice
4 cups boiling water
1 long red chili, seeded and
    finely chopped
¾-inch piece ginger, peeled and
    grated
2 garlic cloves, crushed
3 cups green beans cut into
    2-inch lengths
½ cup hoisin sauce
1 tablespoon soft brown sugar
2 tablespoons mirin

Soak the almonds in a bowl with enough tamari to cover, for 30 minutes. Drain and dry with paper towels. Heat a nonstick frying pan with oil. Add the almonds and toss for 2–3 minutes, then drain. Roughly chop and set aside.

Preheat the oven to 400°F. Heat 1 tablespoon of sesame oil in a deep baking dish, add the rice and stir until well coated. Stir in the boiling water. Cover and cook for 20 minutes or until all the water is absorbed. Keep warm.

Meanwhile, heat the remaining sesame oil in a wok or large frying pan and cook the chili, ginger, and garlic for 1 minute. Add the beans, hoisin sauce, and sugar and cook for a few minutes. Stir in the mirin and cook for 1 minute or until the beans are just tender; they should be a little crunchy. Remove from the heat and stir in the almonds. Serve with the rice.

ajo blanco

serves 4–6

1 loaf day-old white Italian bread,
    crusts removed
3–4 garlic cloves, chopped
1 cup blanched almonds
½ cup extra virgin olive oil
⅓ cup dry sherry
1¼ cups vegetable stock
2 tablespoons olive oil
2 cups cubed day-old white
    Italian bread, extra
1 cup seedless green grapes

Soak the bread in cold water for 5 minutes, then squeeze out any excess liquid. Chop the garlic and almonds in a food processor until well ground. Add the soaked bread and continue to process until smooth. With the motor running, add the extra virgin olive oil in a slow steady stream until the mixture resembes thick mayonnaise. Slowly add the sherry and vegetable stock. Season to taste. Refrigerate for at least 2 hours.

When ready to serve, heat the olive oil in a frying pan, add the bread cubes and toss over medium heat for 3 minutes or until golden. Drain on paper towels. Serve the soup very cold—you may need to add extra stock or water to thin it. Garnish with the grapes and bread cubes.

almond, orange, and cardamom biscotti

Preheat the oven to 315°F and line a baking sheet with baking paper.

Beat the eggs and sugar in a bowl until pale and creamy. Sift the flours into the bowl, then add the almonds, orange zest, and cardamom and mix to a soft dough.

Turn out the dough onto a lightly floured work surface. Divide the mixture into equal portions, shaping it into two 2 x 8-inch loaves. Place on the prepared baking sheet and bake for 35–40 minutes or until lightly golden. Transfer to a wire rack to cool. Cut the loaves into 1/2-inch diagonal slices with a large serrated bread knife. The biscotti will be crumbly on the edges so work slowly and, if possible, try to hold the sides as you cut.

Arrange the slices on the baking sheet in a single layer (you may need to use two sheets or do this in batches). Return to the oven and bake for an additional 10 minutes on each side. Don't worry if they don't seem fully dry as they will become crisp on cooling. Transfer to a wire rack to cool. Store in an airtight container for up to 3 weeks.

2 eggs
3/4 cup soft brown sugar
1 cup self-rising flour
3/4 cup all-purpose flour
1 cup almonds
1 tablespoon finely grated orange zest
1/4 teaspoon ground cardamom

nuts ■ almonds

For other almond recipes see:

figs with rose water, almonds, and honey 56

trout stuffed with dates 86

broccoli and almond stir-fry 285

chestnuts

produce ▪ **nuts**
season ▪ **harvested in fall**

With their low fat and calorie content, sweet, starchy flesh and quite significant vitamin C levels, the chestnut is hardly a typical nut. In fact, many food cultures have long used the chestnut as a vegetable, mashing the mealy flesh like potato, braising it with meats, or cooking it with cabbage or Brussels sprouts. Chestnuts also star in traditional sweet preparations. Think of monte bianco where piles of sweetened chestnut puree are pushed through a mouli into long strands then lavished with cream, or the hopelessly luxurious *marrons glacés* (candied chestnuts) from France. Chestnuts are also dried, made into flour for baked goods, and widely enjoyed roasted as a hot snack.

As well as starch (they contain twice as much as potatoes), chestnuts are rich in potassium and contain reasonable amounts of vitamin B.

selection and storage

Mature chestnuts simply fall to the ground when ready for eating and need only to be gathered up. When buying chestnuts, choose those with glossy and smooth shells (their prickly outer casing will generally have been removed) and that feel heavy for their size.

Avoid nuts that rattle in their shells as this indicates they are starting to dry out. Store fresh chestnuts for up to 1 month in a perforated plastic bag in the refrigerator; they'll also be fine frozen, for up to 4 months. Cooked chestnut flesh can also be frozen successfully for up to 4 months.

preparation

Chestnuts contain high levels of tannic acid so do need to be fully cooked—never eat them raw. To prepare chestnuts, make a cross-shaped incision in their flat side with a small, sharp knife. Boil the nuts in water for 15–20 minutes, then peel them while still hot—the tough inner skin will come off more easily than when cold. Work with a few nuts at a time, keeping the remaining nuts warm in their cooking water.

To roast chestnuts, make the same incision, then cook them in a 400°F oven for 20 minutes or until soft, then peel.

chestnut, pancetta, and cabbage soup

Cook the cabbage in 6 cups boiling salted water over high heat for about 10 minutes. Drain, reserving the water. Cool cabbage slightly and finely chop.

Heat the oil in a large saucepan, add the onion and pancetta and cook over medium-high heat for 4–5 minutes, until the onion is soft and the pancetta lightly browned. Add the garlic and rosemary and cook for a few more minutes.

Using your hands, break up the chestnuts and add to the pan with the cabbage. Stir to combine, season to taste, then add the wine. Bring to a boil and cook for 2 minutes. Add the cabbage water, reduce the heat and simmer for 15 minutes. Remove half the soup mixture from the saucepan and allow to cool slightly before blending to a puree in a food processor. Return puree to heat and stir to combine. Serve with a drizzle of extra virgin olive oil.

1¼ cups roughly chopped savoy cabbage
2 tablespoons olive oil
1 large onion, finely chopped
1¼ cups diced pancetta
3 garlic cloves, crushed
2 tablespoons chopped rosemary
2 cups cooked, peeled chestnuts
⅔ cup red wine
extra virgin olive oil, to serve

nuts ■ chestnuts

chestnut cake

Preheat the oven to 350°F. Grease and flour an 8-inch round cake pan. Boil the chestnuts in a saucepan of water over high heat for 15–20 minutes or until tender. Drain and peel the chestnuts while still hot. Put peeled chestnuts into a food processor and puree. Push the puree through a sieve so that the mixture is smooth.

Whisk the egg yolks and sugar until light and fluffy. Add the butter, lemon zest, chestnut puree, ground almonds, and flour and stir well. Whisk the egg whites until soft peaks form and fold into the mixture. Pour into the pan and bake for 50–60 minutes. Turn out onto a wire rack to cool. Serve with whipped cream.

14 ounces (about 24) chestnuts
5 egg yolks
heaping ¾ cup superfine sugar
⅓ cup unsalted butter, softened
1 tablespoon grated lemon zest
1½ cups ground almonds
2 tablespoons all-purpose flour
4 egg whites
whipped cream, to serve

hazelnuts

selection and storage

Purchase hazelnuts that feel full and heavy in their shells—the nuts inside should be plump; the fine brown skin that covers it should be tight. Hazelnuts, like all nuts, are highly perishable so store them away from heat and humidity—in the refrigerator is ideal.

produce ■ **nuts**
season ■ **harvested in summer**

Hazelnut lore is legion—ancient Greek texts assert the nut is effective as a cure for colds as well as for hair loss. Some people in Spain still insist that a dozen hazelnuts eaten before sleep will discourage bed-wetting. The Romans burned torches of hazelnut wood at weddings as a fertility rite and magicians' wands are traditionally made of hazelnut wood, a member of the birch (Betulaceae) family.

Today, much of the world's hazelnut crop is supplied by Turkey, although the state of Oregon in the United States claims it grows the world's best. Italy has given us some of the most adored hazelnut treats—the hazelnut-flavored liqueur Frangelico, and *gianduja* (a divine chocolate-hazelnut paste used in desserts and confectionery). Hazelnuts, as the Italians discovered, have a special affinity with chocolate and are delicious in all manner of chocolate cakes, cookies, tarts, sauces, and desserts.

preparation

Shelled hazelnuts benefit from the removal of their fine skin as this is slightly bitter. To do this, roast the nuts in a 350°F oven for 10–12 minutes or until skins are beginning to lift. Transfer them to a paper towel (or dishtowel) and wrap them in this to steam for several minutes, then rub vigorously to remove skins—not all will be removed but most will come off.

chocolate and hazelnut semifreddo

Line a 6-cup loaf pan with two long strips of foil. Heat ¾ cup of the cream in a small saucepan. Combine the sugar, cocoa, and egg yolks in a bowl. Pour the hot cream on top and mix well. Pour the mixture back into the saucepan and cook over low heat, stirring continuously, until the mixture is thick enough to coat the back of a wooden spoon—do not allow the custard to boil. Stir in the brandy and remove from the heat. Cover the surface with plastic wrap and cool.

Using electric beaters, whisk the egg whites in a clean, dry glass bowl until stiff peaks form. Add the confectioners' sugar and continue whisking until stiff and glossy. Whip the remaining cream in a large bowl until soft peaks form. Lightly fold the chocolate custard into the whipped cream, then fold in the egg whites. Gently fold in the hazelnuts. Spoon into the pan, smooth the surface and cover with foil. Freeze for at least 24 hours. Leave at room temperature for 5 minutes before serving in slices. Semifreddo will keep, frozen, for up to 5 days.

2 cups heavy cream
⅔ cup superfine sugar
½ cup unsweetened cocoa powder
4 eggs, separated
3 tablespoons brandy
3 tablespoons confectioners' sugar
1¼ cups skinned, roughly chopped hazelnuts

nuts ■ hazelnuts

Confusingly, in the United States hazelnuts are also called "filberts," while in Europe "filbert" and "cob" are used to indicate varieties of cultivated hazelnuts, possibly because they are harvested around St Philbert's feast day on August 20.

For other hazelnut recipes see:
orange, hazelnut, and goat
  cheese salad....................................37
mixed nut tartlets.............................171

macadamias

produce ■ nuts
season ■ available year-round

Macadamia nuts are native to Australia, where the indigenous peoples had eaten them long before European settlement. In fact, the colonizers of Australia initially paid little notice to the macadamia and it wasn't until the 1880s that the first orchard was planted. By then the nut had already been taken to Hawaii where it was found to grow spectacularly well—today, Hawaii is a significant producer of quality macadamias.

preparation

Macadamias are difficult to shell at home and are generally purchased out of their shell, although a nutcracker has been developed specifically for this purpose. Macadamias are relatively expensive, as their nut yield in relation to their weight when unshelled is quite high—about 55 pounds of unshelled nuts yields an average amount of 13–15 pounds of nut meat.

culinary uses

With their subtle, rich, buttery taste and singularly smooth texture, macadamias are quite unlike any other nut. A light roasting brings out their flavor, as does a sprinkling of salt, in which state they make an indulgent snack to eat with drinks. Their delicate, creamy flavor and their silky texture make macadamias an ideal partner for other nuts and tropical fruits and, intriguingly, white chocolate. They can be chopped and tossed in salads and can also be used in a crust for chicken or fish—finely ground and combined with bread crumbs, parsley, and a touch of grated lemon or lime zest, the mixture can be used to coat chicken or firm white fish fillets before shallow-frying for a delicious outcome.

selection and storage

The macadamia has the hardest shell of all commercially grown nuts, and indicates its ripeness by falling to the ground after the green husk that surrounds it has split—it is then collected, dried, and shelled. Because of their very high oil content (up to 80 percent), macadamias can quickly turn rancid, so store them in an airtight container in the refrigerator for up to 6 months, or in the freezer for up to 1 year.

macadamia-crusted chicken bites

Cut the chicken into strips and dust with the flour. Dip the strips in the egg, then coat them in the combined nuts and bread crumbs. Refrigerate for at least 30 minutes to firm the crust.

Fill a large, heavy-bottomed saucepan one third full of oil and heat to 350°F or until a cube of bread dropped into the oil browns in 15 seconds. Cook the chicken strips in batches for 2–3 minutes or until golden brown all over, taking care not to burn the nuts. Drain well on paper towels. Serve warm with mango salsa.

12 chicken tenderloins
seasoned all-purpose flour, for coating
2 eggs, lightly beaten
1½ cups macadamias, finely chopped
2 cups fresh bread crumbs
oil, for deep-frying
mango salsa (see page 417), to serve

nuts ■ macadamias

macadamia blondies

makes 25 pieces

Preheat the oven to 350°F. Lightly grease an 8-inch square cake pan and line with baking paper, leaving the paper hanging over on two opposite sides.

Put the butter and white chocolate in a heatproof bowl. Half fill a saucepan with water and bring to a boil. Remove from the heat. Put the bowl over the saucepan, making sure the base of the bowl does not touch the water. Stir until the butter and chocolate have melted and are smooth.

Put the sugar into the bowl and gradually stir in the eggs. Add the vanilla extract, fold in the flour and macadamia nuts, then pour into the pan. Bake for 35–40 minutes. If the top starts to brown too quickly, cover with foil. When cooked, cool in the pan before lifting out, using the paper as handles, and cutting into squares to serve.

⅓ cup unsalted butter, cubed
⅓ cup chopped white chocolate
heaping ½ cup superfine sugar
2 eggs, lightly beaten
1 teaspoon natural vanilla extract
1 cup self-rising flour
½ cup macadamia nuts, roughly chopped

peanuts

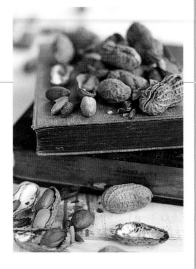

produce ■ **nuts**
season ■ **harvested fall–winter**

The peanut isn't a nut at all but rather a legume, related to peas and beans. Peanuts are technically seeds in pods, which grow on tendrils below the ground, hence their common name, groundnut.

To say the peanut is a significant worldwide food crop is something of an understatement—an estimated half a billion people, mainly in Africa, rely on peanuts as their main protein. From the satay sauces of Southeast Asia, to the peanut-based stews and soups of Africa and the Caribbean, to the spicy stir-fries of Sichuan in China's southwest, and the ever-popular peanut butter, the peanut is a truly global food. Nutritionally, it's a powerhouse, offering 26 percent of its mass as protein and containing a veritable smorgasbord of vitamins and essential minerals.

selection and storage

Like all nuts, peanuts contain a high ratio of oil and are prone to rancidity so need to be stored carefully. Buy them in their shells (look closely for any sign of mold as this is common in peanuts) and store them in a well-aerated bag (not in plastic or they could turn moldy).

preparation

roasting To roast peanuts in their shell, simply spread them on a baking sheet, in a single layer, and bake them in a 350°F oven for 30 minutes, turning them often and testing after about 20 minutes. The peanuts can be served hot, warm, or at room temperature.

blanching To blanch shelled peanuts, put them in a bowl, pour boiling water over them, stand for 5 minutes, then drain well. The skins should just slip off. In China, peanuts are boiled, either in their shells or skins. Simmered for 40 minutes in water fragranced with star anise, cinnamon, cloves, Sichuan pepper, fennel seed, and salt, they swell, soften, and absorb the delicious flavors, making a wonderfully different snack.

satay sauce

Put the roasted peanuts in a food processor and process until finely chopped.

Heat the oil in a frying pan. Add the onion and cook over medium heat for 5 minutes or until softened. Add the garlic, ginger, chili powder, curry powder, and ground cumin and cook, stirring, for 2 minutes. Add the coconut milk, brown sugar and the chopped peanuts. Reduce the heat and cook for 5 minutes or until the sauce thickens. Add the lemon juice and season with sea salt and freshly ground black pepper. Serve as a dip or a sauce for barbecued meats, pork, lamb, beef, or chicken.

note For a smoother sauce, wait until the mixture has cooled slightly and then process in a food processor for 30 seconds. Return to the heat to warm the sauce.

1 cup unsalted peanuts, roasted
2 tablespoons oil
1 onion, chopped
2 garlic cloves, crushed
2 teaspoons grated ginger
½ teaspoon chili powder
2 teaspoons curry powder
1 teaspoon ground cumin
1 ⅔ cups coconut milk
3 tablespoons soft brown sugar
1 tablespoon lemon juice

jumbo shrimp with peanuts

serves 4

Peel and devein the jumbo shrimp, leaving the tails intact.

Combine the shrimp with the scallion, garlic, ginger, sambal oelek, coriander, turmeric, lemon zest, lemon juice, and peanuts. Cover and refrigerate for 1 hour.

Heat the oil in a frying pan, add the shrimp mixture and stir-fry over high heat for about 3 minutes or until the shrimp are cooked. Serve with rice.

2 pounds 12 ounces raw jumbo
  shrimp
4 scallions, chopped
1 garlic clove, crushed
1 teaspoon grated ginger
1 teaspoon sambal oelek
1 teaspoon ground coriander
½ teaspoon ground turmeric
1 teaspoon grated lemon zest
1 tablespoon lemon juice
⅔ cup chopped unsalted
  roasted peanuts
2 tablespoons peanut oil
steamed rice, to serve

nuts ■ peanuts

pecans

produce ■ nuts
season ■ harvested in fall

A North American native, the pecan was an important food for the indigenous peoples; the Algonquin called it *paccan*, which French settlers later turned into "pecan." Botanists assumed, because of the huge numbers growing there, that the pecan tree was originally from Illinois—hence the scientific name *Carya illinoinensis*, although its original home is more likely to have been Texas or Louisiana.

There are hundreds of varieties of pecan grown today, many of which have been specially developed to produce large nuts with thin shells, generally better-tasting and with a longer shelf life than their ancestors. Pecans are grown now in Australia, Israel, Brazil, and South Africa although the United States still grows most of the world's supply.

Like other nuts, pecans are incredibly nutritious. They contain no less than nineteen different vitamins and minerals, including high levels of zinc, which helps in the generation of testosterone. They also contain antioxidants.

culinary uses

Pecans are used in similar ways to their walnut relative, although their flavor is somewhat smoother and sweeter. Toss them into salads or include them in breads, cakes, tarts, and stuffing for meats, although they are arguably at their most memorable in decadent classics such as pecan pie and butter pecan ice cream.

selection and storage

The freshest pecans are those available in fall, when the nut meat is sweet and moist. Keep the nuts cool as their high monounsaturated fat content (around 75 percent) can quickly cause rancidity.

Shelled nuts are best stored in the refrigerator where they will maintain freshness for up to 3 months. Unshelled nuts will store at cool room temperature for up to 3 months—for longer storage times, both shelled and unshelled nuts should be frozen.

mixed nut tartlets

Preheat the oven to 350°F. Spread the nuts on a baking sheet and roast for 7 minutes or until light golden.

Put the sifted flour and butter in a food processor. Pulse for 10 seconds or until the mixture resembles fine bread crumbs. Add about 1/3 cup water and process until the mixture just comes together. Add another tablespoon of water if needed, but do not overprocess as the pastry will be tough. Turn out onto a lightly floured surface and gather into a ball. Refrigerate for 20 minutes.

Lightly grease ten 3 1/4-inch fluted tartlet pans. Divide the pastry into ten equal-size portions. Roll each portion out on a lightly floured surface to fit the tartlet pans. Trim excess pastry, then refrigerate the pastry cases for 10 minutes.

Put the pans on two baking sheets. Cut sheets of baking paper to line the base and side of each pan. Put baking beads or uncooked rice in the pans and bake for 10 minutes. Remove the beads and paper and bake for an additional 10–12 minutes or until dry to touch and golden.

Divide the nuts among the pastry shells. Whisk together the brown sugar, sugar, corn syrup, extra butter, and eggs and drizzle the mixture over the nuts. Bake for 15–20 minutes or until just set and golden. Cool completely before serving.

2 cups mixed nuts (pecans, macadamias, and hazelnuts)
3 cups all-purpose flour
1 cup unsalted butter, chopped
3 tablespoons soft brown sugar
2 tablespoons sugar
3 tablespoons light corn syrup
1½ tablespoons butter, extra, melted
2 eggs, lightly beaten

nuts ■ pecans

Perhaps no dish is associated with a particular nut as is pecan pie, that staple of the American south. Its invention was suprisingly recent—it wasn't mentioned in cookbooks until the 1940s. Composed of pastry and a corn-syrup based, pecan-studded filling, pecan pie is incredibly sweet and best enjoyed ocassionally and in thin slices.

pistachios

produce ▪ nuts
season ▪ harvested late summer–early fall

selection and storage

Some processors open their pistachios mechanically, so make sure any nuts you buy have been allowed to open naturally on the tree, as their flavor will be superior. Once the pistachios' shells have split, the nuts have a limited shelf life, so store them carefully. This is best done in a container in the refrigerator (for up to 3 months) or frozen, for up to 6 months.

The Queen of Sheba knew a good thing when she saw it—she decreed that all pistachios grown in her domains be sent for the exclusive use of her court. An ancient food, the pistachio nut is just one of two nuts given mention in the Old Testament (the other is the almond) and is reputed to have been a feature of Nebuchadnezzar's fabled Hanging Gardens of Babylon. Certainly the pistachio was a founding crop in the Fertile Crescent of today's Middle East region where until recent decades it was almost exclusively grown—most notably in Iran.

Technically, the pistachio does not produce nuts at all but rather drupes, of which the pale green "nuts," or kernels, are the edible seeds. These grow in grapelike clusters and are enclosed in a pale shell. When the kernels ripen, they expand inside their shells causing them to split open at one end (prompting the Chinese to call them the "happy nut" and the Arabs the "smiling pistachio")—they are ready to eat when this happens.

Good pistachios should taste delicately sweet and buttery and be quite green—their characteristic pigment comes from chlorophyll and the greener the pistachios are the better the flavor. The brownish skin that covers the kernels is perfectly edible but can be removed by blanching in boiling water, if desired.

pistachio, yogurt, and cardamom cake

Preheat the oven to 350°F. Grease an 8-inch round cake pan and line the base with baking paper. Put the pistachios and cardamom in a food processor and, using the pulse action, process the mixture until pistachios are coarsely chopped. Add the butter, flour, and sugar and pulse for 20 seconds or until crumbly. Add the combined eggs and yogurt and pulse for 10 seconds or until just combined. Spoon into the pan and smooth the surface.

Bake for 45–50 minutes or until a skewer comes out clean when inserted into the center of the cake. Allow to cool in the pan for 10 minutes before turning out onto a wire rack.

To make the syrup, peel the zest off the lime with a vegetable peeler—remove any white pith from the zest. Put the sugar and 1/2 cup water in a saucepan and stir over low heat until the sugar has dissolved. Bring to a boil, then add the lime zest and cook for 5 minutes. Strain and cool slightly. Put the cake on a serving plate, pierce with a skewer, and pour the hot syrup over the cooled cake.

1 cup unsalted pistachio nuts
1/2 teaspoon ground cardamom
2/3 cup unsalted butter, chopped
1 1/2 cups self-rising flour
3/4 cup superfine sugar
3 eggs
1/2 cup plain yogurt

syrup
1 lime
heaping 1/2 cup superfine sugar

nuts ▪ pistachios

Fresh, soft, immature pistachios are available, fleetingly, in late summer and early fall. Their soft pink shell is stripped away to reveal a soft, sweet, green kernel. Serve these as a snack with a snifter of arak (a Lebanese liqueur that tastes of aniseed) or toss them through Middle Eastern-style salads.

walnuts

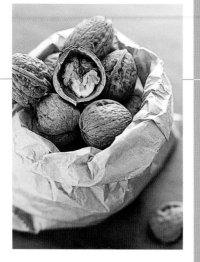

produce ▪ **nuts**
season ▪ **available year-round**

Purchase walnuts in the shell, crack them yourself and taste the sweet difference—the majority of shelled, packaged nuts are bitter and less than fresh, giving this delicious and versatile nut a bad reputation. The walnut fruits are classified as drupes. The nut we are most familiar with is that produced by the *Juglans regia* tree, one of over a dozen edible species of *Juglans*, of which the *regia* walnut is the largest and the most easily cracked. The name derives from the latin *Jovis glans*, meaning "regal nut of the Gods," although the name "walnut" is an English corruption of Gaul (or French) nut.

preparation

For certain uses (for pickling in the English manner or infusing into alcohol to make the delicious Italian digestive Nocino, for example) walnuts are picked while the shell is soft and immature and surrounded by a fleshy, green layer. Generally though, walnuts are used when fully mature and completely dried after harvesting. As a rough guide, 1 pound of walnuts in the shell will yield about 2 cups nut meat.

culinary uses

The world of cookery is awash with ways to use this delicious nut. In Italy it turns up in a version of pesto, whole in honey to spoon over gorgonzola and, in the north, in regional tarts and breads. Everyone knows the Greek sweet baklava, and is familiar with the English notion of serving cracked walnuts with Stilton cheese and port. In Asia and the Middle East the walnut is used in numerous sauces, including the famous taratoor.

selection and storage

Buy walnuts with undamaged shells and shake them first—if any rattle, it means the meat has withered inside the shell. The shells protect the meat from insects and light, and the nuts will keep, unshelled, for up to 1 year stored in a cool, dark place. Shelled nuts should be refrigerated for up to 3 months or frozen for up to 6 months.

walnut taratoor

Finely chop the walnuts in a blender or food processor. Set aside 1/2 teaspoon of the walnuts for a garnish. Add the bread crumbs, garlic, vinegar, and 3 tablespoons water and blend well. With the motor running, gradually add the olive oil in a thin steady stream until smooth. Add a little more water if the sauce appears to be too thick. Season to taste, then transfer to a serving bowl and refrigerate. Combine the reserved walnuts and parsley and sprinkle on top. Serve with seafood, salads, fried vegetables, or bread.

variation A taratoor can be made with almonds, hazelnuts, or pine nuts instead of the walnuts. Lemon juice can be used as a substitute for the vinegar.

2 1/2 cups shelled walnuts
1 cup fresh white bread crumbs
3 garlic cloves
1/4 cup white wine vinegar
1 cup olive oil
parsley, chopped, to garnish

nuts ■ walnuts

walnut and cheddar soda bread

makes 1 loaf

Preheat the oven to 350°F and line a baking sheet with baking paper.

Sift the flours, baking powder, and baking soda into a large bowl (tip any husks from the whole-wheat flour left in the sieve back into the mixture). Stir in the sugar, walnuts, and cheese. Make a well in the center. Combine the butter, eggs, and buttermilk in a bowl and pour into the well. Stir with a wooden spoon until a soft dough forms, then turn out onto a lightly floured work surface. Knead briefly just until smooth, then shape the dough into an 8-inch round. Transfer to the baking sheet.

Using a sharp knife, cut a 1/2-inch deep cross into the top of the loaf. Bake for 30–40 minutes or until golden. Remove from the tray and cool. Serve cut into slices, with butter.

2 cups all-purpose flour
1 1/2 cups whole-wheat flour
1 tablespoon baking powder
1 teaspoon baking soda
1 tablespoon soft brown sugar
1/2 cup walnuts, chopped
1 1/2 cups grated mature cheddar
   cheese
2 tablespoons butter, melted and
   cooled
2 eggs, lightly beaten
1 cup buttermilk

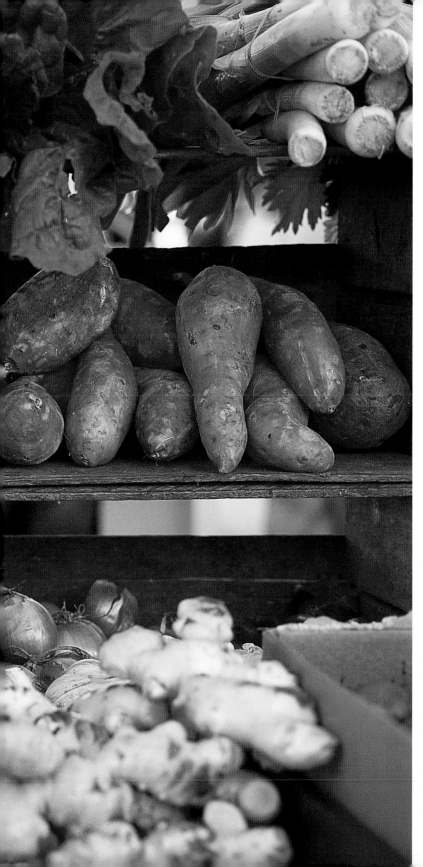

vegetables

beet
carrot
celeriac
ginger
horseradish
jerusalem artichoke
jicama
kohlrabi
parsnip
potato
radish
sweet potato
taro
turnip and rutabaga
asparagus
celery
fennel
garlic
leek
onion
rhubarb
scallion
shallot
sprouts
artichoke
broccoli
cauliflower
arugula
asian greens
belgian endive
brussels sprouts
cabbage
lettuce
radicchio
sorrel
spinach
swiss chard
watercress
avocado
bell pepper
chili
cucumber
eggplant
tomato
winter squash
zucchini
zucchini blossom
fava beans
green beans
okra
peas
soybeans
sugar snap and snow peas
sweet corn
cultivated and wild mushrooms
exotic mushrooms

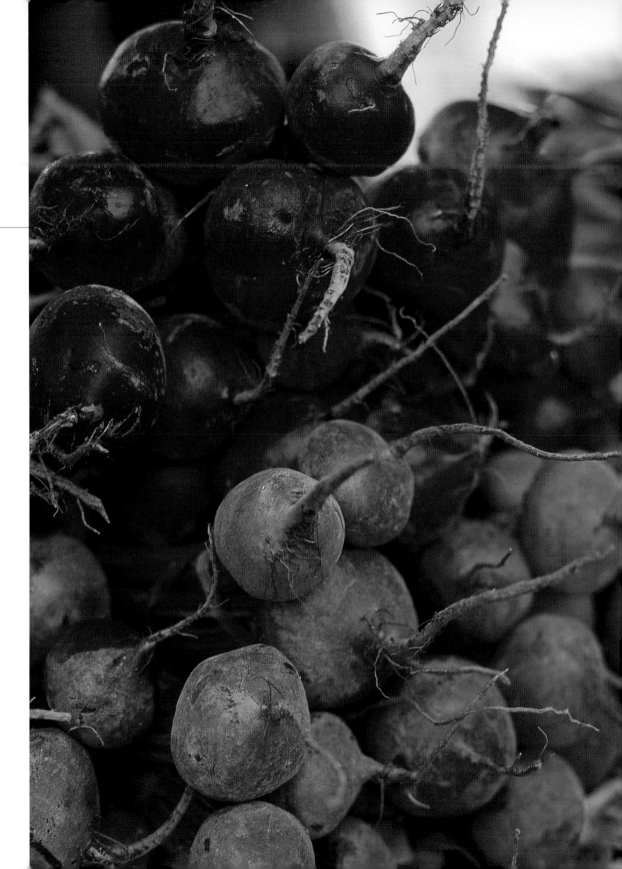

beet

vegetable ■ roots and tubers
season ■ available year-round

Beets are believed to be a vegetable from pre-history, once occurring wild over vast swathes of the northern hemisphere, from Britain all the way to India. Initially it was just their leaves that were appreciated—the Romans and Greeks consigned the roots to medicinal uses and Pliny the Elder (A.D. 23–79) referred to them as "those crimson, nether parts."

It wasn't until the third century AD that the roots were declared to taste "better than cabbage," as was noted at the time. And little wonder they were pronounced so good—beets contain more sucrose than any other vegetable.

Beets, although generally rounded, come in less-common elongated varieties and, increasingly, in "baby" golf-ball sizes. Recent hybrids have golden orange or white interiors while others, known as chioggia, are layered inside with concentric rings of pink and white. These hybrids have a more delicate flavor than the standard red sort, whose startling carmine color is due to the pigment betacyanin, to which some people are intolerant. In these individuals, the maroon color passes all the way through their systems without being absorbed, which, given its resemblance to blood, can prove a little disconcerting.

selection and storage

Always buy beets with the stems and leaves attached. These should look fresh and bright—a sign that the beets have been recently dug.
Try to choose bulbs that are approximately the same size (otherwise they'll all have different cooking times) and that have smooth, unblemished, tight skin.
Avoid any that are very big as these may be woody inside.

Use the leaves and stems within 2 days of purchase—these are delicious when chopped and stewed in olive oil with garlic, anchovies, currants, and a splash of red wine vinegar. Trimmed beets will keep, stored in a plastic bag in the refrigerator, for up to 10 days.

preparation

Sweet, earthy beets are unavoidably messy to prepare, leaving vivid, hard-to-remove trails of deep red on whatever their juices touch; chopping boards, hands, work surface. They also take what seems like an age to cook and perhaps this is why many people know beets only from their more user-friendly canned guise—which is a great pity, as these are but a pallid stand-in for the real thing.

Beets can be boiled, roasted, or steamed. It is advisable to cook them in their skins, as this preserves both flavor and color (much of the color bleeds out into cooking water if peeled). Don't cut off the long roots and only peel beets if you are using them in certain soup recipes that demand this.

Of all the ways to cook beets, baking or roasting results in the sweetest, most intense flavor as this dry method of cooking concentrates the flavors. Once tender, beets can be sliced, diced, or cut into wedges and used in salads, risottos, dips, and vegetable side dishes. Not all recipes require beets to be precooked, though. Certain soups, chutneys and even thin, crisp-fried "chips" are prepared using the raw vegetable, while finely grated, raw beet is often the basis for deliciously fresh-tasting salads. Whichever method of cooking you opt for, the preparation is identical. Simply cut off the stems and leaves, reserving these for some other use. Scrub the beets to remove all dirt; if roasting, pat dry.

boiling Cook large-medium beets in simmering, salted water for up to 1½ hours or until tender all the way through —a thin skewer is perfect for testing them. Baby beets will take only 20–30 minutes to cook. Drain well and allow to cool, then use your hands to slip the skins off (a pair of rubber gloves is useful here).

roasting Put beets in a roasting pan in a single layer and brush lightly with olive oil. Cook in a 350°F oven for about 1½–2 hours, depending on size or until tender when tested with a knife. Peel when cool enough to handle but still quite warm. Beets can also be wrapped tightly in foil before baking, which has a steaming effect—the beets won't shrivel as much and will be easier to peel but won't have the same concentrated flavor (see recipe on page 182).

steaming Cook beets over boiling water in a perforated, double-boiler arrangement or an electric steamer—large ones will take around 1¼ hours to reach tenderness, while baby beets will take about 20 minutes.

beet hummus

Put the chickpeas in a large bowl, cover with cold water and soak overnight.

Drain the chickpeas and put them in a large, heavy-bottomed saucepan with the onion. Cover with water and bring to a boil. Cook for 1 hour or until the chickpeas are very soft. Drain, reserving 1 cup of cooking liquid. Allow the chickpeas to cool.

Cook the unpeeled beets in a large saucepan of boiling water for 1½ hours or until tender. Drain and allow to cool slightly before removing skins.

Chop the beets and place in a food processor, in batches if necessary. Add the chickpea and onion mixture, tahini, garlic, lemon juice, and cumin and process until smooth. Slowly add the reserved cooking liquid and olive oil while the machine is running. Blend until mixture is thoroughly combined. Drizzle with a little olive oil to serve.

1 cup dried chickpeas
1 large onion, chopped
1 pound (about 3) beets
½ cup tahini (sesame seed paste)
3 garlic cloves, crushed
¼ cup lemon juice
1 tablespoon ground cumin
¼ cup olive oil, plus extra, to serve

roots and tubers ■ beet

beet chips

Use a sharp knife to cut the beets into paper-thin slices. Preheat the oven to 235°F.

Heat the oil in a frying pan over high heat and cook the beet slices, in batches, until they are crisp and browned. Drain on paper towels and keep warm in the oven while cooking the remainder of the chips.

Serve the beet chips with aïoli.

1 pound (about 3) beets, peeled
3 cups vegetable oil
aïoli (page 253), to serve

roasted beets with horseradish cream

8 beets
2 tablespoons olive oil
2 teaspoons honey
½ quantity horseradish cream
    (see page 199), to serve
chopped parsley, to garnish

Preheat the oven to 400°F. Scrub and peel the beets, trim the ends, and cut into quarters. Put the oil and honey in a small bowl and mix well. Season with salt and freshly ground black pepper. Divide the beets among four large squares of foil and drizzle with the honey mixture, turning to coat well. Wrap the beets loosely in the foil. Bake for 1 hour or until the beets are tender when pierced with a skewer.

Once the beets are cooked, remove from the oven and leave in the foil for 5 minutes. Remove from the foil and serve with a dollop of horseradish cream, and parsley to garnish.

beets and goat cheese salad

dressing
1 tablespoon red wine vinegar
2 tablespoons extra virgin
    olive oil
1 garlic clove, crushed
1 tablespoon salted capers,
    rinsed, drained, and chopped

4 beets, with leaves
2 cups green beans
⅔ cup crumbled goat cheese

To make the dressing, put all the ingredients into a screwtop jar, season with sea salt and freshly ground black pepper and shake. Trim the leaves from the beets. Scrub the bulbs and wash the leaves. Simmer the whole bulbs in a large saucepan of boiling water, covered, for 30 minutes or until tender.

Meanwhile, bring a separate saucepan of water to a boil, add the beans and cook for 3 minutes or until just tender. Remove with a slotted spoon and plunge into a bowl of cold water. Drain well. Add the beet leaves to the same saucepan and cook for 3–5 minutes or until the leaves and stems are tender. Drain and plunge into a bowl of cold water, then drain again. Peel the skins off the beets and cut into thin wedges.

To serve, put the beans, beet leaves, and beet wedges into a serving bowl. Sprinkle the goat cheese over the top and drizzle with the dressing.

carrot

vegetable ▪ **roots and tubers**
season ▪ **available year-round**

Carrots are essential to kitchens the world over;
there is barely a cuisine that does not rely on their
sweet, earthy presence in stocks, soups, stews,
salads, stir-fries, and sauces. Even in drinks
(consider the recent mainstream popularity of
carrot juice), preserves, cakes, and baked desserts,
carrots are an indispensable ingredient. And,
unlike many other root vegetables, carrots are
as delicious raw as they are cooked.

While we think of the carrot as a distinctively
orange-hued vegetable, the original carrots
(including some wild and heirloom varieties
available today) were white, yellow, pink, black, or
purple. Believed to have originated in Afghanistan,
carrots moved gradually westward over the
centuries, eventually ending up, via Arab traders, in
twelfth-century Spain. It is believed that the purple
carrot was being cultivated in Italy and other corners
of Europe in the fourteenth century—the orange
version, so familiar to us now, didn't come on the
scene until the 1700s. The orange carrot was
developed by the Dutch, motivated, it is believed,
out of patriotism for the ruling House of Orange.

The high vitamin A content of carrots (it
contains more than any other vegetable) is,
among other things, beneficial for retinal function.

baby carrots

Baby carrots, sometimes called Dutch carrots, are those which have been specially bred to mature when small, or are a larger variety that have been thinned out of the main crop. Most often these are sold in bunches with their green, feathery tops still on. You do not need to peel baby carrots, just give them a good scrub—with their cute size and sweet, juicy interior, they are perfect for serving raw or steaming whole.

preparation

roasting Although we tend to boil carrots, they are delicious when roasted, as this concentrates their sugars, which caramelize in dry heat. To do this, peel, then cut them into "pennies." Put them in a roasting pan with olive oil to coat and roast them for about 35 minutes, turning once, in a 350°F oven or until deep golden. Serve them at room temperature, doused in balsamic vinegar and sprinkled with sea salt and a handful of chopped mint.

culinary uses

Carrots generally play a support role in cookery, as one of many components in sauces, stews, or soups. Examples do abound though, of dishes where carrots are the star feature. In North Africa, a coarse, highly spiced, and lemony puree of carrot is served as an appetizer. The Indians make a carrot-based halva, a concentrated sweet dessert involving highly reduced, thickened milk, loads of grated carrot, and sweet spices.

A pureed carrot soup is delicious flavored with a little orange juice and finished with cream. To make such a soup, sauté 1 chopped onion and 2 pounds peeled, chopped carrots in a large saucepan over medium-low heat for 20–25 minutes or until completely tender. Cooking in their own juices renders carrots much sweeter than if they are simply boiled to softness in stock. Add 3¼ cups chicken or vegetable stock and 2 cups orange juice and simmer for 10 minutes. Puree the soup, adding more stock or juice if necessary. Season with sea salt and freshly ground black pepper and nutmeg, and finish with a dash of whipping cream.

Although there are few flavor scenarios the versatile carrot won't fit into, it has a special affinity with the following—dill, parsley, mint, butter, cream, walnuts, honey, raisins, cinnamon, and nutmeg.

selection and storage

Today, carrots are bred for consistency of color and size. Gone, it seems, are the days of wiggly, misshapen carrots—they all seem to be uniformly straight and thick. Choose mature carrots with smooth, unblemished skin, exhibiting no soft, shrivelled, brown, or wrinkled spots. The deeper the orange color, the higher in betacarotene the carrots are.

Avoid any with green "shoulders" as these have been exposed to sunlight and will be bitter. Don't buy overly large carrots either as these will have a tough, woody core and won't taste as sweet.

Generally, carrots are marketed without their luxurious, green tops—if you do happen to buy some with tops on, which should be green and fresh-looking with no signs of wilting or yellowing, cut these off for storage as they will drain the carrots of nutrients and moisture. Greens from extremely fresh young carrots have a distinctive, spicy taste and can be eaten chopped and tossed into a salad or soup.

serves 4

carrot and winter squash risotto

1/3 cup butter
1 onion, finely chopped
13/4 cups diced winter squash
2 carrots, diced
8 cups vegetable stock, heated
2 cups risotto (arborio) rice
1 cup shaved Romano or
　　Parmesan cheese
1/4 teaspoon freshly grated
　　nutmeg

Heat 3 tablespoon of the butter in a large, heavy-bottomed frying pan. Add the onion and fry for 1–2 minutes or until soft. Add the diced winter squash and carrot and cook for 6–8 minutes or until tender. Mash slightly with a potato masher. In a separate saucepan, heat the stock over medium heat and keep the stock at simmering point.

Add the rice to the vegetables and cook for 1 minute, stirring constantly, until the grains are translucent. Ladle in 1/2 cup of hot stock and stir well. Reduce the heat and add the stock little by little, stirring constantly for 20–25 minutes, until the rice is tender and creamy. You may not need to add all the stock, or you may run out and need to use a little water—every risotto is different.

Remove from the heat, add the remaining butter, the cheese, and nutmeg, season with freshly ground black pepper and stir thoroughly. Cover and leave for 5 minutes before serving.

The original, wild carrots were quite bitter and their first uses were medicinal. Their seeds were used as a spice, hardly surprising given that close carrot relatives include caraway, cumin, and cilantro. In ancient Greek and Roman times, carrots were used as a cure for everything from ulcerous sores, snakebite, and tumors, to bladder infections; during the Middle Ages they were thought to be a remedy for a miscellany of ills from syphilis to dog bite.

serves 4 # spicy carrot soup

2 tablespoons olive oil
1 onion, chopped
1 pound 12 ounces (about 8)
  carrots, chopped
1 bay leaf
1 teaspoon ground cumin
1 teaspoon cayenne pepper
1 teaspoon ground coriander
2 teaspoons paprika
5 cups vegetable stock
1 cup plain yogurt
cilantro leaves, to serve

Heat the olive oil in a saucepan, add the onion and carrot and cook over low heat for 30 minutes.

Add the bay leaf and spices and cook for 2 minutes. Add the stock, bring to a boil, then reduce the heat and simmer, uncovered, for 40 minutes or until the carrot is tender. Cool slightly, then blend in batches in a food processor. Return to the saucepan and gently reheat. Season with sea salt and freshly ground black pepper.

Mix the yogurt with the cilantro leaves. Pour the soup into bowls and top with a dollop of the yogurt mixture.

serves 4 # carrot pesto bake

1/4 cup butter
1/4 cup all-purpose flour
3 cups milk
2/3 cup sour cream
3/4 cup grated cheddar cheese
4 eggs, lightly beaten
2 tablespoons pesto (see
  page 411)
1 pound 10 ounces (about 7)
  carrots, grated
9 ounces (about 15 sheets)
  instant lasagna sheets
1/3 cup grated cheddar cheese,
  extra

Grease a 12 x 8-inch baking dish. Heat the butter in a large saucepan and add the flour. Stir over low heat until mixture is bubbling. Gradually add the combined milk, sour cream, and 1 teaspoon freshly ground black pepper. Stir constantly over medium heat for 5 minutes until the mixture boils and thickens. Remove from heat, stir in the cheese and cool slightly. Gradually add the beaten eggs, stirring constantly.

Preheat the oven to 300°F. Pour one third of the sauce into a separate bowl and set aside. Add the pesto and grated carrot to the remaining sauce, stirring to combine.

Put one third of the carrot mixture into the dish, followed by an even layer of lasagna sheets. Repeat this layering twice more, finishing with a layer of lasagna sheets. Spread the reserved sauce evenly over the top. Sprinkle with the extra cheese and bake for 40 minutes. Remove from the oven and set aside for 15 minutes before serving.

carrot cake with lemon frosting

Preheat the oven to 315°F. Lightly grease a 9-inch round cake pan and line the base and side with baking paper.

Sift the flours, spices, and baking soda into a large bowl and make a well in the center. Whisk together the oil, sugar, eggs, and corn syrup in a bowl until combined. Add this mixture to the well in the flour and gradually stir into the dry ingredients with a metal spoon until smooth. Stir in the carrot and nuts, mixing thoroughly.

Spoon the batter into the prepared pan and smooth the surface. Bake for 1½ hours or until a skewer comes out clean when inserted into the center of the cake. Leave the cake in the pan for at least 15 minutes before turning out onto a wire rack to cool completely.

To make the lemon frosting, beat the cream cheese and butter with electric beaters until smooth. Gradually add the confectioners' sugar alternately with the vanilla and lemon juice, beating until light and creamy. Spread the icing over the cooled cake using a flat-bladed knife. As an option you can serve it sprinkled with freshly grated nutmeg.

1 cup self-rising flour
1 cup all-purpose flour
2 teaspoons ground cinnamon
1 teaspoon ground ginger
½ teaspoon ground nutmeg
1 teaspoon baking soda
1 cup vegetable oil
1 cup soft brown sugar
4 eggs
½ cup dark corn syrup
2½ cups grated carrot
½ cup chopped pecans or
  walnuts

lemon frosting
¾ cup cream cheese, softened
¼ cup unsalted butter, softened
1½ cups confectioners' sugar
1 teaspoon natural vanilla extract
1–2 teaspoons lemon juice
freshly ground nutmeg, to dust,
  optional

roots and tubers ▪ carrot

The carrot was a favorite of Queen Elizabeth I (1533–1603). During the reign of James I, carrot leaves and flowers became a fashion statement— ladies even wore them in their hair and festooned their clothing with them. Carrots were also once favored as a powerful love potion—their effects were thought to make men more passionate and women more willing.

celeriac

A relative of the carrot family, as is celery, celeriac is an unpromising-looking brute of a vegetable. It has a bumpy surface, a brackish-colored skin, and tough, largely inedible stalks sprouting from its top, balanced by a hairy tangle of roots at its base. But with its subtle, celery-like flavor, celeriac is thoroughly delicious and suited to a range of cooking purposes.

It is believed celeriac was first cultivated in the Mediterranean, where it was used medicinally until the seventeenth century, and then as a food only sparingly. However, somewhere along the food-history line somebody discovered the possibilities of this root—celeriac makes dreamy puree, either solo or in tandem with potato, ditto creamy gratins and smooth soups (celeriac and chestnut soup is simply heavenly).

Celeriac is also extremely delicious raw, cut into matchsticks and tossed with mayonnaise, mustard, lemon juice, and parsley (as in the classic French salad, celeriac remoulade), or cut into very thin slices and fried, to become chips.

selection and storage

Celeriac keeps well, in fact it will keep in the ground long after the stalks are killed off by the first frosts.

Avoid buying celeriac that are overly large, as these tend to have cottony centers. Select bulbs that are very heavy for their size, that feel firm and are about the size of a baseball; these will have the crispest, most dense interior. If they still have their leaves, these should be bright green, and bulbs that are freshly harvested will have a green tinge around their tops.

Celeriac bulbs, trimmed of their stalks, will keep in a bag in the coolest part of the refrigerator for up to 10 days.

preparation

To prepare celeriac you need to remove and discard the stalks and leaves, then remove all of the thick skin with a sharp knife. This can seem like quite a wasteful exercise, as rather a lot of trimming is necessary to get rid of all the root material at the base. Put cut or sliced pieces of celeriac into a bowl of acidulated water (water with lemon juice) as you go, as the flesh quickly oxidizes on contact with the air.

Celeriac can be grated or cut into matchsticks for putting in salads—good partners for its aniseed taste include watercress, crumbled goat or blue cheese, walnuts, hazelnuts, apples, capers, anchovies, olives, boiled eggs, and oranges. As its flavor tends to dominate, celeriac can be tempered by a quick blanching in boiling salted water before tossing in a salad.
boiled Peeled chunks of celeriac can be boiled in salted water for about 15 minutes or until tender. They can then be mashed with butter and cream or tossed with a little butter and black pepper and served as a side dish with sausages, smoked meats, chicken, or fish. Celeriac can also be cut into matchsticks and deep-fried in hot oil until golden and crisp. If using this method, it is best to parboil the celeriac first for quicker cooking. The matchsticks go well served with fish, chicken, or beef.
roasted Celeriac can be roasted much like potatoes, in olive oil or butter. Peel celeriac, then cut into 5/8-inch wedges. Toss generously in olive oil to coat, then arrange in a large roasting pan in a single layer. Cook in a 400°F oven for 20–25 minutes, or until tender and golden.

culinary uses

Celeriac mash is brilliant—you can also cook celeriac and potato together, then mash them for a milder flavor, or cook peeled and cored Granny Smith apples with celeriac and mash together for a sweet-tasting variant. Either of these scenarios also make for winning soups of the pureed, creamy sort.

celeriac remoulade

To make the mustard mayonnaise, whisk the egg yolks, vinegar, and mustard together. Add the oil, drop by drop from the tip of a teaspoon, whisking constantly until it begins to thicken, then add the remaining oil in a very thin stream. If you're using a food processor, pour the oil in a thin stream with the motor running. Season with sea salt and freshly ground black pepper and, if necessary, thin with a little warm water. Set aside until required.

To make the remoulade, put 4 cups cold water in a large bowl and add half the lemon juice. Roughly grate the celeriac and place in the acidulated water. Bring a saucepan of water to a boil over high heat and add the remaining lemon juice. Drain the celeriac and add to the saucepan. After 1 minute, drain again and cool under running water. Pat dry with paper towels. Toss with the mayonnaise, capers, gherkins, and parsley. Serve with a baguette.

mustard mayonnaise
2 egg yolks
1 tablespoon white wine vinegar
 or lemon juice
1 tablespoon Dijon mustard
⅔ cup light olive oil

juice of 1 lemon
2 celeriac, trimmed and peeled
2 tablespoons capers, rinsed and
 drained
5 gherkins (cornichons),
 chopped
2 tablespoons finely chopped
 parsley
baguette, to serve

celeriac mash

serves 4

Put 2 cups cold water in a large bowl and add half the lemon juice. Chop the celeriac into cubes the same size as the potatoes, then put in the acidulated water until ready to use.

Put the potato and celeriac in a saucepan with the milk and bring to a boil over high heat. Cover and cook for 15 minutes or until the celeriac and potato are tender. Mash together with the milk. Season with sea salt and freshly ground black pepper and stir in the butter to serve.

variation To make celeriac and apple mash, add 2 peeled, cored, and coarsley chopped apples to the potato and celeriac; boil with the milk and continue as above.

juice of ½ lemon
1 celeriac, trimmed and peeled
1 potato, cut into cubes
1 cup milk
1 tablespoon butter

roots and tubers ■ celeriac

ginger

vegetables ■ roots and tubers
season ■ available year-round

Ginger is one of the world's most popular spices and has been known and used for so long that its wild origins are not clear. It is believed to be native to the south of India, from where it spread to the Western world at least 2,000 years ago; the Romans traded in ginger and by the time of the Norman Conquest in 1066 it was familiar to the tables of England. Botanically, the edible part of the ginger plant is a fat rhizome, which creeps under the ground, sprouting new stalks as it goes. The plant produces no seeds, and one theory about this is that it has been cultivated for so long the plant has forgotten how!

Ginger has some powerful culinary, medicinal, and preservative properties. Its ability to combat nausea is legendary, hence the use of ginger ale or ginger tea to treat mild gastro illnesses, motion and morning sickness, and recent research shows it can also play a role in reducing cholesterol. It contains a substance called protease, a protein-digesting enzyme, which tenderizes meats, while powerful antioxidants in ginger have been shown to retard food spoilage. This, it has been conjectured, is why ginger was initially used so heavily in baked items in England and Europe—not only does gingerbread in its many guises taste sensational, it is extremely long-keeping as well.

For other ginger recipes see:

selection and storage

Ginger should feel solid and heavy—the harder the rhizomes are, the better. Don't purchase ginger that is soft or shows signs of withering (indicating dryness and old age) or mold.

The age of the ginger when harvested has a distinct bearing on flavor. Young or "early-harvest" ginger has a light, thin, tan-colored skin with pinkish tips, and is juicier, crisper and milder than more mature ginger. Ginger that has a late harvesting has thicker and dark-tan skin, with hard, quite fibrous flesh and a far stronger flavor.

The size of the "hands" of ginger are not indicative of quality or age but are the result of where, and under what conditions, it was grown.

Ginger will store in an airtight container in the refrigerator for several weeks.

preparation

Fresh ginger bears little resemblance to its dried, powdered counterpart, which is only good for baking. Fresh ginger can be sliced, cut into matchsticks, chopped, grated, or ground to a paste.

Unless you have very young ginger, it is necessary to peel it before use—a small, sharp paring knife is best for this. To cut ginger into matchsticks, slice ginger thinly, then stack the slices on top of each other, in batches, and cut these into fine strips. To chop these, turn the strips 90 degrees on your board and, holding them together, cut them into very small pieces.

Alternatively, use the finest hole of a grater to grate ginger; you can also purchase purpose-made ginger graters from Asian food stores or kitchenware store. These are generally either wooden or ceramic. A small food processor is ideal for reducing chopped ginger to a fine paste, as is often required when making Indian or Southeast Asian curries.

Some recipes call for ginger juice—this is easily extracted by placing freshly grated ginger in a piece of cheesecloth and squeezing firmly to collect the juices.

culinary uses

Fresh ginger is most useful in Asian-style dishes; it is a vital component of stir-fries, curries, condiments, and braises from Burma to Beijing, Seoul to Surabaya. Generally it is sautéed first, perhaps with garlic or onion, which tempers its hot edge somewhat.

The longer ginger cooks, the mellower it becomes. Fine shreds of young ginger can be sprinkled over fish to be briefly steamed or added to a quick-cooking stir-fry, while older, hotter tasting ginger is best used in slow-simmering dishes such as curries and braises. Raw, it adds a healthy zing to freshly made juices, such as carrot, apple, and ginger juice.

fish in ginger broth

Heat the oil in a large saucepan, add the scallions and ginger and cook over low heat for 2 minutes, stirring occasionally. Add the fish sauce, jaggery, and 6 cups water and bring to a boil. Reduce the heat, add the fish and poach gently for 3–4 minutes or until the fish is just cooked and flakes easily when tested with a fork. Lift the fish out with a slotted spoon and put in a warm shallow bowl. Cover with foil to keep warm.

Bring the liquid in the saucepan to a boil, reduce the heat and simmer until reduced by half. Add the lime juice.

Cook the peas in a separate saucepan of boiling water for 5 minutes or until tender, then drain well. To serve, put the fish in bowls, ladle the broth over the top, then divide the peas among the bowls. Garnish with cilantro.

1 tablespoon oil
8 scallions, sliced diagonally
2 tablespoons finely chopped ginger
1/3 cup fish sauce
4 tablespoons grated jaggery or soft brown sugar
4 (7-ounce) salmon or ocean trout fillets
2 tablespoons lime juice
1 1/3 cups fresh peas (about 14 ounces unpodded)
cilantro leaves, to garnish

roots and tubers ▪ ginger

pickled ginger

makes 1 cup

Peel and cut the ginger into 1-inch pieces. Sprinkle with 2 teaspoons salt, then cover and refrigerate for 1 week.

With a sharp knife, cut the ginger into paper-thin slices across the grain. In a saucepan over low heat, dissolve the sugar in the rice vinegar and 2 tablespoons water. Bring to a boil and simmer for 1 minute.

Put the ginger into a hot sterilized jar, cover with the marinade, seal and refrigerate for 1 week before using. The ginger will turn pale pink or it can be colored using 1 teaspoon grenadine. Store in the refrigerator for up to 3 months.

4 1/2-inch piece ginger
2 tablespoons sugar
1/2 cup rice vinegar
1 teaspoon grenadine, optional

horseradish

vegetables ▪ **roots and tubers**
season ▪ **spring–fall**

Horseradish belongs to the mustard family, which will hardly surprise anyone acquainted with its hot, peppery flavor. Generally sold in jars, often prepared as a creamy condiment to eat with roast beef, horseradish is available in limited supply fresh each season and is well worth trying in this form. It presents as a hard, gnarly root—sometimes so hard and fibrous it can barely be cut with a knife.

selection and storage

Fresh horseradish is usually sold in short sections—entire roots measure up to 20 inches in length and 1–2 inches in diameter. Choose roots, or sections of them, that are very firm with no damp or moldy patches, nor any green or shrivelled-looking areas. Horseradish needs to be stored in the refrigerator, in a sealed plastic bag in the crisper section, where it will last for 7–10 days, although it will decrease in pungency somewhat during storage.

preparation

Before using horseradish you need to peel off the tough skin and, if the roots are older, remove the fibrous central core, as well as any green bits. Horseradish is best used finely chopped or grated and, in common with garlic and onions, the finer it is chopped, the more volatile compounds it releases and the stronger it tastes. Horseradish devotees insist that it should be prepared just before it is needed as the flavor starts to dissipate the moment the cut flesh has contact with the air. Perhaps the easiest way to finely chop horseradish is in the food processor, after first cutting it into pieces; the vapors from it can seriously hurt your eyes and throat, so beware of breathing these in.

culinary uses

Horseradish can be used in soups and stews (cooking renders it quite mild so add it near the end of cooking if you want a mustardy hit of flavor) although it is, arguably, at its best in sauces and condiments to accompany meats and fish. Grated horseradish in a vinaigrette dressing is great over raw oysters or a salad with beef, beets, spinach leaves, and walnuts, or one with dill in a potato, fennel, steamed mussel, and watercress salad. An apple sauce spiked subtly with horseradish is sublime with smoked eel, smoked mackerel, or smoked trout.

horseradish cream

Whip the cream until it starts to thicken, then fold in the horseradish, lemon juice, sugar, and a pinch of salt. Don't overwhip the cream as the acid from the lemon juice and horseradish will act as a thickener—if the cream is heavily whisked from the start it may split. Store horseradish cream in a hot sterilized jar and serve with beets, smoked salmon, or roast beef dishes.

⅔ cup heavy cream
2 tablespoons grated fresh horseradish
2 teaspoons lemon juice
1 pinch sugar

roots and tubers ▪ horseradish

If you have more fresh horseradish than you can easily use, you have a few options. One is to finely grate the flesh and freeze it in small, usable quantities—it will lose some pungency in the freezer but will last for 6–8 weeks. Another is to finely grate or process it and to add a little sugar, some salt, and a good slosh or two of white wine vinegar, stir to mix well, then store in a tightly sealed jar in the refrigerator. It will keep for 4–5 weeks and you can use it in sauces, condiments, and dressings as you would fresh.

jerusalem artichoke

vegetables ▪ roots and tubers
season ▪ late fall–early spring

selection and storage

Jerusalem artichokes look rather like large fresh ginger rhizomes, but with lighter, more translucent, thin skin. They can be plump, rounded and beige or longer, much knobbier and a reddish color.

The very warty, protuberant ones can be time-consuming to prepare, as getting rid of all the skin (either by peeling or scrubbing) with its attendant detritus, takes patience. The skin, however, is perfectly edible so if you find smoother specimens, a good wash and light scrub will suffice.

Choose tubers that are firm, of even size (so they will all be cooked at the same time), and show no signs of softness, green, or sprouting. Store them, in a plastic bag, for up to 2 weeks, in the refrigerator.

In a reverse of the usual trend, the Jerusalem artichoke was sent to the Old World in 1616 by North American settlers who thought the Europeans might like it. They were quite right and now this tuber is more popular there than in its homeland, where Native Americans had cultivated it for aeons.

The name is confusing—it is not an artichoke at all but a member of the sunflower family, nor is there any connection to Jerusalem—this is an English corruption of the Spanish *gerasol* and Italian *girasole*, which mean "turn to the sun," or "sunflower." Whatever the etymology, the Jerusalem artichoke, also called the sunchoke, has a deliciously sweet, nutty, and earthy flavor and, when raw, a pleasantly crisp texture. It has a high calcium content and appreciable levels of vitamins A, C, and some of the B group, plus the minerals iron, magnesium, and phosphorus.

culinary uses

Jerusalem artichokes make delicious soup, especially when pureed with a finishing touch of cream. They can be roasted in butter, or boiled and mashed with potatoes. They can also just be boiled or steamed and served as an accompaniment to simple meat or fish dishes. They collapse when overcooked so check them regularly to guard against this. Jerusalem artichokes can be used raw in salads, as a crudité with dips, or pickled in vinegar. Peeled, cut into very thin rounds, then patted dry, they can be deep-fried and salted and served as a snack with drinks.

warm salad of jerusalem artichoke, radicchio, and pastrami

Peel the Jerusalem artichokes. Cut any large ones to give pieces of roughly the same size. Put the artichokes in a nonreactive saucepan of boiling salted water with the lemon juice. Simmer for 12 minutes or until tender, then drain. When cool, slice the artichokes on a diagonal.

Preheat the broiler to hot. Trim off any coarse outer leaves from the radicchio and quarter it lengthwise. Put the radicchio, cut side up, in a medium, shallow heatproof dish, sprinkle with walnuts and drizzle with half the oil. Broil for 1–2 minutes or until the leaves start to pucker and the edges start to brown. Remove from the heat and set aside to cool for 2–3 minutes.

Cut off the radicchio stems and return the leaves to the dish. Add the artichokes, orange juice, and parsley and season with salt and freshly ground black pepper. Toss lightly. Scrunch the pastrami pieces into loose balls and arrange them among the artichokes. Drizzle with the remaining walnut oil and return to the broiler. Broil for 1–2 minutes or until just beginning to brown. Top with the orange zest and serve immediately.

1 pound (about 7) Jerusalem
  artichokes (sunchokes)
juice of 1/2 lemon
1 Treviso radicchio
1/3 cup golden walnut pieces
1/4 cup walnut oil
juice of 1 orange
1 tablespoon chopped parsley
9 pastrami slices, halved
zest of 1 orange

Like jicama, Jerusalem artichokes can be grated, sliced, or cut into matchsticks and used raw in salads; their lovely flavor goes well with other nutty tastes (walnut, hazelnuts, pecans), with the sweetness of seafoods such as scallops, salmon and shrimp, and with the bracing flavors of mint, lemon, chives, or mustard—serve them tossed with mustard mayonnaise as a variation to the usual celeriac remoulade.

jicama

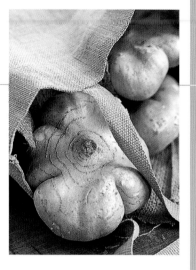

vegetables ▪ **roots and tubers**
season ▪ **fall–spring**

Called yam bean in parts of Asia, on account of the pods that develop on the vine it grows on, jicama is a Central American native and its name (pronounced HEE-kama) is Mexican. Part of the morning glory family, the plant was taken by the Spanish to the Philippines from where it spread throughout Asia. There is, though, just one variety of jicama, which can come in a variety of sizes—from a 7-ounce to a 5-pound, smooth, tan-skinned tuber. The appeal of jicama lies in its exceptionally crisp, juicy flesh. Ivory-white, the flesh is rather like that of a water chestnut but has a subtle, alluring flavor all its own. Jicama is most useful as a salad vegetable, when its delicious and refreshing crunch can be put to great use.

preparation

Jicama must first be peeled. If you have chosen your tubers well, the skin will be thin and come off easily. A paring knife is best for this as there is a layer of fibrous flesh just under the skin that also needs to be removed. In very fresh tubers the skin will simply pull off.

Unlike other root vegetables (such as potatoes or celeriac), jicama won't discolor with advance preparation so you can prepare it before you need it. Once peeled, you can slice it, grate it, fashion it into matchsticks, batons, or cubes, depending on your requirements. Jicama can be used in stir-fries, braises, and soups, or steamed with a selection of other vegetables—unusually, it absorbs flavors without losing its characteristic crunch.

selection and storage

Choose jicama with smooth, tight, silky skins that feel heavy and dense for their size. Blemished, raggy-looking tubers, or those with dull skin are likely to be old—their interior will yield fibrous, tasteless, starchy flesh.

This vegetable keeps well and can be stored in the refrigerator for up to 2 weeks—do not store them in plastic as they need air to circulate around them.

tuna and jicama remoulade rolls

To make the jicama remoulade, combine the garlic, ginger, cilantro, and mayonnaise in a bowl and stir to mix well. Add the jicama, season with sea salt and freshly ground black pepper and stir to combine. Set aside until required.

Using a thin, sharp knife, cut the tuna into 1/16–1/8-inch thick slices. Place each slice on a work surface and, using the heel of your hand, gently flatten them. Divide the remoulade amongst the tuna slices, placing it down the middle of each piece, then roll the tuna around the filling to form tight rolls. Serve the tuna rolls immediately, with lime wedges and soy sauce passed separately.

jicama remoulade
1 garlic clove, crushed
2½ teaspoons very finely chopped ginger
1 large handful cilantro leaves, chopped
½ cup ready-made egg mayonnaise
1 pound 10 ounces (about 2) jicama, peeled and cut into fine matchsticks

1 pound sashimi-grade tuna, blood line removed
lime wedges, to serve
soy sauce, to serve

roots and tubers ■ jicama

The jicama is used in Mexican cookery, where its blandness is complemented well by the flavors of chili, lime juice, orange, or cilantro. Elsewhere its crunch takes well to the textures of avocado, pineapple, and peanuts. In Vietnam, the tuber is pickled and served as an accompaniment on the lunch or dinner table, while in Indonesia and Malaysia it is included in the vigorously flavored salad rojak, *an intriguing mix of fruits and vegetables in a sweet-sour tamarind dressing.*

kohlrabi

vegetables ■ roots and tubers
season ■ peak season late summer–early winter

Kohlrabi, with its crisp texture and broccoli-stalk-crossed-with-cucumber flavor, is relatively young as far as vegetables go—the first record of it was in 1554 and today, in many parts of the world, it remains a little-known oddity. A curious-looking specimen, kohlrabi is one of the very few vegetables to have originated in Northern Europe.

It is technically not a root vegetable at all since the fleshy part isn't a tuber—rather, it is a swollen, above-ground stem. Kohlrabi is a member of the brassica family and theories abound that it, along with other family members (such as broccoli and Brussels sprouts), is descended from wild cabbage. Over the centuries, selective breeding has emphasized aspects of the original plant (leaves, flowers, stems), depending on local preferences.

"Kohlrabi" is German for "cabbage turnip" and, not surprisingly, that nation has the distinction of being the world's largest consumer of it. Kohlrabi has, historically, been used medicinally to strengthen and repair gums, teeth, and bones. It does contain significant amounts of bone-building compounds (calcium, iron and phosphorus) as well as vitamins A and C.

It occurs in two colors—pale green and purple. The purple sort has a sweeter, more pronounced flavor—both varieties have pale greenish, crisp flesh.

selection and storage

Larger kohlrabi tend to be woody so select small to medium globes that are free of surface cracks, bruises, or splits.

Leaves, if they have been left on, should be green and fresh-looking with no yellowing or wilting. The leaves are edible but need to be stored separately, so cut them off and store in a ventilated bag in the refrigerator.

The leaves will last just a few days, while the bulbs, stored in the same manner, will keep for several weeks.

preparation

Kohlrabi is enormously versatile; the only constant is that it needs to be peeled. Cut off stems, saving the tender leaves, if desired. Used raw, kohlrabi is delicious on a vegetable platter—slice it into half-moons or thick batons if using this way. Grated, finely diced, or cut into matchsticks, it is wonderful in salads, especially slaw-type ones that are dressed with rich, homemade mayonnaise.

blanching A quick blanching of prepared kohlrabi intensifies its flavor somewhat—blanch peeled, whole, small kohlrabi or halved, larger vegetables for 3–4 minutes in boiling water. Drain, then slice, dice, or grate and use in salads or other cold dishes.

steaming Kohlrabi can be steamed or boiled. Depending on their size they will take 15–30 minutes to become tender. Once they are tender, they can be sautéed, stir-fried, or added to soups and braises during the last 20 minutes of cooking.

culinary uses

Kohlrabi pairs well with creamy, cheesy sauces (Gruyère and blue cheese especially), and can be hollowed out, stuffed (with meat and breadcrumb mixtures or rice, cheese, and the blanched, chopped flesh and trimmed stems) then baked or braised in stock. Kohlrabi has also become popular in certain Asian cuisines, notably Vietnamese, where it is used in everything from salads to spring roll fillings, and in Chinese cookery where it is a winner in stir-fries and braises.

The leaves, trimmed of tough stems, can be blanched then sautéed in a little butter and served as a side dish with mushrooms. They can also be put to nutritious use in soups and stews and also in stuffings for baked kohlrabi, tasting not unlike Swiss chard.

szechuan-style kohlrabi braise

Dry-roast the peppercorns in a heavy-bottomed frying pan over low heat for 3 minutes or until fragrant—take care not to burn the peppercorns. Using an electric spice grinder or in a mortar using a pestle, very finely grind the peppercorns. Set aside.

Heat 2 tablepoons of oil in a large frying pan, add half the pork and cook over medium-high heat for 5–6 minutes, turning often or until golden all over. Transfer pork to a bowl. Add remaining pork and repeat this process, adding more oil to pan if necessary, then remove second batch of pork to bowl, reserving the pan.

Add most of the stock, the wine, soy sauce, bean paste, rock sugar, star anise, garlic, and ginger to the pan. Slowly bring to a boil, stirring occasionally, until all the sugar is dissolved. Return the pork and a little more chicken stock to just cover, if necessary, then reduce heat to low. Gently simmer mixture for 1 hour or until pork is tender. Add the kohlrabi, stir to combine, then cook for an additional 20 minutes or until kohlrabi is cooked. Serve with steamed rice and Asian greens—braises taste better if left for a day, refrigerated, as the flavors will develop and deepen.

2½ tablespoons Szechuan peppercorns
peanut oil, to fry
2 pounds 12 ounces boneless, skinned pork leg or shoulder, trimmed and cut into 1¼-inch pieces
2 cups chicken stock
⅓ cup Shaoxing wine
1½ tablespoons soy sauce
⅓ cup Szechuan chili-bean paste, or to taste
⅓ cup coarsely crushed Chinese rock sugar
1 star anise
5 garlic cloves, peeled and bruised
1½-inch piece ginger, sliced
1 pound (about 2 small) kohlrabi, trimmed, peeled, and cut into ¾-inch pieces
steamed rice and Asian greens, to serve

roots and tubers ■ kohlrabi

parsnip

vegetables ▪ roots and tubers
season ▪ late fall–winter

The parsnip is closely related to carrots and celeriac, and has been utilized as a food for thousands of years. In fact, it was Europe's preeminent winter vegetable until the potato was introduced in the eighteenth century and ultimately usurped its position; from then on its popularity at the European table dwindled.

Like all produce of ancient origins, the parsnip has a fascinating history. Parsnips were so esteemed that the Roman emperor Tiberius had them brought to his Capri villa all the way from France and Germany. During the Middle Ages, parents gave their babies a parsnip to suck on when they needed pacifying—by this time the vegetable was enjoyed in savory as well as sweet dishes. Colonists took the parsnip to the New World where the early settlers used it to make everything from wines, pies, breads, and puddings, to chips and stews.

The parsnip has a unique, sweet-earthy flavor like that of no other vegetable, and it also has an interesting nutritional profile, being especially high in potassium, folic acid, and vitamin C.

preparation

Cut larger parsnips in half lengthwise and inspect the core; larger ones are likely to have a woody core, which is best removed before cooking. Peel parsnips just before cooking them as they discolor slightly on contact with the air; do not put them into acidulated water to prevent this or they will turn soggy.

While you may need to preboil parsnips in order to then use them in some other way (in a mash or baked into a gratin, for example), boiling isn't generally a good treatment for parsnips as they become water-logged and unpalatable.

steaming To steam parsnips, place peeled 2-inch thick rounds of parsnips in a steamer basket over boiling water. Cover and cook for about 10 minutes or until tender.

roasting To roast parsnips, peel and halve them lengthwise, then place in a large roasting pan in a single layer and drizzle liberally with olive oil, tossing to coat. Cook in a 400°F oven for 30–45 minutes (depending on size) or until golden and tender.

culinary uses

Home cooks tend to use parsnip largely as a roast vegetable to accompany meat or in a mash, classically, with potatoes or carrots. Parsnip has enjoyed something of a renaissance thanks to restaurant chefs rediscovering its sweet, nutty, earthy flavor, and putting it to more sophisticated uses.

Parsnips need richness to bring out their silky texture and nutty flavor; roasting in butter or olive oil, for example, or baking or pureeing with cream, are ideal. Roasted, cooled parsnips taste great in a salad—consider a combination such as roast parsnip tossed with arugula, walnuts, and prosciutto. They also pair beautifully with rustic pork sausage, roasted or broiled lamb or beef, bacon, and certain seafoods (scallops and salt cod, for example). They take well to the flavors of nutmeg, Gruyère cheese, ginger, orange, balsamic vinegar, and curry.

selection and storage

Parsnips taste best during the colder months; their quality falls off once the weather warms up. They are always sold without their green tops as these contain an irritating juice that can cause a serious rash on some people.

The freshest parsnips will have smooth, creamy-beige skin; avoid any with browning on their skin or with tops that have started to sprout. The latter indicates they will be woody in the middle. Select ones that feel heavy for their size and try to pick them of a similar size so they will all cook at the same time. They should feel very hard and not be even slightly bendy, which indicates age.

Parsnips come in a variety of shapes—from very elongated and tapering, to fat, short, and stumpy; maximize meatiness by choosing fatter, stumpy ones. Generally, toughness and the presence of fibers is due to long storage and not size, so if possible, taste for sweetness and tenderness before you purchase. Parsnips will keep, refrigerated in a loosely sealed plastic bag, for up to 1 week.

serves 4–6

parsnip and leek puree

1 leek, white part only, thinly
    sliced
3 large parsnips, peeled and
    chopped
2 tablespoons snipped chives
2 tablespoons butter
3 tablespoons crème fraîche

Put the leek and parsnips in a saucepan of boiling salted water. Cook for about 10 minutes or until tender. Drain well and allow to cool slightly before blending in food processor. Process to a smooth puree.

Put the puree in a clean saucepan and add the chives and butter. Season with sea salt and freshly ground black pepper. Cook until the puree is heated through. Remove from the heat and stir in the crème fraîche (you may not need to use all of it). Serve with grilled lamb cutlets, roast beef, or pork.

serves 4–6

parsnip and mustard soup

2 tablespoons butter
1 onion, chopped
1 pound 10 ounces (about 6)
    parsnips, chopped
4 cups vegetable stock
½ cup milk
½ cup whipping cream
2–3 tablespoons wholegrain
    mustard
2 tablespoons chopped Italian
    parsley

Melt the butter in a large saucepan, add the onion and cook over medium heat, stirring often, until soft but not brown.

Add the parsnip and stock and bring to a boil. Simmer, covered, for 25 minutes or until the parsnip is tender. Set aside to cool slightly.

Blend the soup in batches in a blender or food processor. Return to the pan, add the milk and cream and reheat gently, but do not allow the soup to boil. Stir in the mustard and season to taste with salt and freshly ground black pepper. Serve with chopped parsley as a garnish.

parsnip and pecan fritters

To make the dipping sauce, combine the sour cream, chives, lemon juice, and sweet chili sauce in a serving bowl. Add the Tabasco sauce to taste. Set aside.

Peel the parsnips, cut them into chunks and immediately place in a saucepan of water. Bring to a boil. Add ½ teaspoon salt, reduce the heat and simmer for 15–20 minutes or until tender, then drain and allow to cool slightly.

Puree the parsnip with a potato ricer or mouli, discarding any tough bits. Transfer to a bowl and mix with the egg, flour, parsley, butter, milk, pecans, and cayenne pepper. Season with sea salt and freshly ground black pepper.

Heat the oil in a nonstick frying pan over medium heat. Drop in large tablespoons of the mixture, in batches, and flatten slightly with the back of a spoon. Cook, turning once, for 15–20 seconds on each side or until golden. Remove with a slotted spoon and drain on paper towels. Serve hot, with the dipping sauce.

dipping sauce
heaping ¾ cup sour cream
1 tablespoon finely snipped chives
1 teaspoon lemon juice
2 tablespoons sweet chili sauce
3–4 drops Tabasco sauce

3 parsnips
1 egg
¼ cup all-purpose flour
1 tablespoon chopped parsley
3 tablespoons butter, melted
¼ cup milk
⅔ cup pecans, coarsely chopped
1 pinch cayenne pepper
1 cup oil

roots and tubers ■ parsnip

The Romans adored parsnips—they ate them for dessert with honey and fruits, and baked them into sweet cakes. According to the Roman epicure Apicius, parsnips were also combined with a sauce containing celery seed, honey, rue, raisin wine, stock, and oil and, unusually, included in a vegetable sausage that they roasted and served with wine sauce.

potato

For such a poisonous plant (only the tubers are edible), the potato has made an incalculable impact on the global diet, providing more protein and energy than any other food crop, per unit of land. And who doesn't love the humble potato? From Chile to China, from Ireland to Idaho, potato dishes furnish countless societies with goodness, calories, and comfort.

We have the sixteenth-century Spanish explorers to thank for bringing this nightshade (as in "deadly") family member out from its South American obscurity and into the wider gastronomic world—although until it was discovered that their vitamin C content was a worthy cure for scurvy, potatoes were mainly fed to pigs.

The potato has come a long way since then. It's the "little black dress" of the food world—or, as American food writer Linda Wells observed, it is to food "what sensible shoes are to fashion." Dependable and adaptable, with the ability to move between dressed-up glamour and simple, satisfying understatement, the potato is equally tempting whether dolloped with caviar, mashed with cream to an unctuous puree, roasted with rosemary to crisped perfection, curried in a slew of exotic spices, or simply baked to tenderness in its earthy jacket then topped with chips of cold butter.

selection and storage

Avoid potatoes that feel soft or spongy or have any discoloration, bruises, or blemishes. Also, don't buy any that are showing signs of sprouting as these have simply been stored for too long.

Any green areas (and you may not detect these until you peel your potatoes) should be cut away and discarded—they contain a toxic substance called solanine. The greening occurs through excessive exposure to light; similiarly, cut off any eyes that are starting to sprout.

Light and humidity are enemies of the potato, so for good storage, dark, dry conditions are best. Avoid refrigeration, plastic bags, and sunlight at all costs as these promote softening, sprouting, and spoiling.

During storage (and in the correct conditions potatoes will keep for 10–12 weeks), the starch in potatoes slowly converts to sugar. New potatoes, and small, thin-skinned varieties, should not be stored but used quickly within a few days.

new potatoes

"New" potatoes are those that are a little immature and have been harvested from plants that still have their green leaves, usually during the winter months. The skin of the new potato is fragile, thin, and "feathery"; their flesh dense, fresh-tasting, and moist. The singular flavor and texture of new potatoes is best showcased by the simplest cooking methods—they require only boiling or steaming and perhaps enhancing with the flavors of mint, sea salt, or butter.

nutrition

Potatoes are a rich source of vitamin B6, contain more vitamin C than your average orange, have very decent amounts of niacin, iodine, folic acid, copper, and magnesium and offer around 5 percent of their mass in protein.

Much of the potato's nutritional goodness is stored in (or just under) the skin, so don't peel unless necessary for aesthetic reasons (if making a potato salad, for example, or mashed potatoes). Alternatively, boil potatoes whole first, in their skins, then cool slightly, peel, and prepare. When boiled or baked whole with skins intact, potatoes retain most of their vitamins and nutrients.

varieties

Before exploring the names of specific potatoes it is worthwhile understanding the different "types" of potatoes, which are quite separate to their variety. Floury potatoes are dry, have a low sugar content but are high in starch—these are perfect for baking, mashing, and frying. Waxy potatoes have moist, dense flesh and are low in starch—ideal for boiling, using in salads and gratins, or adding raw to stews, as they will not lose their shape when cooked. All-purpose potatoes (and many of the varieties commonly available from supermarkets fall into this category) have been specially bred to span all possible uses.

Most new potatoes, red-skinned potatoes, and many of the fingerling varieties are waxy, while most old potatoes are floury. Because of starch, sugar, and moisture variations (due to growing and storage conditions and the season a particular potato is harvested) there can be floury and waxy examples of the same variety available. With increasing "heirloom" and "boutique" potato varieties available, and more suppliers selling potatoes by named variety, it is easy to buy the best potato for the particular purpose (boiling, mashing, roasting, frying) you have in mind.

Varieties of potatoes and their growing seasons vary the world over but, loosely, potatoes can be divided into the following categories.

blue-fleshed Although of ancient origin, blue and purple-fleshed potatoes are a novel addition to the modern potato scene and are a fun thing to serve at dinner parties—serve lilac-hued mashed potatoes and watch reactions around the table! These varieties vary in color and texture enormously—the eccentric color is their only commonality, so it may require some experimentation to see how they behave when cooked.

fingerlings These types are small and long and tend to have superior flavor and texture, making them ideal for steaming and boiling and for use in salads.

old potatoes

"Old" or maincrop potatoes are those harvested when their vines are blooming; the flesh of these specimens is drier and their skins thicker than their "new" counterparts. They are generally stored in cool, dark conditions to extend their availability—the majority of potatoes purchased in supermarkets are "old." Any of the potato varieties, however, can be harvested new or old.

golden (tan-skinned) Within this category are an enormous number of varieties, which run the entire gamut of cooking and preparation possibilities: from frying, boiling, and mashing to roasting, baking, and steaming.

red-skinned This group generally represents waxy, full-flavored varieties that are great for boiling, baking, or steaming.

preparation

Unless cooking them immediately, place peeled or cut potatoes into a bowl of water, as the flesh will discolor slightly.

boiling Place potatoes, either whole and unpeeled, cut and unpeeled (if very large), or peeled and cut, into a saucepan and cover with cold water. Add salt and bring to a boil, then simmer, uncovered, for 15–20 minutes (depending on size) until tender. Drain potatoes well the minute they are cooked or they will become unappetizingly soggy.

baking Scrub unpeeled potatoes, prick them several times with the point of a small, sharp knife, then place directly on a rack in an oven at 400°F. Cook them until they are tender when tested with a thin metal skewer—depending on the size and the variety, this will take between 50 minutes and 1¼ hours. Do not wrap potatoes for baking in foil first as this will steam them, not bake them.

roasting Parboil small, unpeeled potatoes, or halved medium-size potatoes, for 20 minutes or until tender but still quite firm. Drain very well and leave in the colander for about 15 minutes to allow as much moisture as possible to evaporate. Toss potatoes into the roasting pan with whatever you are roasting (chicken, lamb, pork, beef), turning them occasionally to coat well in the rich cooking fats and juices and to let them brown and crisp on all sides—this will take 45–55 minutes in a 350°F oven. To roast them on their own, toss to coat in olive oil and cook them as above.

united states

Bintje
Concord
Early Chio
German Butterball
La Ratte
Purple Peruvian
Russet
Yukon Gold

united kingdom

Jersey Royal
Kerrs Pink
King Edward
Maris Piper
Pink Fir Apple

australia

Chat
Coliban
Desiree
Kipfler
Nicola
Pontiac
Purple Congo
Sebago
Toolangi Delight
Spunta

potato masala

serves 4 as a side dish

2 tablespoons oil
1 teaspoon black mustard seeds
10 curry leaves
1/4 teaspoon ground turmeric
1/2-inch piece of ginger, grated
2 green chilies, finely chopped
2 onions, chopped
1 pound (about 3) boiling (waxy) potatoes, cut into 3/4-inch cubes
1 tablespoon tamarind puree

Heat the oil in a heavy-bottomed frying pan, add the mustard seeds, cover, and when they start to pop add the curry leaves, turmeric, ginger, chili, and onion. Cook, uncovered, for 5 minutes or until the onion is soft.

Add the potato and 1 cup water to the pan, bring to a boil, cover and cook until the potato is tender and almost breaking up. If there is any liquid left in the pan, simmer, uncovered, until it evaporates. If the potato isn't cooked and there is no liquid left, add a little more water and continue to cook. Add the tamarind puree and mix throughly. Season with sea salt and freshly ground black pepper. Serve hot.

potato croquettes

makes 12

1 pound 10 ounces (about 4) floury potatoes, coarsely chopped
2 tablespoons whipping cream or melted butter
3 eggs, lightly beaten
1/4 teaspoon nutmeg
all-purpose flour, to coat
1 1/2 cups dry bread crumbs
oil, for deep-frying

Cook the potato in a saucepan of boiling salted water for 8–10 minutes or until tender. Drain and return the potato to the hot pan and mash with a fork. Stir in the cream or butter, a third of the beaten egg, and the nutmeg. Season with sea salt and freshly ground black pepper. Spread the potato mixture evenly on a baking sheet, cover and refrigerate for 30 minutes.

Divide the mixture into twelve equal portions, then roll each portion into a sausage shape. Roll in the flour, shaking off the excess. Dip each croquette in the remaining egg, coat evenly in the bread crumbs, shaking off any excess. Cover and refrigerate for at least 2 hours.

Half fill a deep, heavy-bottomed frying pan with oil and heat until a cube of bread dropped into the oil browns in 15 seconds. Cook the croquettes in batches for 5 minutes each or until golden. Drain on paper towels and serve.

potato cake

Put the onion in a bowl, cover with cold water and leave for 1 hour. Drain well. Preheat the oven to 415°F. Line an 8-inch springform pan with foil. Grease the foil.

Melt the butter in a small saucepan, add the garlic and set aside. Put a layer of potato over the base of the pan, followed by layers of onion, butter, mozzarella cheese, and Parmesan cheese. Repeat the layers until you have used up all the ingredients, finishing with potato and keeping a bit of butter to drizzle over at the end. Season the layers as you go. Spoon the milk over the top.

Bake for 1 hour or until the top is golden brown and the potatoes are tender. If the top is overbrowning before the potatoes are done, cover with foil. Cool for 10 minutes before serving. Unclip the base of the pan, peel off the foil and transfer to a warm plate, to serve.

1 small onion, sliced into rings
1/3 cup butter
2 garlic cloves, crushed
2 pounds 4 ounces (about 6) floury potatoes, thinly sliced
2/3 cup grated mozzarella cheese
1/2 cup shaved Parmesan cheese
2 tablespoons milk

roots and tubers ■ potato

crisp potato wedges

serves 4

Preheat the oven to 425°F. Scrub and pat dry the potatoes and cut into thick wedges. Put the wedges in a single layer on a baking sheet.

Brush the wedges lightly with olive oil, sprinkle with sea salt and sweet paprika (or chili powder for a spicier flavor). Cook for 35–40 minutes or until the wedges are crisp and golden. Serve with sweet chili sauce or aïoli as a dipping sauce.

8 floury potatoes
olive oil, to brush
sweet paprika, to dust
sweet chili sauce (see page 339) or aïoli (see page 253), to serve

serves 4

potato gnocchi
with pancetta and sage

gnocchi
2 pounds 4 ounces (about 6)
   floury potatoes, unpeeled
2 egg yolks, lightly beaten
2 tablespoons grated Parmesan
   cheese
1½ cups all-purpose flour
all-purpose flour, extra, to knead

sauce
1 tablespoon butter
½ cup thinly sliced pancetta or
   bacon
8 very small sage or basil leaves
⅔ cup heavy cream
½ cup shaved Parmesan cheese

Prick the potatoes all over, then bake for 1 hour or until tender. Leave to cool for 15 minutes, then peel and mash, or put through a potato ricer or a mouli (do not use a blender or food processor).

Mix in the egg yolks and Parmesan cheese, then gradually stir in the flour. When the mixture gets too firm to use a spoon, work with your hands. Once a loose dough forms, transfer to a lightly floured surface and knead gently. Work in enough extra flour to give a soft, pliable dough that is damp to the touch but not sticky.

Divide the dough into six portions. Working with one portion at a time, roll out on the floured surface to make a rope about ⅝-inch thick. Cut the rope into ⅝-inch lengths. Take one piece of dough and press your finger into it to form a concave shape, then roll the outer surface over the tines of a fork to make deep ridges. Fold the outer lips in toward each other to make a hollow in the middle. Set aside and continue with the remaining dough.

Bring a large saucepan of salted water to a boil. Add the gnocchi in batches, about twenty at a time. Stir gently and cook for 1–2 minutes or until they rise to the surface. Remove with a slotted spoon, drain, then put the gnocchi in a greased shallow casserole dish or baking dish.

Preheat the oven to 400°F. To make the sauce, melt the butter in a frying pan and fry the pancetta or bacon until crisp. Stir in the sage leaves and cream. Season with sea salt and freshly ground black pepper and simmer for 10 minutes or until thickened.

Pour the sauce over the gnocchi, toss gently, then sprinkle the Parmesan cheese on top. Bake for 10–15 minutes or until the cheese melts and turns golden. Serve hot.

radish

vegetables ▪ roots and tubers
season ▪ peak season spring–fall

Radishes (*Raphanus sativus*), although a "root" vegetable, are members of the crucifer, or mustard family—hence their distinctive peppery flavor. Their hot, spicy jolt comes from enzymes in the skin. Peeling a radish would reduce this effect and indeed is necessary in "winter" varieties, but really, that distinctive, mustardy freshness is a large part of the radish's attraction.

Radishes have been eaten, in some form or another, for millennia. Red radishes were popular in ancient Turkey and Persia. The ancient Greeks thought much of the radish, even creating radish replicas made from gold. Their modern name is derived from *radix*, the Latin word for "root."

Today, the main types of radish you are likely to encounter are the familiar round red sort, the long, slender, white "icicle" radish, and the enormous daikon—these can grow up to 20 inches in length and over 4 inches in diameter. Although daikon radish is firmly associated with East Asia (the Japanese are reputed to grow more of this vegetable than any other), they actually originated in the Mediterranean. Some might be fortunate enough to source the black radish, which is popular in Eastern European countries and has black skin, ivory flesh, and a dryish texture with a pronounced, earthy flavor.

culinary uses

Radishes are very easy to grow, making them a favorite with home gardeners. In the main, it is the quick-growing, tender, crisp "spring" varieties that are common—"winter" varieties are harder skinned and require peeling and tend to be cooked rather than consumed raw. Mostly, tender-skinned types of red radish are used raw; once trimmed, washed, and sliced they generally get relegated to the green salad bowl.

Delicious though they are in this guise, they can be used in far more interesting ways. The French, for example, serve perfect little red radishes whole as an appetizer, accompanying them with quality, sweet, unsalted butter, sea salt, and pepper. Sliced radish makes a delicious sandwich filling, especially with cream cheese, dill, and slices of smoked salmon. Red radishes can also be steamed or roasted and served as a side dish with meats; cooking like this renders them soft and nutty. When braised in butter and raspberry or red wine vinegar, they become a sublime accompaniment to roast duck. In Middle Eastern cuisines they are variously pickled and used in colorful salad combinations, often with oranges and black olives, for example.

Black radishes, a winter vegetable, perform extremely well as a roast vegetable to serve with joints of meat, or can be grated raw to use as you would horseradish.

Daikon radishes are an Asian staple, particularly in Japan. Their name is Japanese for "great root" and they come in green, yellow, pink, and black varieties, too. They are said to aid the digestion of fatty foods and can be eaten raw (choose smaller specimens for this), though need to be peeled first, then grated or cut into very fine matchsticks. Daikon can also be used as one would a turnip, put into stews and soups where they provide a bright, refreshing note and offset the richness of meats. They can be stir-fried, finely grated and used as a garnish, pickled, baked, or simmered. The Japanese claim that cooking daikon in rice-soaking water enhances their white color and eliminates any sharp flavors.

selection and storage

Buy radishes with green, fresh-looking tops, as the tops will yellow and wilt very quickly. Not only do the tops indicate the roots are fresh, but they are delicious in their own right. Daikon tops, if you get them, are a rich source of vitamin C, betacarotene, calcium, and iron and can be simmered in soups or blanched, then dressed and used in salads.

Small radish varieties as well as their large daikon cousins should have firm, smooth skin with no signs of growth cracks, browning, or wrinkling.

Black radishes should feel very hard; any softness at all can indicate a "woolly" interior. Once home, cut off radish tops and store these separately—this prolongs the life of the roots. Keep radishes for up to 1 week in the refrigerator, stored in a ventilated plastic bag.

serves 4

crisp-skinned salmon with radish and cucumber salad

salad
1 large cucumber
2 celery sticks, thinly sliced
1 shallot, diced
1 avocado, diced
20 red or white radishes, halved
1 small handful cilantro leaves

dressing
1/3 cup olive oil
2 tablespoons lime juice
1 teaspoon finely grated lime zest
1 garlic clove, crushed
1 teaspoon honey

4 small salmon fillets, skin on
2–3 tablespoons olive oil
1 small handful cilantro leaves,
    extra

To make the salad, peel the cucumber and cut it in half lengthwise. Using a teaspoon, scoop out and discard the seeds. Slice very thinly into half-moon shapes and put in a large bowl. Add the celery, shallot, avocado, radishes, and cilantro.

To make the dressing, put the oil, lime juice, lime zest, garlic, and honey in a small bowl and mix well. Season with sea salt and freshly ground black pepper. Set aside until ready to serve.

Brush the salmon fillets lightly with olive oil and sprinkle the skin with a little salt. Heat the remaining oil in a large frying pan over high heat. When hot, add the salmon, skin side down, and immediately hold a spatula or another frying pan on top of the fillets to keep them flat. Fry for 1–2 minutes or until the skin is crisp and brown all over. Reduce the heat to medium and turn the salmon over. Cook until just opaque, 2–3 minutes, depending on the thickness. Drain on paper towels.

When cool enough to handle, use kitchen scissors to cut each salmon fillet across the grain into three strips. Break each strip into bite-size pieces. Add to the salad with the dressing and extra cilantro. Toss gently to coat and serve immediately.

daikon salad with sashimi

roots and tubers ■ radish

To make the dipping sauce, stir the soy sauce, ginger, and sugar in a small bowl until the sugar has dissolved. Set aside.

To make the salad, shave the daikon, cucumber, and carrot lengthwise into wide thin strips with a mandolin or a vegetable peeler and put in a large bowl. Cut the ginger into fine matchsticks and add to the bowl.

Just before you are ready to serve, add the scallion, sesame seeds, rice vinegar, soy sauce, and mirin and toss to coat. Divide the salad among four serving plates.

Lightly roast the nori by holding the sheet 2 inches above a low flame, moving it around to toast evenly for 2–3 seconds. Alternatively, toast it under the broiler for 2–3 seconds. Cut the nori into thin strips using scissors and sprinkle some over each salad.

Using a very sharp knife, slice the salmon and tuna into even 1/4-inch thick strips. Divide among the plates, arranging them in neat rows. Add a dab of wasabi to the plates and serve immediately with the dipping sauce.

dipping sauce
1/2 cup Japanese soy sauce
1 teaspoon grated ginger
1 pinch sugar

daikon salad
1/3 small (5 ounces) daikon, peeled
1 Lebanese (short) cucumber
1 carrot, peeled
1½-inch piece ginger
3 scallions, thinly sliced diagonally
1/2 teaspoon sesame seeds, roasted
2 teaspoons rice vinegar
2 teaspoons Japanese soy sauce
2 teaspoons mirin
1 sheet nori seaweed

9-ounce piece sashimi-quality salmon
9-ounce piece sashimi-quality tuna
wasabi paste, to serve

The Egyptians were eating red, white, and black radishes 4,000 years ago; laborers working on the great pyramids were sustained by these and other vegetables. Meanwhile in Asia, the Chinese were cultivating the black sort, and Indians and Indonesians were consuming white radishes.

sweet potato

vegetables ■ roots and tubers
season ■ available year-round

selection and storage

Most sweet potatoes are aged for some weeks in order for their sugars to develop—freshly harvested sweet potatoes are generally not sweet. Choose ones with smooth, unblemished skins, exhibiting no bruises, mold, or soft spots.

Only buy as many sweet potatoes as you need because they don't last very long; store them at room temperature in a well-ventilated spot for 2–3 days and not in the refrigerator.

Not a relation to the potato at all, the sweet potato, or *Ipomoea batatas*, is a member of the morning glory family. Sometimes falsely called yams, sweet potatoes are native to tropical parts of Central and South America and are yet another vegetable that Columbus took to Europe during his voyages of exploration. While they were embraced by the Spanish, the sweet potato didn't really catch on throughout Europe and has come to be largely associated with the cooking of the Americas, the Pacific, and the Caribbean. The Portuguese transported it to their Asian and African colonies where it rapidly spread, and today the sweet potato is an important staple in many countries in those regions.

Sweet potatoes are a troublesome lot to classify. There are several hundred different types and there is wide variance in their appearance and behavior when cooked. Their skin may be extremely thin or tough and thick. Skin color ranges from red to purple to orange to deep beige. Their flesh color varies too, depending on type (some are yellow fleshed, some orange and some ivory or white), as does the texture of their flesh and their sweetness once cooked.

varieties

Orange-fleshed sweet potatoes tend to have a pumpkinlike flavor and become very soft when cooked. Their sweetness is variable, depending on where they were grown and the particular cultivar. Those with creamy-white flesh and smooth purplish or rosy skins are classified as "Oriental" types, as they were developed in the Far East. These are quite sweet when cooked—their flesh turns translucent yellow and they are also rather moist, although they do hold their shape well.

Another sort, sometimes called the boniato, is large and heavy-looking with knobbly red-purple skin and pale flesh. This type is less sweet, and is fluffy and dry when cooked, with an appealing, slightly chestnut taste. Beige-skinned sweet potatoes, with their dark cream flesh, are a small, unprepossessing-looking vegetable but when baked, their flesh transforms into an incredibly sweet, moist substance.

preparation

Sweet potatoes can be boiled, mashed, roasted, baked, fried, made into fritters, and even used in baking and desserts. When baking or roasting, which is the method that most concentrates their sweet, nutty flavors, sweet potatoes will hold their shape best if left unpeeled. They can be cooked in much the same way as potatoes (see page 215), but it is important to note that they will take a shorter time to cook—wedges of sweet potato or 3/4-inch slices will take about 40–45 minutes to cook in a 400°F oven.

Similarly, when frying sweet potatoes, their high sugar content means they can easily burn, so do this at a lower temperature than you would for regular potatoes. It is generally better to steam sweet potatoes than to boil them (unless you are making mash), making it much easier to peel the skin after cooking. Sweet potatoes are also delicious when grilled—thinly slice peeled sweet potatoes, brush them with oil, then cook on a medium-hot barbecue grill plate for 2–4 minutes on each side until just tender.

culinary uses

Sweet potatoes are complemented well by the flavors of ginger, cinnamon and nutmeg, bacon, turkey, ham and chicken, and are luscious with butter, maple syrup, or brown sugar. They also go well in curries, especially coconut-cream based ones. The sweet simplicity of a well-roasted sweet potato, cooked to the point of near-collapse, however, is extremely difficult to beat.

sweet potato ravioli

Preheat the oven to 425°F. Put the sweet potato on a baking sheet and drizzle with oil. Bake for 40–45 minutes or until tender. Transfer the sweet potato to a bowl with the ricotta, basil, Parmesan cheese, and a third of the garlic. Mash together until smooth.

Line a baking sheet with baking paper. Cover the wonton wrappers with a damp dishtowel to stop them drying out. Place 2 level teaspoons of the sweet potato mixture into the center of one wonton wrapper and brush the edges with a little water. Top with another wrapper, pressing the edges together to seal. Put onto the prepared baking sheet and cover with a dishtowel. Repeat with the remaining ingredients to make about sixty ravioli, placing a sheet of baking paper between each layer on the tray.

Melt the butter in a frying pan. Add the scallion and remaining garlic and cook over medium heat for 1 minute. Add the cream, bring to a boil, then reduce the heat and simmer for 4–5 minutes or until the cream has reduced and thickened. Keep warm.

Bring a large saucepan of water to a boil. Cook the ravioli, in batches, for 2–4 minutes or until just tender. Drain well. Ladle the hot sauce over the top of the ravioli, garnish with the basil leaves and serve immediately.

1 pound 2 ounces (1 large or 2 small) orange sweet potato, cut into 3/4-inch chunks
1/4 cup olive oil
2/3 cup ricotta cheese
1 tablespoon chopped basil
2 tablespoons grated Parmesan cheese
3 garlic cloves, crushed
120 ready-made egg wonton wrappers (about 1 pound)
1/4 cup butter
4 scallions, sliced diagonally
1 1/4 cups whipping cream
baby basil leaves, to serve

roots and tubers ■ sweet potato

serves 4–6 # beef tagine with sweet potato

2 pounds 4 ounces blade or
  chuck steak
¼ cup olive oil
1 onion, finely chopped
½ teaspoon cayenne pepper
½ teaspoon ground cumin
1 teaspoon ground turmeric
½ teaspoon ground ginger
2 teaspoons paprika
2 tablespoons chopped Italian
  parsley
2 tablespoons chopped cilantro
  leaves
2 tomatoes
1 pound 2 ounces (1 large or
  2 small) orange sweet potato

Trim the steak of any fat and cut into 1-inch pieces. Heat half the oil in a saucepan and brown the beef, in batches, over high heat, adding a little more oil as needed. Set aside in a dish.

Reduce the heat to low, add the onion and the remaining oil to the pan and gently cook for 10 minutes or until the onion is softened. Add the cayenne pepper, cumin, turmeric, ginger, and paprika, cook for a few seconds, then add 1 teaspoon sea salt and freshly ground black pepper. Return the beef to the pan, add the parsley, cilantro, and 1 cup water. Cover and simmer over low heat for 1½ hours or until the beef is almost tender.

Peel the tomatoes. To do this, score a cross in the base of each one using a knife. Put the tomatoes in a bowl of boiling water for 20 seconds, then plunge them into iced water to cool. Remove from the water and peel the skin away from the cross—it should slip off easily. Slice the tomatoes. Peel the sweet potatoes, cut them into ¾-inch dice and leave in water until required.

Preheat the oven to 350°F. Transfer the beef and its sauce to an ovenproof serving dish (the base of a tagine would be ideal). Drain the sweet potato and spread it on top of the beef. Top with the tomato slices. Cover the dish with foil (or the lid of the tagine) and bake for 40 minutes. Remove the foil, increase the oven temperature to 425°F and raise the dish to the upper oven shelf. Cook until the tomato and sweet potato are flecked with brown and are tender. Serve immediately.

sweet potato phyllo pie

Preheat the oven to 400°F. Cut the sweet potato into 1-inch cubes and put in a large roasting pan, along with the shallots and baby potatoes. Combine the olive oil, paprika, ginger, cumin, and cinnamon in a small bowl and pour over the vegetables. Toss to coat. Roast for 25 minutes, then turn the vegetables and roast for an additional 15 minutes. Remove from the oven and reduce the oven temperature to 350°F.

Add the spinach and golden raisins to the vegetables. Toss lightly, then set aside for 5 minutes for the spinach to wilt. Transfer to a large bowl and add the almonds, pistachios, and cilantro. Put 2 tablespoons of the corn syrup, the yogurt, chickpeas, garlic, cayenne pepper, and lemon juice in a food processor and blend until smooth. Season with sea salt and freshly ground black pepper. Stir into the roasted vegetables.

Brush an 11¼ x 8¼-inch loose-bottomed rectangular tart pan with some of the butter. Brush a sheet of phyllo with butter and lay it diagonally over one end of the pan, so that the pastry overhangs on the sides. Don't push the pastry into the sides of the pan, just place it loosely on top. Brush another sheet of phyllo with butter and lay it similarly, at the opposite end of the pan. Brush a third sheet with butter and lay it in the middle of the pan. Continue in this way twice more, until all the phyllo is used.

Pile the sweet potato mixture in the center of the pan. Starting in the middle, bring the opposite sides of the phyllo together, encasing the filling tightly but with the phyllo points sticking up. Brush carefully with the remaining butter and drizzle the remaining corn syrup in zigzags over the top. Place the pan on a baking sheet and bake for 30 minutes or until golden. Set aside for 5 minutes before serving.

1 pound 10 ounces orange sweet potato (about 2 large or 3 small), peeled
12 small shallots, peeled
6 baby potatoes, peeled and halved
½ cup olive oil
1 teaspoon sweet paprika
1 teaspoon ground ginger
2 teaspoons ground cumin
¼ teaspoon ground cinnamon
2 cups baby English spinach leaves
½ cup golden raisins
⅔ cup slivered almonds, toasted
⅔ cup pistachio kernels, roughly chopped
1 cup cilantro leaves, chopped
2½ tablespoons dark corn syrup
⅓ cup plain yogurt
1½ cups drained canned chickpeas
3 garlic cloves, finely chopped
1 pinch cayenne pepper
¼ cup lemon juice
½ cup butter, melted
9 sheets phyllo pastry

roots and tubers ■ sweet potato

taro

vegetables ▪ roots and tubers
season ▪ available year-round

selection and storage

Choose corms that are heavy for their size and check closely for blemishes, signs of mold, or wrinkling; they should smell pleasantly fresh. As taro do not store well, use them quickly once purchased, and store in the refrigerator for no longer than 2 days.

Taro is an old, old food plant, having been cultivated for longer than wheat or barley and predating rice as the starch of choice in parts of China and Southeast Asia. Taro is often sold as dasheen, a corruption of the French, *de la Chine*, meaning "from China." Taro is inedible raw; it contains the toxin calcium oxalate, present as crystals; these are destroyed by cooking. There is only one species but hundreds of varieties. All taro corms are either large, at 3 pounds 5 ounces, or tiny at about 2 ounces—these smaller corms cluster around the "mother" corm.

preparation

Small corms are blander in flavor and moister than the large ones. They are more suitable for plain boiling and steaming. Larger taro can be fibrous, dry, and mealy when cooked, with a nutty sweetness. Expect their flesh to be cream-colored or gray or lilac and, sometimes, flecked with purple or brown fibers.

Protect your hands with gloves when preparing taro as it contains irritating compounds. Remove the thick, slightly hairy skin with a sharp knife, then slip chunks of the vegetable directly into acidulated water, as it rapidly discolors. Taro can be cooked in much the same way as a potato (boil peeled and cut taro chunks in a saucepan of boiling salted water for 15–20 minutes or until tender). Don't boil and then mash them as they will become inedibly gummy. Subsequent roasting after parboiling large chunks for 10 minutes in a 400°F oven, lightens the texture of taro, rendering it pleasantly sweet, dry, and chewy. When cooked in braises and stews, taro absorbs liquid, thus thickening the dish. Always serve taro while it is freshly cooked and hot; as it cools it becomes unappealingly stolid.

black sticky rice with taro

Put the black rice in a bowl and pour in enough cold water to come 2 inches above the rice. Soak for at least 3 hours or overnight if possible.

Drain the rice and add clean water. Scoop the rice through your fingers four or five times to clean it, then drain. Repeat two or three times with clean water to remove the unwanted starch. (The water will never be completely clear when using black rice, even when all the unwanted starch has gone.) Put the rice in a saucepan and add 2½ cups cold water.

Bring to a boil over high heat, stirring the rice frequently as it reaches boiling point. Reduce the heat to medium. Stir and simmer for 30–35 minutes or until nearly all the liquid has been absorbed. The rice should be very moist, but with hardly any water remaining in the bottom of the saucepan. Taste a few grains to check whether the rice is cooked.

Meanwhile, drain the taro, spread it on a plate, then transfer it to a steamer. Taking care not to burn your hands, set the steamer over a saucepan of boiling water over high heat. Cover and steam for 8–10 minutes or until the taro is tender.

When the rice is cooked, add the jaggery and gently stir until the jaggery has dissolved. Add the taro and gently mix.

Mix the salt into the coconut milk. Divide the black sticky rice among individual bowls and drizzle coconut milk on top. Serve warm.

1 cup black sticky rice
1 taro (10 ounces), cut into
 ½-inch squares and soaked
 in cold water
1 cup chopped jaggery
1 teaspoon salt
¾ cup coconut milk

roots and tubers ■ taro

turnip and rutabaga

vegetables ▪ roots and tubers
season ▪ peaking late fall–early spring

selection and storage

The sweetest turnips are those that appear in spring and fall. Winter turnips can have tough, thick skins and be on the large side but their flavor will still be good; it's not worth buying turnips in summer.

Try to buy turnips with their green tops still intact and fresh-looking—this will indicate they have just been harvested. Avoid any with shrivelled, wrinkled, or damaged skins.

Turnips don't suit long storage as they quickly turn bitter, so try to use them within a few days and store them in a plastic bag in the refrigerator.

Rutabagas, on the other hand, will last for more than 1 month in the refrigerator; stored in a dry cellar and packed in sand or sawdust, they can keep for nearly a year.

Choose rutabagas that are heavy for their size as these will be juicy, and that have undamaged skins. If you see them with their tops still attached (and this is rare), snap them up as this means they have been freshly dug.

Close relatives (the turnip is *Brassica rapa* while the rutabaga is *Brassica napus*), these vegetables are celebrated in the cuisines of certain countries, while spurned outright by others. The Scots wouldn't dream of serving haggis without their beloved "bashed neeps" (mashed buttered rutabaga) and the French have made an art out of richly flavored turnip braises (although they do feed rutabaga to cattle). Unfortunately however, many of us have been turned off these vegetables by memories of unappetizing lumps of boiled turnips and rutabagas served during childhood.

Rutabagas are known in other parts of the world as swedes. The name "swede" comes from the fact that this crop is common in Sweden. Rutabagas are not an ancient food; they are the result of a seventeenth-century crossing of a turnip with a cabbage. They have a delightfully sweet, earthy taste, pretty, pale orange flesh and, roughly the size of a baseball, have yellow-tan bases extending into mauve-colored tops, above which sprout stems and leaves.

Turnips, on the other hand, are a very ancient food; experts in such things believe they were first cultivated by man about 5,000 years ago.

roots and tubers ▪ turnip and rutabaga

preparation

Turnips should be peeled before cooking. Cut them into large chunks and boil in salted water. They can also be steamed in a double-boiler arrangement and either way will take the same time, 15–20 minutes.

Rutabagas can be prepared and cooked in exactly the same ways as turnips, but will take slightly longer to cook—about 20–25 minutes. You can also slip uncooked chunks of rutabaga or turnip into braises and stews and allow them to cook slowly in the liquid—give them extra time (almost twice as long) to reach complete tenderness.

culinary uses

Wonderfully versatile, there are many ways to use turnips and rutabagas. Both need to first be trimmed and peeled, although turnip greens can be lightly steamed or stir-fried, blanched, then baked into gratins or incorporated into soups. If the flesh just under the skin is tough and fibrous, you will need to pare this away too.

Both turnips and rutabagas are delicious raw, served with other vegetables with a dip as an appetizer, or cut into very fine slices or matchsticks and tossed through salads (a winter slaw, for example). Both are delicious steamed until *al dente*, then tossed with burnt butter or fruity olive oil—never overcook either vegetable as this ruins both their flavor and texture.

Both vegetables can also be added to the stew-pot (particularly great with lamb or beef) where they will impart sweetness as well as absorbing other flavors, while chunks of either are good when roasted with a leg of lamb. Both vegetables will mash beautifully with potatoes or puree into unctuous, creamy soups. Combined in the latter with winter squash, sweet potato or, unusually, pears or apples, even the most determined rutabaga and turnip detractors will be won over.

duckling with turnips

Preheat the oven to 400°F. Put a roasting pan in the oven to heat up. Truss the duckling by tying the legs together behind the body. Prick all over, put the bouquet garni in the cavity and season.

Heat the clarified butter in a large frying pan and brown the duckling on both sides. Lift the duckling out of the pan and pour all but 1 tablespoon of the fat into a bowl. Add the carrot, celery, and onion to the pan and cook, stirring, for about 10 minutes or until soft. Continue to cook until browned. Remove from the pan.

Add 2 tablespoons of the reserved duck fat to the frying pan over low heat. Add the sugar and cook until dissolved. Increase the heat and add the shallots and turnips. Caramelize over high heat, then remove from the frying pan. Pour in the white wine and boil, stirring, for 30 seconds to deglaze the pan.

Put the carrot, celery, and onion in the middle of the hot roasting pan, place the duckling on top and pour in the wine and stock. Add the turnips to the pan and roast for 45 minutes. Baste well, then add the shallots and roast for 20 minutes. Baste again and roast for another 25 minutes.

Take out the duckling, turnips, and shallots and keep warm. Strain the sauce from the bottom of the pan, pressing the chopped vegetables through a sieve to extract the juices, then discard the chopped vegetables. Pour the strained juice into a small saucepan and boil rapidly to reduce the mixture by half. Mix together the butter and flour. Whisk into the sauce and boil, stirring, for 2 minutes or until thickened.

Put the duckling, turnips, and shallots on a serving plate and pour the sauce over them to serve.

3 pounds 12 ounces whole
  duckling
bouquet garni (see page 413)
2 tablespoons clarified butter
1 carrot, chopped
1 celery stick, chopped
1/2 large onion, chopped
2 teaspoons sugar
8 shallots
8 baby turnips
1/3 cup white wine
2 cups chicken stock
2 teaspoons butter, softened
2 teaspoons all-purpose flour

roots and tubers ■ turnip and rutabaga

serves 4

spiced baby turnips

4 plum tomatoes
¼ cup olive oil
3 small onions, sliced
3 teaspoons ground coriander
1 teaspoon sweet paprika
4 baby turnips, trimmed
1 teaspoon soft brown sugar
1 pound 5 ounces (about
   1 bunch) Swiss chard
1 handful parsley

Score a cross in the top of each tomato, plunge into boiling water for 20 seconds, transfer to a bowl of iced water to cool, and then peel the skin and discard. Cut the tomatoes widthwise into 5/8-inch slices, then gently squeeze out most of the juice and seeds.

Heat the olive oil in a large frying pan over medium heat and fry the onion for 5–6 minutes or until soft. Stir in the coriander and paprika, cook for 1 minute, then add the tomato, turnips, sugar, and 1/3 cup hot water. Season well. Cook over medium heat for 5 minutes. Cover the pan, reduce the heat to low and cook for 4–5 minutes or until the turnips are tender.

Meanwhile, strip the Swiss chard leaves off the stalks (reserving the stalks for another use, if desired). Rinse the leaves under cold water and shake off the excess.

Stir the parsley and Swiss chard into the pan, check the seasoning and cook, covered, for 4 minutes or until the Swiss chard is wilted. Serve hot.

Throughout the Middle East, turnips are turned into exceptionally delicious pickles (as they are in Japan, Korea, and some parts of Russia), while in Finland a Christmas dish called tulaatiko, *where rutabaga is baked into a buttery pudding and flavored with nutmeg, cinnamon, and allspice, is a hearty winter favorite.*

finnish creamy-baked rutabaga

Preheat the oven to 350°F and grease a shallow 7 x 12-inch baking dish.

Cook the rutabagas in boiling salted water for 25 minutes or until tender. Drain well, return to the saucepan and, using a potato masher, mash finely—the mixture should still have some texture. Place the pan over medium heat and stir for 5–7 minutes, until the excess liquid has evaporated. Remove from the heat and cool slightly.

Stir the cream, eggs, egg yolk, flour, and spices into the rutabaga, then season with sea salt and freshly ground black pepper. Pour into the prepared dish, smoothing the top.

Combine the bread crumbs and butter in a food processor and process until fine clumps form, then sprinkle over the rutabaga mixture. Bake for 30–35 minutes or until golden and set in the middle. Serve hot or warm as a side dish to accompany roast or broiled meats.

variation You can substitute the same weight of turnips for rutabagas in this recipe if you prefer.

3 pounds 8 ounces (about 4) rutabagas, peeled and cut into 1½-inch pieces
½ cup whipping cream
2 eggs, lightly beaten
1 egg yolk
¼ cup all-purpose flour
½ teaspoon freshly grated nutmeg
1 small pinch of ground cloves
1¼ cups fresh bread crumbs
¼ cup unsalted butter, cut into cubes

roots and tubers ▪ turnip and rutabaga

By the time of Pliny the Elder in A.D. 23–79, the Greeks had developed many types of turnips, some of which Pliny describes in his writings. The Pantropheon records the way the Romans developed particularly elaborate ways of dealing with turnips—"… they were seasoned with cumin, rue, benzoin, pounded in a mortar, adding to it afterward honey, vinegar, gravy, boiled grapes, and a little oil …"

asparagus

vegetables ■ stems, shoots, and bulbs
season ■ spring–early summer

Resist all temptation to eat imported, out-of-season asparagus. This is a fragile vegetable, subject to moisture loss and damage, its sweetness slowly diminishing from the moment it is harvested. It is best eaten as close to the time and place of harvest as possible; which means waiting until spring, when the first tender spears appear at the market. Asparagus tips are actually leafy buds—if left to their own devices and not picked they develop into a very tall fernlike plant with bright red berries.

There are over 300 species of asparagus, including some wild varieties, which are highly esteemed in the Mediterranean regions where they grow. We are mostly familiar with green asparagus but there are also purple and white varieties. In many parts of Europe, "asparagus" means the white sort, actually the same type as green except for the way it is grown.

White varieties are grown in deep soil trenches or black plastic tunnels, which protect the spears from sunlight, thus interrupting the greening process of photosynthesis. The technique, called "blanching," is labor-intensive, making white asparagus an expensive treat. Purple asparagus, which turns green when cooked, doesn't taste much different to its green counterpart.

preparation

Bend asparagus at their base to find the point at which they naturally snap, break them, then discard the woody ends. Peel the bottom inch of green or purple asparagus using a paring knife or potato peeler, although if large, you may need to peel more—this depends how stringy they are. White asparagus spears always require peeling as their skin is tough and bitter. Take care when doing this as white asparagus is brittle and will easily break. Asparagus is traditionally boiled or steamed, then served as an accompaniment, or cooled and used in salads or other dishes.

boiling To boil asparagus, tie it into bundles of about eight spears each, using string, then cook it in boiling salted water for about 5 minutes or until tender. Drain well. Allow to cool without the use of cold water as this will just dilute its subtle flavor.

steaming To steam asparagus, cook it in bundles, covered, over boiling water for 6–7 minutes or until tender. Hot, cooked asparagus is at its best when tossed in extra virgin olive oil, melted in butter or, of course, served with a dollop of hollandaise sauce variation (see page 36) or a beurre blanc (see page 273).

culinary uses

Roasting in a little oil or brushing with oil, then broiling or barbecuing asparagus concentrates the sweet, herbal flavors. Cooked this way, asparagus become an earthy addition to an antipasti selection and stands up well to robustly flavored partners such as Parmesan cheese, bacon, olives, anchovies, or pesto. A platter of grilled asparagus goes well with aïoli (see page 253) as a party snack, and makes an excellent addition to a big summer salad of other grilled vegetables such as bell peppers, zucchini, eggplant, and Spanish onion.

selection and storage

Inspect the stem end and spurn any asparagus that is wrinkled, dried out, or split. Tips should be tight, bright, and clean—pass over ones that look weepy or floppy. Choose spears roughly the same size so they will cook at the same time.

Debate rages over the pros and cons of fat spears versus thin spears, with some claiming one to be vastly superior to the other—but this is not necessarily the case. By buying the freshest asparagus possible, you can't go too far wrong with either.

Store asparagus for no longer than 2 days in a plastic bag in the refrigerator.

serves 4

asparagus and mint frittata

6 eggs
1/3 cup grated pecorino or
    Parmesan cheese
1 handful mint leaves, finely
    shredded
16 baby asparagus spears
2 tablespoons extra virgin
    olive oil

Break the eggs into a large bowl, beat well, then stir in the cheese and mint and set aside. Trim the woody part of the asparagus, then cut on a diagonal into 2-inch pieces.

Heat the oil in a frying pan that has a heatproof handle. Add the asparagus and cook for 5 minutes or until the asparagus is tender. Season, then reduce the heat to low. Pour the egg mixture over the asparagus and cook for 8–10 minutes. Use a spatula to pull the side of the frittata away from the side of the pan, and tip the pan slightly so the uncooked egg runs underneath the frittata.

When the mixture is nearly set but still slightly runny on top, put the pan under a broiler preheated to low for 1–2 minutes, until the top is set. Serve warm or at room temperature.

tagliatelle with asparagus and herbs

serves 4–6

1 pound 2 ounces tagliatelle
    pasta
2 tablespoons butter
16 asparagus spears, cut into
    short pieces
1 tablespoon chopped parsley
1 tablespoon chopped basil
1 1/4 cups whipping cream
1/2 cup finely grated Parmesan
    cheese
extra Parmesan cheese, shaved,
    to garnish

Cook the pasta in a large saucepan of boiling salted water until *al dente*. Drain and return to the pan.

Heat the butter in a frying pan, add the asparagus and stir over medium heat for 2 minutes or until just tender. Add the parsley, basil, and cream. Season with salt and pepper. Cook for 2 minutes.

Add the grated Parmesan cheese to the pan and stir well. When thoroughly mixed, add the sauce to the warm pasta and toss gently to distribute the ingredients evenly. Serve in warmed bowls with shavings of Parmesan cheese.

celery

Celery is a somewhat utilitarian, underappreciated vegetable. It is one of those greens that most cooks have in their refrigerator, ending up chopped into a soup, a sauce, or a salad. Mainly providing background flavor and texture in dishes, celery is also considered classic dieters' food and, along with raw sticks of carrot, a predictable component of the predinner crudité platter.

There are two main types of celery grown commercially today—self-blanching celery, which is a yellowish color and is favored in Europe, and the green-stalked type, which is common in Asia, Australia, and the United States. Originally, all cultivated celery was "blanched"—grown in deep troughs with soil packed around the stalks to protect them from the greening effect of the sun. This was to produce less fibrous stalks, but modern breeding has made this growing method unnecessary.

Celery contains pthalides, an active component that relaxes the artery muscles that regulate blood pressure—it also reduces stress hormones which have a constricting effect on blood vessels. Celery has powerful diuretic properties and the volatile oils in celery seeds have been credited with effectiveness against a plethora of complaints: from flu and colds to liver and spleen ailments, poor digestion, and arthritis.

In ancient times celery was widely used for a variety of medicinal purposes, never culinary. The Greeks called celery selinon *and as such, it is mentioned in Homer's* Odyssey; *Pliny, Hippocrates, and Theophrastus wrote of it too. Celery was considered a holy plant in ancient Greece and its leaves were worn by victors in the Nemean Games, similar to the use of bay laurel at the more famous Olympic Games.*

selection and storage

The celery you are most likely to encounter at the markets will be vibrant green, with thick, juicy outer stalks and a profusion of leafy tops. The "heart" of a bunch of celery, which is much prized for its delicate flavor and texture, will be a tender, yellow color.

Try to always buy celery with leaves attached, as these are a good indicator of freshness. Take a good look over the outer stalks for signs of browning or limpness and avoid bunches with these. You shouldn't be able to bend the stalks at all (they should be snappingly crisp).

Store celery in the crisper section of the refrigerator in plastic, for up to 1 week—if very fresh, it may keep longer. Take care not to keep it in the coolest part of the refrigerator as, with a 95 percent water content, it may freeze.

preparation

The tough, outer stalks of celery are best suited for stocks, soups, sauces, braising, and baking, although they can, of course, be used in raw dishes such as salads.

Sometimes celery can benefit from peeling to remove the fibrous layer (a regular potato peeler is ideal for this) and discarding the dark green leaves and first inch or so of the stalks, although when washed, these can be utilized in making stocks.

culinary uses

Tender celery hearts, leaves included, are lovely in salads and other raw preparations such as salsa, or chopped with capers, lemon, onion, parsley, and a dash of olive oil and served with fish. Finely chopped and folded into homemade mayonnaise with a few capers and some mustard, they form the basis for an admirable sauce to have with fish or poached chicken.

Celery stands up well to cooking and it is a pity more cooks don't think of solo uses for it. A pureed celery soup (with a potato or two included, for a particularly velvety texture) is delicious, especially if finished with some cream and a crumbling of blue cheese. Continuing on the blue cheese theme, trimmed stalks of celery can be baked into a lush gratin with béchamel sauce and blue or Gruyère cheese; they can also be braised in the Italian sweet-and-sour way, with stock, vinegar, tomato, raisins, pine nuts, and anchovies.

Waldorf salad is legendary, as is the use of a celery stalk swizzle stick in a vodka-based Bloody Mary. Ring the changes by making a salad using celery hearts, crisp pears, and Parmesan and serving with slices of prosciutto, loads of olive oil, and some lemon juice, or serve the hearts simply with walnut bread and sweet cultured butter, as a prelude to an informal dinner or lunch.

waldorf salad

Line a serving bowl with lettuce leaves. Cut the apples into 3/4-inch chunks and place in a large mixing bowl with the celery and walnuts.

In a small bowl, combine the mayonnaise and sour cream and mix well. Fold the dressing into the apple, celery, and walnut mixture, then transfer to the lettuce-lined serving bowl and serve immediately.

lettuce leaves, to serve
2 red apples, quartered and cored
1 large green apple, quartered and cored
1½ celery sticks, sliced
¼ cup halved walnuts
2 tablespoons store-bought egg mayonnaise
1 tablespoon sour cream

braised celery

serves 4

Preheat the oven to 350°F. Grease a shallow baking dish.

Melt the butter in a large frying pan. Add the celery and toss to coat evenly in butter. Cover and cook for 2 minutes. Put the stock, lemon zest, and lemon juice into the pan. Cover the pan and simmer for 10 minutes. Remove the celery with a slotted spoon and place into the prepared dish. Reserve ¼ cup of cooking liquid.

Blend the cream, egg yolks, and cornstarch in a separate bowl. Whisk in the reserved cooking liquid. Return to the heat and cook until the mixture boils and thickens. Add parsley and mace and season with sea salt and freshly ground black pepper.

Pour the sauce over the celery in the dish. Cook in the oven for 15–20 minutes, until the celery softens. Serve warm with poached chicken breast, grilled lamb, or slices of corned beef.

2 tablespoons butter
1 bunch celery, trimmed and cut into 2-inch lengths
2 cups chicken or vegetable stock
2 teaspoons finely grated lemon zest
¼ cup lemon juice
¼ cup whipping cream
2 egg yolks
1 tablespoon cornstarch
1 small handful chopped parsley
½ teaspoon ground mace

stems, shoots, and bulbs ■ celery

fennel

vegetables ■ stems, shoots, and bulbs
season ■ fall, spring–early summer

In 1824, an American official, posted to the
Italian city of Florence, sent some fennel seeds
to the former U.S. president, Thomas Jefferson,
along with a gushing letter: "fennel is beyond every
other vegetable, delicious …" The Americans,
though, along with various other nations, were
slow to catch on to what the Italians have known
forever—that fennel is a wonderful and versatile
vegetable. Although commonly referred to as a
"bulb," cultivated fennel is not a true bulb at all
but rather has thickened leaf stems; it is this
that distinguishes it from wild fennel which,
in favorable conditions, grows like a weed.

In ancient times, the use of fennel was
believed to improve eyesight and, curiously,
Pliny's contemporaries in A.D. 23–79 thought
snakes ate fennel to help them shed their skins.
In 1614, author Giacomo Castelvetro wrote that
fennel "improves the taste of bad wine," claiming
that scurrilous merchants offered fennel to tasting
customers, presumably to mask any vinous
inferiority they might taste.

Fennel has numerous health-giving properties—
it is rich in vitamin C, iron, magnesium, folate,
and phosphorus.

preparation

Fennel can be enjoyed raw or cooked. To serve raw, trim tops and base of smaller bulbs with a small, sharp knife, discarding any outer leaves that are tough and fibrous. The stalks can be sliced and the leaves finely chopped for raw use—soak stalks in iced water to make them crisp. Cut the bulb in half lengthwise and trim the core. Slice fennel into paper-thin slices for salads or slightly wider strips if serving as crudités. Prepare the fennel just before using, or place in a bowl of acidulated water (water with lemon juice), for once it is cut, fennel discolors.

For braising and roasting, cut halved, trimmed bulbs into wedges, but don't trim the core as this will hold the fennel together. Fennel can also be finely chopped or sliced, then sautéed for use in sauces, various vegetable dishes, or stews.

roasting To roast fennel, brush wedges with olive oil, arrange in a tight-fitting single layer in an oiled baking dish and season with sea salt and freshly ground black pepper. Cook in a 350°F oven for 35–40 minutes (depending on size), turning once or until tender.

braising To braise fennel, pour hot chicken stock over wedges in a dish to nearly cover, add a generous amount of olive oil, sprinkle with fresh thyme and season with sea salt and freshly ground black pepper. Cover the dish tightly with foil and cook in a 350°F oven for 35–45 minutes or until tender.

culinary uses

Fennel has many uses. Salads are an obvious one—thin raw slices (or shaved fennel) pair well with any of the following: oranges (especially the voluptuous blood), capers, olives, almonds, watercress, radicchio, Parmesan, pecorino, and goat cheese. It is sublime tossed with homemade anchovy or tuna mayonnaise, or dressed with olive oil and lemon juice and served on a platter with prosciutto or smoked salmon.

Lightly cooked and tossed through pasta, fennel begs for cream, lemon, and parsley. Braised in stock, fennel wedges complement fish or chicken—although it is important to note that cooking does mute its bright aniseed flavors somewhat. Braised fennel is also good with a cheesy sauce, or serve blanched slices baked in cream with nutmeg, thyme, and a sharp cheese.

Finely chopped fennel is excellent cooked in a tomato sauce. Thin slices of fennel, cut lengthwise from the bulb, can be dusted in flour or cornmeal and shallow-fried until golden and tender, making a sensational addition to an antipasti selection.

selection and storage

Never purchase fennel without its tops as these indicate freshness. Tops should be bright green with no signs of wilting; the bulbs should be tight, firm, and a creamy green-white color. Pass over any that look wrinkled, are bruised, or whose outside layers are loose and flabby looking.

The size of bulbs can vary significantly. The smaller ones will be milder and therefore excellent for slicing thinly and serving raw in salads or as crudités—larger ones can also be used this way but are also suitable for cutting into quarters or large wedges and roasting or braising.

Fennel doesn't keep especially well; store it in a plastic bag in the refrigerator for up to 4 days.

stems, shoots, and bulbs ■ fennel

serves 6

florentine roast pork

3 large fennel bulbs
1/2 tablespoon finely chopped
  rosemary
4 garlic cloves, crushed
3 pounds 5 ounces pork loin,
  chined and skinned
3 white onions
1/3 cup olive oil
3/4 cup dry white wine
1/3 cup extra virgin olive oil
1 cup chicken stock
3–4 tablespoons heavy cream

Preheat the oven to 400°F. Cut the green fronds from the tops of the fennel and chop to give 2 tablespoons fronds. Add these to a small bowl with the rosemary, garlic, and plenty of sea salt and freshly ground black pepper. Make deep incisions with a sharp knife all over the pork and rub this mixture into the incisions and the splits in the pork bone. Cut two of the onions in half and place in a roasting pan. Put the pork on top of the onion and drizzle the olive oil over the top.

Roast in the oven for 30 minutes. Baste the pork with the pan juices, then reduce the temperature to 350°F. Roast for another 30 minutes. Baste and lightly salt the surface of the pork. Pour in half the white wine. Continue roasting for 30–45 minutes, basting once or twice.

Meanwhile, remove the tough outer layers of the fennel and discard. Slice the bulbs vertically into 1/2-inch sections and place in a large saucepan. Thinly slice the remaining onion and add to the saucepan with the extra virgin olive oil and a little salt. Add enough water to cover. Put a lid on the saucepan and bring to a boil. Simmer for about 45 minutes or until the fennel is creamy and soft and almost all the liquid has evaporated.

Remove the pork from the roasting pan and leave to rest. Spoon off the excess oil from the pan and discard the onion. Place the pan over high heat on the stovetop and stir in the remaining wine to deglaze. Add the stock and boil the sauce until slightly thickened. Remove from the heat, season with sea salt and freshly ground black pepper, and stir in the cream. Slice the pork and serve on the fennel, with the sauce passed separately.

fennel crumble

Preheat the oven to 350°F. Grease a large ovenproof serving dish. Trim fennel and cut into thin slices. Wash and drain well. Bring a large saucepan of water to a boil over high heat. Add the lemon juice and fennel slices. Cook over medium heat for 3 minutes. Drain and rinse under cold water.

Put the fennel in a large bowl. Add the extra lemon juice and honey and season with freshly ground black pepper; toss to combine. Sprinkle with the flour. Spoon into the prepared dish and pour the cream over the top.

To make the crumble topping, combine the oats, flour, and rye bread crumbs in a bowl. Heat the butter in a small saucepan, add the garlic and cook for 30 seconds. Pour the garlic butter over the dry ingredients and mix well. Sprinkle the crumble over the fennel. Bake for 20–30 minutes or until fennel is tender and crumble is browned.

note White or whole-wheat breadcrumbs can be used in place of rye bread if preferred.

2 fennel bulbs
1/4 cup lemon juice, plus
  2 tablespoons, extra
1 tablespoon honey
1 tablespoon all-purpose flour
1 1/4 cups whipping cream

crumble topping
3/4 cup rolled oats
1/2 cup all-purpose flour
1 cup fresh black rye bread
  crumbs
1/4 cup butter
1 garlic clove, crushed

stems, shoots, and bulbs ■ fennel

garlic

vegetables ▪ stems, shoots, and bulbs
season ▪ peak season spring–late fall

The kitchen would be a lesser place without the sweet pungency of garlic; who could imagine cooking without it? In fact, garlic is the most widely used herb flavoring in the culinary world, with few cuisines not utilizing it.

Garlic, with leeks and onions, is a member of the *Allium*, or lily, family. For a long time it was used only medicinally or was considered a food for the poor—the veritable "stinking rose." Mrs. Beeton, in her famous *Book of Household Management* (1861), pronounced that the smell of garlic "is generally considered offensive, and it is the most acrimonious in its taste of the whole alliaceous tribe."

It is generally accepted that garlic is native to Central Asia, or at least the European sort is— Native Americans were using a form of wild garlic way in advance of European settlers bringing it there. Both good, and good for you, garlic is an essential staple of every good cook's larder.

varieties

There are many, indeed hundreds, of garlic varieties, which all taste essentially the same, they just vary in intensity of flavor. Some have white papery skin around the cloves and bulb, while others have reddish, pink, or mauve-striated coverings. Some have large, fat, rounded cloves (the best-known of this sort being mild-flavored elephant garlic, which is technically not a true garlic at all, being closer botanically to the leek), and others have thin, small, and long cloves.

Our modern word garlic comes from the old English gar *(spear) and* leac *(leek), in reference to the long, spearlike green shoot the plant sends up as it grows. Whatever its etymology, few other members of the vegetal world have attracted as much lore and legend as garlic. All sorts of powers have been attributed to garlic, from Eleanor Roosevelt, who consumed chocolate-coated garlic pills every morning (to help her memory) to Pliny the Elder, who took garlic, spices, and wine-based love potions to improve his manly vigor, to the Central Europeans and Indians who used garlic to ward off demons and vampires.*

selection and storage

When buying garlic, choose bulbs with firm cloves that show no signs of powdery mold or green sprouting. The papery shells should be crisp and crinkly to the touch and the cloves should look as though they are about to burst from tight skins.

It is difficult to tell how large individual cloves are—the size of the bulb is no indication. Store garlic in a dark, well-ventilated place. In general, avoid storing it in plastic or in the refrigerator, although a week or so won't hurt too much.

Well stored, away from light and moisture, garlic will stay fresh for weeks. Garlic cannot be frozen, as this ruins both flavor and texture, and don't prepare garlic until you absolutely need it—exposure to the air causes bitterness to quickly set in.

preparation

The simplest way to peel garlic is to lay the individual cloves on a board, place the flat side of a large knife-blade over each clove and administer a firm tap with the heel of your hand—the skin will then just pull off.

The most effective way to finely chop quantities of garlic is to do this on a board with a little sea salt—the salt helps to break down and soften the garlic and in a relatively short time, you will have a pile of fine pulp. Purists eschew the garlic crusher claiming it alters the flavor, although it is nonetheless a handy device.

The volatile component in garlic responsible for its haunting smell is an enzyme called allinaise, which only asserts itself when cell walls inside the garlic cloves are cut or crushed. The human nose is said to be so sensitive to this compound that it can detect it in the air in as small a concentration as one part per billion. And the more finely the garlic is cut, the more of this sulphurous compound gets released, which has distinct consequences for cooking with garlic. Thus, in the French classic, chicken with forty cloves of garlic, for example, the garlic flavor is actually extremely subdued as the garlic is cooked whole, and for quite some time. On the other hand, just one or two garlic cloves, crushed and added fresh to a salad dressing or mixed into butter, will lend quite a jolt.

Heat destroys allinaise so the longer you cook garlic, and the higher the heat it is cooked at, the milder the resulting flavor. If sautéing garlic in oil or butter, take care not to brown or burn it as this will make it bitter and ruin your dish—cook over a low-medium heat.

As noted above, garlic flesh oxidizes very quickly on contact with the air so avoid preparing garlic in advance—although storing crushed or chopped garlic under a layer of olive oil will slow this process down.

aïoli

Put the egg yolks, garlic, 1/2 teaspoon salt, and half the lemon juice in a mortar or food processor and pound with a pestle or mix until light and creamy. Add the oil, drop by drop from the tip of a teaspoon, whisking constantly until it begins to thicken, then add the oil in a very thin stream. (If you're using a food processor, pour in the oil in a thin stream with the motor running.) Season with sea salt and freshly ground black pepper, add the remaining lemon juice and, if necessary, thin with a little warm water.

Serve the aïoli in a bowl as a dipping sauce. You can keep aïoli sealed in a sterilized jar in the refrigerator for up to 3 weeks. It is delicious served with poached fish, chicken, or seafood. Try it with a selection of crudités—carrots, celery, blanched asparagus, beans, cauliflower—as an appetizer, or spooned beside barbecued or roast beef fillet, or as an accompaniment to whole baked potatoes.

4 egg yolks
8 garlic cloves, crushed
2 tablespoons lemon juice
2 cups olive oil

stems, shoots, and bulbs ∎ garlic

garlic shrimp

serves 4

Heat the butter and olive oil in a large frying pan. When hot, add the garlic and chili. Cook, stirring continuously, for 30 seconds.

Add the shrimp and cook for 3–4 minutes on each side, until they turn pink. Sprinkle the shrimp with the chopped parsley and serve them immediately on hot plates, with the lemon wedges.

2 tablespoons butter
1/3 cup olive oil
2 garlic cloves, finely chopped
1 small red chili, seeded and
   finely chopped
24 large raw shrimp, peeled and
   deveined, tails left intact
3 tablespoons chopped Italian
   parsley
lemon wedges, to serve

leek

vegetables ▪ stems, shoots, and bulbs
season ▪ peak season late spring–fall

Leeks with honey and pepper, leeks in raisin sauce; fish fillets with leek and cilantro; these recipes sound as though they come straight from any modern chef's menu. Yet, they are, in fact, just a few of the many leek recipes that appear in the recipe collection of the famous ancient Roman epicure, Apicius. Which just serves to illustrate how esteemed this vegetable once was and how versatile it was thought to be. Indeed, the leek is still highly valued in many food cultures, while in others, it gets relegated to the soup or stock pot and that's about it.

Leeks have thick, long, white cylindrical stalks of many tightly packed layers, which flow into green, flat, and tightly bunched leaves. Probably native to Central Asia, from where they spread throughout Europe a very long time ago, leeks have come to be mostly associated with Wales, of which country it is the national symbol.

Like all the alliums (shallots, onions, garlic), leeks have great health-promoting properties. They are attributed with lowering high cholesterol levels, protecting against high blood pressure and also against certain cancers—notably prostate and colon.

preparation

The coarse green leek tops are discarded and the white part only is used for cooking, although the green part can be utilized, well washed, in stock-making. The trickiest aspect of preparing leeks for cooking is the removal of all the dirt that hides, trapped between the layers. If you plan to use the leeks sliced or cut into matchsticks, this isn't a problem, as the prepared leeks can be washed in plenty of water to remove any soil.

If planning to serve leeks whole, make a deep, crosswise slit through the leafy end of the leeks, then soak in a bowl of water, shaking them well to dislodge any dirt. Alternatively, you can cut the leeks in half lengthwise, right through the root end, thereby holding the leeks together as they cook.

steaming To steam leeks, cut them into 2-inch rounds, place in a steamer basket over boiling water, cover, then cook for 10–15 minutes or until completely tender. Leeks can also be trimmed and steamed whole—depending on their size, this will take 15–25 minutes.

culinary uses

Leeks suit braising whole, in chicken stock with some aromatic herbs such as thyme. They are also excellent stewed, that is, chopped, cooked in unsalted butter and their own juices, and finished with a dash of cream and some grated nutmeg.

They can be steamed too, but never simply boil leeks; the result will be soggy and tasteless. Leeks go very well with fish and seafood, with vinaigrette dressings, anchovies, mustard, cheeses (Gruyère and blue cheese, especially), chicken, prosciutto, cream, potatoes (think of Vichyssoise soup), walnuts, hazelnuts (and their oils), and parsley.

selection and storage

Leeks should feel very firm and heavy for their size and be straight, bearing dark green leaves. There should be no yellowing or withering in evidence and it is best to choose leeks that have a diameter of no more than 1½ inches—any larger than this and they tend to be fibrous and less sweet.

Never buy leeks that have been trimmed of their leaves. Inspect very closely before buying leeks at the end of the season, as these can have a woody inner core and are best avoided.

Store leeks with leaves attached, in the refrigerator, in a loosely sealed plastic bag, for up to 7 days.

serves 4

chicken and leek pie

¼ cup butter
2 large leeks, white part only, thinly sliced
4 scallions, sliced
1 garlic clove, crushed
¼ cup all-purpose flour
1½ cups chicken stock
½ cup whipping cream
1 barbecued chicken, meat removed from bones and chopped
13-ounce block puff pastry
¼ cup milk

Preheat the oven to 400°F. Grease an 8-inch round pie dish.

Melt the butter in a saucepan and add the leek, scallion, and garlic. Cook over low heat for 6 minutes, until the leek is soft but not browned. Sprinkle with the flour and mix well. Gradually pour in the stock and cook, stirring, until the mixture is thick and smooth.

Stir in the cream and add the chicken. Put the mixture in the pie dish and set aside to cool.

Divide the pastry into two pieces. Roll each piece between two sheets of baking paper to a thickness of ⅛ inch. Cut a circle out of one of the sheets of pastry, to cover the top of the pie. Brush the rim of the pie dish with a little milk. Put the pastry on top and press to seal around the edge. Trim off any excess pastry, then crimp the edge with the back of a fork. Cut the other sheet into ½-inch strips and roll each strip up loosely like a snail. Arrange the pastry on top of the pie, starting from the center and leaving a gap between each one. The spirals may not cover the whole surface of the pie. Make a few small holes between the spirals to let out any steam, and brush the top of the pie lightly with milk.

Bake for 25–30 minutes or until the top is brown and crispy. Make sure the spirals look well cooked and are not raw in the middle.

note Make small chicken pies by dividing the mixture among four greased 1¼-cup round ovenproof dishes. Cut the pastry into four rounds to cover the top of each pie. Bake for 15 minutes or until the pastry is crisp.

leeks à la grecque

Put the oil, wine, tomato paste, sugar, bay leaf, thyme, garlic, coriander seeds, peppercorns, and 1 cup water in a large frying pan with a lid. Bring to a boil, cover, and simmer for 5 minutes.

Add the leeks in a single layer and bring to simmering point. Reduce the heat, cover the pan again, and cook for 20–30 minutes or until the leeks are tender (pierce with a fine skewer to test). Lift out the leeks and put them in a serving dish.

Add the lemon juice to the cooking liquid and boil rapidly until the liquid is slightly syrupy. Remove the bay leaf, thyme, and peppercorns. Season with salt and pour over the leeks. Serve the leeks cold, sprinkled with chopped parsley.

¼ cup extra virgin olive oil
2 tablespoons white wine
1 tablespoon tomato paste
¼ teaspoon sugar
1 bay leaf
1 thyme sprig
1 garlic clove, crushed
4 coriander seeds, crushed
4 peppercorns
8 small leeks, white part only, trimmed
1 teaspoon lemon juice
1 tablespoon chopped parsley

stems, shoots, and bulbs ■ leek

The leek has historically been associated with a beneficial effect on the throat; the Roman emperor, Nero, allegedly took a daily potion of leeks to improve his singing voice, and Aristotle believed the partridge possessed such a clear voice because of its diet of leeks.

For other leek recipes see:
parsnip and leek puree 210

onion

vegetables ■ **stems, shoots, and bulbs**
season ■ **available year-round**

The onion is one of those ancient, venerable foods with a fascinating history. People began using onions way before recorded history, making it one of the earliest of all cultivated crops. It is thought the onion originated in Central Asia, although it has been dispersed over the world for so long, experts aren't really sure.

Through most of history however, onions were considered fit only for the poor—possibly because their strong smell offended the fine sensibilities of the rich. Onions were cheap, easy to grow, and quite frequently eaten raw on bread for breakfast by the less well-off. It wasn't until the Middle Ages, when onions became a hoi-polloi staple, along with cabbage and beans, that the upper classes began to appreciate them. And the rest, as the saying goes, is history.

Aside from a few religious groups who prohibit onion consumption (for example, Jainists and Buddhists both believe certain pungent foods, of which the onion is one, excite the passions), there isn't a culture anywhere that doesn't use onions. American author Maggie Waldron expressed the idea thus: "It's probably illegal to make soup, stews, and casseroles without plenty of onions." Illegal no, but, religious convictions notwithstanding, it's certainly illogical.

varieties

There are over 300 varieties of onions and very few are sold by named variety. Rather, onions are generally sold by types. Some of the most common onion types are listed below.

baby onions These are very small onions, usually brown-skinned but sometimes white, which are perfect for pickling whole. They can also be roasted, braised, or used in stews, such as the French dish coq au vin, to great effect. Baby onions are sometimes called pickling or pearl onions.

red onions A mild, sweet-tasting onion with distinctive red-mauve skin and pink-tinged white flesh. Red onions are wonderful eaten raw—perfect in salads, dressings, salsas, and sandwiches. They are also delicious when broiled or barbecued but they can be disappointing in stews or when long-cooked or roasted.

spanish onions These are a large, round, yellow-skinned variety favored for use in salads or for eating raw, on account of their juicy, mild-tasting flesh. Confusingly, in Australia, red onions are also called Spanish onions.

sweet onions Sweet onions are popular in the United States. Also referred to as "short-day" onions because they are grown over winter months and harvested in spring to summer, they are distinct from "storage" onions (the majority of yellow and white onions are classic "storage" onions), which are harvested in late summer to fall and, because of their firmer texture and lower moisture content, are suited to curing and storing. Storage onions have a sugar content somewhere around 3–5 percent, whereas sweet onions hover around 15 percent. As well as being sweeter, they have a subtle, mild flavor and thin, light-colored skins, which tend to be quite fragile. Some of the best-known examples of sweet onions are the Vidalia, the Walla Walla, and the Maui—they are well-suited to raw use.

white onions As the name suggests, white onions have white skin and white, green-tinged, juicy flesh; their flavor is clean and tangy and tends to be stronger than brown and yellow onions. White onions contain their fair share of pungent sulphur compounds, so beware when peeling. A good choice for sautéing, roasting, baking, and for use in casseroles.

yellow onions About 75 percent of all onions used are the classic brown or yellow-skinned onion that comes in a variety of sizes and degrees of bulbousness. This is a good all-purpose cooking onion, suitable for stewing, frying, roasting, and stuffing. These onions taste quite strong and unless you particularly favor their throat-catching flavor, they are not a good choice to use raw.

selection and storage

Onions should feel firm and heavy. Their skin should be shiny and the skin around the neck should be very tightly closed. There should be no soft or dark spots or sprouting. Onions, even if they taste strong, should smell mild when unpeeled—a strong odor can indicate spoilage. Don't choose onions sporting green areas either as these will taste fairly unpleasant.

Store onions in a cool, dry and well-ventilated place; light can cause bitterness so keep them somewhere dark. They readily absorb moisture so avoid leaving them anywhere damp (in a cupboard under a sink, for example) and also, don't store them near potatoes as these give off moisture and gas and will make onions spoil more rapidly.

It's agreed that onions were cultivated as long as 5,000 years ago. The Egyptians venerated onions, believing them to be a symbol of eternity, on account of their circle-within-a-circle structure. Pharaohs were buried with onions for this reason although it has been conjectured that the strong antiseptic qualities of the onion could have been another contributing factor in this. The laborers of the pyramids were sustained by onions and other vegetables, and in Greece, athletes would drink onion juice, consume raw onions, and rub onions over their bodies to strengthen themselves before competing in the Olympic Games.

nutrition

Onions are something of a wonder food, not so much for their vitamin content (they do contain vitamins C and B6 but not in startling quantities) but for the 150 or so phytochemicals they contain. For example, they contain saponins, which are associated with cholesterol reduction and also inhibiting tumor growth.

Red and yellow onions have been found to contain quercetin, a substance that blocks formation of cancer cells; research has also shown that compounds in onions can prevent certain causes of asthma, kill infectious bacteria, and act to dissolve blood clots. Consumption of onions may also be helpful in preventing gastric ulcers and cataracts.

preparation

Onions contain over 100 volatile sulphur compounds in their cells and these are released when the cell walls are chopped or sliced with a knife. The effects of this are legendary—once caught in the eyes, the potent, compound-laden juices of an onion quickly reduce the cook to tears. The older the onion, the stronger these compounds are.

peeling If you need to peel a quantity of onions, especially baby ones which will be used whole, the best way to do this is to pour boiling water over them in a bowl and let them stand for 5 minutes. This loosens the skins considerably. Whether employing this method or not, peel onions from the neck end down, leaving the root intact, which holds the onion effectively together, facilitating easier chopping. Also, when planning to cook onions whole, halved, or in wedges, they will break up into layers if the root end has been chopped through.

cutting The cooking fraternity abounds with suggestions for reducing the effects of onion chopping and these run the gamut from the whimsical to the utterly ludicrous. Possibly the most effective and convenient method is to refrigerate onions for 30 minutes before chopping them as this seems to subdue their potency. Also, make sure your knife is very sharp as this will slice through cells, causing minimal damage, whereas a blunt knife will bruise and batter its way through the cells, releasing far more sulphur compounds into the air.

The best way to chop an onion is to first peel and halve it, then place it, flat side down, on a board before slicing and chopping. Do not prepare onions in advance as they quickly oxidize and can taste extremely unpleasant.

roasting To roast onions, either peel or leave them unpeeled for different results. When unpeeled, the onion flesh steams to a creamy mass inside the skins, which can then be squeezed or scooped out to eat. Peeled roast onions result in a crusty, crunchy, deeply caramelized exterior and a softish interior.

red onions

Whichever way you choose, trim a little off the base of each onion so they will stand upright in the dish, rub generously with olive oil, then roast in a 350°F oven for about 1 hour or until tender.

grilling To grill onions, cut peeled onions into thin wedges, brush with oil, then cook on a barbecue grill or grill pan for 3 minutes on each side, until lightly charred and tender.

caremelizing To caramelize onions, finely slice 6–8 onions (they lose much of their 90 percent water content during this process so it isn't really worth doing with just one or two), then cook in olive oil over medium heat in a large saucepan for 45–60 minutes, stirring often or until golden and "melted." You can add a dash of sugar, some red wine vinegar, and red wine near the end of cooking if desired to reduce this down to a jammy mess to make a savory "marmalade"—an excellent accompaniment for roast meats.

culinary uses

Onions are an assumed part of practically all savory recipes, and for this reason risk being overlooked as a vegetable in their own right. They are sublime when baked, grilled, or stewed to a caramelized mass—onions contain substances which, when reduced down through long cooking, are many times sweeter than table sugar.

Grilled onions are wonderful doused with good balsamic vinegar and sprinkled with sea salt and chopped mint, and served at room temperature as a side dish. Expand this idea into a salad by adding some arugula, black olives, and slices of medium-rare lamb and you have a delicious, light main course meal.

onion and thyme marmalade

4 pounds 8 ounces (about 12)
   onions, cut into rings
3 cups malt vinegar
6 black peppercorns
2 bay leaves
4-inch square of cheesecloth
4⅓ cups soft brown sugar
2 tablespoons thyme leaves
10 thyme sprigs, about
   1¼-inches long

Put the sliced onions in a large saucepan with the vinegar. Put the peppercorns and bay leaves in the cheesecloth and tie securely with string. Add to the saucepan. Bring to a boil, then reduce the heat and simmer for 40–45 minutes or until the onion is very soft.

Add the sugar, thyme leaves, and 1 teaspoon salt. Stir for 7–8 minutes or until all the sugar has dissolved. Bring to a boil, then reduce the heat and simmer for 20–30 minutes or until thick and syrupy. Remove any scum from the surface with a slotted spoon. Discard the cheesecloth bag and stir in the thyme sprigs.

Carefully ladle into hot sterilized jars and seal. Allow to cool, then label and date each jar. Store in a cool, dark place for 6–12 months. Refrigerate after opening for up to 6 weeks.

The term "to know one's onions" was developed in the United States in the 1920s—one suggested meaning of this is that, with so many varieties of this easily hybridized vegetable being developed at the time, to "know your onions" became synonymous with expertise in a given field.

stifatho (beef and onion stew)

Preheat the oven to 315°F. Cut the beef into ¾-inch thick slices, then into 1¼-inch chunks. Heat half the olive oil in a large frying pan over high heat. Fry the beef, in batches, for 7–8 minutes or until browned, then transfer to a bowl.

Add the remaining oil, chopped onion, and garlic to the frying pan, reduce the heat to low and fry for 5–6 minutes, until soft. Add the allspice and cumin and cook for 1 minute. Return the beef to the frying pan, increase the heat and stir well to coat with the spices. Add the tomato paste, wine, and vinegar and cook for 1 minute. Add the bay leaf, cinnamon stick, stock, and enough hot water to cover the beef. Bring to a boil, then quickly transfer to a casserole dish with a lid. Cover and cook in the oven for 1 hour.

Remove the loose outer skin of the baby onions but do not peel them entirely or top and tail them. Cut a cross in the root. Bring a large saucepan of water to a boil and add the onions. Boil for 1 minute, then drain. The inner skins will have been loosened and will peel off easily.

Add the baby onions to the casserole dish, along with the golden raisins, and toss lightly. If necessary, top up with hot water to keep the meat and onions just covered. Bake for another 1 hour or until the meat and onions are tender but not breaking up. Discard the pieces of bay leaf and cinnamon stick before serving.

2 pounds 4 ounces blade or
  chuck steak, trimmed
⅓ cup olive oil
1 large brown onion, finely
  chopped
2 garlic cloves, thinly sliced
¼ teaspoon ground allspice
½ teaspoon ground cumin
¼ cup tomato paste
⅔ cup dry red wine
2 tablespoons red wine vinegar
1 bay leaf, torn in half
1 cinnamon stick, broken in half
1 cup beef stock
1 pound 12 ounces (16–20) baby
  onions
2 tablespoons golden raisins

For other onion recipes see:

rhubarb

vegetables ■ stems, shoots, and bulbs
season ■ available year-round

The use of rhubarb as a food crop is relatively recent. For millennia the root of this cold-weather plant was an important medicine crop in China, and from there it was eventually exported to Europe, where it became incredibly popular. In sixteenth-century France, rhubarb was reputed to be ten times as expensive as cinnamon—in 1650's England it sold for over two and a half times the price of opium! Culinary rhubarb was developed in the pre-Islamic East where it was a much-favored ingredient for drinks and meat stews—such preparations are still a striking feature of Middle Eastern cuisines.

Technically a vegetable, only the stalks of the rhubarb, called "petioles," are edible—the leaves contain oxalic acid (the stalks do too but, unless great amounts are ingested, in nonharmful quantities). Supposedly this feature is responsible for its slowness to gain popularity in Europe, as early experimenters consumed the leaves with dire results. Not until the nineteenth century, when strains of the plant were developed that had juicy, tender stalks, did cultivation and consumption begin in earnest—particularly in England and North America.

selection and storage

The first rhubarb stalks to appear in early spring are the most tender. Field-grown rhubarb tends to be juicier, sourer, less tender, and more deeply red than that grown in greenhouses. Both field-grown and indoor-grown rhubarb have their fans, some preferring the fuller flavor and thicker stems of the former, others prizing the softer texture and gentler flavor of the latter.

Stalks can range in color from pink and red to green; color is no indicator of maturity although generally the red stalks are sweeter than the others.

Rhubarb dries out quickly once picked and becomes flaccid, so look for stalks that are firm and upright, avoiding very thick ones as these will be fibrous. Discard the leaves before wrapping the stalks in plastic wrap—they will keep for up to 1 week in the refrigerator.

preparation

Rhubarb is generally cooked, or stewed, with sugar for use in sweet dishes such as fools, jams, compotes, and a range of baked desserts, such as cobblers, crumbles, and pies.

stewing Simply slice 2 pounds rhubarb into 3/4-inch pieces —if stalks are fibrous, remove these first (a potato peeler is ideal for this but beware of the fine red juices, which are likely to spurt and can stain clothing). Put the chopped stalks in a saucepan with 1/4 cup superfine sugar and 2 tablespoons water—add the sugar in small amounts to begin with, then increase to taste as the rhubarb cooks; rhubarb can vary widely in sourness so no two batches will necessarily need the same amount. Cover the saucepan and simmer, stirring occasionally, for 5–8 minutes or until the rhubarb is tender. Serve the stewed rhubarb with vanilla or strawberry ice cream, or with whipped cream and a shortbread-style cookie on the side.

culinary uses

Rhubarb can be flavored with a little rose water or cinnamon, sweetened with honey instead of sugar, or cooked with a little orange juice and finely grated orange zest. Stewed rhubarb is equally delicious whether served hot, warm, or chilled, and needs little more than some cream, custard, or ice cream to cut the acid edge. Rhubarb and orange marmalade is lush, as is rhubarb and strawberry jam (or rhubarb and strawberry pie filling or crumble base—the two have a great affinity).

Rhubarb is also used in savory dishes—notably in the spiced meat koreshes of Iran, lamb stews of Georgia (in the former Soviet Union), and fragrant tagines of North Africa. Lightly sweetened and pureed, rhubarb makes a wonderful sauce for pork and, cooked with apple into a rich chutney, a perfect foil for smoked meats such as ham.

rhubarb and ginger jam

Chop the rhubarb into small pieces. Layer the rhubarb, sugar, and lemon juice in a large nonmetallic bowl. Cover and leave overnight.

Put two small plates in the freezer. Place the rhubarb mixture in a large saucepan. Put the ginger in the cheesecloth, tie securely with string and add to the pan. Stir over low heat for 5 minutes or until all the sugar has dissolved. Bring to a boil and boil rapidly for 20–30 minutes, stirring often. When the jam falls from the back of a tilted wooden spoon in thick sheets without dripping, start testing for setting point. To do this, remove from the heat, put a little jam onto one of the cold plates and place in the freezer for 30 seconds. A skin should form on the surface and the jam should wrinkle when pushed with your finger. If not, continue to reduce the syrup over heat, then use the second testing plate to test for setting point. Discard the cheesecloth bag and add the glacé ginger.

Carefully ladle the jam into hot sterilized jars and seal. Allow to cool, then label and date each jar. Store in a cool, dark place for 6–12 months. Refrigerate after opening for up to 6 weeks.

note To warm sugar, preheat the oven to 300°F. Spread the sugar evenly in a baking dish and put in the oven for about 10–15 minutes or until warmed through. Do not overheat the sugar or it will start to lump together.

3 pounds 5 ounces rhubarb, trimmed
6¾ cups sugar, warmed (see note)
½ cup lemon juice
1½-inch piece ginger, roughly chopped
4-inch square of cheesecloth
½ cup glacé ginger, finely chopped

stems, shoots, and bulbs ■ rhubarb

rhubarb and apple
upside-down cake

Preheat the oven to 350°F. Lightly grease a deep 8-inch round cake pan and line the base with baking paper.

Put the sugar in a saucepan with 1/3 cup water and heat gently, shaking occasionally, until the sugar has dissolved. Increase the heat and cook until it turns a pale caramel color—it will turn a deeper color in the oven. Pour into the pan and then press the rhubarb and apple into the caramel.

Beat the eggs, confectioners' sugar, and vanilla extract in a small bowl with electric beaters until the mixture is frothy. Fold in the melted butter. Sift the flour over the top and stir (the mixture will be soft). Spoon gently over the fruit, being careful not to dislodge it.

Bake for about 45 minutes or until set on top. Run a knife around the side of the cake and turn out very carefully onto a wire rack to cool. Be sure to do this straight away, otherwise the caramel will cool and stick to the pan. Serve warm with cream as a dessert, or cool as a teacake.

variation Fresh plums can be substituted for the apple and rhubarb in this recipe. The plums should be halved and cored, then sliced and pressed into the caramel in a decorative spiral pattern, or randomly. Bake the cake as for the original recipe and serve either warm or cold.

1 cup sugar
2 cups rhubarb chopped into 3/4-inch pieces
1 small apple, peeled, cored, and chopped
2 eggs
1/3 cup confectioners' sugar
1/2 teaspoon natural vanilla extract
1/3 cup unsalted butter, melted and cooled
1 cup self-rising flour

stems, shoots, and bulbs ■ rhubarb

For other rhubarb recipes see:

scallion

vegetables ▪ **stems, shoots, and bulbs**
season ▪ **available year-round**

selection and storage

Choose bunches of scallions with deep green shoot ends and firm, unblemished white root ends. Avoid any with signs of wilting or with yellowing green ends.

Wrap bunches of scallions in plastic wrap and store in the crisper section of the refrigerator —they are fairly perishable so use within 2–3 days.

This member of the onion family has a confusing number of names. Along with scallion, it is also called the green onion, and in some places, and quite erroneously, the spring onion (spring onions are similar but have slightly bulbous white ends). The scallion, with its long, elegant green end atop a bright white stem end, is much-used around the world, particularly in Asian climes from where it was thought to have come. Indeed, this is the only onion commonly used in traditional Japanese cooking. The green part is highly nutritious, being particularly high in vitamins A and C. Generally, the scallion is used finely sliced or cut into thin matchsticks, raw, or very lightly cooked only; it is not suited to long cooking.

preparation

The root end needs to be removed, as does the fine, tough membrane that invariably covers the white parts of the onion. Cut off the top 1½ inches or so, then finely slice on a diagonal, widthwise, or cut into 2-inch long sections and cut these into fine matchsticks.

culinary uses

Use scallions in stir-fries (they are particularly compatible with garlic and ginger), stirred through salads, or sprinkled on soups as a garnish. The finely chopped green tops work well, with their mild-hot flavor, stirred into vegetable fritter mixtures, potato (and other root vegetable) purees, and gratins.

scallion pancakes

Place the flour and 1/2 teaspoon salt in a bowl and stir to combine. Add the oil and 7 fluid ounces water and mix into a rough dough using a wooden spoon. Turn the dough out onto a lightly floured surface and knead for 5 minutes or until smooth and elastic. Cover the dough with a cloth and rest for 20 minutes.

On a lightly floured surface, use your hands to roll the dough into a long roll. Divide the dough into 24 pieces. Working with one portion of dough at a time, place the dough, cut edge down, on the work surface. Using a small rolling pin, roll it out to a 4-inch circle. Brush the surface with sesame oil and sprinkle on some scallion. Starting with the edge closest to you, roll up the dough into a log and pinch the ends to seal. Lightly flatten the roll, then roll it up lengthwise to form a snail, pinching the ends to seal. Repeat with the remaining dough, sesame oil, and scallion. Let the rolls rest for 20 minutes.

Place each roll flat on the work surface and press down with the palm of your hand. Roll out to a 4-inch circle with a rolling pin. Place on a lightly floured baking sheet. Stack the pancakes between lightly floured sheets of baking paper and leave to rest for 20 minutes.

Heat a frying pan over medium heat, brush the surface with oil and add two or three pancakes at a time. Cook for 2–3 minutes on each side, turning once, until the pancakes are light golden and crisp. Remove and drain on paper towels. Serve immediately.

note You can reheat pancakes, wrapped in foil, in a 350°F oven for 15 minutes if you want to prepare and cook them in advance.

2 cups all-purpose flour
1 tablespoon oil
3 tablespoons roasted
   sesame oil
2 scallions, green part only,
   finely chopped
oil, for frying

stems, shoots, and bulbs ▪ scallion

shallot

vegetables ■ **stems, shoots, and bulbs**
season ■ **peak season summer**

Shallots have papery, thin, brittle skins which range in color from copper and gold to grayish with flesh that can be yellowy, pink-tinged, or white. The pink-fleshed sort is held to have the best flavor. Prized for their distinct but polite flavor, shallots never "take over" a dish in the way onions or garlic can, and are valued by good cooks everywhere.

Another member of the allium family, true shallots grow not from seed but from a bulb. A "mother" bulb is planted and produces endless "daughters"—in France it is against the law to label anything but bulb-grown shallots as shallots. Seed-propagated shallots look, to many, like "proper" shallots. They do not, however, possess that singular flavor (elegant, sweet, and intense) for which shallots are so valued.

preparation

If using shallots in any quantity, the skins can be tedious to peel. Pour boiling water over shallots in a bowl, weight them with a plate to submerge, then stand for 5 minutes. Drain well and cool slightly. To peel, slice across the skin from the very top of each bulb, then, using a small, sharp knife, pull a section of skin away from flesh, then pull it down to the root end.

Trim the root ends but don't cut them off completely, especially if you want to cook shallots whole, as this will help them stay together. Although shallots are generally used finely sliced, chopped, or minced, they can also be cooked whole.

selection and storage

Choose bulbs that feel hard and whose papery skins are shiny and brittle. Be vigilant in not purchasing any that are sprouting, soft (which could indicate a powdery mold), or withered. Shallots will store very well (for several months) if they are fresh when bought.

Keep them in a dark, well-ventilated place at cool room temperature; if you must refrigerate them, do so after you have loosely wrapped them in paper towels to protect them from damp and humidity.

shallot, bacon, and cheddar breakfast muffins

Preheat the oven to 400°F. Grease a 6-hole giant muffin pan. Slice 1 of the shallots into rings. Heat the 2 teaspoons of extra oil in a frying pan over low heat. Add the shallot and fry for 3 minutes. Remove and drain on paper towels. Set aside.

Finely chop the remaining 4 shallots. Increase the heat to medium and add these shallots and bacon to the pan. Fry for 5 minutes or until the shallots are soft. Drain on paper towels.

Sift the flour, baking powder, sugar, mustard, and 1/2 teaspoon salt into a bowl. Add 3/4 cup of the cheddar cheese. Stir in the fried bacon and shallots. Combine the milk, egg, and remaining 1/4 cup of oil. Pour into the bowl and fold gently—the batter should be lumpy.

Divide the batter among the muffin holes. Top with the fried shallot and remaining cheddar cheese. Bake for 20–25 minutes or until the muffins are golden and a skewer inserted into the center of the muffin comes out clean. Cool in the pan before turning out on a wire rack. Sprinkle paprika on top to serve.

1/4 cup oil, plus 2 teaspoons, extra
5 shallots, peeled
2 bacon slices, finely chopped
2 cups all-purpose flour
1 tablespoon baking powder
1 tablespoon superfine sugar
1 teaspoon dry mustard
1 1/4 cups grated mature cheddar cheese
3/4 cup milk
1 egg
sweet paprika, to serve

stems, shoots, and bulbs ■ shallot

beurre blanc

makes 1 cup

Put the white wine vinegar, white wine, and shallots into a saucepan and bring to a boil over high heat. Simmer for 6–7 minutes or until the liquid has reduced to 1/4 cup. Strain the liquid and return to the saucepan. Discard the shallots.

Whisk in the butter, one cube at a time, over low heat, so the butter melts into the sauce and doesn't split. Season with sea salt and freshly ground black pepper. Serve with fish, chicken, eggs, asparagus, or artichoke.

2 1/2 tablespoons white wine vinegar
1/2 cup white wine
2 shallots, finely chopped
1 cup unsalted butter, cubed

sprouts

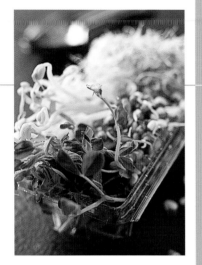

vegetables ■ stems, shoots, and bulbs
season ■ available year-round

selection and storage

Look for seed sprouts with fresh, bright colors that are dry-looking, with no damp or brown patches. Often these types of sprouts are sold ventilated in plastic boxes—keep them in these, in the refrigerator, until ready to use and use quickly (within 2 days) as they are highly perishable.

Bean sprouts should have shoots that are crisp, clear-colored, and with no mushy, brown or soft spots. Bean sprouts should be stored in a roomy, sealed plastic bag in the refrigerator and used within 2 days of purchase, as they are at their nutritional peak and flavor for only a short time.

The Chinese have long been sprouting beans and seeds; for millennia Chinese physicians have been prescribing them on account of their health-giving properties and particularly high nutritional value. Their use in Western cuisines is fairly recent—it has only been in the last 30 years or so that they have become widely popular.

Sprouts are seeds that have just started to grow. Loosely, there are those sprouts that come from beans and those that are sprouted from vegetable seeds. The most common bean sprouts are the mung bean and soybean, while well-known vegetable seed sprouts include radish, cress, alfalfa, and mustard. Both types are eaten whole—the only sprout that requires cooking is the soybean sprout, while certain others (notably the mung bean sprout) can be lightly cooked (by steaming, stir-frying, blanching); mostly though, they are used raw.

Seed sprouts are diminutive, with fine, silvery shoots topped with several tiny green leaves. Their soft, delicate texture makes them perfect in salads or sandwich fillings.

Bean sprouts are less starchy than the beans they sprout from as the sprouting process causes starches and sugars to be used up. Sprouts from beans (adzuki, mung, and soy) typically have long, translucent ends and tiny, light yellow leaves.

pear and sprout salad with sesame dressing

Put all the sesame dressing ingredients in a small screwtop jar and shake well to dissolve the sugar. Set aside.

Peel and core the pears, then slice them into thin strips. Put the pear strips in a bowl and cover with water to prevent discoloration.

Drain the pears and put in a large serving bowl with the snow pea sprouts, bean sprouts, chives, snow peas, celery, and cilantro. Pour the dressing over, toss lightly, sprinkle with sesame seeds and serve.

sesame dressing
1½ tablespoons soy sauce
1 teaspoon sesame oil
3 teaspoons soft brown sugar
1½ tablespoons peanut oil
3 teaspoons rice vinegar

2 small firm, ripe pears
2 cups snow pea sprouts
2½ cups bean sprouts, tails trimmed
1 handful chives, snipped into 1½-inch pieces
1 cup snow peas, cut into matchsticks
1 celery stalk, cut into matchsticks
1 small handful cilantro sprigs
1 teaspoon sesame seeds

tropical sprout salad

Peel the papaya, cut in half and scoop out the seeds. Cut the flesh into ½-inch slices and arrange in a single layer. Drizzle with lime juice and allow to sit for 10 minutes.

Arrange half the papaya slices in a serving bowl, then add half the snow pea sprouts, half the kiwifruit slices, and half the alfafa sprouts. Repeat with the remaining ingredients and serve immediately.

1 small papaya
2 tablespoons lime juice
½ cup snow pea sprouts
2 small kiwifruit, peeled and thinly sliced
½ cup alfalfa sprouts

artichoke

vegetables ■ flowers
season ■ spring

storage and selection

Globe artichokes are in peak condition when their leaves are green and tight and they feel heavy for their size. The best test for freshness is to rub the leaves together to check for a characteristic "squeak." This is often considered a more reliable indicator than color alone, as artichokes with some bronzing on the tips of their leaves (called the "winter kiss" in some countries) have been touched by frost, which actually enhances their flavor and makes them the most highly prized of all.

Artichokes are dry and well past their prime when their leaves appear to be opening. They start deteriorating from the moment they are picked so freshness is of the essence. While best used on the day of purchase, unwashed artichokes can be stored in a sealed plastic bag in the refrigerator for up to 2 days.

Synonymous with spring, globe artichokes are the unopened flowers and stems of an edible thistle. Along with broccoli and cauliflower, they are classified as an inflorescent vegetable, that is, one with an edible flower, which in the case of the artichoke, if allowed to bloom, transforms into a magnificent large purple blossom. They grow on perennial plants that only produce the edible flowers in their second and third years. This, coupled with the fact that they are a low yield per acreage crop, explains their status as a delicacy and their relatively high price tag.

First thought to have been cultivated in Sicily, artichokes appear in ancient Greek and Roman literature and were grown in Granada by the Moors from around A.D. 800. Globe artichokes are entirely unrelated to the tuberous Jerusalem (which is not only not an artichoke, it is not even from Jerusalem) and Chinese artichokes, which are thus named as their flavor is said to resemble that of the globe artichoke. The main types of commonly available artichoke are the green globe, purple globe, and purple Roman varieties.

Artichokes contain limited levels of vitamin A and potassium, and fair amounts of folate.

preparation

Much of a mature artichoke is inedible. The fleshy base of each leaf is succulent, while the prickly tops are cut off and discarded, as is the hairy "choke" inside each artichoke. The tender "heart" of the artichoke is the most prized part, although there is a ritualistic element attached to eating the outer leaves—customarily you tear off individual leaves from a boiled artichoke, dip the base into melted butter and then pull the flesh away with your teeth, discarding the leaf, thus working your way toward the heart.

Although home cooks often find the thought of preparing artichokes off-putting, it is really quite a straightforward process requiring no particular skill, just a little time. Working with one artichoke at a time and using a small, sharp knife, trim the stalks, leaving 1½–2½ inches of stalk, then snap off the tough outer leaves until you start to see leaves with a tender, yellow base. Cut off about 1½ inches across the tops of each artichoke. The stems can then be peeled, and the hairy choke scooped out from the top of the bulb with a teaspoon and discarded.

Alternately, you can trim the artichokes right down to the tender heart, discarding all the outer leaves. As you go, place the artichokes in acidulated water (water with lemon juice) to prevent discoloration until ready to use. They should not be cooked in iron or aluminum pans, as this can cause them to brown.

boiling To boil artichokes, cook them in a saucepan of boiling salted water for 20–25 minutes or until tender through the thickest part (a skewer is ideal for this)—cover the vegetables with an upturned plate to keep them submerged. Drain, then serve whole with butter or sauce; provide finger bowls and paper towels for dealing with the aftermath.

culinary uses

Luxuriant artichokes are most often served simply boiled or steamed with mayonnaise, hollandaise, or vinaigrette for dipping their tender inner leaves, but they can also be stuffed and braised or baked, enjoyed raw, grilled, fried, marinated, and preserved in oil, or even added to spring stews.

Their brief spring season begs for their use with other quintessentially spring ingredients like asparagus, fava beans, peas, and lamb, veal, and capretto. Herbs such as Italian parsley, marjoram, thyme, and sage complement artichoke's fine flavor and delicate texture, and they pair well with butter, shrimp, pancetta, prosciutto, saffron, and cheeses such as Parmesan, pecorino, and Gruyère.

artichokes vinaigrette

To prepare the artichokes, bring a large saucepan of salted water to a boil and add the lemon juice. Break the stalks from the artichokes, pulling out any strings at the same time, and then trim the bases flat. Add the artichokes to the water and put a small plate on top of them to keep them submerged. Cook at a simmer for 20–25 minutes or until a leaf from the base comes away easily. (The base will be tender when pierced with a skewer.) Cool quickly under cold running water, then drain upside down on a tray.

To make the vinaigrette, heat 1 tablespoon of the oil in a small saucepan, add the scallion and cook over low heat for 2 minutes. Leave to cool a little, then add the white wine, vinegar, mustard, and sugar. Gradually whisk in the remaining oil. Season with sea salt and freshly ground black pepper and stir in half the parsley.

Put an artichoke on each plate and gently prise it open a little. Spoon the dressing over the top, allowing it to drizzle into the artichoke and around the plate. Pour the remaining dressing into a small bowl for people to dip the leaves. Sprinkle each artichoke with the remaining parsley.

Eat the leaves one by one, dipping them in the vinaigrette and scraping the flesh off the leaves between your teeth. When you reach the middle, pull off any really small leaves and then use a teaspoon to remove the furry choke. Once you've got rid of the choke, you can eat the tender base or "heart" of the artichoke.

juice of 1 lemon
4 artichokes

vinaigrette
5 tablespoons olive oil
2 scallions, finely chopped
2 tablespoons white wine
2 tablespoons white wine vinegar
1/4 teaspoon Dijon mustard
pinch of sugar
1 tablespoon finely chopped parsley

flowers ■ artichoke

lamb and artichoke fricassee

To prepare the artichokes, bring a large saucepan of salted water to a boil and add the lemon juice. Trim the stems from the artichokes and remove the tough outer leaves. Cut the hard tips off the remaining leaves using scissors. Cook the artichokes for 5 minutes. Remove and turn upside down to drain. When cool enough to handle, use a small spoon to remove the choke from the center of each. Scrape the bases well to remove all the membrane. Cut the artichokes into quarters and set aside.

Score a cross in the top of each tomato, plunge them into boiling water for 20 seconds, transfer to a bowl of iced water to cool, and then peel the skin and discard it. Cut each tomato in half and scoop out the seeds with a teaspoon. Chop the tomatoes.

Heat half the oil in a deep, flameproof casserole dish and fry batches of the lamb until golden. Add the remaining oil and cook the onion for about 8 minutes or until soft and caramelized. Add the flour and cook for 1 minute. Add the tomato, garlic, wine, and chicken stock. Return the lamb to the dish, add the bouquet garni and simmer, covered, for 1 hour.

Put the artichokes in the dish and simmer, uncovered, for 15 minutes. Remove the lamb and artichokes with a slotted spoon and place in a serving dish. Keep warm. Discard the bouquet garni. Cook the sauce left in the casserole dish over high heat until it thickens. Pour the sauce over the lamb and garnish with parsley. Serve with lemon wedges.

1/4 cup lemon juice
6 artichokes
2 large tomatoes
1/3 cup olive oil
4 pounds 8 ounces diced lamb
1 pound 10 ounces (4–5) brown onions, thinly sliced
1 tablespoon all-purpose flour
2 garlic cloves, crushed
3/4 cup white wine
1 1/3 cups chicken stock
1 bouquet garni (see page 413)
chopped Italian parsley, to garnish
lemon wedges, to serve

flowers ■ artichoke

broccoli

selection and storage

When buying broccoli, look for heads with tightly closed, compact, deep green florets, with no signs of yellowing. Broccoli with yellow flowers attached is overmature and should be avoided. The stalks should be firm and not too thick or they will be woody. Any leaves attached to the stalk should be green and sprightly.

A fairly perishable vegetable, broccoli should be stored in a perforated or open plastic bag in the refrigerator crisper and used within 3–4 days. It should not be washed before storing, as water clinging to its surface will cause it to rapidly deteriorate.

Broccolini, which is a recent innovation and an Australian-developed hybrid, should have long, firm, clean stems topped with a smallish, compact head. Florets should be blue-green or green-purple in color and leaves should be healthy looking (no wilting or browning) and olive green. A few yellow flowers per bunch are acceptable (about six or so) but more than this indicate overmaturity. Store in the same manner as broccoli.

Like others in the brassica family, broccoli began its life in the Mediterranean. It originated as a form of wild cabbage that eventually evolved to develop buds rather than large leaves. The most common sort of broccoli is the familiar emerald green variety with tightly clustered tiny buds sitting atop thick stalks.

The less well-known Calabrese broccoli, named after the southern Italian region of Calabria, is an heirloom variety with a deep bluish-green color. Prized for its succulence and delicate flavor, it is often compared to asparagus. The Italians also eat broccoli raab (alternately known as rabe or *brocoletti di rape*), which despite its name and appearance is not directly related to broccoli, although it is a member of the cabbage family.

A more recent addition to the broccoli line-up is broccolini, a cross between broccoli and Chinese kale. Broccolini is gaining in popularity due to its slender, tender long stalks, deliciously subtle flavor and loose, small buds.

Broccoli is one of the healthiest of vegetables, containing excellent doses of folate, phytonutrients including betacarotene and lutein, manganese, and potassium. A single cup of broccoli boasts as much calcium as a cup of milk. Broccolini is especially rich in vitamins A and C, folate, and potassium.

The purple sprouting variety was the first form of broccoli, featuring tender green stems and edible purple buds. This was the type cultivated and eaten by the ancient Romans, who typically cooked it in wine, added it to a hearty chickpea and lentil soup or dressed it with olive oil and garum, a pungent fermented fish sauce. This primitive variety of broccoli can still occasionally be found today. It turns green when cooked and is especially delicious when picked young, then cooked whole and served with melted butter and a squeeze of lemon juice.

preparation

When preparing broccoli, use a small sharp knife to separate the florets from the stalks, cutting the florets into roughly even-size pieces if large, then soak them in salted water to drive out any caterpillars—broccoli seems very susceptible to these.

It is the habit of many cooks to throw away the thick stalks, however, peeled, sliced, and steamed, these are actually delicious and it is a waste to not use them. Stalks take longer to cook than the florets, so they need to be cooked separately or put into the steamer about 2–3 minutes before the florets.

boiling To boil broccoli, use plenty of boiling salted water and boil them, uncovered, for 3–4 minutes or until tender but still bright green. Drain well as cooking water can sit, trapped among the tiny buds, causing the eating experience to be a soggy one. Broccolini requires just a wash and the trimming of the very base of the stem. It can be steamed or boiled whole for about 3–4 minutes, or chopped and stir-fried.

culinary uses

Broccoli tends to be treated in a fairly one-dimensional way (boiled, steamed, or topped with cheese sauce, perhaps) but one need only look to the Italians for inspiration for how best to cook and consume broccoli—after all, they were the first to cultivate it. In Italy, they might slowly braise chopped broccoli in garlic, lemon juice, and loads of olive oil until it collapses into a delicious mass, then serve it at room temperature with rustic bread as an antipasto offering, or tossed warm with pasta and grated pecorino cheese.

The Asian lineage of broccolini makes it a perfect choice for steaming, then drizzling with oyster sauce thinned with chicken stock, as an accompaniment to poached salmon or teriyaki-glazed ocean trout fillets. Broccolini also makes excellent tempura and it gives a crisp burst of green when added to a gingery beef and sweet soy sauce (or kecap manis) stir-fry.

broccoli and ricotta soufflé

Preheat the oven to 375°F. Cook the broccoli florets in boiling salted water for 4 minutes, then drain.

Heat the olive oil and butter in a frying pan over medium heat. Fry the onion for 6 minutes or until soft. Transfer to a large bowl and add the broccoli, ricotta cheese, Parmesan cheese, eggs, nutmeg, and cayenne pepper. Season with sea salt and freshly ground black pepper. Mix well.

Whisk the egg whites with a pinch of salt and the cream of tartar in a bowl until stiff peaks form. Gently fold a third of the egg white into the broccoli mixture, then gently incorporate the remainder.

Grease a 4-cup soufflé dish and sprinkle with the dry bread crumbs. Turn the dish to coat with the crumbs, then shake out the excess. Spoon the broccoli mixture into the dish and bake for 35–40 minutes or until puffed and golden brown.

- 1 cup small broccoli florets
- 2 tablespoons olive oil
- 2 tablespoons butter
- 1 onion, finely chopped
- 1¾ cups ricotta cheese
- ½ cup grated Parmesan cheese
- 3 eggs, lightly beaten
- 1 pinch ground nutmeg
- 1 pinch cayenne pepper
- 4 egg whites
- 1 pinch cream of tartar
- ¼ cup dry bread crumbs

flowers ■ broccoli

broccoli and almond stir-fry

serves 4

Lightly crush the coriander seeds in a mortar, using a pestle. Cut the broccoli into small florets.

Heat the oil in a wok or a large, heavy-bottomed frying pan. Add the coriander and almonds. Stir quickly over medium heat for 1 minute or until the almonds are golden.

Add the garlic, ginger, and broccoli to the pan. Stir-fry over high heat for 2 minutes. Remove the pan from the heat. Pour the combined vinegar, soy sauce, and sesame oil into the pan. Toss until the broccoli is well coated in the sauce. Serve immediately, sprinkled with toasted sesame seeds.

- 1 teaspoon coriander seeds
- 1 head (1 pound) broccoli
- 3 tablespoons olive oil
- 2 tablespoons slivered almonds
- 1 garlic clove, crushed
- 1 teaspoon finely shredded ginger
- 2 tablespoons red wine vinegar
- 1 tablespoon soy sauce
- 2 teaspoons sesame oil
- 1 teaspoon sesame seeds, toasted

cauliflower

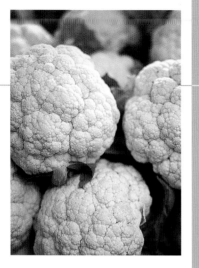

vegetables ▪ **flowers**
season ▪ **peak season winter**

Like its close relation broccoli, the edible part of cauliflower is composed of tightly clustered florets of immature flower buds called the "curd," which is hugged by tight green leaves. The leaves serve to shield the curd from the sun. Unlike broccoli though, the leaves prevent the development of chlorophyll, which would turn it green, thus explaining the cauliflower's characteristic, milky-white color.

Like other members of the brassica family, cauliflower is high in vitamin C, folate, potassium, and cancer-fighting antioxidants. Take note though, cauliflower also contains naturally occurring compounds called purines, which break down to form uric acid, so people with gout are often advised to avoid eating it in copious quantities.

varieties

Although cauliflowers are now generally quite enormous, the restaurant-driven trend for "baby" vegetables has seen the cultivation of miniature cauliflowers, which is quite ironic considering that early cauliflowers were no larger than tennis balls, and over time, were bred to be bigger.

Occasionally, lesser known purple and green versions (such as Romanesco cauliflower) can be found, with the purple turning green upon cooking. Broccoflower, as its name suggests, is a cross between broccoli and cauliflower. Originating in the Netherlands, it is light green, with a milder taste than either of its progenitors.

preparation

To prepare cauliflower, first remove the outer leaves and any tough stalk then, using a small, sharp knife, cut florets from the base. The stems and leaves are completely edible and can be added to vegetable soups and braises if desired. Cauliflower should generally be cooked only until just tender, as it contains phytochemicals which release an unpleasant sulphurous smell when cooked for too long. For the same reason, it is best to cook cauliflower in nonreactive cookware, as the reaction with aluminum and iron can cause it to develop an unsightly brownish hue.

steaming To steam cauliflower, place small florets of the vegetable in a steaming basket over boiling water, cover, then cook for 10–12 minutes or until just tender.

roasting While most cooks wouldn't think to roast cauliflower, it tastes wonderful prepared this way, with all of its nutty sweetness concentrated and none of the trademark sulphurous smell. Simply lay the cauliflower florets in a single layer in a roasting dish, drizzle generously with olive oil, then cook in a 350°F oven for about 30 minutes, turning the cauliflower often or until soft and golden.

culinary uses

Cauliflower is popular in many cuisines. It appears in numerous guises in Indian cooking—cooked with potatoes, mustard seeds, cumin, ginger, and fresh cilantro to become aloo gobi, a north Indian standard. When cooked with lentils and basmati rice, it transforms into a satisfying pilaf; and coated with a turmeric and coriander-spiced chickpea flour batter, then fried, it becomes crisp little fritters called pakoras.

In Sicily, cauliflower finds itself matched with pasta, pine nuts, capers, anchovies, and raisins in a dish typical of the sweet-sour flavors the region favors. Braised in a tomato, garlic, and Italian parsley sauce and finished with lots of grated Parmesan cheese, it makes a great accompaniment for the boiled meat dishes of the country's north.

Serve roasted cauliflower with a tasty dip or spread, or combine with arugula, cooked bacon, and some crumbled blue cheese, and dress with a little balsamic vinegar to make a delicious salad. The English make many variants of cream of cauliflower soup, arguably the best of which includes a decent amount of sharp Stilton cheese to add pungency. Cauliflower is also essential to that very English of pickles, piccalilli.

selection and storage

Choose cauliflower with compact, creamy white curds that are surrounded by perky green leaves. Cauliflower will remain fresh for longer if the leaves are intact. Avoid any with black spots as this signifies spoilage or water damage.

Raw cauliflower should be stored, stem side down (to prevent condensation), in a perforated plastic or paper bag in the refrigerator for up to 5 days.

flowers ■ cauliflower

serves 6

cauliflower and pasta bake

1²/₃ cups short pasta (such as penne)
1 head (about 1 pound 5 ounces) cauliflower, cut into florets
2 tablespoons olive oil
2 red onions, chopped
2 garlic cloves, finely chopped
1/3 cup butter
4 tablespoons all-purpose flour
4 cups milk
2 cups grated Parmesan cheese
3 handfuls basil, torn
5 slices of day-old bread, crusts removed
1/4 cup butter, extra, melted

Preheat the oven to 350°F. Cook the pasta in boiling salted water until *al dente*. Drain and set aside. Steam the cauliflower for 10 minutes or until just tender.

Heat the olive oil in a frying pan. Fry the onions and garlic over medium heat for 5 minutes or until the onions are soft. Combine in a bowl with the cauliflower.

Melt the butter in a large frying pan. Blend in the flour and cook, stirring constantly, for 1 minute. Gradually whisk in the milk. Stir constantly until the mixture boils and thickens. Remove from the heat and stir in 1¼ cups of the grated Parmesan cheese and the basil. Add the cauliflower, pasta, and onions to the sauce and mix thoroughly.

Spoon the cauliflower and pasta mixture into a large ovenproof dish. Cut the bread into large cubes. Toss the cubes in the extra melted butter and sprinkle them over the cauliflower mixture. Sprinkle with the remaining Parmesan cheese. Bake for 35–40 minutes until the top is golden.

Originating in Asia Minor, cauliflower traces its antecedents to wild cabbage, and was initially cultivated by the ancient Romans around 600 B.C. It remained an almost exclusively Italian vegetable until the 1600s, when it became somewhat fashionable in France for a brief period. From there its use spread to Northern Europe and the United Kingdom, where it flourished.

cauliflower pilaf

Put the rice in a sieve and rinse under cold running water. Set aside to drain. Heat the oil in a saucepan that has a tightly fitting lid. Cook the onion over medium heat, stirring frequently, for 5 minutes or until soft and lightly golden. Add the spices and cook, stirring, for 1 minute.

Add the rice to the pan and stir to coat in the spices. Add the stock and cauliflower, stirring to combine. Cover with the lid and bring to a boil. Reduce the heat to very low and cook for 15 minutes, until the rice and cauliflower are tender and all the stock has been absorbed. Stir in the cilantro and serve.

2 cups basmati rice
2 tablespoons olive oil
1 large onion, thinly sliced
¼ teaspoon cardamom seeds
½ teaspoon ground turmeric
1 cinnamon stick
1 teaspoon cumin seeds
¼ teaspoon cayenne pepper
2 cups vegetable or chicken stock
1 large (1 pound 12 ounces) cauliflower, trimmed and cut into florets
2 large handfuls cilantro leaves, chopped

flowers ▪ cauliflower

aloo gobi

serves 4

Heat the oil in a large, heavy-bottomed frying pan over low heat. Add the mustard seeds, cover the pan and wait for the seeds to pop. Add the onion and potato and fry until lightly browned.

Add the turmeric, cumin, coriander, and garam masala to the pan and cook for a couple of seconds. Add the tomato and stir until the spices are well mixed. Add the cauliflower florets and stir until thoroughly coated. Stir in the ginger, sugar, and ½ cup water, increase the heat to medium and bring to a boil. Reduce the heat, cover the pan and simmer for 15 minutes or until the vegetables are tender. Season with sea salt and freshly ground black pepper.

Uncover the pan and if the sauce is too runny, simmer for 1–2 minutes before serving.

3 tablespoons oil
½ teaspoon black mustard seeds
½ onion, finely chopped
2 potatoes, cut into ¾-inch cubes
¼ teaspoon ground turmeric
1 teaspoon ground cumin
1 teaspoon ground coriander
1½ teaspoons garam masala
4 tomatoes, chopped
1 large cauliflower, cut into florets
¾-inch piece of ginger, grated
1 teaspoon sugar

arugula

vegetables ■ **leaves**
season ■ **winter–spring**

Whether called by its British and Australian name of rocket, its Italian tag *rucola*, or French name *roquette*, arugula by any other name is still a peppery, mustard-flavored leafy green, used to best advantage raw in salads or lightly wilted in pasta dishes or risotto. The Italian fondness for this native vegetable is widely celebrated—one need go no further than the simple combination of arugula and shaved Parmesan cheese, drizzled with fruity extra virgin olive oil, to experience it in all its pungent glory.

The ancient Romans were the first to appreciate the fiery flavor of arugula; they used its seeds to infuse oil, and, along with the ancient Egyptians, considered it to have aphrodisiac qualities. Cultivated arugula has much larger, broader leaves (it is sold as baby arugula in its immature state), while wild arugula has small, thin, serrated leaves. Arugula is rich in vitamins A and C, and iron.

selection and storage

Choose arugula with deep green, dry, unblemished leaves, which are not wilted or torn. The smaller the leaves, the milder the flavor, as arugula has a tendency to go quickly to seed and these larger, rampant leaves can be extremely biting.

Store arugula in a loosely sealed plastic bag in the crisper section of the refrigerator and use within 1–2 days, as it is extremely perishable. Wash thoroughly to remove any grit before using and dry carefully using a salad spinner or by blotting the leaves on absorbent paper towels.

culinary uses

In Italy, arugula is not just relegated to the salad bowl, but used to add a fresh, sharp note to endless cooked dishes as well; sprinkled over a crisp pizza along with prosciutto after it appears bubbling from the oven, or included at the last minute in a creamy potato soup, or wilted in pasta sauces. The intense flavor of arugula pairs well with many ingredients, among them avocado, beef, lamb, balsamic vinegar, butter, bresaola, cheese, garlic, lemon juice, olive oil, pasta, pears, pine nuts, potatoes, radicchio, seafood, tomatoes, and walnuts.

For other arugula recipes see:
grilled vegetable terrine 366

arugula tarts

Preheat the oven to 350°F. Cut out four 6-inch circles from the sheets of puff pastry and use them to line four greased 4-inch loose-bottomed tartlet pans.

Prick the pastry bases with a fork. Line the pastry with baking paper, fill with baking beads or dried beans and bake for 15 minutes. Remove the weights and baking paper and bake for an additonal 5 minutes. Remove from the oven and set aside.

Heat the olive oil in a frying pan over medium heat and gently cook the onion for 5 minutes. Stir in the arugula and remove from the heat.

Put the beaten eggs, ricotta cheese, and nutmeg into a small bowl. Season with sea salt and freshly ground black pepper. Beat lightly, leaving some of the ricotta in lumps. Stir in the arugula mixture. Spoon into the pastry shells and bake for about 25 minutes or until set.

2 sheets puff pastry
1 tablespoon olive oil
½ small onion, finely diced
1 large handful baby arugula
   leaves
3 eggs, beaten
½ cup ricotta cheese
1 pinch ground nutmeg

leaves ∎ arugula

spaghetti with arugula and chili

serves 4

Cook the pasta in a large saucepan of boiling salted water until *al dente*. Drain the pasta and return it to the pan.

Meanwhile, heat the olive oil in a large, heavy-bottomed frying pan. Add the chili and cook for 1 minute over low heat. Add the arugula and cook, stirring often, for an additional 2–3 minutes or until softened. Add the lemon juice and season with sea salt and freshly ground black pepper. Add the arugula mixture to the pasta and toss until combined. Serve immediately.

1 pound 2 ounces spaghetti or
   spaghettini
2 tablespoons olive oil
2 teaspoons finely chopped small
   red chili
2 small bunches arugula (about
   1 pound leaves)
1 tablespoon lemon juice

asian greens

vegetables ▪ **leaves**
season ▪ **peak season winter–spring**

Although Asian greens, in their myriad varieties, are eaten by more than half the world's population up to three times every day, they have only fairly recently become familiar to Western countries. Migration and international travel have inspired an appreciation of Asian cuisines, cooking methods, and ingredients, including Asian greens, which now take pride of place alongside broccoli, peas, and beans on dining tables the Western world over. Extremely versatile, highly nutritious, and easy to cook, Asian greens suit stir-frying, steaming, poaching, or adding to braises, curries, and soups. All you need for the makings of a satisfyingly quick meal are a bunch of Asian greens, some seafood, meat, or tofu, and steamed rice or boiled noodles.

Excluding water spinach, Asian greens are cruciferous vegetables that belong to the brassica family. As a group, Asian greens, like other leafy green vegetables, are high in antioxidants, folate, and vitamins A and C. Chinese kale, also called gai larn or Chinese broccoli, boasts the highest concentration of calcium of any green vegetable, with the added plus of also being high in iron and fiber. Baby bok choy and choy sum are ideal vegetables for pregnant women, as they are rich in folate. Water spinach is especially high in iron.

varieties

baby bok choy Also known as Shanghai bok choy or mei quing choi, this popular Asian vegetable is a squat, bulbous-based, small variety of bok choy featuring upright spoon-shaped green leaves and crunchy pale green stems. The succulent leaves have a mild, mustard-like flavor.

Baby bok choy are at their peak during fall and spring—this is the time to steam or braise them whole, then drizzle with oyster sauce and serve as an accompaniment to Asian meals, or halve lengthwise and stir-fry with julienned ginger, then finish with a little chicken stock and light soy sauce.

boy choy Also known as pak choy and Chinese white cabbage, these have a rounded base, lustrous dark green leaves and long ivory-colored stems. Bok choy are the Asian green with the longest cultivation pedigree, appreciated for their crisp thick stems and pleasantly cabbage-flavored, slightly tangy leaves. Separate the stems and leaves before cooking, as the stems take slightly longer to cook, then cook quickly to retain their green color and crunchy texture, as they quickly become soggy due to their high water content. A biennial plant at its best in early summer and late fall, bok choy leaves are a fine addition to clear Asian soups or stir-fries.

choy sum Also called Chinese flowering cabbage due to the usually yellow (but sometimes purple) flowers attached to pale green, slender stems, choy sum has long oval green leaves. While the leaves have a pleasingly sweet mustard flavor, the stems maintain a crunch when properly (that is, briefly) cooked. They are the Asian green of choice for steaming, stir-frying, or poaching.

chinese cabbage Variously known also as Peking or napa cabbage, and wom bok or wong bok, this actually belongs to a different species of brassicas to the European cabbage varieties. Shaped like a cylindrical barrel, Chinese cabbage has tightly packed layers of crinkled green and white leaves that are softer and thinner than those of European cabbage, and a thick white midrib. Its delicate flavor is excellent shredded and eaten raw in salads, lightly steamed, stir-fried, or added to hotpots and clear Asian soups.

chinese kale Also called Chinese broccoli and gai larn, this is one of the most nutritious vegetables available; one cup of cooked Chinese kale has as much calcium as a glass of milk. This healthy vegetable has dark green leaves, delicate white flowers, and green extended broccoli-like stems that should be peeled and halved lengthwise before cooking. Chinese kale best suits parboiling, stir-frying, steaming, or adding to soups just before serving, but ensure that it is briefly cooked until just tender.

gai choy Also called mustard cabbage thanks to its distinctly mustardy flavor, gai choy should have thick, bulbous, pale green stems with crinkled, broad, light green leaves. Traditionally braised, added to soups, or pickled, gai choy can also be stir-fried, although some prefer to blanch it first to temper its strong, tangy flavor.

water spinach A member of the morning glory (*Convolvulaceae*) family, water spinach is an edible aquatic vine that grows rampantly in very moist garden beds or suspended in water. Alternately called water convolvus, ong choi, kang kung or pak bung, depending on where you are, water spinach has numerous dark green, pointy, elongated, narrow leaves radiating from its succulent, hollow, long stems. To cook water spinach, wash well, cut into 2-inch lengths and add to Thai-style curries, Asian soups, or stir-fries.

preparation

When cooking varieties of Asian greens with thick stems, it is best to separate the leaves from the stems and cook the stems first, as they take longer to cook. Asian greens should be trimmed before cooking, then soaked in cold water to remove any traces of dirt clinging to their bases.

To stir-fry Chinese kale, cut trimmed stems into 3/4-inch pieces and cook in a wok over high heat for 1–2 minutes—they should still be crunchy. To steam it, cut the wide stems in half lengthwise and steam for 5 minutes or until just tender. More delicate greens, like Chinese cabbage and bok choy, require just brief stir-frying—sliced leaves will wilt in about 1 minute. Baby bok choy can be steamed whole, which will take 6–10 minutes.

culinary uses

Unless braising whole or halved bok choy or gai choy, or steaming or poaching Chinese kale, Asian greens generally require little cooking—a brief steam or stir-fry is all that is required. Asian greens work best when matched with other defining flavors of Asian cuisines, especially rice, noodles, chili, garlic, ginger, black bean sauce, hoisin sauce, oyster sauce, soy sauce, pork, chicken, duck, seafood, coconut milk, fish sauce, rice wine, tofu, shiitake mushrooms, and sesame oil. They are at their best when simply prepared—sliced bok choy stir-fried with ginger and garlic, for instance, or steamed Chinese kale dressed with black bean or oyster sauce.

storage and selection

Generally speaking, Asian greens should have dark green leaves with no signs of limpness, wilting, tears, or blemishes. Their bases should be dry and firm.

Because of their high water content they generally don't store well, so if possible it is best to use them on the day of purchasing. Otherwise, they can be stored in a perforated plastic bag in the crisper section of the refrigerator for 1–2 days.

leaves ■ asian greens

serves 4

stir-fried tofu with asian greens

2 tablespoons lime juice
3 tablespoons vegetable oil
1½ tablespoons fish sauce
1 teaspoon sambal oelek
½ teaspoon soft brown sugar
7 ounces smoked tofu
1 bunch (14 ounces) choy sum
(Chinese flowering cabbage),
trimmed
4 cups torn English spinach
leaves
2 teaspoons sesame seeds,
toasted
1 small handful cilantro leaves

To make the dressing, put the lime juice and 2 tablespoons of vegetable oil, the fish sauce, sambal oelek, and brown sugar in a bowl and whisk well.

Cut the smoked tofu into ¾-inch cubes. Trim the choy sum and cut into 3¼-inch lengths.

Heat the remaining 1 tablespoon oil in a large wok over medium heat and gently stir-fry the tofu for 2–3 minutes or until golden brown. Add half the dressing and toss to coat. Remove from the wok and set aside.

Add the choy sum to the wok and stir-fry for 1 minute. Add the spinach leaves and stir-fry for 1 minute. Return the tofu to the wok, add the sesame seeds and the remaining dressing and toss lightly. Serve with the cilantro leaves piled on top.

Cultivated in China since the fifth century, pak choy and its descendants did not make their way west to Europe until the mid 1700s, where they did not make much of a mark until the twentieth century. The average person in China consumes about 1 pound of Asian greens each day, most of which are cruciferous.

chinese kale with ginger, lime, and peanuts

97

Put the tamarind in a bowl and pour in the boiling water. Allow to steep for 5 minutes, then strain. Discard the solids.

Heat a nonstick frying pan over high heat, add the peanut oil and swirl to coat the pan. Add the Chinese kale and stir-fry for 2–3 minutes or until wilted. Add the chili, garlic, and ginger and cook for 1 minute, then add the sugar, lime juice, and 1 tablespoon of the tamarind liquid and simmer for 1 minute. Transfer to a plate and drizzle with the sesame oil. Sprinkle with peanuts to serve.

2 tablespoons tamarind pulp
1/4 cup boiling water
1 tablespoon peanut oil
1 large bunch (about 1 pound 5 ounces) Chinese kale (gai larn), trimmed and halved widthwise
1 small red chili, seeded and finely chopped
2 garlic cloves, finely chopped
3 teaspoons finely grated ginger
1 tablespoon sugar
1 tablespoon lime juice
1 teaspoon sesame oil
1 tablespoon finely chopped roasted unsalted peanuts

leaves ■ asian greens

beef and bok choy

serves 4

Wash the bok choy and drain. Cut the leaves into thin strips. Heat 1 tablespoon of oil in a frying pan or wok. Add the garlic and stir-fry for 30 seconds.

Heat the remaining oil; add the meat in small batches, and stir-fry for 3 minutes over high heat until the meat has browned but not cooked through. Remove from the pan.

Stir-fry the bok choy for 30 seconds or until it is just wilted. Add the meat, soy sauce, and sherry. Stir-fry for 2–3 minutes or until the meat is tender. Add the basil and sesame oil and toss well. Serve immediately. Garnish with strips of red bell pepper, if desired.

1 large bunch (about 1 pound 5 ounces) bok choy
2 tablespoons oil
2 garlic cloves, crushed
9 ounces rump steak, thinly sliced
2 tablespoons soy sauce
1 tablespoon sweet sherry
2 tablespoons chopped basil
2 teaspoons sesame oil
1/4 red bell pepper, sliced, to serve, optional

belgian endive

selection and storage

Look for crisp, tightly packed heads with pale, yellow-green or pink tips. Belgian endive is highly perishable and increases in bitterness the longer it is stored, so wrap it in a paper towel, place inside a plastic bag, then keep in the refrigerator vegetable crisper for no more than 1 day.

vegetables ▪ **leaves**
season ▪ **winter–early spring**

Noted for its slightly bittersweet flavor and featuring compact, slender, elongated heads consisting of yellow (or pink) tipped, cream leaves, Belgian endive (also called French endive and witlof) did not really take off until the twentieth century when its cultivation began in earnest.

Expensive and labor-intensive to harvest, Belgian endive is grown in the dark, using a technique called blanching, to prevent sunlight from creating chlorophyll, which would turn its white leaves green. It is then hand-picked and stored carefully wrapped to prevent exposure to light, which even at this stage would turn it green and make it bitter. While not as nutrient rich as green vegetables, Belgian endive contains vitamin A, potassium, dietary fiber, vitamin C, folate, and some iron.

preparation

To prepare Belgian endive, cut away the base, then separate leaves and wash under cold running water; do not soak as this tips the balance of the flavor to the sour side of bittersweet. Do not use cast-iron utensils for cooking, as they will turn the leaves an unappealing shade of gray.

braising Cut heads in half and pack snugly into an ovenproof dish. Add hot chicken stock to cover to halfway, cover the dish with foil and cook in a 350°F oven for 40 minutes until tender.

sautéing To sauté Belgian endive, simply cut into chunks and toss in a large frying pan with plenty of butter over medium-high heat for 5–6 minutes or until softened and golden.

belgian endive with olives, anchovies, and caperberries

Chop the olives and put them in a small bowl. Finely chop the anchovies and add them to the olives. Chop two of the caperberries to the size of baby capers and add to the olives. Add half the olive oil and mix together.

Discard the outer leaves and cut the heads of the Belgian endives in half lengthwise. Open out the leaves a little and spoon the olive mixture over and between the leaves. Join the two halves together again and tie to secure with string.

Heat the remaining oil and the butter in a saucepan over low heat. Add the Belgian endives, garlic, and chili flakes, if using them, then cover and braise for 8–10 minutes, turning halfway through. Add a little hot water if necessary to prevent sticking.

To serve, untie the string and arrange four equal portions of Belgian endive, cut side up, on a serving plate. Spoon over any pan juices. Slice the remaining caperberries in half lengthwise and sprinkle them over the top. Serve hot.

¼ cup pitted Kalamata olives
2 anchovy fillets
5 small caperberries
1 tablespoon olive oil
2 heads pale cream or red Belgian endives
1 tablespoon butter
1 garlic clove, crushed
1 pinch chili flakes, optional

leaves ■ belgian endive

Introduced to Paris to rave reviews in 1872, Belgian endive was so revered that it became known as "white gold." There is a restaurant called Traiteur Restaurant Veilinghof, in the Belgian town of Kampenhout, the hometown of Belgian endive, whose menu is entirely devoted to the vegetable. On the menu are fifty Belgian endive dishes, heaven for the true aficionado.

brussels sprouts

vegetables ▪ **leaves**
season ▪ **winter–spring**

Guaranteed to evoke a passionate response—of either love or loathing—Brussels sprouts are undoubtedly one of the most misunderstood and maligned members of the vegetable kingdom. Overboiled, sulphurous smelling Brussels sprouts may have prejudiced many from their childhoods; yet like their cabbage cousins, when handled correctly they can be a sweet revelation.

Resembling Lilliputian cabbages, Brussels sprouts are actually compact buds that grow in clusters along the stems of the *Brassica oleracea* plant. Like other brassicas, Brussels sprouts are an excellent source of vitamin C and also contain healthy quantities of fiber, iron, phosphorus, potassium, and vitamin A.

selection and storage

Choose firm, verdant green, uniform-size Brussels sprouts with no splitting, browning, or mottling of the outer leaves.

The smaller the Brussels sprout, the sweeter and more tender they will be to eat.
To store, loosely wrap them in absorbent paper, then place in a perforated plastic bag and refrigerate in the vegetable crisper for up to 3 days; their flavor intensifies the longer they are kept.

preparation

As well as boiling, steaming is a good way to parcook Brussels sprouts if you intend to sauté them, bake them in a gratin, or want to finish them in a reduced, creamy sauce. Slice them finely to stir-fry or to use raw in salads. Before cooking, wash the sprouts well, and, if they have come directly from the garden, soak them in cold water in case they contain a few worms. Remove any discolored outer leaves and score a cross into their base to promote even cooking.

boiling To boil sprouts, cook them whole, uncovered, in plenty of boiling salted water for 6–8 minutes or until just tender, then drain well. To steam, cook them halved or whole, for 8–12 minutes or until just tender.

brussels sprouts with pancetta

Preheat the broiler to high. Spread the pancetta on a baking sheet or on a broiler tray lined with foil and put the tray about 3–4 inches under the heat source. Broil for 45–60 seconds or until crisp. Set aside to cool.

Peel the shallots and cut them into thick rings. Heat the butter and oil in a large frying pan over medium heat. Add the shallots and garlic and cook for 3–4 minutes or until just starting to brown. Add the Brussels sprouts and season with freshly ground black pepper. Cook, stirring often, for about 4–5 minutes or until partly golden and crisp. Turn off the heat, cover and set aside for 5 minutes.

Break the pancetta into large shards. Add to the Brussels sprouts and toss lightly; some will break up into smaller pieces. Serve immediately.

¾ cup thinly sliced pancetta
4 shallots
1 tablespoon butter
1 tablespoon olive oil
1 garlic clove, crushed
1 pound (about 20) Brussels sprouts, trimmed and thickly sliced

leaves ■ brussels sprouts

Although there is not an endless array of Brussels sprouts recipes to try, they match brilliantly with bacon, butter, caraway seeds, chives, cream, garlic, horseradish, mace, mustard, nutmeg, roast pork, and shallots. Tiny whole sprouts can be blanched and added to the French classic poached chicken dish, poule au pot, *or stir-fried with garlic, soy sauce, and sesame seeds.*

cabbage

vegetables ■ leaves
season ■ red–fall; green–winter; savoy–spring

Although cabbage tends to be regarded as a rather dreary, soggy excuse for a vegetable, when treated with restraint (not overcooked, that is), it can be most agreeable to eat. Crisp coleslaw is a case in point (the Dutch, incidentally, invented coleslaw or *koolsla,* which in that language simply means "cabbage salad"), as is ribollita, the robust Tuscan bean and cavolo nero or black cabbage soup. Wine-braised red cabbage with apples, brown sugar, and caraway seeds; savoy cabbage with speck; and potato bubble and squeak are other cabbage-based delicacies—there really is no excuse for badly cooked cabbage.

Along with Brussels sprouts, broccoli, and cauliflower, cabbages are members of the extended brassica family. This has long been known for its therapeutic properties; in the Middle Ages, stems of brassicas were applied as a tonic for fractures and wounds, while the seafaring explorers who ate cabbage to guard against scurvy were on to something, as modern science now tells us that it is relatively rich in vitamin C. As a general rule, cabbage also contains potassium, manganese, folate (especially savoy cabbage), vitamins B6 and K, and to a lesser degree, iron, thiamine, and riboflavin. Savoy cabbage also boasts five times more betacarotene than its green and red counterparts.

The Romans adored cabbage, believing it fended off melancholy, and tradition has it that workers on the Great Wall of China were sustained by preserved cabbage. Apparently it was the Chinese who imported preserved cabbage know-how into Europe, where today it is a mainstay of many countries—witness the popularity of sauerkraut.

varieties

cavolo nero This dark blackish cabbage with thick, long, curly leaves originated in Italy, where it is prized for its slightly bitter, yet rich flavor. The Tuscans in particular favor this handsome vegetable, utilizing it in stews and soups, most notably the aforementioned ribollita and various hearty lentil soups. When sautéed or braised with garlic and chili and drizzled with peppery olive oil, it is a magnificent accompaniment to poached, broiled, and roast meat or, along with crumbled Gorgonzola cheese, an easy bruschetta topping.

green or white The most common of all the cabbages, the green and white varieties have rounded heads consisting of tightly packed leaves, thick stems, and largish cores.

Sometimes called Dutch cabbage, the white cabbage's smooth, crisp, and crunchy leaves suit use raw in salads. They are also good cooked in lashings of butter and sprinkled with freshly ground black pepper, or cut into wedges and poached along with corned beef. This type is also the cabbage of choice for making sauerkraut.

The more delicately flavored baby or dwarf green cabbages, which can also occasionally be found, require minimal cooking, and are suited to stir-frying, blanching, or steaming, while larger green cabbages are also ideal for stuffing.

red With a unique purple hue and mellow taste, red cabbage is a vibrant addition to wintry salads, stir-fries, soups, and stews. It is best to cook this cabbage with an acidic ingredient, such as lemons or apples, wine or vinegar, to preserve the distinct color; otherwise, upon cooking, it turns a curious color somewhere between gray, blue, and purple.

Red cabbage makes a vinegary pickle popularly served with cold meat and game; it is also a commendable accompaniment to pork or beef casseroles when baked in a casserole dish with red wine vinegar, onions, and prunes.

For other cabbage recipes see:

savoy The distinctive, dark green, loose heads of savoy cabbage contain large crinkled leaves with tough inner stalks. Savoy cabbage is often regarded as the king of the cabbages due to its milder flavor and attractive leaves; blanched savoy cabbage leaves are the perfect vehicle for a rice, ground pork and veal, and dill stuffing. Its Italian origins also make it perfect for sautéing with porcini mushrooms, potatoes, and sage, then served with short pasta, or added to a creamy fontina cheese and pancetta risotto.

preparation

A whole cabbage is best dealt with by removing all the tough outer leaves, then cutting the vegetable in half lengthwise. Using a large, sharp knife, cut out the hard central core, then thinly slice for use in salads, to braise, steam, or stir-fry. Any unused cabbage will store in the refrigerator, in a plastic bag, for 2–3 days.

If you require whole leaves for stuffing, cut these away at the base, easing them off the head with your fingers—tears are inevitable and you will always need more than a recipe requires to compensate for this. To prepare leaves for stuffing, simply cook them a few at a time in a large saucepan of boiling water for 3–5 minutes or until tender, then drain well and pat dry. Boiled cabbage exudes an unpleasant, sulphurous smell, which possibly explains the legions of non-cabbage eaters. Cabbages contain sulphur compounds which are released when the vegetable is boiled; in fact, the longer the boiling, the more of these compounds are released into the air. For this reason boiling cabbage, and certainly overboiling it, is the least preferred method of cooking. It is far more pleasant to eat cabbage that has been thinly sliced and cooked, covered, with butter and its natural juices—it takes about 7 minutes to cook to tenderness this way.

culinary uses

Cabbage leaves wrapped around various permutations of rice, ground meat, herbs, and spices are a time-honored tradition from Eastern Europe to the Middle East, while life minus the fermented cabbage staple, sauerkraut, would be unimaginable for many Central Europeans. Cabbage pairs admirably with anchovies, apples, bacon, butter, caraway seeds, cheese, chestnuts, chicken, cider vinegar, corned beef, cream, duck, mayonnaise, nutmeg, pancetta, pasta, potatoes, pulses, pork, rice, salmon, smoked meat, sour cream, veal, and walnuts.

selection and storage

Cabbages should be firm and heavy for their size with no yellow or brown patches. Tight-leaf cabbages such as green and red varieties should have tightly closed outer leaves enclosing the heads. They can be stored in a plastic bag in the crisper section of the refrigerator for up to 1 week.

Their loose-leaf cousins, like savoy cabbage and cavolo nero, should have crisp, strongly colored leaves that show no signs of wilting or browning. More perishable than the tight-leaved versions, these should only be refrigerated in a plastic bag in the crisper section for 2–3 days.

Any discolored or wilted external leaves, as well as tough stalks, should be removed and discarded before cooking or eating raw.

leaves ■ cabbage

pork chops with braised red cabbage

To braise the cabbage, heat the clarified butter in a large saucepan, add the onion and garlic and cook, stirring often, over medium heat for 6 minutes or until softened but not browned. Add the cabbage, apple, wine, vinegar, cloves, and sage. Season with salt and pepper. Cover the pan and cook for 30 minutes over very low heat. Uncover the pan and cook, stirring, for 5 minutes, increasing the heat if necessary, to evaporate any liquid.

Meanwhile, trim the pork chops. Heat the clarified butter in a frying pan, season the meat and cook for 4–5 minutes, turning once, over medium-high heat, until the pork is brown on both sides. Add the wine and stock, cover and simmer for 20 minutes or until the pork is tender.

Remove the meat from the frying pan and strain the liquid. Return the liquid to the pan, bring to a boil and cook until reduced by two thirds. Add the cream and mustard and stir over very low heat, without boiling, until the sauce has thickened slightly. Pour over the pork chops and garnish with sage. Serve with the red cabbage.

braised red cabbage
2 tablespoons clarified butter
1 onion, finely chopped
1 garlic clove, crushed
1 small red cabbage, shredded
1 dessert apple, peeled, cored, and finely sliced
1/3 cup red wine
1 tablespoon red wine vinegar
1/4 teaspoon ground cloves
1 tablespoon chopped sage

4 (7-ounce) pork chops
1 tablespoon clarified butter
1/3 cup white wine
1 1/2 cups chicken stock
3 tablespoons heavy cream
1 1/2 tablespoons Dijon mustard
4 sage leaves

classic coleslaw

serves 4

Remove the hard core from the cabbages and shred the leaves with a sharp knife. Toss in a large bowl and add the carrot, radish, bell pepper, scallions, and parsley. Refrigerate until ready to serve.

Just before serving, add the mayonnaise, season to taste with sea salt and freshly ground black pepper, and toss until well combined.

1/2 small green cabbage
1/4 small red cabbage
2 carrots, coarsely grated
4 radishes, coarsely grated
1/2 red bell pepper, chopped
3 scallions, sliced
3 tablespoons chopped parsley
2/3 cup egg mayonnaise

leaves ■ cabbage

lettuce

vegetables ■ **leaves**
season ■ **spring-summer**

Lettuce is without a doubt one of the world's favorite vegetables, and with good reason. Whether adding crunchy interest to an anchovy-spiked Caesar salad, a spicy Thai beef salad, or a simple vinaigrette-dressed garden salad, long summer days are unthinkable without the refreshing presence of lettuce.

Allegedly, lettuces originated in Asia Minor. A member of the sunflower family, lettuce was enjoyed by the ancient Romans and Egyptians, and even graced the tables of Persian kings. The original wild lettuce contained a narcotic similar to opium, and the Romans ate lettuce in the evening to induce sleep—however, the ancients also believed lettuce sparked the appetite so, confusingly, also ate it before dining. Although these civilizations declined, the fortunes of lettuce continued to prosper. Some form of lettuce has been known in China since the fifth century. There it is generally eaten cooked, although the Cantonese made a culinary art form out of raw lettuce with their invention of san choy bau (trimmed crisp leaves filled with aromatic pork, water chestnuts and shiitake mushrooms).

Consisting of approximately 95 percent water, the darker varieties of lettuce are the most nutritious, with the highest concentrations of vitamins A and C, betacarotene, folate, and calcium.

leaves ■ lettuce

selection and storage

When buying lettuce, look for crisp-looking, brightly colored heads and avoid any that are wilted, blemished, or slimy.

Keep lettuces in perforated plastic bags in the refrigerator crisper for up to 2 days. Lettuces need to be washed well before using—they should not be soaked in water as this can make the leaves limp and soggy, particularly the loose-leaved varieties.

A salad spinner is excellent for eliminating excess water from the leaves, which is especially useful if using in a salad, as the drier the leaves, the better the dressing will adhere to them. Remove and discard tough, outer leaves before using.

For other lettuce recipes see:

varieties

With varieties grown around the globe numbering in the hundreds, cultivated lettuces can be divided into four categories.
butterhead As the name suggests, this lettuce has a mild buttery flavor, with smaller, looser heads than their crisphead cousins, and leaves with a soft, thin texture, said to resemble a blossoming rose. With soft, pale green leaves, butter lettuce is the definitive example of this variety, which also contains the curly, reddish purple-tinged, dark green-leaved mignonette. In the U.S. the Bibbs and Boston varieties are popular.
crisphead Generally rotund and consisting of tightly packed layers of juicy, crisp leaves, the most famous member of the crisphead clan is the iceberg—so named because it was first developed in the United States before widespread refrigeration, so the heads were packed in boxes and covered with ice for transport and said to resemble icebergs. The English favor Webb lettuce, while in the U.S. the Imperial, Western, and Vanguard lettuce are popular.
loose-leaf Distinguished by the fact that they do not form a distinct heart or head, loose-leaf lettuces have soft, eclectically colored and shaped leaves emanating directly from their core. Main varieties include the earthy, pale green to rose tinted oakleaf (*feuille de chêne*); the tender, frilly, light green or reddish-leaved coral; and the magenta ruffle-tipped and slightly bitter lollo rosso.
romaine Because it originated on the Greek island of Cos, where it was discovered by the ancient Romans, this lettuce is also known as Cos lettuce. Its narrow, upright, elongated, deep green leaves boast a sweet, crisp, almost nutty flavor. The small, crisp, and tender leaves at the center of the lettuce are sold as "romaine hearts."

culinary uses

Lettuce is undeniably at its best when served as the star ingredient of a simple salad. While we remain hooked on the classics, the diversity and versatility of lettuce provides ample opportunities for thinking beyond the usual lettuce-tomato-cucumber-radish assemblages. For instance, some cuisines cook the leafy green to great effect. The French serve lettuce braised with peas and mint with fish or fowl, while the Greeks use romaine lettuce in a summery lemon and dill-infused lamb stew. However you wish to eat lettuce, it works best with avocado, bacon, beef, bread, cheese, chicken, chili, crème fraîche, cucumber, fish sauce, herbs, lobster, mayonnaise, mustard, noodles, olive oil, peas, pork, shrimp, radishes, tomatoes, turkey, vinaigrette, and vinegar.

salata baladi

To make the dressing, whisk together the oil and lemon juice in a bowl. Season well with salt and freshly ground black pepper.

Put the lettuce, tomato, bell pepper, cucumber, radish, onion, and herbs in a large serving bowl and toss together well. Add the dressing and toss again. Serve at once, while the salad is crisp.

1½ tablespoons extra virgin olive oil
1½ tablespoons lemon juice
1 baby romaine lettuce, leaves torn
2 tomatoes, each cut into 8 wedges
1 small green bell pepper, chopped
2 Lebanese (short) cucumbers, seeded and chopped
4 radishes, sliced
1 small red onion, thinly sliced
2 tablespoons chopped Italian parsley
1 small handful mint leaves

leaves ■ lettuce

red leaf salad

serves 4 as a side salad

Wash and dry the lettuce leaves, then tear them into bite-size pieces.

Finely slice the fennel and onion and toss into a serving bowl with the shredded lettuce. Just before serving, drizzle the olive oil over the salad, then the vinegar. Toss lightly and serve.

5½ ounces mixed red lettuce leaves (such as coral lettuce or lollo rosso lettuce)
1 baby fennel bulb
1 small red onion
2 tablespoons olive oil
1 tablespoon balsamic vinegar

radicchio

vegetables ▪ **leaves**
season ▪ **late fall–winter**

The bold magenta color and distinctive bitter flavor of radicchio add vigor to any dish it adorns; from striking salads to rich risottos, radicchio makes a handsome impression. Along with chicory, curly endive, and Belgian endive, radicchio belongs to the *Cichorium* branch of the daisy (Compositae) family. All radicchio begin their lives green, turning various shades of purple-red as they mature and the weather cools.

Radicchio is associated with the Veneto region of Italy. The ancient Roman author and philosopher, Pliny the Elder, referred to the region's red-flushed lettuces in his authoritative tome of the time, *Naturalis Historia*. Although Pliny credited the Egyptians with cultivating radicchio from wild chicory, it was the Italians who cultivated the numerous modern variants. The original radicchio wasn't red at all—the technique for turning the plants red involves a rather complex process of "blanching" the plants after premature harvesting, in darkened rooms, with the root ends placed in water—resulting in its deep red-colored leaves.

The characteristic bitter flavor of radicchio is due to a chemical called intybin, which both stimulates the appetite and digestive system and assists the functioning of the liver and blood.

selection and storage

Choose radicchio that shows no signs of browning, wilting, or sliminess, and with unbroken, crisp and brightly colored leaves. Inspect the stem end to make sure it looks fresh and not slimy or browned. Like lettuces, radicchio is best stored whole in perforated plastic bags in the vegetable crisper section of the refrigerator, and should be used within 1–2 days.

varieties

The four most common varieties of radicchio are the deep garnet-colored, round-headed radicchio di Chioggia; the more elongated and slender-headed radicchio di Treviso, which has thick white ribs and splayed, crisp, maroon leaves; the soft, crumpled, and speckle-leaved Castelfranco; and America's favorite, the elongated, bright red radicchio di Verona.

In homage to their birthplace, all of these are named after towns in the Veneto region of Italy. Treviso radicchio is the variety best suited to cooking. Castelfranco and Chioggia radicchio are most often found in salads, as their decorative, red-tinged green leaves and pale hearts are milder in flavor.

preparation

As with lettuces, remove the tough, outer leaves and discard. Remove inner leaves and carefully wash them to remove all dirt, then gently dry—do this in a salad spinner having first shaken off excess water, or pat dry on paper towels.

culinary uses

While most people are familiar with a splash of radicchio in a salad, its bold flavor mellows and sweetens when cooked and it is suited to other uses besides brightening up the salad bowl. Try halving Treviso radicchio lengthwise, drizzling with olive oil and grilling, then serving with barbecued quail, tuna steaks, or lamb. Sauté strips of radicchio with butter, garlic, and prosciutto and toss through *al dente* spaghettini. Thinly sliced radicchio also makes an invigorating last-minute addition to a hearty barley soup.

Almonds, artichokes, arugula, butter, cheese (especially goat, Gorgonzola, and Parmesan), chicken, duck, duck livers, hazelnut oil, pasta, rice, swordfish, tuna, or watercress are all good partners to radicchio.

grilled radicchio

Trim the radicchio, discarding the outer leaves. Slice into quarters lengthwise and rinse well. Drain, then pat dry with paper towels.

Heat a barbecue grill plate or grill pan to hot. Lightly sprinkle the radicchio with some of the olive oil and season with sea salt and freshly ground black pepper. Cook for 2–3 minutes, until the under leaves soften and darken, then turn to cook the other side. Transfer to a dish and drizzle with the remaining oil and vinegar.

Serve the radicchio hot with grilled meats, or cold as part of an antipasti selection.

2 heads radicchio
¼ cup olive oil
1 teaspoon balsamic vinegar

radicchio with figs and ginger vinaigrette

serves 4

Wash the radicchio and curly endive thoroughly and drain well. Tear any large leaves into bite-size pieces and toss in a salad bowl.

Peel and segment the oranges, discarding all the bitter white pith. Add to the salad leaves, along with the onion and eight of the fig quarters, reserving the remaining fig quarters.

Whisk the oil, vinegar, cinnamon, orange juice, ginger, and ginger syrup in a small bowl. Season with sea salt and freshly ground black pepper. Pour over the salad and toss.

Arrange the reserved figs in pairs over the salad. If you are using the pomegranates, scoop out the seeds, sprinkle them over the salad and serve.

1 head radicchio
1 baby curly endive
3 oranges or mandarins
½ small red onion, thinly sliced into rings
8 small green figs, cut into quarters
3 tablespoons extra virgin olive oil
1 teaspoon red wine vinegar
1 pinch ground cinnamon
2 tablespoons orange juice
2 tablespoons very finely chopped glacé ginger, plus 2 teaspoons syrup
2 pomegranates, halved, optional

leaves ■ radicchio

sorrel

vegetables ■ **leaves**
season ■ **spring**

Of all the different types of sorrel, it is the cultivated French one that is the best for eating. Its lemony flavor extends a tangy note to salads, sauces, soups, and vegetable purees, and is a particularly good addition to omelettes.

Belonging to the buckwheat family, sorrel is a hardy perennial that has grown wild across Europe, Asia, and the United States for centuries. Similar in shape to spinach, but more elongated and paler green in color, the young leaves are the most tender and have the finest flavor. Extremely rich in oxalic acid, sorrel should be enjoyed in moderation. Sorrel also contains quantities of vitamin A, and to a lesser extent, vitamin C, calcium, magnesium, phosphorus, and potassium.

selection and storage

Sorrel is highly perishable and wilts quickly, so choose bunches with crisp-looking, brightly colored leaves. Those with yellowing, saggy leaves and woody stems are best avoided as they are well past their prime. Store sorrel in perforated plastic bags in the crisper section of the refrigerator, then use within 3 days.

Utilize young sorrel in salads, and more mature leaves in soups and sauces. When cooking sorrel, be sure to add it to your dish at the very last moment, as overcooking turns it an unappealing shade of khaki.

culinary uses

The sharpness of sorrel acts as a great foil for sweet and delicate and very rich ingredients like chicken, cream, eggs, and salmon. In combination with dandelion leaves, young sorrel makes a refreshing salad when dressed with a walnut oil-based vinaigrette.

Buttered, just-wilted sorrel is an ideal accompaniment for ocean trout fillets poached in stock, and, when combined with herbs such as thyme, Italian parsley, chervil, fresh bread crumbs, and butter to moisten, it makes an intriguing crust for baked chicken breasts. Add sorrel to a potato-based cucumber Vichyssoise, then chill and serve as a refreshingly simple first course for an alfresco summer meal; top with a dollop of crème fraîche and salmon roe for a wow-factor finish.

sorrel and asparagus risotto

Combine the stock and wine in a large saucepan and bring to a boil, covered, over high heat. Reduce heat to low and keep at a gentle simmer.

Melt half the butter in a large, heavy-bottomed saucepan, add olive oil, onion, and garlic. Cook, stirring often, over medium heat for 5 minutes or until onion is soft. Add the rice and cook, stirring, for 2 minutes or until rice is hot and coated in oil. Add 1 cup of stock mixture and stir the rice until the stock has been absorbed. Add another cup of stock, stirring until liquid has been absorbed, then repeat the process using another cup of stock.

Add the asparagus and sorrel, then continue adding stock to the rice, 1 cup at a time, stirring until completely absorbed before adding more. Stir in the remaining butter and the Parmesan cheese. Season with sea salt and freshly ground black pepper and serve immediately.

4 cups chicken stock
1 cup dry white wine
1/4 cup unsalted butter, cut into cubes
1/4 cup extra virgin olive oil
1 onion, peeled and finely chopped
2 garlic cloves, peeled and crushed
1 1/3 cups risotto (arborio) rice
24 asparagus spears, trimmed and cut into 3/4-inch pieces
3 1/2 ounces sorrel, washed, trimmed, and finely chopped
2/3 cup grated Parmesan cheese

leaves ■ sorrel

Sorrel is a source of oxalic acid, as is rhubarb. Oxalic acid combines in the body with calcium to form oxalate crsystals, which can be a stomach and kidney irritant and can lead to the formation of kidney stones. Sorrel therefore, although high in various nutrients and utterly delicious, should be consumed in moderation.

spinach

vegetables ■ **leaves**
season ■ available year-round but best winter–spring

Although childhood memories of spinach revolve around the comic strip character Popeye, exhorting us to eat the healthy vegetable, humans can't readily assimilate the high iron content for which it is so fabled. Nonetheless, it is an excellent source of vitamin C, betacarotene, folate, and calcium.

Eaten since antiquity, spinach is thought to have originated in the temperate climes of ancient Persia, where it is still eaten in vast quantities as an integral part of the modern-day Iranian diet. In the Arab world, spinach is considered the "prince of vegetables," featuring in many permutations—combined with eggs and bounteous herbs in thick omelettes, added to lamb stews, consumed in conjunction with pulses, or enjoyed as a side dish with pine nuts and raisins.

From Persia, spinach travelled eastward to China. The Moors took spinach with them to Spain in the twelfth century, but it did not really find favor in Europe until the sixteenth century, when Catherine de Medici brought her favorite vegetables (and Italian chefs to cook them) with her from Florence to France upon her marriage to Henry of Orleans. Since this time, French dishes including a high spinach quotient have come to be known as "a la Florentine"—this description is most applied to eggs, chicken, sole, and quiche.

selection and storage

When buying bunches of spinach, look for those with broad, spade-shaped, jade leaves and undamaged stems. Baby English spinach leaves can also be bought either loose or in prepacked bags. These are an ideal salad green, but take care to choose small, dry leaves with no bruising, wilting, or yellowing as they are extremely perishable.

Spinach needs to be washed carefully in several changes of cold water to eliminate any muddy residue; first remove all the leaves and discard the stalks.

A delicate green, prone to bruising and other leaf damage, spinach shouldn't be stored for longer than 2 days in a plastic bag in the refrigerator.

preparation

Once washed, spinach leaves can be simply cooked, covered, in a saucepan, with the water from washing still clinging to the leaves until just wilted—this will take 3–4 minutes over medium-high heat. It should then be drained in a colander, using a large spoon to press down on the spinach to rid it of as much water as possible. The spinach can be served as is, or returned to a pan with a little butter or cream and perhaps some freshly grated nutmeg, and cooked until the butter melts and the spinach is coated, or the cream is reduced and thickened slightly.

To make spinach puree, simply process the cooked spinach in a food processor and treat it in the same manner as above—serve it as it is, or cook it in a little cream or with some butter.

Whether sautéed, steamed, pureed, or added to stuffings, soups, braises, sauces, or egg dishes, spinach reduces in volume dramatically when cooked, so be sure to buy plenty. As a general guide, two bunches (about 2 pounds) of spinach will suffice for four to six spinach-loving adults.

culinary uses

Matching well with anchovies, butter, cheese, cream, eggs, ham, mushrooms, olive oil, pasta, pastry, prosciutto, soy sauce, sesame seeds, walnuts, and yogurt, spinach's tender, sweet flavor also has a natural affinity with allspice, black pepper, garlic, ginger, lemon juice, mace, mustard, nutmeg, and paprika.

For a Japanese take on spinach, try dressing cooled, wilted baby leaves with soy sauce, rice vinegar, and sesame oil, then sprinkling with toasted sesame seeds and serving with yakitori chicken or grilled salmon skewers. The classic European preparation of creamed spinach is a sumptuous way to deal with a glut of the leafy green and makes an elegant companion for meatloaf.

spinach and feta triangles

Trim any coarse stems from the spinach. Wash the leaves thoroughly, roughly chop, then place in a large frying pan with just a little water clinging to the leaves. Cover and cook gently over low heat for 5 minutes or until the leaves have wilted. Drain well and allow to cool slightly before squeezing tightly to remove excess water.

Heat the oil in a heavy-bottomed frying pan. Add the onion and cook over low heat for 10 minutes or until golden. Add the scallions and cook for 3 minutes. Remove from the heat. Stir in the drained spinach, parsley, dill, nutmeg, Parmesan cheese, feta, ricotta, and beaten eggs. Season with sea salt and freshly ground black pepper.

Preheat the oven to 350°F and grease two baking sheets. Combine the melted butter with the extra oil. Work with three sheets of pastry at a time, keeping the rest covered with a damp dishtowel. Brush each sheet with the butter mixture and lay them on top of each other, then cut them in half lengthwise.

Spoon 4 tablespoons of the filling at the end of each strip, placing the filling on an angle. Fold the pastry over to enclose the filling and form a triangle. Continue folding the triangle over until you reach the end of the pastry. Put the triangles on the baking sheets and brush with the remaining butter mixture. Bake for 20–25 minutes or until the pastry is golden brown.

2 pounds English spinach
1/4 cup olive oil
1 onion, chopped
10 scallions, sliced
1 handful parsley, chopped
1 tablespoon chopped dill
1 pinch ground nutmeg
1/3 cup grated Parmesan cheese
1 cup crumbled feta cheese
1/3 cup ricotta cheese
4 eggs, lightly beaten
2 tablespoons butter, melted
1 tablespoon olive oil, extra
12 sheets phyllo pastry

leaves ■ spinach

For other spinach recipes see:
stir-fried tofu with Asian greens 294

makes 2 x 12-inch pizzas

pizza spinaci

pizza dough
1 tablespoon superfine sugar
2 teaspoons dried yeast or
    1/2 ounce fresh yeast
7 1/2 fluid ounces lukewarm water
3 2/3 cups all-purpose flour
3 tablespoons olive oil

topping
4 tablespoons olive oil
4 garlic cloves, crushed
4 tablespoons pine nuts
4 pounds 8 ounces English
    spinach, trimmed and roughly
    chopped
cornstarch, to dust
2 quantities tomato sauce (see
    page 356)
3 cups grated mozzarella cheese
30 very small black olives
6 tablespoons grated Parmesan
    cheese

To make the pizza dough, put the sugar and yeast in a bowl, then stir in 3 fluid ounces water. Leave in a draft-free spot to activate. If the yeast does not bubble and foam in 5 minutes, throw it away and start again.

Mix the flour and 1/4 teaspoon salt in a bowl or food processor fitted with a plastic blade. Add the olive oil, remaining water, and the yeast mixture. Mix until the dough loosely clumps together. Transfer to a lightly floured surface and knead for 8 minutes, adding a little flour or warm water if necessary, until you have a soft dough that is not sticky but is dry to the touch.

Rub the inside of a large bowl with olive oil. Roll the ball of dough around in the bowl to coat it with oil, then cut a shallow cross on the top with a sharp knife. Cover with a dishtowel or put in a plastic bag and leave in a draft-free spot for 1–1 1/2 hours or until doubled in size.

Punch down the dough to its original size, then divide into two portions. Working with one portion at a time, push the dough out to fit a 12-inch lightly oiled circular tray. Preheat the oven to 475°F.

To make the topping, heat the oil in a frying pan and fry the garlic and pine nuts, stirring often, over low heat for 5–6 minutes until golden. Add the spinach, increase the heat and stir until wilted. Season with salt and pepper.

Dust each pizza base with cornstarch and spoon over half the tomato sauce on each base, spreading to cover. Sprinkle with half the mozzarella. Spread the spinach mixture and olives over the top, followed by the remaining mozzarella and the Parmesan cheese. Bake for 12–15 minutes or until golden and puffed. Brush the rim with a little extra olive oil before serving.

swiss chard

vegetables ▪ **leaves**
season ▪ **spring–fall**

Swiss chard (also called silverbeet), like beets and other members of the *Beta vulgaris* family, actually originated in the Mediterranean, not Switzerland, as the name might suggest. A Swiss botanist named Koch gave it its scientific name, hence the "Swiss" in its common name.

While many people cook just the leaves and the tender white ribs, in many parts of Europe the tougher stalks are actually considered the most prized part of the plant. Unless these are particularly young and tender though, they are best cooked separately, as they take longer to cook. Occasionally, so-called rainbow chard, featuring alternating red, yellow, and white stalks and green leaves, can be found.

Thanks to modern science, we now know that Swiss chard is one of the healthiest of vegetables, rich in folate, vitamins, A, K and C, magnesium, potassium, iron, and fiber. However, it is useful to note that Swiss chard also contains decent amounts of oxalates, natural substances which, when excessively ingested, can concentrate in one's body fluids, exacerbating kidney or gallbladder problems. The oxalates can also interfere with the absorption of calcium.

selection and storage

This hardy perennial vegetable will grow under diverse conditions and even thrive if neglected, but once picked, is not quite so robust. Its vivid, deep green leaves are easily bruised, and it is best not to store it for too long.

Favor Swiss chard with shiny, firm leaves that show no signs of wilting, browning, or yellowing. The ivory colored stalks of common Swiss chard should be unblemished and crisp-looking, while the ruby version should have firm, slender, deep red stalks and scarlet leaves.

Store Swiss chard in a perforated plastic bag in the vegetable crisper for up to 3 days—for ease of storage, you may want to cut off the stalks and store these separately.

preparation

Wash the leaves very well before using, as dirt can lurk in their many folds. Lay several leaves on top of each other, roll up tightly and slice. Cook the leaves, covered, in a very small quantity of boiling water for 5 minutes or until tender, then drain very well. To do this, transfer the Swiss chard to a colander and press down on it with the back of a large metal spoon to extract as much liquid as possible.

To cook the stalks, trim 2 inches or so from the root end of stalks and, using a small, sharp knife, remove any tough strings. Steam or simmer stalks for 8–10 minutes or until tender, then drain well and dress with melted butter or olive oil.

culinary uses

Swiss chard can be used to fill myriad dough-based dishes such as ravioli, phyllo pastry pies such as the *spanakopites* of Greece, and quiche. The Italians make much of it in frittatas, and shredded Swiss chard adds vim to the many cumin-spiced, lemony lentil soups and chickpea casseroles of the Middle East.

Blanched, whole leaves can be used to wrap spiced rice and ground meat combinations, or even used to enclose salmon fillets before steaming. The stalks can also be blanched, then baked into a gratin with cream, nutmeg, and cheese (Parmesan, pecorino, Gruyère, or a blue, for preference), and they can also be diced, sautéed in oil or butter, and included in dishes where the leaves feature, such as risotto, pasta sauces, and vegetable tagines—it is such a shame to waste them!

For other Swiss chard recipes see:

spiced baby turnips 236

sautéed swiss chard

Trim the leaves from the stalks of the Swiss chard and rinse them in cold water. Blanch the leaves in a large saucepan of boiling salted water for 1–2 minutes or until tender but still firm. Drain well in a colander, lay out on a dishtowel, then, using your hands, gently wring out any excess water.

Heat the oil in a heavy-bottomed frying pan and cook the garlic over low heat until just starting to turn golden. Add the Swiss chard, season with sea salt and freshly ground black pepper, and cook over medium heat for 3–4 minutes or until warmed through. Transfer to a serving plate and drizzle with extra virgin olive oil, to serve.

2 pounds Swiss chard (about 2 bunches)
2 tablespoons olive oil
3 garlic cloves, finely sliced
extra virgin olive oil, to serve

warm swiss chard and chickpea salad with sumac

serves 4

Put the chickpeas in a large bowl, cover with water and leave to soak overnight. Drain and place in a large saucepan. Cover with water and bring to a boil, then simmer for 1 3/4 hours or until tender. Drain and set aside.

Heat the oil in a heavy-bottomed frying pan, add the onion and cook over low heat for 5 minutes or until softened and just starting to brown. Cut the tomatoes in half, scrape out the seeds with a teaspoon, then dice the flesh. Add the tomato flesh to the pan with the sugar, cinnamon, and garlic. Cook for 2–3 minutes or until softened.

Wash the Swiss chard and pat dry with paper towels. Trim the stems and finely shred the leaves. Add to the tomato mixture with the chickpeas and cook for 3–4 minutes or until the Swiss chard wilts. Add the mint, lemon juice, and sumac, season, then cook for 1 minute. Serve immediately.

1 cup dried chickpeas
1/2 cup olive oil
1 onion, cut into thin wedges
2 tomatoes
1 teaspoon sugar
1/4 teaspoon ground cinnamon
2 garlic cloves, chopped
3 pounds 5 ounces Swiss chard (about 3 bunches)
3 tablespoons chopped mint
2–3 tablespoons lemon juice
1 1/2 tablespoons ground sumac

watercress

vegetables ■ **leaves**
season ■ **available year-round**

The natural habitat of watercress, as its name would suggest, is in countryside streams and brooks. Like other cruciferous vegetables, watercress is characterized by a tangy, mustard-like flavor. Believed to have originated in the Mediterranean and Asia Minor, its small, embossed leaves have a faintly tart, peppery bite (which becomes distinctly pronounced as it matures) that has been appreciated since ancient times.

Brimming with vitamins C, A, and K, plus potassium, iron, calcium, and copper, watercress was so highly rated by the "father" of modern medicine, Hippocrates, that he sited his very first hospital by a stream in order to have the vegetable close at hand.

selection and storage

Choose vibrant, glossy green watercress, with no wilted, yellowing, brown, or slimy leaves or bruised stems. Darker leaves and thicker stems identify older watercress, which has an overly intense flavor.

Store watercress in a plastic bag in the crisper section of the refrigerator for up to 2 days, or refrigerate with the stalks placed in water and the leaves loosely covered by a plastic bag.

preparation

When ready to use watercress, pick through the bunch and remove the sprigs and the single, tender stalks that occur further down the central stems. Discard any thick, tough stems and gently wash and pat dry.

culinary uses

Watercress is often relegated to the minor role of garnish, but it is deserving of far more attention than this. It lends itself to various other uses—pureed into a potato-based soup, for example, or tossed into all manner of salads. Use it like wilted spinach in a quiche filling or add chopped handfuls at the last moment to Asian-style noodle broths. Watercress cuts the richness of roast meats and pâtés, and a sprig or two served alongside these is a nice touch.

warm spring lamb, watercress, and citrus salad

To make the dressing, put all the ingredients in a small bowl, season with sea salt and freshly ground black pepper and whisk to combine.

Cut the lamb fillets in half and season with freshly ground black pepper. Heat the olive oil in a frying pan over high heat and cook the lamb for 3–4 minutes or until browned all over but still a little pink in the middle. Turn the lamb once or twice during this time. Season with sea salt and remove from the heat.

Peel the oranges and grapefruit, removing all the white pith. Holding them over a bowl to catch the juice, segment them by using a small, sharp knife to cut between the membranes. Put the segments in the bowl with the juices.

Cut the lamb on a diagonal into 1-inch thick slices and add to the bowl, along with the watercress and red onion. Pour the dressing over the salad and lightly toss to coat.

dressing
1 tablespoon red wine vinegar
1 garlic clove, crushed
½ teaspoon honey
2 teaspoons walnut oil
1½ tablespoons olive oil

10½ ounces lamb fillets
1 tablespoon olive oil
2 oranges
1 small pink grapefruit
3 large handfuls watercress, picked over
½ small red onion, finely sliced

leaves ■ watercress

Watercress became a staple part of the working class English diet in the 1800s, when it was eaten in sandwiches for breakfast. Those too poor to buy bread often ate it on its own; hence it came to be known as "poor man's bread." The British still hold watercress sandwiches in high esteem, although they have now entered more illustrious realms, and these days often include boiled eggs, chopped shrimp, or smoked salmon.

avocado

Indigenous to Mexico and tropical Central America, the avocado is an incredible vegetable—although more correctly it is classified as a fruit. With its unique buttery green flesh, which increases in unsaturated fat content and decreases in sugar content as it ripens, there is nothing else quite like it. The avocado is the only member of the laurel family to bear edible fruit; the fruit is also an oddity as it only ripens, or softens, once it has left the tree. The fruit will keep, mature but hard, on the tree for up to seven months without deteriorating, with a single tree bearing up to 120 fruit in a season.

The name "avocado" is a derivation of the Spanish word for the fruit, *ahuacate*, which itself comes from the Aztec name, *ahuacatl*; intriguingly, this word is also Aztec for "testicle." Perhaps because of this, the avocado has long been considered an aphrodisiac.

Avocados have the decadent richness of a dairy food but their fat is mainly of the "good" sort, that is, monounsaturated. This type of fat can actually play a part in lowering certain types of cholesterol in the body. The avocado is also particularly rich in vitamin E and other powerful antioxidants, as well as providing good quantities of potassium, betacarotene, B vitamins, and calcium.

selection and storage

Avocados should only be used when fully ripe, otherwise they are hard and completely tasteless. To determine ripeness, cradle the fruit in your hands and apply slight pressure—it should "give" slightly.

Avocados are perishable so, unless you plan to use them straight away, it is best to purchase them a little under-ripe—they will take 2–3 days to fully soften at room temperature. Once ripe, store them in the refrigerator and plan on using them within 1–2 days.

varieties

Spanish explorers took enthusiastically to the avocado and by the 1650s the three principal strains had been cataloged; these are the Mexican, Guatemalan, and West Indian. Some of the most favored varieties we enjoy today (such as the Hass and the Feurte) are hybrids of Mexican and Guatemalan types.

The Mexican avocado strain is typified by plum-size fruits with very dark, smooth skin and particularly aromatic, anise-scented leaves. Guatemalan types are larger, with green or purple skin, while the lesser-known West Indian varieties are very large, producing fruits that weigh in at over 2 pounds.

hass This is the only variety that grows year-round. Discovered by chance in the 1920s in California, it has gone on to become one of the world's favorite avocados. The fruit features knobbly green skin which turns inky-purple when fully ripe and has rich green, buttery flesh. The skin can be difficult to remove.

fuerte Fuertes have smooth green skin which remains that color when ripe. The flesh is a creamy, pale yellow; make sure they are really ripe as their subtle flavor can be lost to blandness if not fully ready for eating.

reed Reeds are large, rounded fruits with thin, shiny green, easy-peeling skin, and appear in the summer months. Inside, their pale yellow flesh is mild flavored and buttery.

zutano An attractive, pear-shaped fruit with yellow-green skin and rich green flesh; this avocado is particularly easy to peel.

preparation

The easiest way to deal with an avocado is to cut it in half lengthwise around the large central seed. Rotate the halves to separate them, then nudge out the seed with the tip of a spoon—this can also be done by striking the seed with a sharp knife while cradling the avocado half in your other hand—care needs to be employed with this method though, as you can cut yourself if the seed is soft (unlikely) or splits.

Once cut, an avocado browns quickly on exposure to the air —brush it with lemon or lime juice to slow the process down. The skin of some avocados can be brittle or reluctant to come off. In this instance you can employ a large metal spoon to scoop the halved avocado out of its shell or, if you wish to slice or dice it first, do this while still in its skin. Then, using the large spoon, scoop the pieces out in one swoop and use immediately.

Avocado varieties can be used interchangeably in recipes. Don't cook avocados as heat brings out bitter tannins.

avocado salsa

Finely chop the onion. Cut the avocados in half; remove the seed, and cut the flesh into cubes while still in the skin. Use a large spoon to scoop the cubes into a bowl and toss lightly with lime juice.

Cut the tomato in half widthwise, squeeze gently to remove the seeds, then chop finely. Remove the seeds and membrane from the bell pepper and finely dice.

Put the ground coriander and cumin in a small frying pan; stir over medium heat for 1 minute to enhance fragrance and flavor. Allow to cool. Add all the ingredients to a bowl with the avocado and gently combine, so that the avocado retains its shape and is not mashed. Refrigerate until required and serve at room temperature with corn chips.

1 red onion
2 large avocados
1 tablespoon lime juice
1 tomato
1 small red bell pepper
1 teaspoon ground coriander
1 teaspoon ground cumin
3 tablespoons chopped cilantro
   leaves
2 tablespoons olive oil
4–5 drops Tabasco sauce
corn chips, to serve

fruit vegetables ■ avocado

avocado, bacon, and tomato salad

serves 2

Preheat the oven to 350°F. Put the unpeeled garlic cloves on a baking sheet and roast for 30 minutes. Remove, allow to cool, then squeeze the flesh out of the skins and mash in a small bowl. Add the oil, vinegar, and mustard, then whisk to combine well.

Chop the bacon into bite-size pieces, then cook under a medium-hot broiler or dry-fry in a frying pan over medium heat for 3–5 minutes, until crisp. Gently toss the bacon, salad leaves, onion, avocado, and tomato in a bowl. Drizzle the garlic mixture over the salad just before serving.

3 garlic cloves, unpeeled
2 tablespoons olive oil
3 teaspoons balsamic vinegar
1 teaspoon Dijon mustard
3 bacon slices
2 cups mixed green salad leaves
1/2 small red onion, finely sliced
1 avocado, cut into chunks
2 small tomatoes, cut into chunks

bell pepper

vegetables ▪ fruit vegetables
season ▪ **peak season mid-summer–fall**

The large, non-pungent members of the capsicum or chili family are variously called capsicums or, in the United States, "bell peppers," so-named for their squat, blocky, bell shape. They contain a recessive gene which means they don't contain any capsaicin, the heat-producing compound common to all other chilies.

Fleshy, crisp, and (the non-green ones, at least) sweet, bell peppers show up in all sorts of culinary guises. They can be eaten raw (as a crudité or in salads), stir-fried, broiled, braised, stuffed and baked, or roasted.

A member of the nightshade family, bell peppers are native to Central America where they have been cultivated by indigenous populations from around 3500 B.C. They were introduced to Spain and Portugal by returning explorers during the thirteenth century and were quickly embraced in Europe.

They are a feature of many of the world's great ethnic cuisines—Italian, Spanish, Chinese, and Mexican among them. There are a number of famous sweet bell pepper dishes; ratatouille and piperade, both tomato-based vegetable stews from the South of France, are two such examples. Mechouia, a popular salad in Tunisia, and Mahamurra, a hauntingly flavored sauce from Turkey, also use bell peppers to great effect.

varieties

Sweet bell peppers come in a variety of colors—green, red, orange, yellow, purple, and brown. Green bell peppers are actually mature but not quite ripe yellow or red bell peppers, therefore they tend to be less sweet than fully ripe fruits. Green bell peppers also contain less vitamin C than their more brightly colored counterparts, although they are hardly deficient in this department, containing twice as much vitamin C, by weight, than the equivalent in citrus. Red bell peppers contain three times as much vitamin C as green ones and they also contain good quantities of betacarotene.

preparation

peeling Sweet peppers can be used peeled or unpeeled—some find the skin difficult to digest so if in doubt, take it off. If using sweet bell peppers raw, or preparing them for a stir-fry, you can take off the skin using a potato peeler (avoid very creviced peppers for peeling raw). Then slice off the fleshy lobes or sides of the pepper, leaving just the seed-filled core and hard stem end. Discard these, then slice, dice, or chop the flesh and use as desired. The skin can also be removed by grilling, broiling, or roasting the peppers, a common way to prepare the vegetable, as these cooking methods render it particularly tender and sweet. Thus prepared, the cooked, peeled flesh can be used in salads, sauces, chutneys, and stews.

roasting To roast bell peppers, brush whole peppers lightly with oil, place in a single layer in a roasting pan, then cook in a 425°F oven for 15–20 minutes, turning occasionally or until flesh has softened and skin is burnt-looking and will pull away from the flesh. Cool for 10 minutes in a paper bag, or in a large bowl covered with a dishtowel, after which the skin will be particularly easy to remove. Once peeled, cut away the stem end, pull out seeds and tough inner ribs, then cut or tear the flesh into the desired size.

grilling To grill peppers, place them whole on a hot barbecue grill or in a grill pan and cook, turning frequently, until the skin blackens and blisters. This will take about 10 minutes. Cool in the same manner as roasted ones, then pull off all the black skin. Always resist any temptation to wash away skin and seeds under running water, as you will greatly dilute the taste of the vegetable—far better to discover an occasional seed or piece of skin in your food than to eat peppers washed of their flavor.

selection and storage

Choose bell peppers that are heavy for their size and that have bright, tight, smooth, glossy skin with no watery-looking spots or wrinkly patches. Because they are prone to mold and wrinkling, store them in a ventilated bag in the crisper section of the refrigerator for up to 1 week.

bell pepper and bean stew

Put the beans in a large bowl, cover with cold water and soak overnight. Rinse well, then transfer to a saucepan, cover with cold water, bring to a boil, then simmer for 45 minutes or until just tender. Drain and set aside.

Heat the oil in a large saucepan. Cook the garlic and onion over medium heat for 2–3 minutes or until the onion is soft. Add the bell peppers and cook for 5 minutes.

Stir in the tomato, tomato paste, stock, and beans. Simmer, covered, for 40 minutes or until the beans are cooked. Stir in the basil, olives, and sugar. Season with sea salt and freshly ground black pepper. Serve hot with crusty bread.

note 1 cup of dried haricot beans yields about 2 1/2 cups cooked beans. Use 2 1/2 cups of drained canned haricot or cranberry beans instead if you prefer, but add these at the end with the basil, olives, and sugar, and just heat through.

- 1 cup dried haricot beans (see note)
- 2 tablespoons olive oil
- 2 large garlic cloves, crushed
- 1 red onion, halved and cut into thin wedges
- 1 red bell pepper, cubed
- 1 green bell pepper, cubed
- 2 (14-ounce) cans chopped tomatoes
- 2 tablespoons tomato paste
- 2 cups vegetable stock
- 2 tablespoons chopped basil
- 3/4 cup Kalamata olives, pitted
- 1–2 teaspoons soft brown sugar

red bell pepper puree

makes 1 1/4 cups

Broil the bell peppers under high heat for 10 minutes, turning often, until the skin blisters and blackens all over. Place in a paper bag or a bowl covered with a dishtowel, cool slightly, then peel, remove the seeds, and roughly chop.

Put the bell peppers into a food processor and add the scallions, garlic, and chili. Process until smooth. Transfer the puree to a saucepan and stir in the fish sauce (if using), lime juice, and cilantro. Cook over medium heat until slightly thickened. Serve as a dip with an antipasti selection or as a pasta sauce.

- 3 large red bell peppers
- 4 scallions, chopped
- 2 garlic cloves, crushed
- 2 small red chilies, finely chopped
- 2 tablespoons fish sauce, optional
- 2 tablespoons lime juice
- 2 tablespoons chopped cilantro leaves

chili

vegetables ■ **fruit vegetables**
season ■ **available year-round**

storage and selection

Choose chilies that have tight, glossy skins with no trace of bruising or soft, wet spots.

Store them in a loosely sealed plastic bag in the refrigerator—they will keep for up to 1 week.

There are hundreds of varieties of chilies—not all provide a distinctive wallop of heat; some are rather tame—but they are all very nutritious, high in vitamins C and A and betacarotene levels, and are also mildly antibacterial. The heat factor comes from the presence of capsaicin, a compound that causes burning sensations in the mouth and throat. Extreme care should be taken when handling chilies, as the volatile juices can be transferred to eyes and other sensitive parts of the body via your hands. In general, red chilies are hotter than green or yellow chilies, and the smaller the chili, the hotter it will be.

varieties

banana A mild-tasting chili, practically benign when immature and only pleasantly tangy when fully red. They are sold with pale yellow, waxy-looking skin. They are a conical-shaped, tapering chili, about 7 inches long.

bird's eye These are either green or red and are a very small, bullet-shaped chili with smooth, glossy skin and are very hot.

habanero An extremely hot, fruity-tasting chili with a rounded lantern shape, these small chilies have thin, waxy flesh.

jalapeño A famous, moderately hot green chili with a red blush (later in the season they mature and turn red). They are 2–3 inches long.

serrano A small, cylindrical chili with a blunt end. They are thin-skinned with meaty flesh and are bright green, ripening to red-brown or orange. They are reputed to be five times hotter than the jalapeños.

chili con queso

Melt the butter in a saucepan over medium heat. Add the onion and green and red chilies and cook for 5 minutes or until softened. Increase the heat to high, add the garlic and paprika and cook for 1 minute until fragrant.

Add the beer, bring to a boil and cook until the beer has almost evaporated. Reduce the heat to low and add the sour cream, stirring until smooth. Add the cheese and stir until the cheese is just melted and the mixture is smooth. Remove from the heat, stir in the cilantro and jalapeño and season to taste. Serve with corn or tortilla chips, for dipping.

1½ tablespoons butter
½ red onion
2 large green chilies, seeded and finely chopped
2 small red chilies, seeded and finely chopped
1 garlic clove, crushed
½ teaspoon sweet paprika
1½ tablespoons beer
½ cup sour cream
1⅔ cups grated cheddar cheese
1 tablespoon chopped cilantro leaves
1 tablespoon sliced jalapeños
corn or tortilla chips, to serve

fruit vegetables ■ chili

sweet chili sauce

makes ¼ cup

In a mortar using a pestle or in a blender, pound or blend the chilies into a rough paste.

Put the vinegar, sugar, and ½ teaspoon salt in a small pan over high heat and bring to a boil, stirring constantly. Reduce the heat to medium and simmer for 15–20 minutes, until the mixture forms a thick syrup. Spoon the chili paste into the syrup and cook for 1–2 minutes. Remove from the heat and pour into a serving dish to serve as a dipping sauce.

7 long red chilies, seeded and roughly chopped
¾ cup white vinegar
8 tablespoons sugar

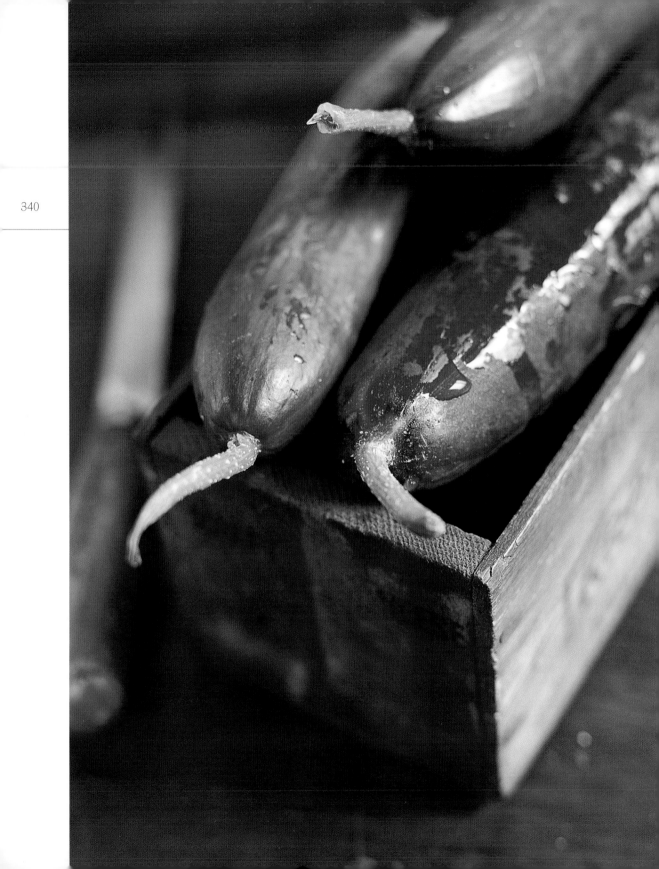

cucumber

vegetables ■ **fruit vegetables**
season ■ **peak season summer**

Belonging to the same botanical family as melons and gourds, cucumbers have suffered somewhat during modern cultivation processes, in much the same way as has the tomato. Major varieties are grown and packaged for supermarket supply, requiring that cucumbers be uniform in size and are able to transport and store well. With their shiny, shrink-wrapped (or worse, waxed) skins and bland interiors, they often end up as nothing more than an innocuous, crunchy presence in the salad bowl.

There are boundless cucumber varieties though, coming in round and oval shapes, yellow, pale green and bronze colors, and various sizes, from gherkins that are barely over 1 inch long, to mammoth English types that can be over 20 inches long. Do try to search out those produced by a caring grower, and a whole world of herbal, sweet, grassy flavors will be opened up.

Cucumbers contain silica, an essential component of healthy connective tissue and therefore very good for the skin. Over the centuries cucumber has been used topically to treat dermatitis, sunburn, and eye-swelling. Containing significant amounts of ascorbic and caffeic acids, the cucumber is also helpful in preventing fluid retention, no mean feat considering it is comprised of 96 percent water itself.

selection and storage

Select cucumbers that are heavy for their size and that are firm and unblemished. Inspect ends closely to check for softness or wrinkling (a sign of age or poor storage) and go for ones that are small and slender for their type. These will be younger and therefore sweeter than more mature cucumbers. Green varieties should have little, if any, signs of yellowing.

Store unwashed cucumbers in the vegetable crisper section of the refrigerator in a ventilated plastic bag—note that they do not like excessive cold so don't store them in the coldest part of the refrigerator.

varieties

garden Also called the common cucumber, this variety is generally sold waxed, and is a slicing cucumber. It is stumpy and has rounded ends and a thick, slightly bitter skin with large seeds. It is best to peel and seed this cucumber. The chopped or grated flesh is good in soups and dips or tossed at the last moment into a reduced cream and tarragon (or dill) sauce for serving with fish.

gherkin The classic pickling cucumber, these short, slightly warty-skinned specimens have been bred specifically for this purpose. They are pickled whole—no peeling, slicing, or seeding is required before use.

lebanese (short) These are smallish, about 4 inches in length, and sweetly mild-tasting—they can be eaten out of hand, skin, seeds and all, as a refreshing snack. These cucumbers are especially juicy and are great in salads or any recipe that calls for raw, unpeeled cucumber.

telegraph (long) This is also called the English, continental, or "burpless" cucumber and invariably comes plastic-wrapped (to protect against drying out). It is long and slim with tapered ends and has glossy green, quite thin skin and small seeds. This cucumber can be used without being peeled or seeded and is therefore great in salads and salsas. Check with your supplier though, that the skin is not waxed—if it has been, you will need to peel before using.

preparation

To seed cucumbers, simply slice them in half lengthwise, then use a teaspoon to scoop out all the seeds. If adding sliced or grated cucumbers to a yogurt or sour-cream based dip or soup, do so at the last moment as they will release a lot of water upon standing.

culinary uses

Generally speaking, the flavor and texture of cucumber goes very well with mint, parsley, chives and tarragon, vinegar, chili, ginger, sour cream and cream, butter, yogurt, lemon, and seafood. Also think of putting it with certain cheeses, particularly the likes of feta or sharp, soft-textured goat cheese, which makes a fine match.

cucumber, feta,
mint, and dill salad

Put the crumbled feta in a large bowl. Peel and seed the cucumbers, then cut into 1/2-inch dice. Add to the bowl along with the onion and dill.

Grind the mint in a mortar using a pestle until powdered. Combine with the oil and lemon juice, then season with sea salt and freshly ground black pepper. Pour over the salad and toss well.

3/4 cup roughly crumbled feta cheese
4 Lebanese (short) cucumbers
1 small red onion, thinly sliced
1 1/2 tablespoons finely chopped dill
1 tablespoon dried mint
3 tablespoons olive oil
1 1/2 tablespoons lemon juice

fruit vegetables ■ cucumber

tsatsiki

makes 2 cups

Cut the cucumbers in half lengthwise, scoop out the seeds with a teaspoon and discard. Leaving the skin on, coarsely grate the cucumber into a small colander. Sprinkle with a little salt and leave to stand over a large bowl for 15 minutes to drain off any bitter juices.

Meanwhile, stir together the yogurt, garlic, mint, and lemon juice in a bowl. Rinse the cucumber under cold water, then, taking small handfuls, squeeze out any excess moisture. Combine the cucumber with the yogurt mixture and season to taste. Serve immediately or refrigerate until ready to serve. Garnish with mint. Can be served as a dip with flat bread or as a sauce for seafood and meat dishes.

2 Lebanese (short) cucumbers
1 2/3 cups plain yogurt
4 garlic cloves, crushed
3 tablespoons finely chopped mint
1 tablespoon lemon juice
chopped mint, extra, to garnish

eggplant

vegetables ▪ **fruit vegetables**
season ▪ **peak season mid-summer–early fall**

The eggplant is often thought of as a Mediterranean vegetable, and with good reason; some of the world's most iconic eggplant dishes come from that region. There's caponata and eggplant parmigiano from Italy, ratatouille from the south of France, and moussaka from Greece. Turkey is thought to have over 1,000 recipes for eggplant of which imam bayildi is perhaps the most famous. So it may surprise some to learn that the eggplant is native to Asia, probably originating in India or Burma (experts can't quite agree).

The only member of the deadly nightshade clan to be native to the East, the eggplant was once viewed with enormous suspicion in certain parts of Europe. Arab traders took the vegetable west, first to Spain. The Spanish warmed to it quite readily and called it the "apple of love" as they believed it to possess aphrodisiac powers. The Italians also, cautiously, developed an appreciation for the culinary possibilities of the eggplant, but in northern Europe and England it was used ornamentally only, as superstition held that eating it would induce insanity, which explains why some called it the "mad apple."

varieties

There are many eggplant varieties. They come in more shapes, sizes, and skin colors than most of us are likely to encounter—some are yellowish or orange or brown, black, pink-and-white striped, lavender, or green. They vary in size from well over 1 pound in weight to the diminutive pea eggplants used in Thai cookery. Some of the most commonly grown varieties are listed below.

japanese These eggplants are long, 6–8 inches, and slim, about 1¼ inches in diameter. They are usually purple-skinned but can also be light mauve. Their flesh is cream-colored and mildly sweet-tasting. Japanese eggplants are great for stuffing and baking, pickling, stir-frying, broiling, and steaming. It doesn't require peeling.

pea These grow in tiny clusters and come in a variety of colors—red, orange, green, and purple. They have an assertive, bitter flavor and are used in Asian cuisines, mainly in pickles and curries, although in Thailand they are eaten raw, accompanied by chili jam.

thai These are small and round (about the size of a ping pong ball), lavender with green striations, or green or cream. They have tough skin, a seedy interior, and a strong flavor—they are used, unpeeled and sliced in Thai soups, salads, and curries where they add a pleasantly bitter note.

western or globe This is the classic, large, dark purple eggplant and the sort most commonly available. These vary in size from around 12 ounces to 1 pound and, when in perfect condition, have pale flesh with few visible seeds. When they are past their prime, the flesh becomes darker, the seeds become more numerous and the flavor deteriorates into bitterness. These are the most versatile eggplant and can be sliced for frying or broiling, or cut into chunks for roasting, stewing, or sautéing. They can be peeled or not—many prefer to peel—as the skin can be tough.

preparation

salting Debate rages over the necessity of salting eggplant flesh before cooking it. The reason generally given for salting is that salt extracts bitterness, but generally commercially grown eggplants are not bitter unless they are old and past their best. However, there are other reasons to salt eggplant.

The food scientist Harold McGee believes that salting collapses air pockets in the spongy flesh, resulting in eggplant less prone to soaking up excess oil when cooked. Salting also seems to improve the cooked texture of eggplant, especially when it is to be sliced and broiled or barbecued.

To salt, remove the green calyx (which is spiky, so be careful), then slice the eggplant into the desired thickness or cut into chunks. Layer these in a colander, sprinkling with sea salt as you go, then stand the colander over a sink or bowl to collect juices, for 30–40 minutes. Discard the juices and rinse eggplant well in plenty of cold water, drain then pat dry on paper towels. You can then proceed with your recipe. Note that eggplant is one vegetable that should never be undercooked—it needs to be cooked to the point of sweet collapse.

baking To bake eggplant, toss chunks or wedges of eggplant in oil, arrange in a single layer in a baking dish, then cook in a 350°F oven for 40–50 minutes (depending on size) or until golden and soft.

chargrilling To chargrill whole eggplant (useful for making dips and spreads) prick a whole, unpeeled eggplant several times with a thin metal skewer, then cook directly over a gas flame, turning often, for 25 minutes or until the skin is completely blackened and the eggplant is soft. (You can also do this on the barbecue.) When cool enough to handle, remove all of the skin, then drain the flesh well in a colander, squeezing to remove excess moisture. This method results in wonderfully smoky-flavored eggplant but can be somewhat messy (put foil around the gas element to catch juices).

This can also be done with less mess in the oven, although the cooked eggplant flesh won't have that smoky flavor. Brush a whole eggplant lightly with oil, prick several times with a thin metal skewer, place in a roasting pan, then cook in a 350°F oven for 45 minutes or until very soft. Allow to cool before peeling.

grilling To grill eggplant, cut it into slices and brush with oil. Cook over medium heat on a barbecue grill for about 3 minutes each side or until well-marked and tender.

selection and storage

Eggplants are quite perishable, so it is important to choose them at their peak. They should be firm and heavy for their size and have taut, shiny, smooth skins. When you press the skin of a larger eggplant, a dent should form but should disappear soon after.

The smaller, tender Japanese eggplants may not spring back when pressed. The calyx end should be a little moist and firmly attached. Store eggplants for no more than 2–3 days, and at cool room temperature in preference to refrigerating. Eggplants don't like cold, and can brown and alter in flavor if refrigerated.

serves 4

moroccan eggplant
with couscous

1 cup instant couscous
¾ cup olive oil
1 onion, halved and sliced
1 eggplant
3 teaspoons ground cumin
¼ teaspoon ground cinnamon
1 teaspoon paprika
¼ teaspoon ground cloves
¼ cup butter
1 handful parsley, roughly
   chopped

Put the couscous in a large bowl and add 1½ cups boiling water. Leave for 10 minutes, then fluff with a fork.

Add 2 tablespoons of oil to a large frying pan and cook the onion for 8–10 minutes or until browned. Remove from the pan using a slotted spoon, retaining the cooking oil.

Cut the eggplant into ½-inch slices, then into quarters, and place in a large bowl. Combine the cumin, cinnamon, paprika, cloves, and ½ teaspoon salt and sprinkle over the eggplant, tossing until it is well coated. Add the remaining oil to the pan and reheat over medium heat. Cook the eggplant, turning once, for 20–25 minutes or until browned. Remove from the pan and cool.

Using the same pan, melt the butter, then add the couscous and cook, stirring, for 2–3 minutes or until warmed through. Stir in the onion, eggplant, and parsley, allow to cool, then serve.

For other eggplant recipes see:

grilled vegetable terrine 366

eggplant marinated in chermoula

Cut the eggplants into 1/2-inch thick slices and sprinkle with salt. Set aside for 30 minutes, then rinse and pat dry. Brush the eggplant slices liberally with olive oil and cook under a preheated broiler until golden brown on both sides. Drain on paper towels.

To make the chermoula, combine all the ingredients. Add the eggplant and toss. Cover and refrigerate for 1 hour. Serve at room temperature.

note Chermoula is also used to marinate fish. The fish, either whole fillets or pieces, is left to marinate overnight, then can be fried, grilled, or baked.

2 eggplants
olive oil

chermoula
2 garlic cloves, crushed
1 tablespoon ground cumin
1 teaspoon ground cinnamon
1/4 teaspoon cayenne pepper
1 teaspoon allspice
1/4 cup lemon juice
3 tablespoons chopped cilantro
  leaves
2 tablespoons chopped mint
1/2 cup olive oil

fruit vegetables ■ eggplant

eggplant jam

serves 6–8

Cut the eggplants into 1/2-inch thick slices. Sprinkle with salt and drain in a colander for 30 minutes. Rinse well, squeeze gently and pat dry. Fill a large frying pan with 1/4 inch of olive oil. Place over medium heat and fry the eggplant in batches for 4–5 minutes, turning once or until golden brown on both sides. Drain on paper towels, then chop finely.

Put the eggplant in a colander and leave it until most of the oil has drained off, then transfer to a bowl and add the garlic, paprika, cumin, cilantro, and sugar.

Wipe out the frying pan, add the eggplant mixture and stir constantly over medium heat for 2 minutes. Transfer to a bowl, stir in the lemon juice and season. Serve at room temperature as a dip or with other salads.

2 eggplants
olive oil, for shallow-frying
2 garlic cloves, crushed
1 teaspoon paprika
1 1/2 teaspoons ground cumin
2 tablespoons chopped cilantro
  leaves
1/2 teaspoon sugar
1 tablespoon lemon juice

tomato

fruit vegetables ▪ tomato

Thanks (or, more accurately, no thanks) to year-round supply, tomatoes have all but lost their association with the arrival of summer. Not, however, for the legions of home gardeners who lovingly tend their vines and anticipate the summer's crop; in fact, only by growing your own tomatoes, or buying seasonally from a local grower, can you hope to experience that sweet-acid, fragrant, juicy hit of a "real" tomato. In her worthy *Vegetable Book*, the late Jane Grigson declared the tomato "needs someone to save it from the dragon of commerce," and it is indisputable that the vast majority of tomatoes that adorn supermarket shelves are pallid, flavorless specimens; one is better off using a good canned product in cooking instead.

Although the tomato is associated closely with Italy, it is interesting to note that tomato sauce wasn't paired with pasta until the mid-1700s and the tomato didn't become widely popular (and then, only in Italy's south) until the late 1800s. Also of interest is the fact that the Italian name for tomato, *pomodoro*, comes from the earliest name they coined for it, *pomi d'oro* (golden apple), hinting at its original color. The English name comes ultimately from the Aztec name *tomatl*, while the fruit's Latin nomenclature, *Lycopersicon esculentum*, means "edible wolf's peach."

nutrition

There's been a lot of press in recent years for the health-promoting properties of tomatoes. This has mainly concerned the lycopene they contain, a substance that gives tomatoes their red color. Lycopene is a potent antioxidant and is believed to be an effective protector against the development of cancers (particularly prostate cancer in men) and heart disease.

Lycopene is particularly abundant near the skin of the tomato and is said to be more readily absorbed when cooked with certain oils—particularly olive oil.

Tomatoes are also generous providers of vitamins A and C and, in their raw state, vitamin E. They contain a veritable brew of minerals, including potassium, calcium, and folic acid.

selection

The best test of a great tomato, even more than its color, is aroma—smell the stem end and you should be able to inhale strong, sweet-acid tomato wafts. If not, then don't bother buying.

Tomatoes that have been fully ripened on their vines by the sun are terribly perishable, which is exactly the reason that, for supermarket sale, they are picked while green. These tomatoes are then ripened to redness, or sunny yellowness, in controlled environments using ethylene gas and, even though they may look the part, their flavor, aroma, and texture never fully develop.

Choose tomatoes that are plump-looking and shiny and that "give" slightly to pressure when pressed. They should feel heavy for their size and, needless to say, be free of soft spots, blemishes, and bruises.

Tomatoes with such skin damage will quickly turn moldy and spoil.

varieties

It would be near-impossible to comment on every variety of tomato—even to include all those which are commonly available worldwide would require a lengthy discourse. It is perhaps more helpful to talk generally of types of tomatoes. Each tomato variety has unique characteristics. Variables include skin thickness, flesh density, juiciness, and the size and quantity of seeds, making some more suitable for certain uses over others.

cherry Cherry tomatoes have the greatest amount of sugar of all the tomato types and their taste is a concentrated burst of tomato sweetness. These are a good choice for eating raw whether tossed through salads, coarsely chopped into a salsa, or pureed to form an uncooked sauce or used to flavor vinaigrette. They can, of course, be cooked and are perfect when halved and used to top a homemade pizza or, tossed with a little olive oil, briefly roasted and served as a vegetable side dish with fish, chicken, or meat. They can also be cooked in the pan with quick-cooking meat cuts (a lamb loin for example) or fillets of fish.

beefsteak These are the giants of the tomato world, needing hot, late-summer sun to fully ripen. Beefsteaks have a unique ribbed shape and their firm, juicy flesh (of which their name is highly descriptive) is punctuated throughout by little pockets of seeds. Because of their shape and size, they lend themselves to being sliced and slipped into hamburgers or sandwiches. They can be used in salads—cut into pieces or baton shapes—and are also a good choice for cooking.

green Some heirloom varieties are green when ripe but generally, tomatoes sold as "green" are those at the end of the season, which will fail to fully ripen in the cooling weather. If set on a sunny ledge, though, they may continue to ripen; however green tomatoes have special characteristics and uses of their own. Firm, not as juicy as their ripe counterparts, and piquant-tasting, green tomatoes are wonderful when made into relishes and chutneys, and their suitability for frying is legendary.

golden or yellow Most red varieties have a golden equivalent, from cherry tomatoes through to plums and the large beefsteaks. These taste more or less identical to red tomatoes (although some claim that yellow cherry tomatoes are sweeter than red) and can be used in exactly the same ways.

round or salad These rounded, squat, medium-size tomatoes are the best known and most used, perhaps, of all the tomato types. Generally they have quite juicy interiors with large seed cavities and are a good all-purpose tomato; their shape lends itself to slicing, dicing or cutting into wedges for salads, to hollowing out for stuffing and baking, or to cutting in half (either width or lengthwise) or quarters and roasting, broiling, pan-frying, or semidrying in a coolish oven. These tomatoes are also suitable for chopping, and using in sauces, stews and soups.

plum These tomatoes are characterized by their thickish skin, elongated shape, and large interior "core." They are variously called "egg," "Italian," "Roma," and "paste" tomatoes and are great for cooking as their flesh is particularly dense and firm—they hold their shape well when cooked. They have fewer seeds than other sorts of tomatoes and have less juicy (but no less flavorsome), meaty flesh. Use these wherever it is necessary to cook tomatoes—in pasta and other sauces, in casseroles, soups, and braises. They are also very good for ovendrying or sun drying and also for preserving for winter use.

preparation

So many recipes tell the cook to peel the tomatoes, but many neglect to explain how. In most dishes that utilize tomatoes, removing the skin is a necessary refinement, as is, on occasion, the removal of the seeds. Author Marcella Hazan puts it thus, "A tomato's skin is a veil which obscures the wonders of its flesh. If you leave it on, the tomatoes will eventually shed their skin as they cook and later you will either have to spit it out or, since it is not pleasant to chew on, swallow it."

peeling Using a small, sharp knife, cut a small cross-shape incision into the base of your tomatoes (some people cut quite large ones; this is unnecessary), then drop them, a few at a time, into a saucepan of boiling water. Leave them for about 20 seconds (the time is variable depending on tomato ripeness and variety), then remove them with a slotted spoon and immediately plunge them into iced water. Pull the skin away, starting from the cross-shape incision (a small knife can be useful here); it should come off very easily. If not, the tomatoes have not been blanched for long enough. Beware of leaving them in the boiling water for too long as this will cause the flesh to become mushy—it should still be firm and "suedelike" when the skin is peeled.

seeding To seed tomatoes, cut them into quarters after they have been blanched and the stem end removed. You can use your fingers to nudge the seeds and their flavorsome, jellylike surrounds out. Collect the seeds and reserve for some other use—in stockmaking, soups, or pasta sauces for example. To seed a whole tomato for baking, cut the top 1/2 inch or so off an unseeded tomato, then use a teaspoon to scoop out the seeds and soft pulp.

storage

Tomatoes should be stored at cool room temperature, out of their packaging and definitely not in the refrigerator—and used within a few days.

The refrigerator diminishes the flavor of tomatoes; as a subtropical fruit, they do not like the cold. If you purchase under-ripe tomatoes (those with green "shoulders" or the occasional green patch, for example) they will ripen fully, given the right conditions. Leave them somewhere warm and in full sunlight if possible.

The best way to store a glut of tomatoes for future use is by freezing. This can most easily be done by simply freezing them whole—once they thaw, the skins will easily slip off and you just need to cut away the stem end. Alternatively, they can be frozen peeled and chopped, or peeled and pureed.

serves 4

tomato tarte tatin

12 plum tomatoes
4 tablespoons olive oil
3 red onions, finely sliced
2 garlic cloves, finely sliced
1 tablespoon balsamic vinegar
1 teaspoon soft brown sugar
1 handful basil, finely chopped
1/3 cup crumbled goat cheese
1 sheet puff pastry

Preheat the oven to 300°F. Score a cross in the top of each tomato, plunge into boiling water for 20 seconds, transfer to a bowl of iced water to cool, and then peel the skin and discard. Cut tomatoes in half lengthwise, and season well. Place the tomatoes, cut side up, on a rack in a baking dish. Cook in the oven for 3 hours.

Heat 2 tablespoons of oil in a heavy-bottomed saucepan, add the onions and cook over very low heat, stirring often, for 1 hour or until caramelized.

When the tomatoes are ready, remove from the oven and increase the oven temperature to 400°F.

Heat the remaining olive oil in an 8-inch ovenproof frying pan over medium heat. Add the garlic, vinegar, sugar, and 1 tablespoon water and cook until the sugar dissolves. Remove from the heat. Arrange the tomatoes in concentric circles inside the pan, cut side up, in one layer. Top with the onions, basil, and crumbled goat cheese. Cover with the puff pastry, trim the edges, and tuck the pastry into the side of the pan around the tomatoes. Bake for 25–30 minutes or until the pastry is golden. Carefully invert the tart onto a plate, cool to room temperature and serve.

The tomato is an Andean native. It grew wild in various regions of South America and, although eaten by pre-Colombian peoples, wasn't considered worthy of domestication. These early tomatoes were small (about the size of the cherry tomato we know today) and yellow.

fennel, tomato, and garlic gratin

Preheat the oven to 400°F. Grease an 8½-inch square gratin dish. Cut the fennel in half lengthwise, then slice thinly.

Heat the olive oil in a large frying pan. Cook the onion for 3–4 minutes until softened but not browned. Add the garlic and cook for 2 minutes. Add the fennel and cook, stirring frequently, for 7 minutes or until softened and golden brown.

Score a cross in the top of each tomato, plunge into boiling water for 20 seconds, transfer to a bowl of iced water to cool, and then peel the skin and discard it. Chop the flesh roughly and add to the fennel. Cook, stirring frequently, for 5 minutes or until the tomato is softened. Season well and transfer the vegetables to the dish.

To make the gratin topping, mix together all the ingredients, sprinkle over the vegetables and bake for 15 minutes or until golden brown and crisp. Serve immediately.

2 fennel bulbs
⅓ cup olive oil
1 large red onion, halved and
   thinly sliced
2 garlic cloves, crushed
3 tomatoes

gratin topping
¾ cup fresh white bread crumbs
⅔ cup grated Parmesan cheese
2 teaspoons grated lemon zest
1 garlic clove, crushed

fruit vegetables ▪ tomato

For many centuries it was believed the tomato was poisonous (not an unreasonable assumption given that it is a nightshade family member and its leaves are, in fact, toxic) and an aphrodisiac. The wealthy, in particular, spurned the tomato although they did grow them for ornamental purposes—poorer classes started eating them out of necessity. Eventually, seeds of red tomatoes were taken to Italy from Mexico and then the tomato really started to take off as a culinary item.

makes 40 slow-roasted balsamic tomatoes

10 firm plum tomatoes
8 garlic cloves, crushed
⅓ cup superfine sugar
4 tablespoons torn basil leaves
4 teaspoons chopped oregano
  leaves
few drops good-quality balsamic
  vinegar

Preheat the oven to 275°F. Line two baking sheets with baking paper. Cut each tomato lengthwise into quarters and put the quarters in rows on the baking sheets.

Mix the garlic with the sugar, basil, oregano, and balsamic vinegar. Using clean fingers, put a little of the mixture onto the sides of each tomato quarter and season with sea salt and freshly ground black pepper.

Bake in the oven for 2½ hours. The tomatoes are ready when they are slightly shrivelled at the edge and semidried (they should still be soft in the middle). Eat warm or cold and store in the refrigerator. Serve with barbecued lamb cutlets, beef steak, or as part of an antipasti selection.

makes 7 fluid ounces tomato sauce

1 large plum tomato
3 basil leaves
2 garlic cloves, crushed
1 tablespoon canned tomato
  puree
2 teaspoons extra virgin olive oil

Core the tomato and puree in a food processor with the basil leaves (or chop the tomato and basil very finely and stir together).

Stir in the garlic, tomato puree, and olive oil and season well. Leave for at least 30 minutes to allow the flavors to blend. Use the tomato sauce on pizzas, toss through pasta, or serve as a sauce with arancini.

winter squash

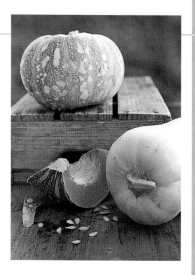

vegetables ▪ **fruit vegetables**
season ▪ **peak season fall–winter**

Winter squash must surely be one of the most versatile of all vegetables. What other vegetable can be baked alongside the Sunday roast, pureed into the silkiest of soups, can take on intense spices to be cooked in a curry, or baked into the sweetest of dessert pies? The flesh can even be candied and made into jams and other preserves.

Winter squash are members of the gourd family. In some countries all winter squash are referred to as pumpkins, but in the United States, pumpkin refers only to the large, segmented ones, often seen around Thanksgiving. The word "pumpkin" ultimately traces back to the Greek word for "melon," *pepon*. American settlers are credited with coining the word, deriving it from "pompion," the English name for pumpkin.

In Mexico, the flowers are enjoyed as a delicacy and pumpkin seeds, pepitas, were roasted and used as a snack, or ground for use as a thickener for pastes and sauces. The seeds provide oil too and in the pre-Columbian Americas the shells of some varieties were used to make containers and spoons.

One of the few things you wouldn't do with a pumpkin is serve it raw—other than this caveat, the sky is the limit. Whether it appears in a risotto or a gratin, a mash, a warm salad, or in a cake, the mellow flavor of pumpkin is a sweet treat.

varieties

There are myriad varieties of winter squash. They come in all shapes, sizes and colors, from hand-small miniatures to 100-pound monsters. Their skin can be smooth, segmented, ridged, or warty and in color they can range from blue to gray to green and yellow striped to creamy tan. Some are squat and round while others are oblong or bell-shaped.

Generally, winter squash have very similar flavor although sweetness, flavor intensity, water content, and color of the flesh will vary from type to type. Exceptions to this are the very small types, which are ideal for stuffing, baking, and serving as an individual portion—their flavor tends to not be very developed. The highly distinctive spaghetti squash, with its bland, watery flesh that cooks magically into long strands resembling spaghetti, is actually something of a squash-family oddity.

preparation

Thin-skinned varieties don't need peeling—the skin is quite edible although many prefer to remove it before cooking. Thick skin should be peeled away, best done with a large, sharp knife (sometimes brute strength is required to do this). When cutting away the skin, ensure that you have the squash sitting firmly on a cut side so it can't wobble while you peel.

roasting Winter squash is sublime when roasted, as this method of cooking concentrates its sweetness better than any other. For this purpose the squash should be cut into chunks, about 2-inch cubes, depending on preference—then tossed in olive oil or butter and cooked in a roasting pan at 400°F for 20–30 minutes, until golden and very soft. Even winter squash that is destined for soup benefits from roasting before being pureed with stock and other ingredients—boiling winter squash in liquid seems to dull its flavor significantly.

steaming Squash is also good when steamed, after which it can be mashed or pureed—steam large chunks for 15 minutes in a perforated double-boiler arrangement. Any excess moisture in steamed squash (especially if it is to be mashed) can be driven out by heating it in a saucepan over medium-high heat for 3–4 minutes. Make sure you stir it continuously though, as it will easily catch and burn. For pumpkin pie or other recipes where mashed pumkin is required, do steam it, as boiling will lead to disappointingly tasteless results.

selection and storage

Buy what is locally grown and seasonally available, according to your needs. For example, a hubbard can weigh over 11 pounds and once cut, needs to be used within a few days or it will quickly become moldy—so decide how much you can deal with at a time before you buy. Butternut squash or the so-called Jap (Kent) pumpkins are a more manageable size, if storing leftovers is an issue.

Whole squash are very good keepers if stored in the right conditions. They should be unblemished and have thick skin, with an amount of stalk remaining to protect the interior from damp.

In a cool, well-ventilated place, they will last for several months; cut winter squash, as previously noted, is very perishable and should be refrigerated, then eaten within a few days. If purchasing cut pieces of winter squash, select those with bright, gleaming flesh and healthy looking, moist interiors.

winter squash, feta, and pine nut pastie

serves 4

1 pound 12 ounces winter
  squash, skin removed, cut into
  ½-inch thick slices
2 tablespoons olive oil
3 garlic cloves, crushed
4 sheets puff pastry, cut into
  6-inch squares
3½ ounces marinated feta
  cheese in oil
3 tablespoons oregano leaves,
  roughly chopped
2 tablespoons pine nuts, toasted
1 egg yolk
1 tablespoon milk
1 tablespoon sesame seeds

Preheat the oven to 425°F. Put the squash on a baking sheet and toss with the oil and garlic. Season with sea salt and freshly ground black pepper. Roast for 40 minutes or until tender and golden. Remove from the oven and cool.

Evenly divide the squash among the four pastry squares, placing it in the center. Combine the feta, oregano, and pine nuts, then divide into four, placing them on top of squash. Drizzle with a little of the feta marinating oil. Bring two of the diagonally opposite corners together and pinch in the center above the filling. Bring the other two diagonally opposite corners together and pinch to seal along the edges. The base will be square and the top will form a pyramid. Twist the top to seal where all four corners meet.

Place the egg yolk and milk in a small bowl and whisk with a fork to make an eggwash for the pastry.

Place the pasties on a greased baking sheet and brush with the eggwash mixture. Sprinkle with sesame seeds and sea salt and bake for 15 minutes or until golden brown.

Native Americans have been growing and using winter squash for centuries, as have the Mexicans. In Mexico, Columbus collected the seeds, taking them back to Europe where initially the fruits of the plant were used to nourish pigs. The Europeans ultimately did embrace the winter squash, although not with as much fervor as the American colonists did—witness its association with festivities such as Halloween and Thanksgiving Day.

spiced winter squash
and lentil tagine

Rinse the lentils in a sieve. Tip into a saucepan and add 4 cups cold water. Bring to a boil, skim the surface to remove any scum, then cover and simmer over low heat for 20 minutes or until tender.

Meanwhile, halve the tomatoes widthwise and squeeze out the seeds. Coarsely grate the tomatoes into a bowl down to the skin. Set the tomato aside. Peel and seed the winter squash and cut into 1¼-inch cubes. Set aside.

Heat the oil in a large saucepan, add the onion and cook over low heat until softened. Add the garlic, cook for a few seconds, then stir in the cumin, turmeric, and cayenne pepper. Cook for 30 seconds, then add the grated tomato, paprika, tomato paste, sugar, half the parsley, and half the cilantro. Season with sea salt and freshly ground black pepper. Add the drained lentils and chopped winter squash, stir well, then cover and simmer for 20 minutes or until the squash and lentils are tender. Adjust the seasoning and sprinkle with the remaining parsley and cilantro. Serve hot or warm with a baguette.

1½ cups brown lentils
2 tomatoes
1 pound 5 ounces firm winter
  squash or butternut squash
¼ cup olive oil
1 onion, finely chopped
3 garlic cloves, finely chopped
½ teaspoon ground cumin
½ teaspoon ground turmeric
⅛ teaspoon cayenne pepper
1 teaspoon paprika
3 teaspoons tomato paste
½ teaspoon sugar
1 tablespoon finely chopped
  Italian parsley
2 tablespoons chopped cilantro
  leaves
baguette, to serve

fruit vegetables ■ winter squash

For other winter squash recipes see:
carrot and winter squash risotto.....186

zucchini

Despite their distinctly Italian name, these members of the summer squash family are Mexican natives. Since ancient times, squash, beans, and maize have been an integral part of the indigenous diet in the Americas, and are a mainstay even today. Squash were one of the many foodstuffs taken back to Europe by Spanish explorers; although embraced in parts of the continent, it has taken a while for them to become mainstream in England and the United States.

Essentially, zucchini are immature vine fruits which, if left to grow, will do so to a prodigious size, very quickly becoming a marrow with tough skin, bland, watery flesh and large, hard seeds. When young and small, they instead have a delicate sweetness and every part is edible—skin, seeds, and flesh. They are generally cylindrical, although there are round varieties too, and the pattypan squash, with its flat, round shape and pretty scalloped edge, is a close, and similar-tasting, relative.

Zucchini come in green, yellow, and so-called "white" varieties; this latter is in reality a pale green color and is slightly bulbous in shape, whereas the others are slim and cylindrical. Another newish variety is the round globe which, at about 3 inches in diameter, is perfect for scooping out, stuffing and baking.

squash

Zucchini represent just one of the many "summer" or "tender" squashes available —there is also the crookneck squash; the round globe squash; and the oval squash, such as the pattypan (scallopini) squash. Pattypan squash are prized for their flesh which, when young and in prime condition, is buttery and dense. These squash are usually a distinctive yellow color, but can also be either deep bright or pale green.

Choose small firm squash and steam them whole, for about 8–10 minutes or until tender. Larger ones can be parboiled for a few minutes, the insides scooped out, replaced with a stuffing and then baked—a fresh bread crumb stuffing, with plenty of chopped fresh herbs (basil, parsley, oregano) and Parmesan cheese works beautifully.

selection and storage

Zucchinis should be firm and have shiny, tight, unblemished skins with no bruises or brown spots. The skin is very delicate (you should be able to pierce it with your fingernail), so a few scratches from harvesting and transporting are probably inevitable. Inside, the flesh should be creamy and bright and have the tiniest of seeds.

Don't store these vegetables for long as their delicate, sweet flavor is marred by storage—no longer than 2 days in a ventilated bag in the crisper section of the refrigerator. Don't wash zucchini until you are about to cook them or they may start to spoil.

preparation

Zucchinis are a breeze to prepare. They require washing, need their stem-end trimmed, then just have to be sliced, grated, chopped, or halved lengthwise, depending on the use. They are quickly cooked and the methods they are best suited to are steaming, stir-frying, baking, sautéing, braising, or barbecuing.

steaming Steamed zucchini will be tender in about 3 minutes in a double-boiler arrangement. Stir-frying and sautéing are equally quick to accomplish.

grilling To grill zucchini, slice them lengthwise into strips about 1/4-inch thick, brush all over with olive oil, then cook for about 1 minute on each side on a medium-hot grill. You can also cook them in a grill pan.

culinary uses

There are a plethora of fabulous, zucchini-based recipes to cook. And to *not* cook—they can after all be served raw, as the Italians do, thinly sliced and dressed with oil, lemon juice, mint, and salt and pepper. Grated zucchini can be bound with a little flour and egg and cooked into delicious fritters—there are even recipes for zucchini cakes and sweet zucchini muffins, similar in spirit to the ever-popular carrot cake.

Zucchinis can be employed, along with other summer produce, such as tomatoes, eggplant, and bell peppers, in sunny vegetable salads or soups, but are arguably at their best when simply sliced into thin rounds and quickly sautéed in olive oil with garlic and fresh thyme.

Mild-tasting zucchinis take well to the robust flavors of garlic, ginger, good-quality vinegars (balsamic, red wine, and sherry, for example), lemon, and anchovies. Classic Mediterranean ingredients like oregano, mint, tomatoes, pine nuts, Parmesan and pecorino cheeses, basil, and mint also complement zucchini.

zucchini fritters

Put the zucchini and onion in the middle of a clean dishtowel, gather the corners together and twist as tightly as possible to remove all the juices. Combine the zucchini, onion, flour, cheese, mint, parsley, nutmeg, bread crumbs, and egg in a large bowl. Season with sea salt and freshly ground black pepper, then mix with your hands to a stiff mixture that clumps together.

Heat the oil in a large frying pan over medium heat. When the oil is hot, drop tablespoons of mixture into the pan and shallow-fry for 2–3 minutes or until well browned all over. Drain well on crumpled paper towels and serve hot with lemon wedges or tsatsiki.

2¼ cups grated zucchini
1 small onion, finely chopped
¼ cup self-rising flour
⅓ cup grated Parmesan cheese
1 tablespoon chopped mint
2 teaspoons chopped Italian
   parsley
1 pinch ground nutmeg
¼ cup dry bread crumbs
1 egg, lightly beaten
olive oil, for shallow-frying
lemon wedges or tsatsiki (see
   page 343), to serve

fruit vegetables ■ zucchini

zucchini, radish, and feta salad

serves 4

To make the dressing, combine the white wine vinegar, olive oil, and mustard. Season with sea salt and freshly ground black pepper.

Shave the zucchini into strips from top to bottom. Place in a colander, sprinkle with 2 teaspoons sea salt, then set aside to drain for 30 minutes. Do not rinse. Gently dry with paper towels and put in a large bowl, along with the radish and onion. Tear the inner leaves of the lettuce into smaller pieces and add to the bowl with the dressing and toss lightly. Transfer to a serving dish and sprinkle the crumbled feta cheese over the top before serving.

dressing
1 tablespoon white wine vinegar
2 tablespoons olive oil
2–3 teaspoons wholegrain
   mustard

5 small zucchini
6 radishes, finely sliced
½ small red onion, finely sliced
1 small romaine lettuce
⅔ cup crumbled feta cheese

serves 8

grilled vegetable terrine

8 large slices grilled eggplant
(see page 347 or store-bought)
10 slices grilled red bell pepper
(see page 336 or store-bought)
8 slices grilled zucchini (see
page 364 or store-bought)
1⅓ cups ricotta cheese
2 garlic cloves, crushed
2 handfuls arugula
3 marinated artichokes, drained
and sliced
½ cup semidried tomatoes,
drained and chopped
⅔ cup marinated mushrooms,
drained and halved

Line a 9 x 5 x 2½ inch loaf tin with plastic wrap, leaving a generous overhang on all sides. Line the base with half the eggplant, cutting to fit. Next, layer in half the bell peppers, then all of the zucchini.

Beat the ricotta cheese and garlic together until smooth. Season with sea salt and freshly ground black pepper, then spread evenly over the zucchini. Press down firmly and top with the arugula leaves. Arrange the marinated artichoke, tomato, and mushrooms in three strips over the arugula. Top with another layer of peppers and finish with the eggplant.

Cover securely with the overhanging plastic wrap. Top with a piece of cardboard and a weight to weigh down the vegetables (canned food is good for this). Chill the terrine in the refrigerator overnight.

Peel back the plastic wrap and carefully turn out the terrine onto a plate. Remove the plastic wrap and cut into thick slices to serve.

note If using store-bought grilled eggplant, bell peppers, and zucchini, drain them of any oil or marinating liquid before use.

For other zucchini recipes see:
papardelle with zucchini flowers
and goat cheese............................369

The word zucchini is from the Italian zuccherino meaning "small squash;" the French name courgette, which is also used in England, is from courge, for marrow. "Squash" is from the American Indian word askutasquash, which means "green thing eaten green" or "raw."

zucchini blossom

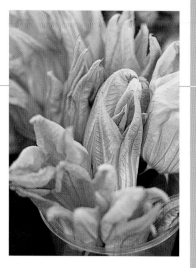

vegetables ▪ **fruit vegetables**
season ▪ **summer**

The Italians have known, since they started growing zucchinis, that the blossoms are an absolute treat—slowly but surely, the rest of the zucchini-loving world is catching on too. They are very perishable (they need to be eaten within a day or two of picking) and actually rather nutritious, containing decent amounts of folic acid.

There are male and female blossoms, with females being more robust and requiring a slightly longer cooking time than their more delicate male counterparts. Whichever sex is on offer, only buy zucchini blossoms that look firm and fresh, with petals that are only slightly open. Brush them gently to remove their furry down covering and gently rinse the insides to flush out any insect life. Some people detach the pistils, while others don't bother.

The blossoms can be put to myriad uses—they can be lightly battered and fried, stuffed and baked, or sautéed with a few aromatics, such as garlic, anchovies, and herbs. They can be sliced and stirred through pastas, risottos, and soups, or cooked into a frittata. Should you need to store your blossoms for a day or so, place them in a damp cloth-lined dish, lay in a single layer, then cover and refrigerate.

papardelle with zucchini blossoms and goat cheese

Combine the ricotta, cream, thyme, and nutmeg in a bowl and season well with sea salt and white pepper. Set aside in a cool place (do not refrigerate) for 1 hour.

Cook the pasta in a saucepan of boiling salted water until *al dente*. Meanwhile, heat the olive oil in a large frying pan over medium-high heat and cook the zucchini for 4 minutes or until lightly golden. Remove the zucchini with a slotted spoon and drain on paper towels.

Dust the zucchini blossoms with flour, shake off the excess, then fry for about 1 minute or until lightly golden.

Drain the pasta and transfer to a large serving dish. Add the zucchini, zucchini blossoms, and ricotta mixture and toss lightly. Dot with small pieces of goat cheese, to serve.

¾ cup ricotta cheese
½ cup heavy cream
2 teaspoons fresh thyme
¼ teaspoon ground nutmeg
10½ ounces dried papardelle pasta or 14 ounces fresh papardelle or other ribbon pasta
¼ cup olive oil
4 small zucchini, cut into thin batons
16 zucchini blossoms, no vegetable attached
all-purpose flour, for dusting
⅔ cup crumbled goat cheese

fruit vegetables ■ zucchini blossom

Any variety of squash, not just the zucchini, provides edible blossoms and in many countries (Mexico, Italy, and France, for example), these are used as everyday fare, not as a rarified treat, which is often the case. Often, advice is given to remove the pistils and stamens (the upright inner parts of the bloom) but this isn't really necessary—they are perfectly edible, just a little crunchy.

fava beans

vegetables ▪ **seeds and pods**
season ▪ **early spring–early summer**

selection and storage

Select pods that are smooth and pale green and without blackening on their ends, or any wrinkles. Also avoid any that are bulgy as this indicates large, hard beans within, which will not make for memorable bean feasting. If possible, break a pod open and check that the pillowy white lining is moist and the beans have taut, smooth skins.

Store fava beans, in their pods, in a ventilated plastic bag in the refrigerator for up to 3 days. Podded, the beans can be frozen for up to 3 months—you can cook them while still frozen.

Before green beans and all the other varieties of bean came to Europe out of the New World, fava beans were *the* bean. Fava beans have been around for so long that it isn't known exactly where they came from—they have become very widespread, common to the cuisines of the Mediterranean, the Middle East, China, and South America. These are the beans of *Jack and the Beanstalk*, "spilling the beans" and being "full of beans."

Fava beans are enclosed in a soft, downy substance, inside a large, slightly dimpled, green pod. Pods vary in length from 7–9 inches and can contain up to eight fleshy seeds. The first fava beans of spring are small and tender; as the season progresses, they become larger and take on starchier, less sweet characteristics. The first fresh fava beans of spring have an almost cult following among chefs and certain ethnic populations; if these are very young and tender, peeling is not necessary. Nothing else comes close to their nutty, vegetal sweetness.

Since ancient times, fava beans (or faba beans or broad beans, as they are also called) have been an invaluable source of nonmeat protein, although to provide this they need to be eaten in tandem with grains, such as pearl barley, dried legumes (dried peas and beans), or seeds.

Fava beans have long been associated with the supernatural and were once placed on gravesites in England to repel ghosts. In Scotland, for example, it was believed witches rode not on broomsticks but on bean stalks, and in some cultures it was believed that dead souls could transmigrate into fava beans.

preparation

Fava beans require two steps of preparation—first they must be podded and then you need to peel them. If you intend to serve your beans pretty much straight after cooking as a simple side dish or in a recipe that requires them to be fully tender (a puree or dip, for example), then simmer the beans until tender (about 10 minutes for young fava beans and 20 minutes for more mature beans). Drain and cool, until they can be handled comfortably, then peel. Reheat them briefly if necessary for a moment or two in a little simmering water or toss in a hot frying pan with some butter or olive oil before serving.

If you intend to add fava beans to a dish such as a risotto or a soup where they will receive additional cooking, just blanch them for 2–3 minutes in boiling water, drain well, then cool in a bowl of iced water. Drain again and peel—the skins will slip off quite willingly.

When buying fresh fava beans it is worth noting that 2 pounds of fava beans will yield about 1½ cups (10½ ounces) of podded beans.

culinary uses

The first fava beans of the season are sweet and tender and are best treated simply—steam them, drizzle with olive oil, and serve with flakes of sea salt as a simple starter—add a few slices of prosciutto or salami and you're practically in Italy. These young tender beans are excellent tossed through fresh pasta with a saffron cream sauce or piled beside a piece of steamed salmon.

Older fava beans have tougher skins, a mealier texture, and a less sweet flavor—use these for a puree (with garlic and some olive oil) to spread on crostini, or cook them in a minestrone-style soup or a mixed spring vegetables stew (think artichoke, peas, asparagus, and new potatoes).

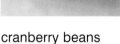

cranberry beans

Cranberry beans are another type of shell bean—a bean with largish seeds inside a glorious red-speckled pod. It is the seeds that are eaten and, in many cases, these are left to reach full maturity, at which point they are dried. When harvested mature, but not yet dried, the beans have a dryish, creamy white flesh inside plump smooth seeds.

Choose cranberry beans with leathery pods that have a lumpy surface. Simmer gently for 15–30 minutes, until tender. Never boil them, as this will only make them tougher.

serves 4

fava bean rotollo
with salad greens

rotollo
1½ cups shelled fava beans
4 eggs
4 egg yolks
2 teaspoons finely chopped mint
2 teaspoons finely chopped basil
1 tablespoon butter
1 cup grated pecorino cheese

salad
1½ tablespoons pine nuts
1 tablespoon chopped basil
⅓ cup olive oil
2 tablespoons lemon juice
2 baby romaine lettuces, trimmed
2 Belgian endives, trimmed

To make the rotollo, bring a medium saucepan of water to a boil. Add a large pinch of salt and the fava beans and simmer for 2 minutes. Drain and plunge into iced water. Drain and peel the skins off the beans, discarding the skins.

Preheat the oven to 315°F. Beat the eggs, egg yolks, mint, and basil together. Season with sea salt and freshly ground black pepper. Melt half the butter in a nonstick frying pan over medium-high heat. Pour in half the egg mixture and cook until the base has set but the top is still a little runny.

Slide the omelette from the pan onto a sheet of baking paper. Sprinkle half the pecorino cheese and half the fava beans over the surface. Using the baking paper as a guide, gently roll the omelette into a tight sausage. Roll the baking paper around the omelette and tie both ends with string to prevent it from unrolling. Place on a baking sheet. Make another roll with the remaining ingredients and put on the baking sheet. Bake for 8 minutes. Remove from the oven, set aside for 2–3 minutes, then unwrap and set aside to cool.

Put the pine nuts in a small dry saucepan over medium heat and toast, stirring and tossing constantly, for 4–5 minutes or until the nuts are golden-brown and fragrant. Tip the nuts into a bowl so they do not cook further from the residual heat, and allow to cool.

To make the salad, put 1 tablespoon of the pine nuts, the basil, olive oil, and lemon juice in a small food processor or blender and process until smooth. Season with sea salt and freshly ground black pepper. Put the romaine and Belgian endive leaves in a bowl and dress with 2 tablespoons of the dressing. Serve the rotollo, cut into slices, over the salad.

green beans

Green beans are another New World native—most likely from Peru—and are related to kidney beans, pinto beans, black beans, and all those other beans that arc only used once reconstituted from a dried state. In fact, the various green beans are among the few from the bean family that are consumed fresh, and the only ones used pod and all.

Green beans are actually picked when immature —if allowed to keep growing, their tiny seeds would become large and their pods very tough— the "green" in their name refers to their immaturity when picked and not their color. In fact, these beans come in a range of hues, from light to bright to deep green; from yellow to purple to mottled cream and russet. They also vary greatly in pod size and shape, from the tiniest, tenderest *haricots verts* (green string bean), so prized by the French and just an inch or so long, to the large Italian flat beans, which can be up to 10 inches in length. Green beans are also called "snap" beans (and indeed, a fresh bean should "snap" when you bend it) and "string" beans because of the fibrous string that ran down the length of earlier varieties and needed to be removed. Most beans these days are bred to be stringless so this is no longer necessary.

selection and storage

If beans are bendable, leave them behind; they should break crisply. The pods should be smooth and uniformly colored with almost imperceptible seed bumps underneath; swellings where the seeds are indicate they are overmature and will not taste great. The pointy ends should be perky and undamaged and there should be no wrinkling, bruises, or shrivelled spots.

Store beans in a ventilated plastic bag in the refrigerator for up to 3 days.

varieties

flat Sometimes called Italian beans, these beans are flat and long, full flavored and meaty textured. They are suited to long cooking in soups, stews, and braises and can even be barbecued until tender.

green Often called French beans, there are many types of green beans—from short and slim to fat and long. Green beans are best boiled in plenty of salted water or steamed; they can also be roasted in olive oil, which concentrates their sweet, grassy flavors.

purple Like green beans only a lovely dark mauve color, purple beans, unfortunately, don't keep their fabulous color when cooked, turning green. Use them as you would green beans.

wax These beans are sometimes called yellow beans on account of their pretty yellow color. Buy wax beans that have a slight green tinge, as these are younger and better tasting than those that are yellow all over. These beans have a gentler flavor than green beans so serve them simply; steamed and dressed with butter is perfect.

preparation

"If you know how to cook a green bean you know how to cook anything," Australian food personality Joan Campbell once famously declared, possibly in reaction to all those overly crisp, undercooked bright green beans so often served up in fashionable restaurants. In stark contrast, some ethnic cooks aren't afraid to braise green beans for 20 minutes until they are deep olive green and incredibly tender.

boiling The best way to cook beans for most uses is to boil them in plenty of salted water for 4–7 minutes, depending on the size of the bean and whether they are whole, halved, or sliced. Before cooking, check there are no strings on your beans—remove these if they are present.

Trim the "top" end of each bean (where it was attached to the plant). It is not necessary to trim the "tail" end. To prepare beans for use in salads it is best to sightly undercook them, drain them well, then leave to cool. Many sources tell you to plunge the just-cooked beans into iced water to cool them—this preserves their bright green color but compromizes their flavor.

roasting Beans can also be roasted whole. Trim them, then toss in generous amounts of olive oil and roast in a 350°F oven, in a single layer in a roasting pan. They will take 20 minutes to cook.

niçoise salad with green beans and seared tuna

Whisk together the olive oil, garlic, mustard, and vinegar. Season well. Brush the tuna with olive oil. Fry on a hot barbecue grill plate or in a frying pan until browned, about 1½–2 minutes each side. Remove from the heat.

Cook the beans in boiling salted water for 3 minutes or until just tender. Remove with tongs and drain. Scrub the baby potatoes, cut in half and add to the saucepan. Boil for 12 minutes or until tender. Drain and put in a shallow salad bowl with the lettuce leaves. Add 2 tablespoons of the dressing and toss gently to coat. Place the tomatoes on top.

Slice the tuna on a diagonal into ¼-inch slices and arrange on the tomatoes. Add the cooked beans and black olives. Cut the hard-boiled eggs into wedges and add to the salad. Arrange the anchovy fillets in a cross on top. Top with capers and drizzle with the remaining dressing.

⅓ cup olive oil
2 garlic cloves, crushed
1 teaspoon Dijon mustard
1 tablespoon champagne vinegar
2 (5½-ounce) tuna fillets
2 cups trimmed green beans
1 pound (about 12) baby potatoes
2 large handfuls torn green lettuce leaves
8 cherry tomatoes, halved
12 black olives
2 eggs, hard-boiled
4 anchovies, halved
1 tablespoon salted capers, drained and rinsed

wax beans with sundried tomatoes and capers

serves 4

Slice the sundried tomatoes into long, thin strips. Heat the oil from the sundried tomatoes in a small frying pan over medium heat and fry the capers, stirring often, for about 1 minute or until darkened and crisp. Drain on paper towels.

Bring a saucepan of salted water to a boil. Add the beans and simmer for 3–4 minutes or until just tender. Drain, season with freshly ground black pepper, then toss with the sun-dried tomatoes, capers, olive oil, and strips of lemon zest. Serve hot or at room temperature.

2 sundried tomatoes in oil, plus 1 teaspoon of oil, extra
2 teaspoons capers, drained and rinsed
2½ cups trimmed young wax beans
1 teaspoon light olive oil
zest of 1 lemon, cut into thin strips

seeds and pods ▪ green beans

okra

vegetables ▪ seeds and pods
season ▪ summer–fall

The world is divided firmly into two types of people—the okra lovers and the okra haters. Few other vegetables seem to spark such polarization and the number one reason for it is, in a word, ooze. Okra contains mucilaginous juices that give it its renowned texture and although there are claims that okra can be purged of its sliminess, really, it can't. One has to either embrace the gummy characteristics of okra, along with its utterly delicious flavor (which is faintly sweet and reminiscent of both eggplant and asparagus), or avoid it altogether.

Okra is the immature seed pod of an annual, tropical herb, which is a member of the mallow family. Okra is related to the hibiscus, the hollyhock, and cotton, and indeed, it produces a hibiscuslike flower—it is believed to be native to Ethiopia and parts of the Sudan.

There are two types of okra, one with green skin and one with red. The latter tends to be larger than the former but no different in flavor, but its gorgeous maroon color, unfortunately, disappears when cooked (it becomes green).

You are most likely to encounter the green sort, which can have ridged or smooth skin. Pods can vary from 3–10 inches in length.

It is surmised that the conquering Moors took okra to Spain and North Africa. Somehow it also ended up in India (perhaps the Moguls were responsible), where it is immensely popular today. African slaves almost certainly conveyed it to the Caribbean and the southern states of America where it is a much-loved feature of the culinary landscape today, as it is in Greece and Turkey, Middle Eastern countries, and South America.

selection and storage

Only buy okra that are super-fresh, as they do not store particularly well. A good test of this is whether they snap cleanly and crisply in half.

Avoid any that are dull-looking or are limp or dry. Mature okra pods are used to make paper and rope in some parts of the world. so you don't wish to be eating these—try to get young ones and if in doubt, choose the smallest on offer.

Okra doesn't like very cold temperatures, so store pods in the crisper section of the refrigerator in a paper bag and try to use them within 1–2 days.

preparation

Perfectly fresh okra requires nothing more than washing—it can then be steamed or braised whole (which has the advantage of containing the juices), but by all means snip off the stem end if preferred. It is possible to remove the "cap" at the stem end without exposing the interior and thus encouraging the juices to escape, although many recipes require sliced okra.

Okra cooks quickly, reaching tenderness when steamed in about 3 minutes, although it can also be braised for longer—witness the classic gumbo of the southern United States, in which it is simmered for a couple of hours. Whole, small okra can also be deep-fried, coated lightly first in cornstarch.

culinary uses

There are a number of iconic okra dishes from various parts of the world apart from those mentioned above. In the Middle East, where it is called *bamia*, okra is stewed to luscious effect with lamb, tomatoes, and cilantro, or with dried limes, tomato, lemon, garlic, and parsley. In India, they stuff okra pods with spices then slowly fry them. They also stir-fry them with mustard seeds and green chili and add them sliced and cooked, with ginger, curry leaves, and an assortment of spices, to yogurt. On the Bahia coast of Brazil, okra is used in a rich dish called *carurú*, a complex brew of fresh and dried shrimp, coconut milk, tomatoes, peanuts, lime juice, and okra, while in Senegal it is used in a substantial fish stew called *soupokandia*.

okra and chicken curry

Grind the chili flakes, turmeric, cumin, peppercorns, and coconut in a spice mill or in a mortar using a pestle until uniform. Trim the okra by cutting off the tip and tough stem end, being careful not to cut into the body of the okra.

Heat the oil in a deep frying pan over medium heat. Fry the onion and garlic for about 5 minutes or until the onion is light brown. Stir in the spice mixture and fry for 1 minute. Add the okra, chicken, tomato, sugar, coconut milk, and chicken stock and bring to a boil.

Reduce the heat and simmer gently for 20 minutes. Add the vinegar and 1 teaspoon sea salt and simmer for an additional 5 minutes. Check the seasoning. Serve the curry with steamed rice or flat bread.

1 teaspoon chili flakes
1/2 teaspoon ground turmeric
1/2 teaspoon cumin seeds
4 white peppercorns
1/3 cup dried coconut
1 pound okra
2 tablespoons oil
2 onions, sliced
3 garlic cloves, crushed
14 ounces boneless, skinless chicken thighs, trimmed and cut into quarters
1 large tomato, chopped
1 teaspoon sugar
1 cup coconut milk
1 1/2 cups chicken stock
1 tablespoon malt vinegar
steamed rice or flat bread, to serve

seeds and pods ■ okra

okra with tomato sauce

serves 4–6 as a side dish

Trim the okra by cutting off the tip and tough stem end. Heat the olive oil in a large frying pan over medium heat. Add the onion and cook for 5 minutes or until golden. Add the garlic and cook for 1 minute.

Add the okra and cook, stirring, for 4–5 minutes. Add the tomatoes, sugar, and lemon juice and simmer, stirring occasionally, for 3–4 minutes. Stir in the cilantro. Remove from the heat and serve immediately as a side dish.

1 pound okra
1/4 cup olive oil
1 onion, chopped
2 garlic cloves, crushed
1 (14-ounce) can chopped tomatoes
2 teaspoons sugar
1/4 cup lemon juice
1 1/2 cups finely chopped cilantro leaves

peas

Frozen peas, an innovation in food preservation that dates back to the 1920s, are a blessing and a curse. A blessing because they are generally the closest thing most pea-eaters ever get to the freshest of newly harvested peas and a curse because, thanks to their ubiquity, peas have all but lost the "special" status they fully deserve. Within hours of harvesting, the succulent sugars in peas start turning to starch and unless you purchase straight from a grower it's likely most "fresh" peas are quite past their prime by the time of purchase. Frozen peas, processed just after harvesting, most closely mimic the fresh pea, in color, flavor, and nutritional value.

Debate rages as to exactly where the pea originated but what is agreed is that the pea, along with wheat and barley, is one of the oldest cultivated crops. The pea is a legume, that is, a plant whose fruit is in the form of a seed-bearing pod, and is one of the few that are eaten this way. But it wasn't until around the sixteenth century, when breeding know-how enabled tender varieties to be developed, that peas were eaten fresh. By the late seventeenth century peas had become so trendy that a noblewoman in the court of King Louis XIV was moved to write to a friend, "there are some ladies who, having supped well, take peas at home before going to bed … it is a fashion, a craze!"

For other pea recipes see:

minted peas 423

Catherine de Medici took her beloved piselli novella (sweet, tiny peas) with her to France, where they became a popular novelty and quite the rage. King Louis XIV made petit pois fashionable by featuring them on royal dinner party menus.

selection and storage

Ripe pea pods are vibrant green, fat and anywhere from 1½–4 inches long. They contain up to ten round grayish green seeds. Pods are considered ripe when the seam on the side of the pod has gone from being convex to concave. The pods should be shiny, velvety, and plump—avoid ones that are dull-looking as these are old and will have lost moisture. Also, avoid any that are yellowish or have gray speckles.

Purchase pods that don't rattle when shaken—the peas inside should fill the pods quite tightly but should not cause the unopened pods to bulge (these peas will be too mature).

Peas deteriorate rapidly once picked, quickly turning starchy and dull-flavored. Therefore, store them for as little time as possible—2 days maximum and then in the refrigerator, sealed in a plastic bag. Podded, blanched peas can be frozen for up to 2 months.

Note when purchasing fresh peas that 2 pounds 12 ounces of unpodded peas will yield sufficient for four people, as a side dish.

preparation

Shelling peas is surely one of the most therapeutic of all kitchen chores. To do this, split the pods open along their seam, then run your thumb under the peas to dislodge them into a bowl.

In *The Garrulous Gourmet*, William Wallace Irwin wrote "there is nothing so innocent, so confiding as the small green face of the freshly shelled spring pea … [it is] so helpless and friendly that it makes really sensitive stomachs suffer to see the way it is treated in the average home. Fling him into water and let him boil—and that's that." It's true that mostly we tend to boil peas and, if you do, at least do this in a minimum of water and simmer them for no more than 3 minutes. Overboiled peas are not pleasant. Peas benefit from a slick of melted butter or really good olive oil.

culinary uses

Some 95 percent of the world's pea crop is either frozen or canned so fresh peas really are a seasonal treat. The most common pea is the garden pea, also called the English pea. Very fresh, tiny peas are sublime raw, tossed into salads. At the other end of the cooking spectrum, the French braise peas in stock with lettuce, drastically altering their character but only in the most delicious of ways. Peas are also the star in the classic Venetian dish risi e bisi, little more than a very wet risotto containing the simplest of ingredients (rice, peas, stock, butter) but far more delicious than this description might suggest.

Peas make admirable mash, either on their own or in tandem with some potatoes, and the addition of mint is also favored by many. Otherwise, add peas to soups such as minestrone, pasta dishes, stir-fries, omelettes, and frittatas.

dry potato and pea curry

Dry-roast the mustard seeds in a frying pan over medium heat for 2–3 minutes or until they start to pop. Add the ghee or oil, onion, garlic, and ginger and cook, stirring, until the onion is soft.

Add the spices and potato to the pan and season with sea salt and freshly ground black pepper. Stir until the potato is coated with the spice mixture. Add ½ cup water and simmer, covered, for 15–20 minutes or until the potato is just tender. Stir occasionally to stop the curry sticking to the bottom of the pan.

Add the peas and stir until combined. Simmer, covered, for 3–5 minutes or until the potato is cooked and all the liquid is absorbed. Stir in the mint and season again before serving.

2 teaspoons brown mustard seeds
2 tablespoons ghee or oil
2 onions, sliced
2 garlic cloves, crushed
2 teaspoons grated fresh ginger
1 teaspoon ground turmeric
½ teaspoon chili powder
1 teaspoon ground cumin
1 teaspoon garam masala
5 potatoes, cubed
⅔ cup peas
2 tablespoons chopped mint

seeds and pods ■ peas

risi e bisi

serves 4

Put the stock in a saucepan, bring to a boil and then maintain at a low simmer. Heat the oil and half the butter in a large, wide heavy-bottomed saucepan and cook the onion and pancetta over low heat for 5 minutes, until softened. Stir in the parsley and peas and add 2 ladlefuls of the stock. Simmer for 6–8 minutes.

Add the rice and the remaining stock to the pan. Simmer for 12–15 minutes or until the rice is *al dente* and most of the stock has been absorbed. Stir in the remaining butter and Parmesan cheese, and season with sea salt and freshly ground black pepper, to serve.

6 cups chicken or vegetable stock
2 teaspoons olive oil
2 tablespoons butter
1 small onion, finely chopped
½ cup chopped pancetta
2 tablespoons chopped parsley
2½ cups shelled young peas
scant 1 cup risotto (arborio) rice
½ cup Parmesan cheese, grated

soybeans

selection and storage

Fresh green soybeans are not widely available, although they can, with increasing ease, be purchased whole and frozen. Fresh soybeans should have bright green pods with healthy-looking whitish or brown furry down—avoid any that look dried, withered, or whose seeds rattle when you shake the pods. They should be consumed within 2 days—refrigerate in a ventilated plastic bag for no longer than this.

Soybeans, an East Asian native, have been a vital source of protein in that part of the world for over 5,000 years. Also known as edamame, which means 'branched bean' in Japanese, soybeans present as bright apple-green pods, covered with a slight white or brown hairy fuzz. Inside, the pods are anywhere from two to eight pealike seeds, which have a sweet, nutty, and delicate flavor and buttery texture. They are of the same species as field or grain soy crops (grown for various uses such as miso, tofu, and soy milk).

The soybean is the only vegetable to contain all nine essential amino acids, making it a source of complete protein; soybeans also contain a veritable cocktail of other nutrients including antioxidants, phytochemicals, essential fatty acids, calcium, and B vitamins.

preparation

boiling Soybeans are easier to pod after cooking. To boil them, cook them in their pods for 5 minutes or until beans inside are tender—you may need to test one to determine if they are tender. Drain well, cool slightly, then serve with salt as a snack, or refresh in iced water, pod and use in stir-fries, soups, or salads.

roasting Soybeans can also be roasted. Simply toss whole, unpodded beans with some olive oil and garlic, season them well, then roast in a 350°F oven for 15 minutes or until tender.

soybeans, snow peas, and shrimp noodle stir-fry

To make the dressing, combine the red wine vinegar, kecap manis, soy sauce, sesame oil, ginger, sweet chili sauce, and garlic and set aside.

Cook the egg noodles in boiling water for 2 minutes, then drain and set aside.

Peel and devein the shrimp, leaving some with their tails on, if desired. Heat the oil in a large wok over high heat and add the shrimp, snow peas, pepper, soybeans, and scallion. Stir-fry for 1 minute or until the shrimp are just opaque. Add the noodles and cook for 20–30 seconds. Stir in the dressing and cilantro. Serve immediately.

dressing
1/3 cup red wine vinegar
1/3 cup kecap manis
2 tablespoons soy sauce
2 tablespoons sesame oil
2 tablespoons grated ginger
1 tablespoon sweet chili sauce
1 garlic clove, crushed

9 ounces egg noodles
5 ounces raw shrimp
1 tablespoon oil
2 cups small snow peas
1 red bell pepper, seeded and
   thinly sliced
1 1/3 cups soybeans
6 scallions, sliced
2 large handfuls cilantro leaves

seeds and pods ■ soybeans

A couple of hundred years B.C., the Chinese started using the mature but still-green pods of soybeans as a fresh vegetable, while the Japanese learnt the technology 400 years ago. Although little known in the West (but with interest in fresh, green soybeans growing by the moment), soybeans have reached enormous popularity in Taiwan, Japan, Korea, and China.

sugar snap and snow peas

selection and storage

Buy snow peas with bright, light green skin. The ideal length is about 3 inches—avoid any really large ones as these tend to be tough. Also spurn those with largish seeds inside, as the seeds should make a minimal impression on the pod.

Try to buy snow peas that still have vestiges of petals at the stem end, which are a good indicator, depending on their condition, of super-freshness. Don't store snow peas for too long—2 days in a ventilated plastic bag in the refrigerator at most. They don't like humid conditions so the ventilation factor is important.

Sugar snap peas should have taut, bright green, bulging pods and give out a distinct "snap" when broken in two. Avoid any that are even a little flaccid or damp-looking as these have been too long off the vine. Their flavor diminishes quickly, so they need to be stored in the same way as snow peas.

Also called mangetout, snow peas are widely associated with China and many assume they come from there. But their Chinese name, *hoh laan dau* (Holland pea) holds the clue to their provenance. The Dutch grew snow peas as early as 1536 and somehow (possibly via the English) the snow pea arrived in the Orient—snow peas are the main type of garden pea eaten in China and Japan today. It is believed the name "snow pea" came from Cantonese farmers in the San Francisco area who called them *shii dau*, meaning snow pea, and somehow, the name has stuck.

The sugar snap, also classified as a "shell" pea (denoting an edible pod and seeds), is even newer on the scene; a cross between the snow pea and the regular English podding pea, it was not perfected until 1979 (it was mentioned in seventeenth century gardening journals but never completely took off).

Both types of pea are characterized by a sweet tenderness and a bright green color, although sugar snaps are darker in hue than snow peas. Sugar snaps are around 2½–3 inches in length and have a plump, firm pod holding pealike seeds, while snow peas are somewhat flat, showing the slight bulge of small seeds within.

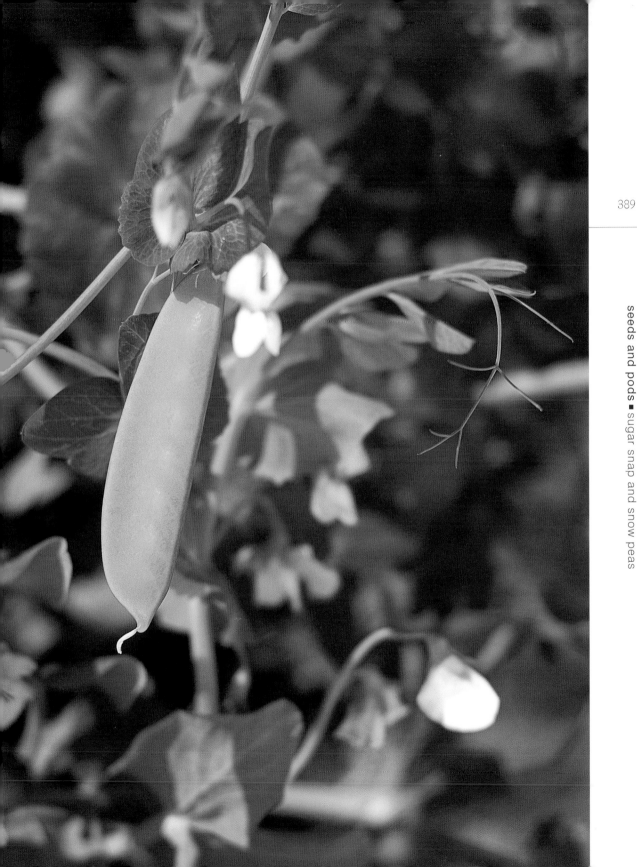

seeds and pods ■ sugar snap and snow peas

preparation

Snow peas require very little preparation. Snip off the stem end and pull away the string that runs down the side of the pod, then cook briefly (1–2 minutes), either by steaming, stir-frying, or simmering

The succulent, sweet juiciness of the sugar snap is best preserved by minimal (and simple) cooking; steam them for about 4 minutes or boil for just 2 minutes. Blanch them briefly before stir-frying or using in salads—although, like snow peas, they can be served raw, a quick cooking brings out their flavor. Some varieties of sugar snaps require stringing—to do this just break off the stem end and pull off the strings that run down the side of the pod.

culinary uses

The sweet, snappy qualities of both snow peas and sugar snaps shouldn't be masked by heavy flavors or long cooking. Hence, steaming, stir-frying, and quick blanching are appropriate treatments—serve either as a simple side dish for meats or fish, or in salads.

They are brilliant with all the classic Asian flavors of ginger, garlic, chili, fish, and soy sauce, and absolutely shine in light oriental-style soups and wok-tossed dishes. Toss blanched snow peas and sugar snaps in a salad bowl with other sweet seasonal greens (peas, beans, asparagus) for a sensational hot-weather dish (chopped mint and slices of bocconcini would be perfect additions). You can also make classic beurre blanc (see page 273) or orange hollandaise sauce (see page 36) and spoon these over warm, just-cooked peas.

sugar snap peas and carrots
in lime butter

Peel the carrot and cut into thin diagonal slices. Wash and string the sugar snap peas. Heat the butter in a large, heavy-bottomed frying pan. Add the garlic and cook over low heat for 1 minute. Add the lime juice and sugar and cook until sugar has completely dissolved. Add the carrots and peas and cook over medium heat for 2–3 minutes or until just cooked. Serve hot with lime strips as a garnish.

variation If limes are unavailable, substitute lemon juice and zest. This dish can be adapted to make a light salad—replace the butter with 2 tablespoons olive oil and cook according to the recipe. Cool to room temperature and sprinkle with finely chopped cashews or toasted pine nuts.

1 large carrot
1¼ cups sugar snap peas
  or snow peas
¼ cup butter
2 garlic cloves, crushed
1 tablespoon lime juice
½ teaspoon soft brown sugar
zest of 1 lime, peeled and cut
  into thin strips

steamed snow peas
with blood orange mayonnaise

serves 4

To make the blood orange mayonnaise, whisk together the egg yolk, white wine vinegar, and Dijon mustard. Whisking constantly, gradually drizzle in the olive oil until you have a thick emulsion. Mix in the blood orange juice, to taste. Season with sea salt and freshly ground black pepper.

Trim the snow peas and put them in a steamer. Add 3–4 very thin strips of fresh ginger. Cover and steam over a rolling boil for 2–5 minutes or until tender. Transfer to a bowl and combine the snow peas with the celery, scallions, and orange segments. Serve with the mayonnaise.

blood orange mayonnaise
1 egg yolk
1 teaspoon white wine vinegar
½ teaspoon Dijon mustard
½ cup olive oil
2 tablespoons blood orange
  juice

1½ cups snow peas
¾-inch piece ginger, cut into
  thin strips
½ celery stick, sliced
4 scallions, sliced
1 orange, broken into segments

seeds and pods ■ sugar snap and snow peas

sweet corn

vegetables ▪ **seeds and pods**
season ▪ **summer**

Few other foods epitomize North America in the
way that corn, or maize, does. Called *mahiz* by the
indigenous peoples, meaning "that which sustains
us," corn was considered one of the vital "three
sisters" of their food supply, the other two being
winter squash and beans. The Native Americans
venerated corn, believing it to be a food-gift from
their gods; their name for it is the source of the
English word "maize."

An exceedingly ancient crop, fossilized remains
of corn have been found in Mexico that are around
80,000 years old. By the time Columbus arrived in
the Americas, large fields of corn were growing
throughout America—corn is credited with the
Native Americans' evolvement from a nomadic to
an agrarian society. It is also thought that the early
settlers of America may have been saved from
starvation by corn; the Native Americans taught
them how to make it into flour, cakes, and soups.

Corn is the most widely grown crop in the
world, second only to rice. There are five main
types of corn grown around the world, of which
sweet corn is the most familiar. This is the classic
"corn on the cob" corn. Over recent decades,
varieties high in sugar content have been
developed. The kernels are most popularly yellow
or white or a mixture of these two colors.

Mark Twain proclaimed that the only way to eat corn is to take your own kettle of water into a corn field, set it over a fire and plop the just-picked, freshly-shucked corn straight into the boiling pot. Sweet corn kernels contain a greater proportion of sugar to starch than any other vegetable, but as soon as it is picked, the sugars in corn begin converting to starch, reducing sweetness. Corn loses 25 percent of its sugars within around 24 hours of harvest; thus Twain was dead right in insisting corn be cooked as soon after harvesting as possible, for the sweetest, most flavorsome results.

preparation

When ready to prepare corn, simply strip away the layers of husk and the silk, rinsing to remove the last of the latter as the fine strands are persistent in sticking to the kernels. An ear or cob of corn contains about 800 kernels, arranged in neat rows; one ear of corn will yield about 3 1/2 ounces (1/2 cup) of kernels. If you wish to remove the kernels for cooking, simply hold each ear upright on a board, then run a sharp knife down the ear, as close to the core as possible—the kernels will come away neatly. Thus prepared, the kernels can be cooked in boiling water for several minutes until tender, then served immediately, tossed with butter.

boiling Corn kernels can be used in any number of ways—in fritters, to make creamed corn, or in soups, risottos, or salads. The classic way to enjoy corn is "on the cob." This involves simmering the whole cobs in lightly salted water (salt toughens the kernels so just use a little) for 5 minutes until tender, drain well, then serve slathered with butter and sprinklings of sea salt and freshly ground black pepper.

grilling and baking Corn can be wrapped in foil with some butter and cooked on the barbecue grill (turn it often, over medium heat, for about 20 minutes), or wrapped in foil and baked in a 350°F oven for 25 minutes, until deliciously tender.

culinary uses

Simmer plenty of corn kernels in whipping cream until the cream has reduced and thickened, and spoon over broiled or barbecued red meats or even poached chicken. Precooked corn kernels are legendarily good in fritters, chowders, and baked into savory cornbread, lovely to eat with sausages and golden fried onion.

On the cob, corn is very good when cut into thick rings and cooked on the barbecue—serve with a flavored butter (garlic, parsley or cumin-flavored) and a steak. Baby corn is a specially bred type of corn and is good in Asian stir-fries and soups.

selection and storage

You can tell by the freshness of the cuts on their stems how long ago corn was harvested—the fresher the cuts, the fresher the corn. The cobs should feel and look moist and plump, with the kernels inside fat and shiny; press against the husk and you should be able to feel the kernels within. The silk of the corn should also be a little sticky and should look glossy, stiff, and moist. Store corn, in its husks, in the refrigerator for 2–3 days only.

seeds and pods ■ sweet corn

corn chowder

serves 8

1/3 cup butter
2 large onions, finely chopped
1 garlic clove, crushed
2 teaspoons cumin seeds
4 cups vegetable stock
2 potatoes, peeled and chopped
1 cup canned creamed corn
2 cups sweet corn kernels (about
    4 cobs)
3 tablespoons chopped parsley
1 cup grated cheddar cheese
3 tablespoons whipping cream,
    optional
2 tablespoons snipped chives

Heat the butter in a large, heavy-bottomed saucepan. Add the onion and cook over medium-high heat for 5 minutes or until golden. Add garlic and cumin seeds and cook for 1 minute, stirring constantly. Add the vegetable stock and bring to a boil. Add the potatoes and reduce heat. Simmer, uncovered, for 10 minutes.

Add the creamed corn, corn kernels, and parsley. Bring to a boil, reduce the heat and simmer for 10 minutes. Stir in the cheese and season with sea salt and freshly ground black pepper. Add the cream, if using. Heat gently until the cheese melts. Serve immediately, sprinkled with snipped chives.

corn and cornmeal pancakes with bacon and maple syrup

serves 4

3/4 cup self-rising flour
3/4 cup fine cornmeal
1 cup milk
1 1/2 cups sweet corn kernels
    (about 3 cobs)
olive oil, for frying
8 bacon slices
1/2 cup maple syrup

Sift the flour into a bowl and stir in the cornmeal. Add the milk and corn and stir until just combined, adding more milk if the batter is too dry. Season with sea salt and black pepper.

Heat the oil in a large frying pan. Using half the batter, spoon it into the pan, in batches, to make four 3 1/2-inch pancakes. Cook for 2 minutes each side or until golden. Repeat with the remaining batter. Keep warm on a plate in a 235°F oven while cooking the bacon.

Add the bacon to the pan and cook for 5 minutes. Put two pancakes and two bacon slices on each plate and drizzle with maple syrup, to serve.

mushrooms

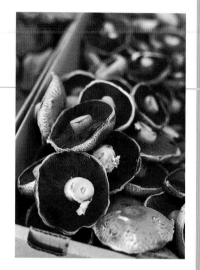

field mushrooms

fungi ▪ cultivated and wild mushrooms
season ▪ cultivated mushrooms available year-round;
wild mushrooms fall–winter

Not technically a vegetable, mushrooms are the fruit-body of a form of fungus, which thrives on dead trees or the roots of living trees. Although there are thousands of fungus varieties around the world, only a tiny fraction of these are edible. Since ancient times, the precious few that are edible have developed and sustained a devoted following. The Egyptian pharaohs forbade commoners from eating them, declaring them an exclusively royal food. Other ancient cultures ascribed all manner of magical properties to mushrooms—some believed they imparted superhuman powers while others thought they could aid in the recovery of lost objects.

An intriguing and diverse ingredient, mushrooms range in size, shape, flavor, and texture from the smallest button mushrooms to enormous puffballs, which can grow up to 40 inches in diameter. While some mushrooms, such as field mushrooms and portobellos, taste almost meaty, others like chanterelles have a mild, delicate flavor.

Mushrooms are rich in proteins, fiber, and B group vitamins including folate, niacin, and riboflavin. Consisting of approximately nine percent water, mushrooms contain enough nutrients to form the main component of a meal. It is worth noting that cultivated mushrooms contain lower levels of vitamins C and K than their wild counterparts.

cultivated mushrooms

Edible fungi can be broadly divided into two categories: cultivated and wild. Cultivated mushrooms are available year-round, are grown in compost in temperature- and moisture-controlled environments and are often hand-harvested in the dead of night.

Although the ancient Egyptians ate mushrooms, and the Romans spread them throughout their empire, mushroom cultivation was initially revolutionized in France in the 1600s, where they were grown in designated caves located close to Paris. All modern-day cultivated mushrooms belong to the *Agaricus bisporus* family and are harvested at different stages of maturity.

button (*A. bisporus*) The most commonly available mushroom, button mushrooms derive from crimini and were bred to be whiter, with closed veils, that is, their caps sit snugly against their stems. Their mild flavor intensifies when cooked, but they are also delicious eaten raw in salads. Whole, they are excellent sautéed and marinated in olive oil, used as the basis for cream of mushroom soup, or they may be added to casseroles, or sliced and used in sauces and pies.

chestnut (*A. bisporus*) Featuring a meaty, firm texture and strong, nutty flavor, chestnut mushrooms look similar to button mushrooms, but are darker in color, with open caps and pink to dark brown gills. They are ideally eaten raw or lightly cooked and suit using in pastry fillings, pâtés, and breads.

cremini (*A. bisporus*) These are actually the original form of the common button mushroom and not a distinct variety in their own right. They are sometimes called Italian brown mushrooms and, outside of the United States, Swiss brown mushrooms. Their caps range in color from light tan to deep brown and their flavor is more intense than that of buttons. Use cremini in meat or game dishes and pasta sauces.

portobello/portabello (*A. bisporus*) Growing up to 4 inches in diameter, these are the largest of the cultivated mushrooms and are in fact cremini mushrooms that have been allowed to continue growing before harvesting. Mushrooms double in size every 24 hours, so they are essentially more mature cremini, whose caps have opened. Boasting a meaty texture and rich flavor, portobello mushrooms are ideal for stuffing and baking, broiling, barbecuing, or pan-frying whole and using as a sandwich filling.

button mushrooms

The odd word "mushroom" is thought to have developed from the French word mousserons, *which was used to describe all mushrooms, poisonous and edible. Nowadays, "mushroom" is used to denote edible fungi and generally just those with a stem and a cap—other sorts are known by their specific names, for example, morels, ceps, and truffles. In these days of widespread mushroom (and other produce) cultivation, their wild equivalents are one of the last remaining, truly seasonal ingredients. Mushroom devotees worship the unique, deep earthy flavors and spongy texture of wild mushrooms.*

pine mushrooms

wild mushrooms

Wild mushrooms are truly seasonal produce, and rely upon the weather conditions of the cooler months to flourish. Both excessive and insufficient rain impedes their growth, so there are some years, such as during droughts, when they are scarce. Fall heralds the start of wild mushroom season (including saffron milk caps and slippery jacks) and extends into late winter, when morels are at their peak. During this eagerly anticipated time, mushroom foragers dot the countryside where the fungi grow wild. Clutching baskets as they embark in a cloak-and-dagger flurry worthy of any detective, most keen mushroom hunters have their own special spot, the secret location of which some even take to the grave.

It is crucial to always look for mushrooms with an experienced mushroom hunter or have the edibility of mushrooms validated by a fungus expert, as there are many more poisonous varieties than edible ones and mistakes can be fatal. Although cultivation guarantees a constant, ready supply of common varieties, it has lead to some compromise in flavor, so it is good to take advantage of wild mushrooms when they are in season.

chanterelles (*Cantharellus cibarius*) Also called girolles, these frilly golden-hued wild mushrooms are prized for their subtle, fruity flavor and firm, rubbery texture. Delicate by nature, they are best added to the cooking process at the last minute to prevent them from toughening, and are excellent in pasta dishes, risotto, sauces for meat, paired with chicken and pheasant, or sautéed in foaming unsalted butter and served with scrambled eggs and warm brioche.

field (*Agaricus campestris*) Characterized by an aniseed-accented flavor, field mushrooms are large, open, and flat-capped wild mushrooms with exposed pinkish brown gills and thick, white flesh. They grow in grassy meadows and cow pastures from late winter to early spring and are the United Kingdom's most popular wild mushroom.

Enjoy this substantial specimen pan-fried, crumbed and deep-fried, roasted, broiled, stuffed, barbecued, pickled and served as antipasto, or added to braised meat dishes. If used in braised poultry recipes, they can turn the dish an unappetizing gray, although this of course does not affect their flavor.

morel (*Morchella vulgaris* and *M. esculenta*) Closely related to the truffle, the most luxurious of all the fungi, morels are one of the few specifically spring mushrooms. Relatively scarce, they come with commensurately steep price tags and are highly prized by mushroom hunters for their earthy, smoky, nutlike flavor.

Their conical, tan to deep brown-black colored, perforated, spongy caps must be cleaned well to remove any bugs lurking in their hollow center. The darker the morel, the more intensely flavored it is. They add a depth of flavor to game, veal, and chicken dishes and are commonly cooked with cream. Morels are also available dried.

pine (*Suillus luteus* and *Lactarius deliciosa*) As the name suggests, pine mushrooms grow wild at the roots of pine trees. This category includes slippery jacks, which have a delicate flavor, moist slippery caps, and spongy flesh; and saffron milk caps, so-named due to their lurid saffron tone and the milky liquid they emit. They have a nutty flavor and firm texture and are excellent when combined with other mushrooms and used in sauces, soups, and stews.

porcini/cèpes (*Boletus edulis*) Indigenous to France and Italy's alpine regions, porcinis are adored by fungus fans for their distinctly sweet, strong mushroom flavor. Available fresh (although only during late summer and fall), dried, or frozen, their pungent aroma invigorates any dish they are added to.

Pale brown in color, porcinis are distinguished by their fleshy dome-shaped caps and thick, bulbous stems. Very young fresh porcini are a delicacy and can be shaved and eaten raw in salads, while older specimens make the best risottos, omelettes, pasta sauces, soups, and stews.

storage and selection

When buying mushrooms, look for unblemished specimens, with no signs of bruising, tearing, or soft spots. The stems should still be intact and the caps firm, not shrivelled, dry, or "tacky," which indicates spoilage.

Store mushrooms in a paper bag (this prevents dehydration and allows them to "breathe") in the refrigerator for up to 3 days. Mushrooms absorb other flavors, so it is best not to store them near strong-smelling foods.

Mushrooms are porous and readily absorb water—they should not be washed before storing or using. Rather, trim stems, then lightly dust with a pastry brush or carefully wipe with a damp cloth to remove any dirt clinging to their surface. As with all rules, there is of course an exception—morels need to be thoroughly washed as bugs can hide in their hollow centers.

If planning to cook mushrooms whole, choose uniform-size specimens so that they cook in approximately the same amount of time.

fungi ■ cultivated and wild mushrooms

preparation

After wiping mushrooms clean, trim the stalks (you can reserve these for use in stocks). If you are intending to stuff mushrooms you will need to remove the stalks completely.

roasting A good method for roasting larger capped mushrooms is to place them in a single layer in a large roasting pan, skin side down, drizzle with oil and sprinkle over some herbs—fresh thyme, marjoram, or rosemary are good. Season with sea salt and freshly ground black pepper and cook, turning once, in a 400°F oven for 12–15 minutes.

sautéing To sauté mushrooms, slice or chop them and cook in oil in a large frying pan over medium-high heat for 5–7 minutes or until soft and golden. Make sure the oil is quite hot before adding the mushrooms and be aware that they will absorb the oil, so don't be tempted to keep adding more; they will release juices and the soaked-up oil as they soften.

broiling To broil mushrooms, brush liberally with oil and place under a medium-high broiler for 7–10 minutes, turning once— the cooking time may vary depending on size.

culinary uses

Mushrooms may well be the ultimate food for fall. A plate laden with garlic and thyme-scented wild mushrooms, with thick slices of buttery, sourdough toast is simplicity personified, but a memorable way to start, or end, a chilly day. Sliced cremini cooked slowly with olive oil and garlic and finished with lots of chopped Italian parsley make a terrific crostini topping or frittata filling. Portobello or field mushroom caps topped with a stuffing of bread crumbs, sage, pancetta, and grated Parmesan cheese, then baked, are the perfect partner for barbecued sirloin steaks. For a sophisticated dinner party, sauté saffron milk caps and slippery jacks in anchovy and chive butter, then serve with wilted spinach as an accompaniment for pan-fried trout, crisp-skinned salmon fillets, or roasted blue eye trevally.

Mushrooms go particularly well with bacon, barley, bread, beef, butter, cheese (for instance Parmesan, Asiago, cheddar, fontina, Boursin, Stilton, Gruyère), chestnuts, chicken, cream, dill, duck, eggs, parsley, garlic, lemon, lentils, Madeira, marjoram, noodles, olive oil, polenta, thyme, pasta, pastry, pork, potatoes, quail, rabbit, rice, rosemary, sage, sherry, speck, spinach, turkey, venison and white and red wine, and seafood such as lobster, kingfish, rainbow trout, and tuna.

mushroom pâté on mini toasts

Heat the butter in a large frying pan. Cook the onion and garlic over medium heat for 2 minutes or until soft. Increase the heat, add the mushrooms and cook for 5 minutes or until the mushrooms are soft and most of the liquid has evaporated. Leave to cool for 10 minutes.

Roughly chop the almonds in a food processor. Add the mushroom mixture and process until smooth. With the motor running, gradually pour in the cream. Stir in the herbs and season with sea salt and freshly ground black pepper. Spoon into two 1-cup ramekins and smooth the surface. Cover and refrigerate for 4–5 hours to let the flavors develop.

To make the toasts, preheat the oven to 350°F. Toast one side of the bread under a hot broiler until golden. Remove the crusts and cut each slice into four triangles. Place on a large baking sheet in a single layer, toasted side down, and cook for 5–10 minutes or until crisp. Serve the toasts immediately with the pâté.

¼ cup butter
1 small onion, chopped
3 garlic cloves, crushed
5 cups quartered button
   mushrooms (13 ounces)
1 cup slivered almonds, toasted
2 tablespoons whipping cream
2 tablespoons finely chopped
   thyme
3 tablespoons finely chopped
   Italian parsley
6 thick slices whole-wheat bread

fungi ■ cultivated and wild mushrooms

Mycophobia is a condition where the sufferer has an extreme fear of, or aversion to, mushrooms. Such fears have their genesis in history —because the mushroom magically appears, from seemingly nowhere, favors damp and dark conditions, and loves to grow near decaying matter—it was regarded with deep suspicion in times past. That it has no leaves, seeds, obvious root structure, or way of gaining nutrients only added to its mysterious aura.

open lasagna of mushrooms, pine nuts, and thyme

serves 4

7 ounces (or 2 medium) fresh
  lasagna sheets
1/3 cup butter
1 tablespoon olive oil
3 1/3 cups sliced assorted
  mushrooms (10 ounces)
2 bacon slices, cut into pieces
  of similar size to the mushroom
  slices
2 garlic cloves, finely sliced
1 tablespoon fresh thyme
1 tablespoon pine nuts, toasted
3 tablespoons heavy cream
3 tablespoons extra virgin
  olive oil
1/3 cup roughly shredded
  pecorino cheese

Bring a large saucepan of salted water to a boil. Cut each
lasagna sheet into eight 3 1/4-inch squares (you will need
sixteen squares in total). Boil half of the pasta squares for
4 minutes or until *al dente*. Using a slotted spoon, transfer
to a bowl of cold water, leave for 15–20 seconds, then drain.
Lay flat on a dry dishtowel and cover with another dishtowel;
it doesn't matter that the squares may have cooked to uneven
sizes. Repeat this process with the remaining pasta squares.

Heat the butter and olive oil in a large frying pan. Add the
mushrooms and bacon and cook over high heat, stirring
often, for 3–4 minutes or until golden brown. Add the
garlic and thyme and cook for 1 minute. Add the pine nuts,
cream, and 2 tablespoons of extra virgin olive oil and stir
until combined. Remove from the heat and season to taste.

Preheat the broiler to medium-high. Put a pasta square in
each of four shallow heatproof pasta bowls. Cover with a
heaping tablespoon of mushroom mixture. Repeat twice
more, then top with the last four pasta squares; the pasta
doesn't have to be in uniform stacks, nor the piles neat.

Drizzle the remaining extra virgin olive oil over the top and
sprinkle with the cheese. Place the bowls under the heat for
1–2 minutes or until cheese has melted. Serve hot or warm.

note Use your favorite type of cap mushroom, such as
chestnut, cremini, portobello, or even shiitake, as long as
they are no bigger than 1 1/2 inches across. To prepare, cut
off the dirty end of the stalks, shake off excess soil, and
wipe the caps with a damp cloth.

exotic
mushrooms

fungi ▪ **exotic mushrooms**
season ▪ **available year-round**

Once exclusive to Japan, China, and Korea, where they originate and have been cultivated for centuries, so-called "exotic" mushrooms are now increasingly available fresh almost everywhere, as demand for their unique flavor spreads.

While edible fungi have been integral to the cuisines of Asian countries for thousands of years, they are also eaten for medicinal purposes. In China, mushrooms are regarded as a symbol of longevity and used to boost immunity. Shiitakes in particular are high in amino acids, thiamine, riboflavin, niacin, and dietary fiber, and contain nutrients not usually found in nonanimal matter, like vitamins B2, B12, and D. In general, like other mushrooms, these exotic varieties contain varying levels of niacin, selenium, riboflavin, and potassium.

culinary uses

With their unique textures, flavors, and character, Asian mushrooms add an interesting note and appealing look to many dishes. Shiitakes contribute a smoky undertone when slowly cooked in a star anise-infused Chinese master stock with pork, chicken, or beef. Braise a mixture of exotic mushrooms in dashi stock, mirin, and soy sauce, or brush oyster mushrooms with tamari and sake and briefly barbecue as an accompaniment for teriyaki beef. Exotic mushrooms work best with flavors favored in the countries they are indigenous to; consider rice, soy sauce, tofu, fish, duck, shrimp, ginger, garlic, cilantro, scallions, Asian greens, soba noodles, and miso.

varieties

enoki (*Flammulina velutipes*) Growing in clusters linked by a communal base, with tiny caps and slender long stems, enoki are named after the hackberry tree of the same name that is their natural habitat. Cultivated enoki are creamy colored, with an almost fruity, sweet flavor and crunchy texture. Extremely delicate, they require only minimal cooking, so should be added at the last minute to Japanese soups and hotpots, or used raw in salads.

king trumpet (*Pleurotus eryngii*) Also called eryngiis or king oysters, these intriguing mushrooms grow in pairs and have small thick caps. Their long, stout stems contain most of their flavor, which is often compared to almonds and abalone and is best when cooked with seafood and meat or used in clear soups.

nameko (*Pholiota nameko*) Indigenous to Japan, these mushrooms are prized for their aromatic flavor. They have a brief shelf life and while they can occasionally be found fresh, they are also sold canned and dried. With slippery, honey-hued rounded caps and gills and paler, thick curved stems, nameko are traditionally added to sushi or used in miso soup and braises.

oyster (*Pleurotus ostreatus*) With pale beige to gray, fluted fan-shaped caps, oyster mushrooms can be enjoyed raw, but gentle cooking elicits their juicy texture and almost peppery, delicate flavor. They are a treat fried in butter and garlic, broiled whole, used in Japanese-style seafood and chicken braises, or added to casseroles or clear soups. They are best matched with clean, unassertive flavors that won't overwhelm their delightful delicacy.

shiitake (*Lentinus edodes*) Indigenous to Japan, shiitake are now the most widely cultivated of all the Asian mushrooms and are increasingly available fresh as well as dried. In their natural habitat their spores grow on oak trees. With broad, plump, and firm tan to dark brown caps and creamy gills, shiitake are intensely flavored with a woodsy aroma. Their assertive flavor best suits braising, sautéing, stir-frying, roasting and adding to soups, or finely chopping and including in fillings for dumplings and stuffed vegetables or fish.

shimeji (*Tricholoma conglobatum*) Confusingly, shimeji refers to around twenty mushroom species. The hon-shimeji is regarded as the "true" shimeji and, as its name suggests, it was first cultivated in Japan. The flavor of the hon-shimeji is nutty and a little sweet and is suited to a wide range of dishes, from soups to stir-fries and sauces. Light gray to taupe in color, it is often sold in the dense cluster in which it grows. The base needs to be cut off and the mushrooms only require wiping—do not wet them or they will become soggy. Shimeji mushrooms aren't suitable for eating raw, but can be cooked whole, sliced, or chopped.

selection and storage

Generally sold on plastic wrapped trays or in disposable conatiners, choose exotic mushrooms that look plump and firm, not dry or shrivelled, then transfer to perforated plastic or paper bags and refrigerate on a shelf, not in the crisper, for up to 3 days.

fungi ▪ exotic mushrooms

shiitake wontons with chili-ginger dipping sauce

makes 24

dipping sauce
2 teaspoons grated ginger
1½ teaspoons sweet chili sauce
⅓ cup light soy sauce
2 tablespoons rice wine
½ teaspoon finely chopped
  cilantro stems

1½ cups finely diced fresh
  shiitake mushrooms
1 teaspoon grated ginger
6 water chestnuts, finely chopped
1 teaspoon chopped cilantro
  leaves
1 teaspoon soy sauce
1 teaspoon rice wine
1 teaspoon sesame oil
3 teaspoons cornstarch
24 ready-made square wheat
  wonton wrappers
vegetable oil, for deep-frying

To make the dipping sauce, combine the ginger, sweet chili sauce, light soy sauce, rice wine, and cilantro stems. Mix thoroughly and set aside.

To make the filling, combine the shiitake mushrooms, ginger, water chestnuts, and cilantro leaves. Stir in the soy sauce, rice wine, sesame oil, and cornstarch. Put a heaping teaspoon of filling in the center of a wonton wrapper. Moisten the edges with water, then gather up the four corners to a peak, encasing the filling. Twist the peak tightly to secure.

In a wok or deep-fryer, heat plenty of vegetable oil to 350°F or until a cube of bread dropped into the oil browns in 15 seconds. Deep-fry the wontons, in batches, for about 1 minute or until golden brown. Drain on paper towels and serve with the dipping sauce.

Since ancient times, traditional physicians throughout Asia have prescribed shiitake mushrooms for a whole gamut of complaints—from sinus ailments to liver disease, from bad eyesight to gastrointestinal conditions. Modern science has identified a phytochemical in shiitake called lentinan, which is believed to assist in the treatment of cancer, coronary disease, and high blood pressure. Little wonder then, that in the East they have long considered it to promote long life and well-being.

exotic mushrooms with dashi

Combine the dashi granules with ½ cup boiling water in a small bowl, then stir in the soy sauce and mirin. Set aside.

Heat a wok or frying pan over high heat, add 1 tablespoon of the oil and swirl to coat. Add the oyster, shiitake, and enoki mushrooms in batches and stir-fry for 1–2 minutes or until wilted and softened.

Heat the remaining oil in the wok, add the ginger and the white part of the scallion and stir-fry for 30 seconds or until fragrant. Return all the cooked mushrooms to the wok, along with the dashi mixture, then bring to a boil. Stir-fry for an additional minute or until the mushrooms are heated through. Remove from the heat, add the shimeji mushrooms and toss until they are wilted with the heat from the other mushrooms. Garnish with the green part of the scallion.

1 teaspoon dashi granules
1 tablespoon Japanese soy sauce
1 tablespoon mirin
1½ tablespoons vegetable oil
5 ounces oyster mushrooms, cut into halves if large
10 ounces fresh shiitake mushrooms, sliced
10 ounces enoki mushrooms, separated into small bunches
1 teaspoon finely grated ginger
1 scallion, white part finely chopped, green part shredded
10 ounces shimeji mushrooms, separated

fungi ▪ exotic mushrooms

tofu and mushroom stir-fry

serves 4

Heat a wok or heavy-bottomed frying pan over high heat. Add 2 teaspoons peanut oil and swirl to coat the wok. Add the tofu in two batches and stir-fry for 2–3 minutes or until golden on all sides, then transfer to a plate.

Heat the remaining oil in the wok, add the sambal oelek, garlic, snow peas, mushrooms, and 1 tablespoon water; stir-fry for 1–2 minutes or until vegetables are cooked but still crunchy.

Return the tofu to the wok, add the kecap manis and stir-fry for 1 minute or until heated through. Serve with steamed rice.

¼ cup peanut oil
1 pound 5 ounces firm tofu, drained and cut into cubes
2 teaspoons sambal oelek
2 garlic cloves, finely chopped
3 cups snow peas, trimmed
5 cups (14 ounces) mixed Asian mushrooms, sliced
¼ cup kecap manis
steamed rice, to serve

herbs

basil

selection and storage

Basil tastes its best when harvested before the plant flowers, so when purchasing, avoid any with flowers in evidence. Leaves should be verdantly green, slightly glossy and devoid of holes or signs of decay.

A bunch of basil should keep for 1 week in the refrigerator—trim the ends of the stalks, then place in a glass of water. Place the whole bunch in a plastic bag and seal. The leaves bruise very easily so don't wash or chop them until just before you need them.

If you grow basil and have more than you can use, excess leaves can easily be frozen. Blanch them briefly in boiling water and drain. Plunge into iced water and drain again, then pat dry and freeze in airtight bags. There is no need to defrost before using.

Basil belongs to the mint family and probably originated in India, from where it was dispersed throughout Mediterranean regions via the ancient spice routes. One of its first important uses was as an embalming agent; basil has been found inside Egyptian mummies and, incredibly, modern research confirms that basil does act as a powerful antibacterial medium. Basil has many other properties too, with high vitamin A and magnesium levels among them. Much legend and lore has sprung up around basil—from Salome hiding John the Baptist's severed head in a pot of basil, to the ancient Greeks and Romans believing that the only way to make it grow was to shout belligerent curses as one planted the seeds.

There are over sixty varieties of basil, each with distinct characteristics, from lemon basil and cinnamon basil to Thai holy basil and the ruffly-edged purple basil, but the most common is the verdant-green sweet basil.

culinary uses

Widely used in many cuisines, basil goes well with summer vegetables like eggplant, tomatoes, and zucchini; cheeses like Parmesan, feta, and mozzarella; with chicken, lamb, pasta, rice, and eggs. It can even be used to great effect in desserts, subtly flavoring custards, creams, ice creams, and syrups, particularly those made with red wine, cinnamon, cloves, or allspice.

pesto

Put the garlic in a large mortar or food processor, add a
pinch of salt and the pine nuts. Pound to a paste using a
pestle, or process. Gradually add the basil leaves and pound
the leaves against the side of the mortar, or continue to
process. Stir in the grated Parmesan cheese, then gradually
add enough of the olive oil to form a thick paste.

Use immediately or store covered in the refrigerator for
1 week. If storing, cover the pesto surface with a thin layer
of olive oil.

2 garlic cloves, crushed
1/3 cup pine nuts
2 1/2 large handfuls basil leaves
3/4 cup grated Parmesan cheese
1/2 cup olive oil

herbs ■ basil

spaghetti puttanesca

serves 4

Cook the spaghetti in a large saucepan of boiling salted
water until *al dente*.

Meanwhile, heat the olive oil in a large frying pan and add
the onion, garlic, and chili. Gently fry for 8 minutes, or until
the onion is soft. Add the anchovies and cook for 1 minute.
Add the tomato, oregano, olive halves, and capers and bring
to a boil. Reduce the heat and simmer for 3 minutes. Season
with sea salt and freshly ground black pepper.

Drain the spaghetti and add it to the sauce. Toss together well
so that the pasta is coated in the sauce. Sprinkle the basil over
the top and serve immediately.

14 ounces spaghetti
2 tablespoons olive oil
1 onion, finely chopped
2 garlic cloves, finely sliced
1 small red chili, seeded and
    sliced
6 anchovy fillets, finely chopped
1 (14-ounce) can chopped
    tomatoes
1 tablespoon oregano, finely
    chopped
16 black olives, halved and pitted
2 tablespoons baby capers,
    rinsed and drained
1 large handful basil leaves,
    to serve

bay leaf

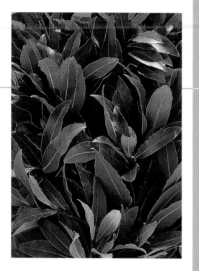

Bay leaves are harvested from the handsome bay laurel tree, which can grow to 60 feet tall. The bay thrives in Mediterranean regions, where the culinary and curative properties of the glossy, deep green leaves have long been appreciated, although it is actually an Asian native.

Bay leaves are common to many food cultures, used in stocks, soups, sauces, stews, marinades, and casseroles. Generally, they are used as a background flavor, lending a warm, woodsy complexity to dishes—there are very few occasions when the flavor of bay would be the predominant one.

preparation

The leaves are large, glossy green and leathery and their flavor is very strong; a single, fresh leaf can go a long way. Drying, the form in which most cooks use them, greatly mellows their flavor. If you have a supply of fresh leaves, it is a simple matter to dry your own. Simply tie small bunches of leaves with string and hang them in a well-ventilated place for several days or until completely dry, then store them in an airtight container and use within a few months.

When using fresh leaves, add them whole and bruised to a dish, or torn into a few large pieces so they can be retrieved before serving—when chopped into small pieces they can cause choking, if eaten.

selection and storage

Fresh leaves will keep, stored in a loosely sealed plastic bag, in the refrigerator for at least 1 week.

For other bay leaf recipes see:

french onion soup

Melt the butter in a heavy-bottomed saucepan over low heat. Add the onions and cook, stirring occasionally, for 25 minutes or until the onions are a deep golden brown and begin to caramelize.

Add the garlic and flour and stir continuously for 2 minutes. Gradually blend in the stock and the wine, stirring all the time, and bring to a boil. Add the bay leaf and thyme and season with sea salt and freshly ground black pepper. Cover the saucepan and simmer for 25 minutes. Remove the bay leaf and thyme and check the seasoning.

Preheat the broiler to high. Toast the baguette slices on the broiler tray, then divide among six warmed heatproof soup bowls. Ladle the soup over the toasts. Sprinkle with the grated cheese and return to the broiler. Broil until the cheese melts and turns a light golden brown. Serve immediately.

¼ cup butter
1 pound 8 ounces onions
 (4–5 onions), finely sliced
2 garlic cloves, finely chopped
⅓ cup all-purpose flour
8 cups beef or chicken stock
1 cup white wine
1 bay leaf
2 thyme sprigs
12 slices day-old baguette
¾ cup grated Gruyère cheese

herbs ■ bay leaf

bouquet garni

makes 1

To make a bouquet garni, wrap the green strip of leek around the bay leaf, thyme sprig, parsley sprig, and celery leaves. Tie the bundle with string, leaving it long at one end for easy removal. Use as directed in recipes.

1 green strip from a leek
1 bay leaf
1 thyme sprig
1 parsley sprig
1 celery top with leaves

chives

selection and storage

Chives are delicate and do not last long once picked. Choose bunches with leaves that show no signs of yellowing, wilting, or decay (water will cause them to start rotting). Store chives, wrapped in damp paper towels, placed in a loosely sealed plastic bag, in the refrigerator for up to 3–4 days.

A member of the lily (allium) family along with leeks, onions, and garlic, the botanical name *Allium schoenoprasum* is Greek for "reedlike leek" whereas the English "chive" is from the Latin for onion, *cepa*.

Chives, which grow in grassy clumps, are graceful and slender, with hollow leaves that grow to about 12 inches in length. They have mauve, puffball-shaped flowers which are also edible (these look lovely strewn over a green salad), although the leaves themselves taste coarse and strong after the plant has flowered. Another variety of chives is the garlic chive, which, as the name suggests, has a pleasant, mild garlic flavor. It has narrow, flat leaves and white flowers and is most used in and best suited to oriental-style dishes.

culinary uses

Chives are best used raw or just warmed through, as strong heat kills both their pleasant, mild-onion flavor as well as their vibrant green color; to preserve color and flavor, they should always be cut and added to dishes at the very last moment. They need to be cut with a very sharp knife or snipped with kitchen scissors otherwise they bruise.

Regular chives (sometimes called "onion" chives to distinguish them from their garlic cousins) have a great affinity with potatoes, eggs, and fish (including smoked salmon), they can be used to excellent effect in savory breads, scones and muffins, vegetable cakes and fritters, and creamy sauces for chicken, veal, and lamb.

cheese and chive scones

Preheat the oven to 415°F. Grease a baking sheet. Sift the flour and a pinch of salt into a bowl. Rub in the butter using your fingertips. Stir in the cheeses and the chives. Make a well in the center, add the milk and 1/2 cup water. Mix lightly with a flat-bladed knife to form a soft dough, adding more liquid if necessary.

Knead the dough briefly on a lightly floured surface until smooth. Press out the dough to a 3/4-inch thickness. Using a floured 2-inch plain round cutter, cut out rounds from the dough. Place rounds on the prepared baking sheet and sprinkle with the extra cheese. Bake for 12 minutes or until cheese is golden and scones have risen. Serve with butter.

2 cups self-rising flour
1 1/2 tablespoons butter
1/2 cup grated cheddar cheese
1/4 cup grated Parmesan cheese
2 tablespoons snipped chives
1/2 cup milk
1/4 cup grated cheddar cheese, extra
butter, to serve

herbs ■ chives

watercress salad

serves 4–6

To make the salad, wash and drain the vegetables. Break the watercress into small sprigs, discarding the coarser stems. Cut the celery into thin 2-inch long sticks. Peel, halve, and seed the cucumber, then cut into thin slices. Peel the oranges, remove the white pith, and cut the oranges into segments between the membranes. Refrigerate until needed.

To make the dressing, combine the oil, lemon juice, orange zest, mustard, and honey in a screwtop jar. Season with black pepper. Shake vigorously to combine well.

Combine all the salad ingredients, except nuts, in a serving bowl. Pour the dressing over and toss. Sprinkle with the pecans or walnuts, to serve.

1 pound (about 2 bunches) watercress, leaves picked
3 celery sticks
1 cucumber
3 oranges
1 red onion, thinly sliced and separated into rings
3/4 cup snipped chives
1/2 cup chopped pecan nuts or walnuts

dressing
1/4 cup olive oil
1/4 cup lemon juice
2 teaspoons grated orange zest
1 teaspoon seeded mustard
1 tablespoon honey

cilantro

Cilantro is one of the world's oldest herbs. It dates back some 5,000 years BC and is actually one of the "bitter herbs" of the traditional Jewish Passover feast. The entire plant can be used—the seeds are dried and used as a spice, the fresh stems and leaves are used in salads, curries, and soups, and in Southeast Asian cooking, the roots are incorporated into wet spice pastes.

Cilantro is so-called after the Spanish name, but also goes by the names of coriander, Chinese parsley, and Mexican parsley. Not surprisingly then, cilantro is related to parsley and carrots, and is much used in cookery all over the globe—it is one of the very few fresh herbs Chinese cooks sanction in their cuisine.

Heat quickly destroys the flavor of cilantro, so when using the chopped leaves in hot dishes, add it at the last moment.

selection and storage

Cilantro does not store well, so should be used within 1–2 days or so of purchase and refrigerated in an airtight container until needed.

When purchasing, look for bunches with bright green, unblemished leaves; avoid overly limp bunches and do not purchase any that are bruised or showing signs of sliminess or yellowing.

culinary uses

Cooks in western Europe tend not to use cilantro, and many people find its smell and taste to be objectionably "soapy." For lovers of the herb though, there is nothing quite like the distinctive, yet mellow, herbaceousness of fresh cilantro. It is used to delicious effect in Mexican dishes such as ceviche and guacamole and in curries, tagines, salads, and vegetable dishes from the Indian, Middle Eastern, and Asian culinary lexicons.

cilantro beef

Combine the garlic, ginger, cilantro, oil, and beef in a large nonmetallic bowl. Cover and refrigerate for 1–2 hours.

Heat a large, heavy-bottomed frying pan or wok over high heat, add the meat in three batches, and stir-fry each batch for 2–3 minutes or until the meat is just cooked. Remove meat from the pan and keep warm.

Heat 1 tablespoon extra oil in the pan, add the onion and cook over medium-high heat for 3–4 minutes or until slightly softened. Add the red and green bell peppers and cook, tossing constantly, for 3–4 minutes or until the peppers have softened slightly.

Return the meat to the pan along with the lime juice and extra cilantro. Toss well, then remove from the heat and season with sea salt and freshly ground black pepper. Serve immediately.

4 garlic cloves, finely chopped
1 tablespoon finely chopped ginger
2 large handfuls cilantro stems, roots, and leaves, finely chopped
1/4 cup vegetable oil
1 pound lean beef fillet, thinly sliced across the grain
oil, extra, for cooking
2 red onions, thinly sliced
1/2 red bell pepper, sliced
1/2 green bell pepper, sliced
1 tablespoon lime juice
2 large handfuls cilantro leaves, extra

herbs ■ cilantro

mango salsa

serves 4 as a side dish

Peel the mango and finely dice the flesh. Remove the seeds from the chili and finely chop the flesh.

Combine all the ingredients in a small bowl. Season with sea salt and freshly ground black pepper and serve as an accompaniment to macadamia-crusted chicken bites (page 167) or lemongrass chicken skewers (page 421).

1 small mango
1 green chili
2 tablespoons finely diced red onion
2 tablespoons roughly chopped cilantro leaves
1 tablespoon lime juice

dill

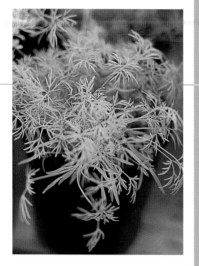

selection and storage

Dill is quite fragile and wilts very quickly after it is picked. To store it, spray with a fine mist of water, wrap carefully in damp paper towels, then seal in a plastic bag and keep in the crisper section of the refrigerator for up to 5 days. You can also freeze dill for up to 8 weeks—it will turn an unattractive dark green color and the flavor won't be as strong as the fresh herb, but is still preferable to using dried dill.

The word "dill" derives from the Norse word *dilla* which means "to lull" or "soothe," and indeed the Greeks placed sprigs of dill over their eyes to induce sleep. Also much used by European herbalists to cure digestive ailments, dill was a common cure for colic during the Middle Ages.

Native to the Mediterranean region, Southern Russia, Central and Southern Asia, dill is a popular culinary herb with diverse uses. It is a vital pickling ingredient in many cuisines (especially with cucumbers; an interesting pairing given that cucumbers have a reputation for being hard to digest and dill can assist with this), and it goes especially well with seafood, chicken, sour cream and yogurt, eggs, potatoes, leeks, cabbage, carrots and, as noted, cucumbers.

Cooking quickly diminishes the fresh anise flavor of this herb so for the best results, chop and add dill to dishes at the final possible moment.

culinary uses

One of the best possible uses for dill is stirred in generous amounts through thick homemade mayonnaise. Serve this with cold steamed shrimp or poached fish, or spread on cucumber sandwiches. Finish a creamy fish chowder with a handful of dill or stir it into softened butter, along with some finely chopped sundried tomatoes, and serve this over chicken, lamb, or beef steak.

sugar-cured salmon

Place the salmon on a board and check for bones. If there are any bones in the salmon it will be impossible to slice the fish thinly, as they will catch on the knife. Any small stubborn bones can be removed using tweezers.

Mix the sugar and salt together and spoon half of the mixture into a shallow, rectangular, nonmetallic dish, large enough to hold the salmon. Place the fish on the mixture. Sprinkle the peppercorns, dill, tarragon, and basil over the fish. Cover with the remaining sugar and salt. Cover loosely with plastic wrap and place a tray, small board, or plate on top of the fish and weigh the tray down with a couple of cans. Refrigerate for 2 days, turning the fish over in the mixture every 12 hours.

To make the mustard sauce, place the egg yolks in a medium bowl with a generous pinch of salt and freshly ground black pepper, and gently whisk together. Mix the oils together. Slowly add the oil to the egg yolks, drop by drop, whisking all the time. Increase to a slow trickle as the sauce thickens. Fold in the lemon zest and juice, dill, and mustard. Whisk the cream to the floppy stage and fold that in too. Taste and season, if desired.

To make the cucumber salad, combine the cucumber, dill, olive oil, and vinegar in a bowl and toss together.

Remove the fish from the dish and brush off the sugar and salt. Discard any brine. Using a sharp knife and cutting along the length of the salmon, slice into paper-thin pieces. Serve with mustard sauce and cucumber salad. The sugar-cured salmon will keep in the refrigerator for 2 days.

variation You can use ocean trout as a substitute for salmon if you prefer.

1 pound middle salmon fillet, skinned
1⅓ cups soft brown sugar
¾ cup coarse sea salt
8 black peppercorns, lightly crushed
1 tablespoon chopped dill
1 tablespoon chopped tarragon
1 tablespoon shredded basil

mustard sauce
3 egg yolks, at room temperature
⅔ cup light olive oil
⅔ cup peanut oil
finely grated zest of 1 lemon
1 tablespoon lemon juice
3 tablespoons chopped dill
2 teaspoons wholegrain mustard
⅓ cup heavy cream

cucumber salad
1 Lebanese (short) cucumber, finely sliced
1 tablespoon finely chopped dill
2 teaspoons extra virgin olive oil
1 teaspoon white wine vinegar

herbs ■ dill

lemongrass

Lemongrass is closely associated with the cooking of Southeast Asian countries like Thailand and Vietnam and is thought to be native to Malaysia (although some think India). It is a member of the grass (Poaceae) family and presents as 2 foot long, very stiff, fibrous green stalks, the outer layers of which are cut off when harvested to reveal the tender, creamy-colored interior core. Culinarily speaking, this is the most usable part of the lemongrass.

Anyone who knows its distinctively haunting, sweet, lemony-lime aroma will be unsurprised to learn that lemongrass is much used in the manufacture of fragrance, soap, and scented candles, and is a close relative of citronella, used widely as an insect repellent. It is widely used for various medicinal purposes; possessing antiviral, antiseptic, and antibacterial properties, it is used for everything from a headache, rheumatism, and malaria cure, to aiding in recovery after childbirth.

selection and storage

Although you can buy dried and powdered lemongrass, these are but pale imitations of the real thing—there really is no comparison.

Choose lemongrass stalks that are plump and firm, with no signs of drying or brittleness. They will keep, stored in a tightly sealed plastic bag in the refrigerator, for 2–3 weeks.

Lemongrass can be successfully frozen. Cut off the tough green ends and wrap stalks tightly in foil and then plastic wrap. Cut from the stalk as you require lemongrass— it will lose a little of its potency but this is a preferable trade-off if the choices are between using frozen or dried alternatives.

preparation

Strip away the inedibly tough outer layers of each stalk to reveal the smooth, pale, round core and cut off and discard the green tops and 3/4–1 1/4 inches from the root end. These off-cuts can be used, whole and bruised, to flavor Asian-style soups, steamed rice or in chicken stock, or chopped finely and steeped to make a delicious tea.

lemongrass chicken skewers

Discard any excess fat from the chicken thighs and cut them in half lengthwise. Combine the sugar, lime juice, curry paste, and 2 of the kaffir lime leaves, shredded, in a bowl. Add the chicken and mix well. Cover and refrigerate for several hours, or overnight.

Trim the lemongrass to measure about 8 inches, leaving the root end intact. Cut each stem along its length into four pieces, to make eight long lemongrass skewers in total. Cut a slit in each of the remaining lime leaves and thread one onto each skewer. Cut two slits in the chicken pieces and thread onto each of the lemongrass skewers, finishing with another lime leaf. Pan-fry or barbecue the skewers until cooked through. Serve with the mango salsa.

4 boneless, skinless chicken thighs
1½ tablespoons soft brown sugar
1½ tablespoons lime juice
2 teaspoons store-bought green curry paste
18 kaffir lime leaves
2 lemongrass stems, white part only
mango salsa (see page 417), to serve

herbs ■ lemongrass

lemongrass ice tea

serves 2

Prepare the lemongrass by removing and discarding the first two tough outer layers. Slice thinly into rings. Put the lemongrass in a heatproof pitcher and cover with the boiling water. Add the lemon slices and cover. Allow to infuse and cool. When cooled to room temperature, strain. Add the honey, to taste. Place the tea in the refrigerator to chill.

To serve, pour the tea into two glasses with extra slices of lemon. Add ice, if desired.

3 lemongrass stems, white part only
2½ cups boiling water
2 lemon slices
3 teaspoons honey, or to taste
lemon slices, extra, to serve
ice, to serve

mint

selection and storage

When buying mint, choose bunches that are sprightly and have bright green leaves that show no signs of drooping or yellowing.

Fresh mint will store for 3–4 days if wrapped carefully in damp paper towels and loosely sealed in a plastic bag in the refrigerator.

There are over 600 varieties of mint and, as the plant readily hybridizes, even experts have trouble separating the many different types. However, the most common sorts are spearmint and peppermint, the latter having squat, rounded leaves with sharp-toothed edges and an intense, clear flavor, while the former is less strong and a more versatile culinary herb. The leaves of spearmint are longish, spearlike, and attractively crinkled.

Mint has been much favored since ancient times for its aromatic, medicinal, and culinary uses. It is thought the Romans were the first to seriously utilize mint in cookery (it was they who introduced mint sauce to Britain) and they also used it to freshen rooms by strewing the leaves over the floor to repel mice and other pests.

culinary uses

The uses of mint are endless, from the simplicity of throwing a handful of leaves into a pot of boiling potatoes, to adding torn leaves at the last minute to salads. It is indispensable in Asian cooking, complementing brilliantly the flavors of chili, fish sauce, jaggery, limes, coconut, and rice noodles. It is also much used in Middle Eastern cuisine, where it works perfectly with the flavors of bulgur wheat, yogurt, lamb, cucumber, and sweet spices that so typify that style of cooking.

Mint owes its clean, cool flavor to the presence of the volatile oil menthol which quickly dissipates so, as is the case with most fresh herbs, avoid cutting or tearing the leaves until just before you use them.

mint sauce

In a small dish, mix together the mint and sugar. Add the boiling water: this sets the color. Then, add the extra sugar, wine vinegar, and a pinch of salt and mix together. Leave to stand for about 1 hour to allow the flavors to develop. Serve with a traditional lamb roast.

4 tablespoons finely chopped
  mint leaves
1 teaspoon sugar
2 tablespoons boiling water
2 teaspoons sugar, extra
3 tablespoons wine vinegar

herbs ■ mint

minted peas

serves 4 as a side dish

Place the peas in a saucepan and pour in water to just cover the peas. Add the mint sprigs.

Bring to a boil and simmer for 5 minutes or until the peas are just tender. Drain and discard the mint. Return the peas to the saucepan, add the butter and shredded mint and stir over low heat until the butter has melted. Season with sea salt and freshly ground black pepper.

4 cups peas
4 mint sprigs
1½ tablespoons butter
2 tablespoons shredded mint
  leaves

oregano and marjoram

selection and storage

As with all fresh herbs, choose oregano and marjoram that show no signs of drooping, yellowing, or drying; stems of these herbs will store well in the refrigerator (up to 1 week) if wrapped in slightly damp paper towels, then loosely sealed in a plastic bag.

When it comes to discussions about these two herbs, confusion often reigns. Marjoram used to have its own genus but has now been subsumed back into that of oregano to become one of the fifty-odd varieties of the parent herb. Oregano itself is often referred to as "wild marjoram" and it is believed that much of the marjoram referred to by the ancients, who used the herb regularly, was actually oregano. Although undoubtedly similar, there are also marked differences.

Marjoram tends to have smaller, softer, more compact leaves than oregano, that are gray-green and ovoid in shape. It bears knotty green buds that open into (edible) white flowers. It has a sweetly pungent flavor. Oregano is considered more "aggressively" flavored (indeed, some varieties are so strong their effect is almost numbing) and has larger leaves (these can be either smooth or slightly furry) and purple blossoms. However, the strength of the flavor is very dependent upon where and how the herb has been grown. All varieties of oregano are members of the mint family, with square stems and opposing pairs of leaves.

Both herbs can be used whole or chopped—it is an easy matter to strip them off their stems for preparation. Long cooking subdues their flavor so, as a general rule, add them near the end of cooking.

greek salad

Chop the tomato and cut the cucumber into rounds. Thinly slice the radishes and onion.

Combine the prepared tomato, cucumber, radishes and onion in a serving bowl, along with the feta and olives. Drizzle with the combined lemon juice, olive oil, and oregano. Serve on a bed of coral lettuce, if desired.

1 large tomato
1 Lebanese (short) cucumber
2 radishes
1 small onion
¾ cup cubed feta cheese
⅓ cup pitted black olives
2 tablespoons lemon juice
3 tablespoons olive oil
½ teaspoon oregano leaves

herbs ■ oregano and marjoram

marjoram salmoriglio (dressing)

serves 4

In a mortar, use a pestle to pound the fresh marjoram. Transfer to a bowl and gradually add the extra virgin olive oil and lemon juice. Season with sea salt and freshly ground black pepper.

note Thyme or oregano can be used instead of marjoram. This simple dressing is used widely in Italy to accompany grilled fish or other seafood.

2 tablespoons marjoram
½ cup extra virgin olive oil
1 tablespoon lemon juice

parsley

selection and storage

When selecting parsley to buy, try to ensure it is young—this is a little easier to do with the Italian variety for as it ages the leaves become large, leathery, and resemble celery leaves; their flavor is coarse.

Store parsley with its stalks in a container of water in the refrigerator and with a plastic bag sealing the cup and leaves—Italian parsley can be stored wrapped in damp paper towels, then loosely sealed in a plastic bag. Thus stored, parsley will keep for about 4 days.

Parsley, which is native to the Mediterranean, must surely be one of the world's most versatile and well-used herbs—there are few savory dishes that do not benefit from its clean, grassy flavor and vivid-green appearance. There are two main culinary varieties of this herb; curly-leafed parsley and flat-leafed Italian parsley—the latter has a stronger flavor as it contains higher levels of essential oils in its leaves.

Parsley is one of the most nutritious herbs, containing power-pack quantities of vitamins A and C, as well as significant amounts of potassium, calcium, phosphorus, magnesium, and iron. Parsley has a very high chlorophyll content which accounts for its bright green color and the way it can "bleed" into white sauces and such—for this reason, and also because prolonged heating kills its flavor, parsley is mostly added to dishes near the end of cooking.

Curly-leafed parsley, which should feel a little soft to touch, not hard and papery, needs thorough washing to remove any trapped dirt and can be washed and then dried in a salad spinner. In the main, though, and with a few notable examples where recipes will specify a particular sort, the two types of parsley are interchangeable, so long as the leaves are young and tender.

tabbouleh

Put the bulgur in a bowl, cover with 2 cups water and leave for 1½ hours.

Cut the tomatoes in half, scoop out the seeds with a teaspoon, then cut into ½-inch cubes. Cut the cucumber in half lengthwise, remove the seeds with a teaspoon, then cut the flesh into ½-inch cubes.

To make the dressing, put the lemon juice and 1½ teaspoons salt in a bowl and whisk until well combined. Season well with freshly ground black pepper, then slowly whisk in the olive oil and extra virgin olive oil.

Drain the bulgur and squeeze out any excess water. Spread the bulgur out on a clean dishtowel or paper towels and leave to dry for about 30 minutes. Put the bulgur in a large salad bowl, add the tomato, cucumber, scallions, parsley, and mint and toss well to combine. Pour the dressing over the salad and toss until evenly coated.

¾ cup bulgur wheat
3 tomatoes
1 telegraph (long) cucumber
4 scallions, sliced
4 cups chopped Italian parsley
2 large handfuls mint leaves, chopped

dressing
⅓ cup lemon juice
¼ cup olive oil
1 tablespoon extra virgin olive oil, extra

herbs ▪ parsley

The health benefits of parsley have long been documented—Hippocrates prescribed parsley to improve general health. The Romans, who ate quantities of parsley, knew it was very good for them; they also believed it relieved drunkenness, placing bouquets of the herb on the banqueting table to absorb "wine vapours."

rosemary

herbs ▪ rosemary
season ▪ available year-round

selection and storage

Rosemary is fairly robust and not subject to the bruising or wilting of other more fragile herbs. When buying rosemary, look for sprightly, green-leafed sprigs with fresh, resinous aromas when a few are rubbed between your fingers. Elderly rosemary looks dried out and somewhat faded and its smell is similarly diminished.

Store fresh rosemary in an airtight container or sealed plastic bag in the refrigerator for up to 1 week.

Rosemary is a venerable plant. It has a fascinating history and, with its unmistakable piney aroma, many uses in the kitchen. Rosemary is native to Mediterranean coastal areas, its Latin name, *Rosmarinus*, means "dew of the sea," possibly in reference to its natural habitat.

When utilized in cooking, rosemary is surprisingly versatile; it can be used in myriad dishes—even certain sweet ones. Its pungent flavor should be unleashed in moderation as it can take over a dish and, as the "needles," or short, spiky leaves of the plant do not soften on cooking, entire sprigs are best used as these can be retrieved and discarded before serving.

Rosemary is used traditionally with meats such as roast pork, lamb, and game—its digestive properties help diners deal with rich flavors. Rosemary is also delicious in soups and braises, particularly those involving dried beans and pulses, and with cuts of stewing meat like shanks, tails, and shins.

Rosemary goes particularly well with potatoes and mushrooms. A sprig of rosemary will perfume a custard or creamy rice pudding wonderfully and the flavor enhances pears, peaches, and apricots—add a sprig to fruit poaching liquid, preferably one based on red wine.

roasted rosemary chicken

Preheat the oven to 425°F. Wipe the chicken inside and out and pat dry with paper towels. Season the chicken cavity and place 4 rosemary sprigs and the garlic cloves inside. Rub the outside of the chicken with 1 tablespoon of oil, season the chicken, then put on its side in a roasting pan. Put the remaining rosemary sprigs in the pan and drizzle with oil.

Put the roasting pan on the middle shelf of the oven. After 20 minutes, turn the chicken onto the other side, baste with the juices and cook for 20 minutes. Turn the chicken, breast side up, baste again, and cook for an additional 15 minutes or until the juices between the body and thigh run clear when pierced with a knife. Transfer the chicken to a warm serving dish and set aside for at least 10 minutes before carving.

Pour off most of the fat from the roasting pan and return the pan to the stove top over high heat. Add 2 tablespoons water and scrape the base of the pan to loosen the residue. Pour over the chicken to serve.

3 pounds 5 ounces whole chicken
6 large sprigs rosemary
4 garlic cloves, peeled
3 tablespoons olive oil

herbs ■ rosemary

bean and rosemary dip

serves 4–6

Rinse and drain the beans and set aside. Heat the olive oil in a saucepan and cook the garlic and rosemary for 1 minute or until the garlic is softened. Add the beans and stock and bring to a boil. Reduce the heat and simmer for 3–4 minutes. Allow to cool.

In a food processor, blend the mixture in batches until smooth. Add the lemon juice and season, to taste. Serve with baguette or crackers. This dip can be kept in the refrigerator in an airtight container for several days.

2¼ cups canned cannellini beans (about 1½ cans)
3 tablespoons olive oil
2 garlic cloves, crushed
1 tablespoon finely chopped rosemary leaves
1 cup chicken or vegetable stock
2 teaspoons lemon juice

sage

herbs ▪ sage
season ▪ available year-round, peak season spring

Sage grows the world over and there are literally hundreds of varieties, but it is common sage (*Salvia officinalis*) with its tapered, silver-green, rough-textured leaves and pretty blue flowers that is most often used for culinary purposes. The genus name *Salvia* comes from the Latin word for "to cure," while the modern French name, *tout bonne*, means "all is well."

Thought to be a Syrian native, sage has, for most of history, been used medicinally; the ancients revered it as a healing herb and used it to treat everything from epilepsy to drunkenness, worms, memory loss, and eye problems. Arab physicians in the tenth century believed sage could extend one's life to immortality.

selection and storage

Sage can be purchased in bunches—the leaves should be fresh-looking with no signs of wilting, brown spots, or bruising. Stored in the refrigerator in a sealed plastic bag, sage will keep for 5–6 days.

culinary uses

Culinarily, its strong, woodsy aroma is most appreciated in Italy, where sage is often paired with veal, chicken, and pork, and is also fried until crisp in butter, then spooned over pasta.

Traditionally, sage has been paired with rich meats—with goose in England, eel in Germany, and sausages and pâté in France. Since ancient times it has been known to be an effective meat preserver, which could account for the French use of it in their charcuterie. Outside Europe, sage is well known as a flavoring in poultry stuffings and is also used to flavor savory muffins, breads, sauces, and marinades.

Because it is so very strong, sage should be used judiciously in cooking as its flavor can completely overpower a dish.

pork with sage and capers

Preheat the oven to 325°F. Heat 1 tablespoon oil and the butter in a frying pan. Add the onion and cook for 5 minutes or until lightly golden.

Put the bread crumbs, chopped sage, parsley, lemon zest, ½ tablespoon capers, and the cooked onion in a bowl. Add the egg and season with sea salt and freshly ground black pepper. Split each pork fillet in half lengthwise, leaving the fillet joined at one side, and open out. Spread the sage stuffing mixture down the length of one fillet and then close.

Stretch the bacon or prosciutto using the back of a knife and wrap each piece (slightly overlapping) around the pork to form a neat rolled parcel. Tie with string at intervals.

Put the pork in a baking pan and drizzle with 1 tablespoon oil. Bake for 1 hour. To test if the meat is cooked, insert a skewer into the thickest part of the meat—the juices should run clear. Remove from the pan, cover with foil and rest.

To make the jus, put the juices in the baking pan on the stove top, add the flour and stir in well. Add the vermouth and allow to bubble for 1 minute. Add the stock and stir while cooking to remove any lumps. Simmer for 5 minutes. Add the remaining capers to the sauce.

In a small saucepan, heat the remaining tablespoon of oil, and when very hot, fry the whole sage leaves until crisp. Drain on paper towels.

Slice the pork into ½-inch slices. Spoon a little sauce over the pork and serve with fried sage leaves on top.

- 3 tablespoons extra virgin olive oil
- 1½ tablespoons unsalted butter
- 1 onion, finely chopped
- 1¼ cups fresh white bread crumbs
- 2 teaspoons chopped fresh sage
- 1 tablespoon chopped Italian parsley
- 2 teaspoons grated lemon zest
- 2½ tablespoons salted baby capers, rinsed and drained
- 1 egg, lightly beaten
- 2 (1-pound) pork fillets
- 8 bacon or prosciutto slices
- 2 teaspoons all-purpose flour
- ½ cup dry vermouth
- 1¼ cups chicken or vegetable stock
- 8 sage leaves, extra, to garnish

herbs ▪ sage

tarragon

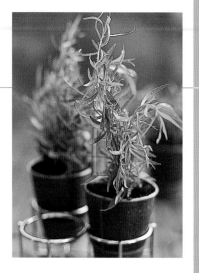

selection and storage

Choose tarragon with fresh-looking, unbruised leaves that show no signs of wilting. Store tarragon, wrapped in damp paper towels, then loosely sealed in a plastic bag, in the refrigerator for up to 4 days.

Tarragon, unlike most of the better known herbs, does not have a long history of culinary use. Many sources claim tarragon came late to European cookery because, as a native of isolated Siberia and Central Asia, it took some time to find its way westward. Whatever the reason, it didn't find common usage in England and France until around the sixteenth century. The French have embraced tarragon like no other culture has—perhaps its most famous uses are in sauce béarnaise and sauce tartare. It is also much used to flavor vinegar and as a vital component in the ubiquitous fines herbes mixture, with chervil, chives, and parsley.

There are two types of tarragon commonly available and it is vital to know the difference as their flavor is very different. French tarragon has delicate, flat, spear-shaped green leaves, which exude a distinctively sweet anise flavor when bruised—this is the tarragon you should choose. Russian tarragon (unfortunately often passed off as French as it is much easier to grow) has narrower, spikier leaves than French, lacks its sweetness, and has an unappealing, harsh, grassy flavor and smell.

Tarragon leaves (strip them off their woody stem just before you plan to use them) are generally chopped and added to a dish near the end of cooking, otherwise the bright flavors will be lost.

asparagus with tarragon vinaigrette

Preheat the oven to 350°F. Spread the walnuts on a baking sheet and place in the oven for 5 minutes. Remove from the oven and cool. Chop the walnuts finely.

Cut any thick, woody ends from the asparagus and discard; trim asparagus with a vegetable peeler. Place in a bowl, cover with boiling water and set aside for 2 minutes. Drain, plunge into iced water, then drain again; pat dry with paper towels. Wash and dry the curly endive and tear into separate leaves.

To make the tarragon vinaigrette, combine the scallion, vinegar, tarragon, and mustard in a small bowl and gradually whisk in the walnut oil. Season with sea salt and freshly ground black pepper.

Arrange the endive in a serving dish. Top with the asparagus spears. Drizzle with the dressing and sprinkle with walnuts.

¼ cup walnuts
24 fresh asparagus spears
3 cups curly endive (frisée)

tarragon vinaigrette
1 scallion, finely chopped
2 tablespoons white wine vinegar
1 tablespoon chopped tarragon
1 teaspoon Dijon mustard
¼ cup walnut oil

herbs ■ tarragon

béarnaise sauce

serves 4

Put the vinegar, scallion, and tarragon in a small saucepan. Bring to a boil, then reduce the heat and simmer until the mixture has reduced by a third. Set aside to cool completely.

Strain the vinegar into a heatproof bowl and add the egg yolks. Place the bowl over a saucepan of barely simmering water and whisk until the mixture is thick and pale.

Add the butter, one cube at a time, and whisk after each addition until the mixture is thick and smooth. Season to taste and serve immediately. Serve with roast beef or lamb, or pan-fried steaks of poached salmon.

⅓ cup white wine vinegar
2 scallions, roughly chopped
2 teaspoons chopped tarragon
2 egg yolks
½ cup butter, cut into cubes

thyme

selection and storage

When buying thyme, select bunches with a profusion of compact, green leaves with no signs of dropping or drying out. Wrap the bunch in damp paper towels and place in a loosely sealed plastic bag—it will keep for up to 1 week in the refrigerator.

Thyme is, unlike most herbs, at home in nearly any dish, except perhaps those of Asian origin, where it is not used. Native to the Mediterranean and North Africa, fresh thyme, with its peppery, piney aroma is one of the most used of all herbs, lifting the flavor of stocks, soups, casseroles, stuffings for meats and vegetables, sauces, pickles, baked goods, sweet custards, and certain fruit dishes. Wild thyme, which grows profusely around the southern Mediterranean region, is the source of the famous thyme honey, which is highly prized in Greece.

Common thyme (*Thymus vulgaris*) has tiny ovoid, tough, deep green leaves which are generally used whole, still attached to a branch as a sprig. Unlike most other herbs, common thyme is best added to dishes at the beginning of cooking and discarded before serving—the flavor subtly perfumes the dish whereas freshly chopped leaves tend to overpower and taste too "green."

Another popular type of thyme is lemon thyme, which has fleshier leaves and a pronounced citrus tang. The two types of thyme are not interchangeable; use lemon thyme in salads and with chicken, veal, and fish, which pair best with its lemony zing.

thyme-flavored semi-dried tomatoes

Preheat the oven to 315°F. Quarter the tomatoes lengthwise and lay, skin side down, in a baking pan.

Sprinkle the tomatoes with 1 teaspoon each of sea salt and freshly ground black pepper. Sprinkle with the thyme and bake for 2½ hours. Check occasionally to make sure the tomatoes don't burn. Toss in the oil and cool before packing into hot sterilized jars and sealing. Refrigerate for 24 hours before serving.

16 plum tomatoes
3 tablespoons thyme, chopped
2 tablespoons olive oil

herbs ■ thyme

lemon, lime, and thyme vinegar

makes 4 cups

Finely grate the zest of the limes and lemons. Squeeze the juice from the limes and two of the lemons.

Put the vinegar, lime juice, lemon juice, lime zest, half the lemon zest, and half the thyme sprigs in a saucepan. Bring to a boil, then reduce the heat and simmer for 5 minutes. Remove from the heat and set aside to cool completely.

Meanwhile, put the remaining lemon zest into a hot sterilized jar and add the remaining thyme. Strain the vinegar and pour it into the jar. Seal and store in a cool place for 1 week.

Line a funnel with cheesecloth and strain the vinegar into warm sterilized bottles. Seal, label, and date each jar. Store for up to 1 year. Use in place of white wine vinegar for a flavored vinaigrette.

2 limes
4 lemons
4 cups white wine vinegar
20 thyme sprigs

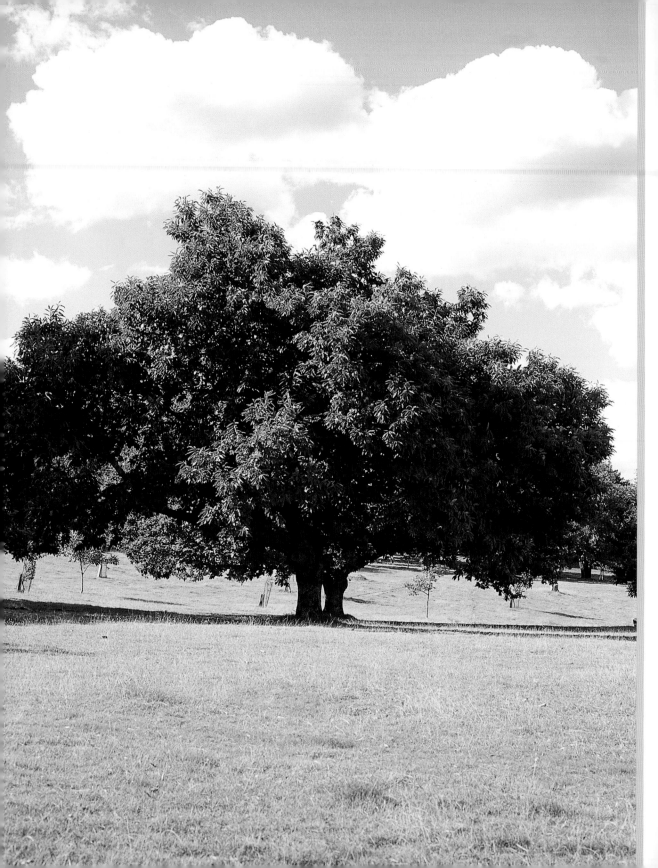

index of topics

index of recipes

445

bibliography

Alexander, S 1996, *The Cook's Companion*, Viking, London.

Alexander, S 2004, *The Cook's Companion*, Rev 2nd edn, Penguin Books, Australia.

Arthur, D & Reeve, D 2002, 'Riding The Citrus Trail: When is a Mandarin a Tangerine', *Perfumer and Flavorist*, July–August.

Bareham, L 1995, *Onions without Tears*. London, Penguin Books, 1995

Bareham, L 2000, *The Big Red Book of Tomatoes*, Penguin Books, London.

Campion, A & Curtis, M 2001, *Fresh—The Seasonal Produce Cookbook*, Purple Egg, Melbourne.

Carluccio, A 2003, *The Complete Mushroom Book; The Quiet Hunt,* Quadrille Publishing, London.

Castelvetro, G 1989, *The Fruit, Herbs & Vegetables of Italy*, forward by Jane Grigson, Viking, London.

Conran, C & Conran, T & Hopkinson, S 1997, *The Conran Cookbook*, Conran Octopus, London.

Davidson, A 1999, *The Oxford Companion to Food*, Oxford University Press, Oxford.

Dinnage, P 1981, *The Book of Fruit and Fruit Cookery*, Sidgwick and Jackson, London.

Fulton, M 1984, *Encyclopaedia of Food and Cookery*, 3rd edn, Octopus Books, London.

Grifith, F & Griffith, L 2003, *Nuts*, St. Martin's Press, New York.

Grigson, J 2000, *Jane Grigson's Fruit Book*, Penguin Books, London.

Grigson, J 1998, *Jane Grigson's Vegetable Book*, Penguin Books, London.

Goldstein, D 1996, *The Vegetarian Hearth: recipes and reflections for the cold season*, Harper Collins, New York.

Hazan, M 1996, *Essentials of Classic Italian Cooking*, Alfred A. Knopf, New York.

Herbst, S T 1995, *The New Food Lover's Companion*, Barron's Educational Series Inc, Pennsylvania.

Kafka, B with Styler, C 2005, *Vegetable Love,* Artisan, New York.

Marks, G 2004 *Olive Trees and Honey—a treasury of vegetarian recipes from Jewish communities around the world*, Wiley Publishing, Hoboken, New Jersey.

Morton, M 1996, *Cupboard Love—A Dictionary of Culinary Curiosities,* Bain & Cox, Winnipeg.

Newton, J ed. 2001, *Food: The Essential A–Z Guide*, Murdoch Books, Australia.

Peterson, J 1998, *Vegetables*, William Morrow and Company, New York.

Rozin, E 1992, *Blue Corn and Chocolate*, Ebury Press, London.

Schneider, E 1998, *Uncommon Fruits and Vegetables*, William Morrow and Company, New York.

Schneider, E 2001, *Vegetables from Amaranth to Zucchini*, William Morrow and Company, New York.

Solomon, C 1996, *Encyclopedia of Asian Food*, William Heinemann, Australia.

Stone, S & Stone, M 1991, *The Essential Root Vegetable Cookbook*, 1st edn, Clarkson Potter, New York.

Trang, C 2003, *Essentials of Asian Cuisine*, Simon & Schuster, New York.

Waters, A 2002, *Chez Panisse Fruit,* Harper Collins, New York.

Waters, A 1996, *Chez Panisse Vegetables*, Harper Collins, New York.

Ward, R 1988, *A Harvest of Apples,* Penguin Books, London.

Wolfert, P 1998, *Mediterranean Grains and Greens: A Book of Savoury Sun-drenched Recipes*, Harper Collins, New York.

Wright, CA 2001, *Mediterranean Vegetables*, The Harvard Common Press, Boston.

acknowledgments

Thanks to Juliet Rogers, Kay Scarlett and Diana Hill at Murdoch Books for providing the opportunity to work on an utterly luscious project such as this book. To have done this with the aid of such a passionate and competent team has been a complete bonus. Special thanks must go to Jacqueline Blanchard, my editor, for her ceaseless enthusiasm and positive energy and to Vivien Valk for making it look so good. Also thanks to my good friend and colleague Kathleen Gandy, without whose help this book would not be what it is. Finally, a rather large thank you to Andrew and Harry Kitchen, who always encourage me to do what I love best in the world, which is to write about beautiful things.

First published by Murdoch Books 2006 Australia
www.murdochbooks.com.au

Published in 2007 by Stewart, Tabori & Chang
An imprint of Harry N. Abrams, Inc.

Library of Congress Cataloging-in-Publication Data is available.

The text of this book was composed in StempelSchneidler and Swiss721BT

Printed and bound by 1010 Printing International Limited. Printed in China.
10 9 8 7 6 5 4 3 2 1

HNA
harry n. abrams, inc.
a subsidiary of La Martinière Groupe

115 West 18th Street
New York, NY 10011
www.hnabooks.com